P9-ECL-695

The Analyzed Bible

G. Campbell Morgan

Fleming H. Revell
A Division of Baker Book House Co
Grand Rapids, Michigan 49516

© 1964 by G. Campbell Morgan

Published by Fleming H. Revell
a division of Baker Book House Company
P.O. Box 6287, Grand Rapids, MI 49516-6287

Paperback published 1995

Printed in the United States of America

ISBN 0-8007-5586-3
Library of Congress Catalog Card Number 64-16600

INTRODUCTION

This work presents an outline of every book of the Bible, and a survey of the book's total message and meaning in broad, clear strokes. *The Analyzed Bible,* here presented for the first time in one volume, is a unique tribute to G. Campbell Morgan's lifetime of Bible study and exposition.

Dr. Morgan once said that if he desired to teach a child geography, he would take a globe, let the child turn it, and point out the land masses and oceans before he proceeded to the special study of separate countries and regions. In this volume he leads us to the world of the Bible and shows us the spiritual landscape of each of its books, preparing the way for a true understanding of the individual chapters, paragraphs, sentences, and words. This method, the "Prince of Expositors" felt very strongly, was fundamental to Bible study: "It is of the utmost importance in the study of any book in the Divine Library to gain primarily a broad and general idea of the scope and main structure thereof."

One marvels at the succinct but comprehensive analysis of each Bible book. Nothing is forced into place; all develops out of the Scripture's own content. The whole is the result of Dr. Morgan's repeated reading of each book of the Bible, sometimes as many as fifty times, over a period of twenty years.

And from beginning to end the reader senses the presence of Jesus Christ. "The roads of the books of the Old Testament," wrote Dr. Morgan, "lead up to Him. The pathways of the New lead out from Him. . . . He, the lonely and perfect Personality of the Gospel narratives, stands at the center, and all the highways meet in Him."

Sometimes the publishers are asked how such a book as *The Analyzed Bible* differs from G. Campbell Morgan's other works. Examination of his other books which relate to the whole Bible reveals the distinctiveness of this one by contrast.

Great Chapters of the Bible consists of expositions of 49 famous Bible chapters such as Genesis 1, Psalm 23, Isaiah 40, and Romans 8. This is obviously a limited work: the 49 chapters are taken from only 17 Bible books.

Searchlights from the Word consists of the exposition of one key verse from each chapter in the Bible.

The Unfolding Message of the Whole Bible emphasizes the harmony and unity of Scripture, its interrelatedness, and the unfolding of the divine revelation. The viewpoint is almost epic; one chapter of *The Unfolding Message* covers the four epistles of Romans, Galatians, and I and II Thessalonians, while another groups five books in one unit.

An Exposition of the Whole Bible consists of a concise exposition of every chapter in the Bible. It is almost a condensation of Scripture, chapter by chapter.

Living Messages of the Books of the Bible is a study of the permanent value of each Bible book, emphasizing the Word's abiding lessons and its application to life.

Since the last-named work would appear to be somewhat like *The Analyzed Bible,* it is of interest that *The Christian Advocate* some years ago compared the two works in these words: "*The Analyzed Bible* has to do with the *facts* of each book; the *Messages* with the *truths* of each book. *The Analyzed Bible* is analytical; the *Messages* synthetical." And *The United Presbyterian* said, "We know of nothing just like this in the entire range of exegetical and theological literature."

The Analyzed Bible offers dependable guidance for personal study of the Bible, for sustained expository preaching, for Bible study groups, for surer understanding of the Word. May it serve in all these areas to the continuing glory of God.

THE PUBLISHERS

PREFACE

This work was originally published by my father in three volumes but it has been out of print for some time. In view of the belief that it will serve the present and future generations, it is being reissued now in this single volume, as a companion volume to *Living Messages of the Books of the Bible* by the same author.

There is contained within these pages that which can be accurately described as *the basic work* of the author, out of which grew all his preaching ministry. Here is to be found a suggested outline for every Book in the Divine Library.

The author's constant method in the study of the Word of God was invariably from the *telescopic* to the *microscopic*, always from that of surveying broad areas to that of the study of passages, texts and words.

The basic nature of this work is evidenced by the fact that in subsequent books from his pen, the author, himself, often quoted passages from it.

After careful consideration it has been decided that the reissue of this work will render valuable help to young students, to ministers desiring to form a Bible School, and to others wishing to gain a bird's-eye view of the contents of each Book in the Divine Library.

I recommend to students of the Word of God that in approaching the study of the Bible they begin by recognizing the fact that it *is* a Library of approximately sixty-six Books. Next let the student select a Book from the Library which he desires to study. Then let him work through that Book in the Bible aided by the chapter in this volume which deals with the content of that particular Book. Finally let him study the chapter on the same Book in the Bible found in *Living Messages of the Books of the Bible*.

This method of procedure, followed through the entire Divine Library, will lay a solid and excellent foundation for further study of the Lively Oracles of God.

F. Crossley Morgan

CONCORD, NORTH CAROLINA

CONTENTS

Part One: THE OLD TESTAMENT

Contents

Part Two: THE NEW TESTAMENT

CONTENTS

Part I:

THE OLD TESTAMENT

GENESIS—*The Book of Beginnings*

A GENERATION *i., ii.*	B DEGENERATION *iii.—xi.*	C REGENERATION *xii.—l.*
I. Of the Material to Man **i.—ii. 3**	**I. Of the Individual** **iii.**	**I. Of Individuals** **xii.—xxxv. 21**

i. Origin.   i. 1
 ii. Ruin.   i. 2a
 iii. The revealed Cosmogony.
     i. 2b—ii. 3
	i. The Serpent and Man. 1-8
	 ii. Jehovah. 9-24
		i. Abraham. xii.—xxv. 10
		     7 Communications
		 ii. Isaac. xxv. 11—xxvi.
		     2 Communications
		 iii. Jacob. xxvii.—xxxv. 21
		     5 Communications

	II. Of the Family **iv., v.**	
II. Of Man, as to Nature and Office **ii. 4-25**	i. The first Family. iv. ii. The Families. v.	**II. Of the Family** **xxxv. 22—xxxviii.**

i. Created.   4-8
 ii. Crowned.   9-15
 iii. Conditioned.   16, 17
 iv. Completed.   18-25
	III. Of Society **vi.**	i. The Sons of Jacob.
		     xxxv. 22-29
		 Generations of Esau.
		     xxxvi.
		 ii. Joseph. xxxvii.
		 iii. Judah's corruption.
		     xxxviii.

	i. Intermixture. ii. Degeneracy.	

	⌈ Destruction and Deliverance
	     vii., viii. ⌋
		III. Of Society
		    xxxix.—l. 21

	New Departure National **ix., x.**	i. History of Joseph. ii. Israel segregated.
	IV. Of the Nations **xi.**	**IV. Of a Nation** **l. 22-26**
	i. Confederacy. ii. Confusion. iii. Continuity. Shem to Abraham.	Prophecy of faith.

GENESIS ✳ ✳ ✳ ✳

THE BOOK OF Genesis is the book of origins. It deals with the beginnings of the facts and forces in the midst of which humanity lives, in so far as it is necessary for man to know them in order to set his life in right relationship to them. There is nothing final in this book. Things created are not seen in perfection, but rather as prepared for development. Evil is revealed neither as to its first origin nor ultimate development, but only in the beginnings of its operation in human life. The Divine plan of redemption is not fully unfolded, but the first movements in history toward its outworking are clearly revealed.

The main divisions of the book are marked by the phrases: "In the beginning God" (i. 1), "Now the serpent" (iii. 1), "Now Jehovah" (xii. 1). The first division tells the story of the beginnings of the material universe. The second division gives an account of how evil entered human history, and traces its first movements. The third division gives the history of the calling of a man, the making of a nation, the creation of a testimony, and thus the preparation for the ultimate coming of a Saviour. These in broad outline are the divisions of the book. The beginnings of created things: Generation, and, at the back of all, God. The beginnings of evil: Degeneration, and, at the back of all, the serpent. The beginnings of the process of restoration: Regeneration, and, at the back of all, Jehovah.

–3

A. GENERATION

In this first division there are two sections, which give an account respectively of the generation of the material to man, and the generation of man as to nature and office.

"In the beginning God created the heaven and the earth." In that simple statement we have the Bible declaration of the origin of the material universe; and it is one in which faith finds reasonable foundation. Interpretations of method may vary, but the essential truth abides. In its dignified and sublime statement reason may rest as it cannot possibly do in any theory which leaves God out of the question, and thus finally declares that the first cause was more or less the result of accident, or the existence of laws without mind, or of order without thought.

"And the earth was waste and void; and darkness was upon the face of the deep." It is not possible that these words describe the condition of the heaven and the earth as they were created by God. Between the original creation and the conditions herein described there had been a cataclysm. Of that revelation has given us no account. Speculations are interesting, but they cannot be final or dogmatic. It may be that behind the material cataclysm there was a moral catastrophe. Probably, if we knew all the history, we should know the truth concerning the origination of evil. In subsequent volumes of the Divine Library there are flashes of light which may afford some clue to the hidden things. The fact that Satan is spoken of as "the god of this world," "the prince of this world," may refer to a relationship he bore to the earth prior to the appearance of man. It may be that here angels "kept not their own principality," and that

A. Generation

in their fall they involved the earth itself in degradation from its primal perfection, and brought it to the condition described as "waste and void."

With the words "The Spirit of God moved upon the face of the waters" begins the story of reconstruction, and this continues through the third verse of the second chapter. The method of the new birth of the earth was that of the brooding over it of the Spirit, and the uttering of the Word of God. The earth was born again by the Spirit and the Word. A careful study of this section and of the following one will reveal the fact that two words are made use of to describe the Divine action. The Revised Version has indicated the difference by the use of our words "created" and "made." The Hebrew words of which these are translations do not indicate the same thing. The first, "created," indicates an essential making, a bringing into existence. The second, "made," suggests rather the origination of new forms by the use of things already created. It is of great interest, and moreover of value, to notice the places where the word "created" is used. It occurs first in the declaration concerning the origin of material things. It occurs again at the point where life rises from the nonsentient to the sentient. It occurs, in the third place, at the story of the coming of man. Between these the word used is always "made." This fact reveals that at the points indicated there was a new act of God, introducing an entirely fresh order of being. It is worthy of notice that these words occur exactly where the evolutionary theory has never yet been able to bridge a gulf. The evolutionary process demands a primal fact from which everything goes forward. It cannot supply it. It is supplied by the declaration, "In the beginning God created." It has never been able to discover

–5

the link between the nonsentient and sentient; that link is here supplied in the affirmation, "God created . . . every living creature." It has never been able finally to discover a link between the highest form of animal life and man; that link is supplied in the affirmation, "God created man in His own image." Whereas according to this account He was ever the immanent God, by His own wisdom and power producing every new form of already existing life, He did also at certain periods in the process by direct, essential, new creation, create a crisis from which the order proceeded anew.

There are those who affirm that in the first two chapters we have two distinct accounts of the creation of man; and moreover, some declare that they contradict each other. As a matter of fact the first story places man in his relation to the material universe. He is seen as the crowning work in creation, the last of a succession, whether a succession of separate events or of evolutionary processes is not declared. Whatever the process, he is seen to be the crown of the material creation. In the second story he is shown to be more than this. There an explanation is given of that spiritual quantity which is found in man and in no other creation. It describes the process by which man became different from, and superior to, everything which had preceded him. He was made of the dust of the ground, that is, he had come from the common origin. His creation as man was due to the fact that God breathed into his nostrils the breath of lives. By the possession of God-breathed lives he was differentiated from everything which had preceded him.

This being, at once related to the material universe, and yet kin of God, was placed at the center of creation, to govern it in co-operation with God. He was to reign over all beneath him. The garden in which he found himself was not the ultimate goal. It was the opportunity for the exercise of the functions of the life bestowed. Within it there lay potentially the city, which man was to build by the cultivation of the forces of the garden, and by exercising authority over creation under the authority of God.

The relation of man to God and Nature was conditioned by a simple and yet perfectly clear command, which indicated the limits of liberty. There were things which he might do. There were bounds beyond which he might not go. His liberty consisted in loyalty to the law of God. Of these fundamental truths the trees of the garden afforded sacramental symbols. Of all save one he might eat; of this one he might not eat. It stood in the presence of his life, marking the bounds of his freedom.

Man was completed by the bringing to him of one who was of himself, and in whom he found the true complement of his own nature. In man and his companion the likeness of God was complete. "In his own image . . . male and female created he them."

B. DEGENERATION

The division here commencing deals with the beginnings of that long process of degeneration, in the midst of which the human race still finds itself. The suggested analysis must not be treated as hard and fast in its separation of parts. It is intended simply to indicate the natural development of thought as to the individual, the family, society, the nation. These divisions indicate the true circles of human interrelationship as they spread out in ever-widening circumference.

Everything commences with the individual. This is a simple story of a man in individual innocence and racial immaturity. Satan appealed to him through a lower form of creation, here spoken of as the serpent. Spiritual evil took material form to reach spiritual man through the material side of his being. The deepest note in the attack was that of its attempt to reflect on God. The deepest note in the fall was that of failure of faith. Faith being lost, fear immediately succeeded.

Man hid from God, but he could not escape Him. He came first for inquisition, and then for pronouncement of sentence. In the sentences pronounced there is evident the differentiation of strictest justice. The curse was for the originator, justice for the deceived. Side by side with the sentence the first prophetic word broke upon human ears. Behind all the movements of law there abides the heart of love, and this is finally seen in the exclusion of man from the tree of life in order that he might not perpetuate the condition into which he had come as the result of sin.

Following swiftly upon the degradation of the individual came that of the family. The sorrow following upon sin was manifest first in the agony of the heart of the first mother. In hope she bore her first-born, and called him Cain, crying, "I have gotten it," that is, I have gotten the promised seed of the Lord. The hope was doomed to disappointment, and she called her next boy Abel, Vanity, because of what she had seen in the first. Thus the first family was broken up, and the first gap in the circle of human society was made by murder.

The race moved on, multiplying into families, but the shadow of the issue of sin was on the whole of them, and with one rare exception through fifteen centuries the knell of death was heard unceasingly.

As families multiplied and branched out into many direc-

C. *Regeneration*

tions, the new relationship of society was created. From the original man two lines proceeded, one through Cain, the other through Seth. These developed around two opposing ideals, the one that of self-consideration and self-advancement, the other that of fear of God and obedience of Him. The lines of difference became less clearly marked until the sons of the godly race intermixed in marriage with the daughters of the people of the materialized ideals, and the issue was most terrible corruption.

This all ended in a Divine interference of swift and overwhelming judgment. The destruction of the race was not total, for while man had failed, the purpose of God moved forward toward consummation. Out of the devastation a remnant was saved, and human history started forward upon a new basis as there emerged a new idea of social relationship, that of the nation.

With an immediateness which startles, the book chronicles the story of the failure of the national idea. The will of God was the peopling of the earth by the separation of those delivered from its primal corruption into nations occupying different territories. Against this separation man rebelled by the formation of a godless confederacy, and an attempt to resist the Divine decree. This was followed by immediate Divine intervention, which issued in the confusion of the confederacy. Finally, the line of continuity from Shem to Abram is declared, and the section setting forth degeneration closes.

C. REGENERATION

In the third division we have the account of the beginnings of Regeneration, that is, of a movement which culminated in the person of the Messiah. The lines of development correspond to those we have already noticed in the previous division. As there we had first the degeneration of the individual, so here the regeneration of the individual is first dealt with, and indeed, at greatest length. We also see the movement in its application to the family, to society, and toward the nation.

The section dealing with the regeneration of the individual gives us the account of the dealings of God with three men: Abraham, Isaac, and Jacob. There is a distinct difference between the Divine communications in these three cases. The difference is to be accounted for by the different quality of faith exemplified in each man. To Abraham there were seven communications, each initiating a new movement. His faith was obedient faith. To Isaac there were two Divine communications, and there does not seem to be any personal or direct relation between the communications of God and Isaac's life. The faith of Isaac was passive. To Jacob there were five communications, each of them coming at the close of a movement in the life of the man by which God arrested and changed the order of his progress. Jacob's faith was restless faith.

The first communication to Abram was of the nature of a call to leave his own country, and to set his face toward a new one, under new conditions of life. "The Lord said unto Abram, Get thee out of thy country . . . unto the land that I will show thee." It may be that this initial call was really to Terah. It is certainly declared that Terah moved, taking Abram and Lot with him. The first intention, however, was not immediately realized. Coming to Haran, Terah remained there. After his death, Abram moved on, and came into the land of Canaan.

C. Regeneration

In the second communication God promised him the land for possession, and he proceeded in faith and obedience.

By the third communication the land was solemnly given to Abram under interesting and remarkable circumstances. The herdsmen of Abram and Lot had quarreled; and the former, with the magnanimity of a great soul, allowed Lot to make his choice. When he had departed God said to Abram, "Lift up now thine eyes," and thus to the man who was content not to choose, but rather to leave himself free for the following of faith, the whole of the land was given.

In the fourth communication God promised him a seed, which should become a great nation.

In connection with the fifth communication God entered into a solemn covenant as between Himself and Abraham.

The sixth communication was in connection with the actual coming to Abraham of his son.

The seventh and final communication was that by which God finally tested this man in the matter of faith, and because of his obedience was able to lead him into a closer and more conscious fellowship with Himself.

By these seven communications God led Abraham step by step through more trying circumstances toward higher experiences, and, because he followed, to larger possessions. In the process of the story we find on the part of Abraham deflections from faith. In a time of difficulty he went down into Egypt and by so doing fell, not merely from the simplicity of faith, but from truth. The method, however, is clearly indicated as being a Divine appearing, an obedient answer, and a consequent advancement.

In the story of Isaac we have first of all an account of the pastoral simplicity of his life. In the midst of this quietness there came to him the first of two Divine communications, in which God told him that the covenant made with Abraham was continued to him. The second communication was for the purpose of ratifying this selfsame covenant. Isaac was a man quiet, restful, and passive. His deflections from faith were fewer than those of his father. His restlessness was less than that of his son. There are no actions of magnificent or daring triumph. God never broke in upon his life with the thick darkness or the alarming struggle by Jabbok, but with quiet messages, showing that he too was included in covenant privilege and purpose. Isaac, the man who dug wells, and lived by them, was necessary in the Divine economy as well as Abraham, the man who blazed the way, and became the pioneer of faith; as well as Jacob, the man of restless activity, who never found final anchorage until he was crippled.

The dealings of God with Jacob were of an entirely different nature because he was an entirely different man. Through all the story it is evident that he was a man who believed in God. That was the deepest fact in his life. He was nevertheless a man of restless activity, and the five communications to him were all for the purpose of checking him, correcting his methods, and keeping him in the pathway of the Divine will.

The first of these culminated a method of duplicity, followed in order to obtain a blessing. By deceit wrought upon his father, under the instigation and with the connivance of his mother, he obtained the blessing which God meant him to have. He believed that it was in the purpose of God for him, but, unable to follow and to wait, by manipulation of events and by the exercise of cunning obtained his father's benediction. As his face was set toward a new country, in

C. Regeneration

consequence of his duplicity, God appeared to him, and with great tenderness, knowing the deepest in him, bridged the gulf between his material life and the spiritual realities by the vision of the ladder and the angels.

Arrived in the land of Laban, by quick wit and ready resource he won his way to material prosperity against all the meanness of his uncle. There was great danger lest such a man should become satisfied with success in an alien land, and God appeared to him the second time, and commanded him to return.

The self-reliance and independence of Jacob are seen in the method of his return. He made his arrangements with Laban, and built a watchtower at Mizpah. He then went forward to meet his brother, and so far as possible prepared for every contingency. Then followed the third Divine communication. God set Himself against Jacob's independence, and in the mystery of that long night revealed Himself as the conquering One, Who breaks in order to make, Who cripples in order to crown.

Having come back into the land, immediately he compromised with the circumstances by which he found himself surrounded, with the result that sorrow entered his house in the wake of sin. Again God appeared to him for purposes of restoration, commanding him to get back to Bethel.

In the last part of this section the faith of Jacob seems to have become obedient, and the fifth communication of God immediately followed.

Subsequently there is an account of another word God spoke to Jacob, but because it was intimately connected with his sons it is omitted in this description of the dealings of God with the man himself.

In this study of the beginnings of the regeneration of the individual the truth is revealed that the one principle through which God is able to operate is that of faith in Himself. Where that is present, even though it may express itself in different ways, according to differeing temperaments, He can act. Obedient faith He leads quietly forward; passive faith He visits to comfort and strengthen; restless faith He checks and corrects toward ultimate realization.

Through the sons of Jacob the circle widens and we see the movement toward the regeneration of the family. Two stories run concurrently, that of Joseph and that of Israel. In the history of Joseph we have a further revelation of the method of God with the individual, but grouped around the man are movements that make toward the regeneration of the family, of society, and the nation. The story of Joseph is in some senses the most wonderful of the Old Testament. Considering it from first to last there is less in him of failure, less of faltering than in any other of the Old Testament characters. Around the story of his life are grouped the events which contributed toward the larger application of the regenerative purposes of God. These events, as they contributed to that purpose, were the result of God's overruling. Apart from that, the process of degeneration moved forward hopelessly.

A list of the sons of Jacob, and a table of the generations of Esau are first given. Then follows the story of Joseph, which is immediately succeeded by an account of the terrible corruption of the family in the case of Judah. The connection here is important in that it indicates the beginning of that movement which culminated in the segregation of the nation, by which they were saved for long years from the contaminating influences of the people of Canaan; and purity of family life, and of society, was made possible.

The history of Joseph shows how God overruled all the failure of man for the ultimate good of man. Joseph was exiled from his father's home by the malice of his brethren, but by the overruling hand of God he was sent into Egypt in order that there he might prepare a place for Israel, that the whole society, which had not yet become a nation, might be brought into circumstances of separation and suffering for their purification. Already, instead of being separate and peculiar, as salt and light in the midst of darkness, they had become corrupted, as the case of Judah proves, and from this corruption it was necessary that they should be delivered. This was accomplished by the overruling of God through the exile of Joseph, the coming of famine, and all those events which issued in their being transferred from Canaan to the land of Goshen, and kept there in separation for centuries. There was nothing more beneficent in the early history of the people than those long years of pain and slavery. Through those years God purged the family and society and so prepared for the nation which was presently to emerge under His wonder-working hand and to enter into possession of the land of His appointment.

In the final verses of the book of Genesis the national idea is seen for a moment as a prophecy and a hope. Joseph, in dying, charged those who were about him that when presently they should return to their land, they should take his bones and carry them with them. In this charge there is revealed one of the greatest triumphs of faith recorded in the whole book. It is the triumph of a man who believed in God, and in the assured establishment of His people; and he therefore was certain that they must ultimately pass back into their own land. The book closes with the account of the burial of the man who had expressed this faith; and the story of beginnings closes with the phrase, "a coffin in Egypt."

EXODUS—*The Emergence of the Nation*

A BONDAGE i.—v.	B DELIVERANCE vi.—xviii.	C ORGANIZATION xix.—xl.
I. Israel in Egypt **i.**	**I. Jehovah and Moses** vi.—vii. 7	**I. Preliminary and Fundamental**
i. Growth of the nation. 1-7	**The Charge**	xix., xx.
ii. Oppression. 8-22		i. The Purpose. Grace. xix.
	i. Self-declaration of Jehovah. vi. 1-9	ii. The Plan. Law. xx.
	ii. The Charge and Fear. vi. 10-12	
II. Moses **ii.—iv.**	(Parenthesis. 13-27)	**II. Laws.** **xxi.—xxiii.**
i. Birth and Preservation. ii. 1-10	iii. The Charge and Faith. vi. 28—vii. 7	i. Of the Person. xxi. 1-32
ii. Flight and Residence in Midian. ii. 11-22		ii. Of Property. xxi. 33—xxii. 15
iii. His Call. ii. 23—iv. 17	**II. Jehovah and Pharaoh** vii. 8—xi.	iii. Of the State. xxii. 16—xxiii. 19
iv. His Obedience. iv. 18-31	**Judgment**	iv. The Angel Promised. xxiii. 20-33
	i. The Approach. vii. 8-13	
III. Israel and Pharaoh **v.**	ii. First cycle—3 Plagues. vii. 14—viii. 19	**III. The System of Worship** **xxiv.—xl.**
i. Moses and Pharaoh. 1-18	iii. Second cycle—3 Plagues. viii. 20—ix. 12	i. Instruction and Equipment. xxiv.—xxxi.
ii. Moses and Israel. 19-21	iv. Third cycle—3 Plagues. ix. 13—x. 29	ii. Interlude. The People's Sin. xxxii.—xxxiv.
iii. Moses and Jehovah. 22-23	v. Final. xi.	iii. Construction and Consecration. xxxv.—xl.
	III. Jehovah and Israel xii.—xviii.	
	i. Deliverance. xii.—xv. 21	
	ii. Guidance. xv. 22—xviii.	

EXODUS   ✳ ✳ ✳ ✳

THE BOOK OF Exodus is a continuation of the story told in the latter part of the book of Genesis. In Exodus nothing is commenced and nothing is finished. It is a link in the chain of the story of God's dealings with the human race. For the sake of linking the subject to that which has gone before, let it be remembered that the book of Genesis was divided into three parts: first, Generation; secondly, Degeneration; thirdly, Regeneration.

In considering Regeneration we saw the work proceeding with regard to the individual, the family, and society. The last note in Genesis indicated the line of the regeneration of the nation.

We now turn to Exodus. The word "Now," with which the first chapter commences, may with perfect accuracy be translated "And." It is a word marking continuity. If we take the book of Genesis away, the book of Exodus becomes meaningless. All the history in Exodus depends upon that in Genesis. We left the children of Israel a people without a national consciousness, or organization. We are now to study the account of the emergence of the nation.

There are three clearly defined divisions in the book: Bondage, Deliverance, and Organization.

A. BONDAGE

Segregated from the corrupting influences of the land of Canaan, the children of Israel rapidly multiplied in the land of Goshen.

This very growth became a menace to Egypt, and from the standpoint of political expediency Pharaoh was justified in resorting to extreme measures to check it. High enthroned over Pharaoh, Jehovah permitted His people to pass through the long period of oppression and suffering, and so stiffened the national fiber, and thereby made the people strong for the campaigns of the future.

As the appointed time for deliverance approached, the instrument of God was found and prepared. The story of Moses occupies the next section. His preservation presents a wonderfully human picture as it manifests the sweet art of mother-love. The inspiration of love's activity was, as we learn from the New Testament, that of faith.

Jehovah's overruling of circumstances toward the accomplishment of His purpose is seen in the coming of Pharaoh's daughter. The history of the human race has been affected by the fact that on a given day a baby cried into the face of a woman. The baby found its way into the woman's heart, and the woman carried the baby into the heart of Egypt's power. There the future leader of Israel received his education, and the first part of the preparation necessary for the work that lay before him.

Forty years passed away, and the child, having become a man, turned his back upon the court of Egypt, and upon all its splendors. His flight was also under the government of God. If he had attempted to deliver Israel at forty years of age, he would have failed. The man, cultured and refined, with all the learning of his time, passed to the next period of his preparation in the majestic loneliness of the Sinaitic peninsula. It was change from lesser to greater grandeur. The solitude of the mountains, under the golden light of sun by day and the stately solemnity of stars by night, is more full of majesty than all the glitter of an earthly court. There Moses was a shepherd, and so received the next part of his preparation for leadership.

Then follows the account of his direct call and commission. In it Jehovah had to meet and deal with the difficulties of Moses' fear. The victory was with God, and Moses turned his back this time upon the loneliness of the wilderness, and set his face toward the court of Pharaoh.

B. DELIVERANCE

In this division Jehovah emerges from the shadows into clear light, and becomes the center of supreme interest. He is seen dealing with Moses by way of preparation, with Pharaoh in judgment, and with His people in deliverance and guidance.

In the first section we have the account of the answer which Jehovah gave to the complaint of His servant when he was discouraged at his first reception both by Pharaoh and his own people.

This answer consisted in the first place of a great Self-declaration. In the course of it the words, "I am Jehovah," are used four times, and surrounding these declarations are affirmations concerning the Divine activity. "I appeared . . . I was not known . . . I have established my covenant . . . I have heard the groaning . . . I have remembered my cove-

nant . . . I will bring you out . . . I will rid you out
. . . I will redeem you . . . I will take you to me . . . I
will be to you a God . . . I will bring you in . . . I will give
it you." The value of this declaration may be gathered by a
recognition of the difficulty of the position which Moses occupied. The man who had been brought up in the court of
Egypt had returned to declare the authority of another
Potentate, an unseen King. He had been treated with contempt by Pharaoh. The very people he had come to deliver
had refused to hear him. He had returned to God with his
complaint, and the method of the Divine dealing with him
was that of unveiling before Him His own glory. Moses was
never afraid again. There were other failures, but no dread of
God was manifest from that moment to the end. He had seen
a new vision of Him, and doubted His power no more.

And yet fear was immediately manifest, but it was fear of
himself. It was difficult to believe that he could be the instrument of such a God. This new fear Jehovah answered by as-
suring His servant that his strength before Pharaoh would
not be that of his own eloquence or power, but rather that of
Divine preparation and equipment. Then faith triumphed
over fear, and Moses went forward to the work appointed
him.

The next section reveals Jehovah dealing with Pharaoh
in judgment. That judgment moves in three cycles, in each
of which three plagues demonstrate the power of God. These
all failing to bring the heart of Pharaoh into willing submission, a fourth and final judgment fell upon him.

In the story of this process of judgment it is necessary to
draw a most careful distinction between Pharaoh's hardening

of his own heart and God's hardening of his heart. This is one of the great passages in Scripture in which the Authorized Version is apt to mislead. There, throughout the account, it is declared that the Lord hardened the heart of Pharaoh. The Hebrew text does not warrant any such translation. As a matter of fact, it is never stated that Jehovah hardened Pharaoh's heart until the end of the second cycle of plagues.

Moreover, two different words are made use of, although both are translated "hardened." One of these means to make strong or courageous. The other means to make stubborn. It is declared from the beginning that God made his heart strong or courageous, thus setting him absolutely free for the unfearing exercise of his own will. It is never declared that God made his heart stubborn until it had been five times affirmed that he hardened his own heart.

There is a moment when God does that with a man. There is no Bible warrant for teaching that a man will be able, whensoever he chooses, throughout the ages, to turn back to God. Every man has his own probation, and his own opportunity, and the Judge of all the earth holds the balances with infinite precision. Whosoever stubbornly refuses to submit himself to God in the day of opportunity, and that repeatedly, finds at last that his own decision has become his destiny. By the outworking of law God seals the choice of the human will.

In this whole process of judgment the patience of God is as clearly manifest as is His power. In spite of persistent lying and deceit by Pharaoh in the promises made to Moses, God patiently waited. It was not until he had repeated opportunities of yielding himself to the Power Who was manifesting Himself that, by the will and decision and act of God, the stubbornness he had cultivated became such that he could not escape therefrom.

The final section in this division is occupied with the account of the actual deliverance of these people, and the commencement of that wonderful guidance which included provision for all their need, and power for all their weakness.

Judgment is seen in its purpose as it merges into deliverance. As they moved on toward the realization of their nationality, the very calendar was altered, and there dawned for them a new year, and a new order began. Before the march to liberty they observed the religious rite of Passover. This rite was called an ordinance, a feast, a sacrifice. It was wholly an ordinance to be observed. It was essentially a feast of rejoicing or deliverance. It was fundamentally a sacrifice perpetuating the memory of vital and essential truths. The night of the exodus was indeed, as the historian declares, "a night to be much observed." The people passed from slavery to liberty, from the lash of oppression to the place of power, from degradation to the realization of national life.

Immediately the nation, delivered and consecrated, is seen under the direct government and guidance of God. "God led them not by the way of the land of the Philistines, although that was near." "God led the people about."

The first march after that from Egypt was back into a place of danger. The definite meaning of that march was declared to Moses. The just judgment of the sin of Pharaoh must be carried out to its last degree, but it must also be carried out in such a way as to make evident its justice. Was ever the madness and blindness of sin persisted in, more manifest than in the proud preparation of chariots and armies to overthrow and destroy a people for whom God had so wondrously wrought?

No comment is necessary on a story so full of life and color and dramatic power as that of the crossing of the sea. In the silent hush of the march through the solemn night there was revealed to the people the fact that, under Divine government, there are no obstacles which cannot be overcome. In fatuous rebellion Pharaoh and his host attempted to walk by the pathway specially prepared for the men of faith. With the morning watch God manifested Himself in some way to the Egyptians. He "looked forth upon the hosts through the pillar of fire and of cloud." There then dawned upon them the consciousness of their folly, and they attempted flight. It was too late. Their doom was sealed, and with the hand of Moses outstretched by Divine authority, the sea broke over them in rushing waves of destruction, and the power of the mighty people that had oppressed God's nation in spite of every opportunity for repentance was broken forever. It was a great and glorious song that rose upon the morning air on the far side of the sea.

There now commences the more direct story of the guidance of the people by Jehovah. Marah afforded an opportunity for the discovery of the resources of God. Elim was an evidence of His tender care for them. As they passed into the wilderness they began to be conscious of the scarcity of some of the things which they had possessed, even in the midst of Egyptian slavery. Again the resources of their God were proved as He supplied them with manna and with meat. Again their faith was tried by lack of water, and notwithstanding their murmuring against Moses, God was proved to be the God of patience.

The march of the people brought down upon them the army of Amalek. Perfect victory was gained by Israel, and in the first battles the principles of their perpetual conflict were revealed. They won by a combination of fighting and faith, a union of practice with prayer.

This division ends with the story of Jethro. His advice to Moses was reverent in its recognition of the Divine authority, "If thou shalt do this thing, and God command thee so." The fact that Moses acted on his advice is almost certain evidence that he recognized that God was speaking to him through this man.

C. ORGANIZATION

The people of Israel, delivered from bondage, were still a promiscuous multitude rather than an organized nation. In this division we have an account of the giving of the constitution, and of the great work of organization. It is divided into three sections, dealing with matters preliminary and fundamental, the moral code, and the established system of worship.

The Divine purpose of grace was first declared. The people were to be His "peculiar possession . . . a kingdom of priests . . . a holy nation." They were not yet prepared for the fulfillment of so great an intention, and their unpreparedness was manifest in their ready declaration that they would keep all the words of Jehovah. Immediately the new method, necessary in view of their condition of mind, was commenced. They were brought face to face with the supreme fact of the majesty of God. The law was given amid the accompaniments of thunders, voices, fire, and smoke. All of this was symbolic of the majesty and holiness of God. By special covenant He had brought the people near to Himself. It was a nearness characterized by untold blessing. Yet they must be reminded of the majesty of their King, and so be filled with reverence for Him.

The ten words of the moral law were preceded by a proclamation of God concerning Himself, first as to His name, "I am Jehovah"; secondly, as to His relation to them, "thy God"; and, thirdly, as to His deliverance of them from bondage. The Decalogue consisted of two parts. The first four commandments constituted the first, and governed the relationship existing between God and man. The last six constituted the second, and conditioned human inter-relationships. These ten words revealed a philosophy of life as well as a law. The true morality was to be learned from this philosophy. Man's first business is with God. His every other relation depends upon that, and will be created by it.

The effect produced upon the people by the uttering of these words was that they were filled with fear. The nearness of God became a terrible thing as they understood His holiness through the spoken words. Their fear was due to ignorance as surely as was their presumption. The Divine answer was full of grace. They were charged to have no other God, and a way of approach to God was at once provided. It was the way of the altar, and of sacrifice. These earliest instructions concerning the altar were deeply significant. It was to be constructed of simple and unmade things, devoid of any workmanship in which the heart of man might make its boast.

Then followed the laws which were to govern the new nation as a state. These had first to do with the person. The relation of slaves to their masters was dealt with, and they were of such a nature that wherever they were obeyed they led ultimately to emancipation.

The sacredness of life was safeguarded by the enactment that any man taking the life of another was to forfeit his own. If the act was premeditated there was to be no escape. Injury or death wrought by cattle on men and women, and also on cattle, was to be punished and compensated. The laws of property were such as to make it patent that no man was to imagine that when he had fulfilled certain direct obligations to God he might live his life without reference to his neighbor. Wrong inflicted by neighbor on neighbor in the material realm was accounted sin against God in the moral realm.

These requirements were characterized by the most careful adjustment of relation between man and man, and revealed the intimate relation of God to all, and His remarkable interest in every phase and department of human life.

There followed a group of laws promiscuously stated, yet all having to do with the bonds which strengthened the state. In two of them sins of unchastity were dealt with. Passion was penalized, in the more natural expression by stern social requirement, and in the more unnatural by death. A blunt, stern word, "Thou shalt not suffer a sorceress to live," revealed how harmful, according to the mind of God, were all attempts to traffic in secret and hidden things. Laws affecting the lending of money and the receiving of pledges followed, and finally such as conditioned the administration of justice.

In this connection the feasts of the Lord were placed in their true relation to the social life of the people. The sabbatic year was arranged in order that the poor might eat.

—28

C. Organization

The rest of the Sabbath was revealed to be a provision of tender care for cattle and servants also, who were included in its intention. This section ends with a gracious promise which Jehovah made to His people of that Presence which should lead and guide them in all the days to come. A study of the subject of this Presence will show that the Person referred to was the Angel-Jehovah.

The third section deals at length and in detail with the preparation for the true worship which followed upon the promise of the Angel Presence, and the warning against false worship. There was a preliminary solemn assembly of the elders of Israel in the presence of God. Perhaps there is nothing more august in the whole book than this account of the approach of the elders. We are told "they saw the God of Israel." No description is given of what they saw. It may be that Jehovah manifested Himself to them in that Angel Presence which He had promised. It is better, however, to leave the statement as it stands, remembering that it can only be interpreted by the facts which followed, namely that Moses went into yet closer communion with God almost immediately afterwards. The vision was characterized for the elders by immunity from judgment, for upon them "he laid not his hand"; and, moreover, by a sacred act of communion in which they "did eat and drink." Finally, Moses was called beyond the people in the valley, and beyond that more select circle of the elders, into the very midst of the mount, where he received in yet fuller detail the law which was to govern them, and saw the heavenly things, and so learned the pattern of the earthly worship.

In examining the structure of the Tabernacle, it will be well to endeavor to understand what it meant to the people for whom it was provided. That detailed study is not within the compass of our present work. We notice now merely the general method of procedure. The first instructions were not concerning the building itself, but concerning its contents. They began at the very center with the ark, which symbolized the fact of the presence of God, and the right of the people to approach Him as their King. Next in order the table of shewbread was described. Two ideas were suggested by this table. To the Eastern mind a table was always a symbol of fellowship and of hospitality. Thus the nation was reminded of the privilege of fellowship with God, and of the fact of a friendship which expressed itself in hospitality. The golden lampstand was the symbol and the figure of the testimony which these people were to bear to the outside world. The curtains and coverings of tabernacle and tent were made of materials which suggested the conditions among which God could make His dwelling-place. The boards and bars, set up in sockets of silver, spoke, in the symbolism of the time, of the standing of these people as a redeemed nation before God. The veil and the screen indicated at once the exclusion of the people from nearness, and yet the way of their approach through mediation. The veil of the outer court, the brazen altar, and all its fittings, reminded them of the life of devotion, based on sacrifice, which they were called to live. The gorgeous robes of the priest are seen to be in common with everything else, full of symbolic teaching. The ceremony of the priests' consecration is described, as is also the altar of incense, and the arrangements for placing the whole of the furniture within the sacred enclosure.

Instructions followed as to the gathering of the half-shekels from the people, which were to be used in the construction

C. Organization

of the foundation sockets; and also as to the preparation of the holy oil to be used in anointing.

The final words of instruction were those of a promise, full of grace and tenderness, that equipment should be granted to certain men which would enable them to do the work necessary for the construction of the tabernacle.

While the lawgiver was yet in the mount receiving this pattern of heavenly things in order to earthly worship, the people in the valley had fallen into grievous sin. This making of the golden calf consisted of a positive violation of the promise they had made to keep the words of the law. When they said, "Up, make us Elohim," it was not that they desired to substitute other gods for the One God, but rather they sought a similitude of God. Their choice of a calf was in itself significant. In Eastern symbolism the ox was ever the type of sacrifice and service, and they had at least some glimmering of the truth concerning the Divine attitude. It is also to be observed that, the day after the calf was erected, they observed a feast to Jehovah. The evil of their action was seen in the attitude of mind produced in them by their creation of a symbol. They "sat down to eat and to drink, and rose up to play." Worship at once became materialized and sensual.

Moses is manifested in all the grandeur of his character in this connection. His pleading with God was not so much on behalf of the people as on behalf of God. He was swayed by an infinite pity for them, but at the back of the pity, and burning through it like a fire, was a passion for the honor of God. Having stood before God for the people, he came to stand before the people for God. In hot anger he broke the tables of stone, and seizing the calf, ground it to powder, and compelled the men who made it to drink of the water into which it was flung. He then proceeded to the ceremony of mediation and restoration, and passed back into the mount. We have no detailed account of the happenings of the second period save that the tables of the law were written anew. During this second absence the people waited patiently until Moses returned, his face shining with the glory of the awful and solemn fellowship of the mount.

The final movement of the book tells the story of the construction and consecration of the Tabernacle. A willing people offered of their substance until there was "much more" than enough. Then, by the hands of specially equipped workmen, the work went speedily forward until all was completed according to the Divine pattern. This is declared in the general statement "thus did Moses; according to all that the Lord commanded him, so did he." Finally it is recorded, "so Moses finished the work." Everything was completed according to the Divine pattern, and in the Divine order.

Everything symbolized the real presence of Jehovah, and that fact was made living in the consciousness of the people when the glory of Jehovah filled the completed place of worship. So great was the glory that Moses was not able to enter the Tent of meeting.

Thus the nation was organized around the presence and power of Jehovah, and the chronicle closes with the simple statement that they went onward in their journeyings guided ever by the presence of God manifested in connection with this center of their life and worship.

LEVITICUS—*The Book of Laws*

A DEDICATION *The Offerings* i.—vii.	B MEDIATION *The Priests* viii.—x.	C SEPARATION *The People* xi.—xxii.	D CONSECRATION *The Feasts* xxiii.—xxiv.	E RATIFICATION *The Signs* xxv.—xxvii.
Provision for Approach	*Appropriation of Provision*	*Conditions of Appropriation*	*Benefits of Approach*	*Symbols of Relation*
I. The Offerings i.—vi. 7 **The Worship** i. Burnt Offering. i. ii. Meal Offering. ii. iii. Peace Offering. iii. iv. Sin Offering. iv. v. Trespass Offering. v.—vi. 7	**I. Consecration of the Priests** viii. i. Preparation. 1-9 ii. Anointing. 10-24 iii. Sacrifice and New Anointing. 25-36	**I. A People Godgoverned** xi.—xvii. i. Of Health. xi.—xv. ii. The Day of Atonement. xvi. iii. General Instructions concerning Sacrifices. xvii.	**I. The Feasts** xxiii. i. The Sabbath. 1-3 ii. The Passover. 4-5 iii. Unleavened Bread. 6-8 iv. First-fruits. 9-14 v. Pentecost. 15-22 vi. Trumpets. 23-25 vii. Atonement. 26-32 viii. Tabernacles. 33-44	**I. Obligatory** xxv.—xxvi. i. The Land Sabbath. xxv. 1-7 ii. Jubilee. xxv. 8-55 iii. Exhortations. xxvi.
II. The Laws of the Offerings vi. 8—vii. **The Worshipper**	**II. The Priests at Work** ix. i. Offerings for Themselves. 1-14 ii. Offerings for the People. 15-24 **III. Nadab and Abihu** x. i. Their Sin. 1-7 ii. Consequent Warnings. 8-20	**II. A People God-manifesting** xviii.—xxii. i. Separation from Evil Practices. xviii. ii. A Call to Holiness. xix. iii. Laws against Unchastity and Uncleanness. xx. iv. Responsibil'ties of the Priests. xxi., xxii.	**II. Symbols of Consecration** xxiv. 1-9 i. The Oil. 1-4 ii. The Shewbread. 5-9 **III. The Blasphemer** xxiv. 10-23	**II. Voluntary** xxvii. **Vows**

LEVITICUS   * * * *

THIS IS A book of laws. It has been aptly called the hand-book of the priests. Its Hebrew title, Vayyikra, which means, "And he called," is the first phrase of the book itself. The first verse indicates the character of what follows. The moral law had been given from amid the splendors of the mountain. The laws regulating worship were spoken from the tent. Thus the content of the book is linked to the subjects dealt with in Exodus, and is in direct continuation thereof.

The nation had been brought out of bondage and organized. At the very center of its life was a provision for worship in the Tabernacle. The whole outlook of Exodus teaches the supreme place of worship in the life of the nation. It, moreover, reveals the fact that there can only be worship through propitiation, because man is a sinner. The fact of sin thus underlies all now to be considered. The fact of redemption in the purpose and economy of God is seen overshadowing the fact of sin and making worship possible. The laws enunciated here have to do with these matters of supreme importance.

The book falls into five parts. First, the setting forth of the Provision for Approach (i.-vii). Secondly, the Institution of the Priesthood through which the Provision might be appropriated (viii.-x.). Thirdly, the Life of Separation, which is the condition of Appropriation (xi.-xxii.). Fourthly, the Feasts, which portrayed the Benefits of Approach (xxiii.-

xxiv.). Lastly, Symbols of Relation which safeguarded the maintenance of the right of Approach (xxv.-xxvii.).

A. DEDICATION: THE OFFERINGS

In this division there is revealed the provision of God for the approach of His people to Himself in worship. The offerings are first described, and then their laws are enunciated.

As to the offerings, five were needed to perfectly unfold the meaning and method of personal dedication. The first was the burnt offering, which suggested the need for perfect dedication. The lamb without blemish consumed by fire indicated the necessity of a dedication perfect in quality and quantity. The meal offering was the work of men's hands, of the fruits of the ground, the result of cultivation, manufacture, and preparation, suggesting that dedication necessitated the offering of a perfect service as well as a perfect life. Of the peace offering, part was burned by fire and part consumed by the worshipper. It was the symbol of communion. In the white light of the Divine holiness, sin is sin, whether it be willful or not; and the sin offering was provided to teach that the failure of those dedicated to God must yet be dealt with on the basis of sacrifice. The trespass offering was provided for definite acts of wrongdoing. Trespass in this connection is more than a mere missing of the mark. It includes the thought of positive and willful wrongdoing.

The Divine provision for worship having been revealed in the offerings, there followed instructions concerning the method of offering, which revealed the true attitude of the worshipper. In connection with each there were detailed instructions which are full of suggestiveness. The ceremonial was Divinely arranged, and nothing was frivolous or unnecessary. Every detail had signification, and was intended to impress upon the mind of the worshipper truths which were of vital importance, in order that he should recognize the solemn nature of his dedication as a member of the nation whose greatness consisted in its intimate relation to Jehovah.

B. MEDIATION: THE PRIESTS

The second division of the book deals with the laws of mediation. It consists of a brief historical portion, which gives an account of the actual ceremony of the consecration of the priests and the tabernacle, and the commencement of worship; and so sets forth God's provision for the approach of His people to Himself through mediation on the basis of sacrifice. In the midst of a solemn assembly the priests were washed, and Aaron was arrayed in the garments of his sacred office. The holy rites of consecration then moved forward. The ceremonies were repeated daily for seven days.

This account of the consecration of the priests is immediately followed by that of the commencement of their work. The people were first gathered together, bringing with them offerings according to the instructions given. While they stood in solemn stillness in the presence of Jehovah, Aaron, in full official capacity, commenced his work. His first act was that of presenting the sin offering and the burnt offering for himself. Then followed immediately his first acts on behalf of the people. First the sin offering, indicating the necessity for expiation of sin; next the burnt offering, indicating the devotion of the whole life to God;

–*37*

following that the meal offering, speaking of the devotion of work and service; finally the peace offering, the symbol of communion. Thus the values of the offerings of approach could only be appropriated through the mediation of the priests.

At the commencement of the history of the official work of the priesthood there were evidences of failure. Nadab and Abihu, two sons of Aaron, offered strange fire before the Lord, and were swiftly slain by fire. Strangely solemn were the words: "Aaron held his peace." They were his own sons, but his relation to God was superior to his relation to them, and the only attitude becoming to him was that of submissive silence. The other priests were solemnly charged to show no signs of mourning, and to abide at their posts.

C. SEPARATION: THE PEOPLE

While provision for approach was made, and the method of appropriation was provided, there were still very definite conditions which must be fulfilled in order that the people might avail themselves of the provision made. These conditions may be summarized as those of entire separation to God. They were to be a people God-governed and God-manifesting. The Divine government must be recognized and obeyed in the matter of health. Minute regulations were given as to food, as to childbirth, as to leprosy, and as to all uncleanness. In the midst of this section instructions were given for the observance of the great Day of Atonement, which was perhaps the most important religious rite of the whole year in the Hebrew economy. It was the day on which the high priest entered into the holy place, all the arrangements for which entry were given in detail. In the ceremonial of this day provision was made for dealing with the whole question of sin, known and unknown. Most particular instructions were given as to the attitude of the people on the great day. They were to rest and afflict their souls. It was to be a day of solemn fasting and humiliation in which they reminded themselves of the fact of their sin, of the provision made for their cleansing, and of their consequent right of approach to God in worship. Strict instructions were next given concerning sacrifices.

The laws of separation then assumed a slightly altered character. So far the principal note had been that of the fundamental matters of relationship to God. The habits of the life of separation are more particularly dealt with. The people were distinctly forbidden to conform to the doings either of Egypt or Canaan.

Then followed a repetition of laws already given, with one reiterated emphasis: "Ye shall be holy, for I, the Lord your God am holy." No less than fourteen times in the course of one chapter (xix.) does the solemn declaration, "I am Jehovah," occur. Yet further laws concerning unchastity and uncleanliness were repeated, and the death penalty was associated with certain forms of disobedience.

The final section in this division deals with the responsibilities of the priest. Standing, as he ever did, in a place of special nearness to God as the appointed mediator of the people, he must of all men manifest in the externals of life and conduct that holiness without which no man can see the Lord.

D. CONSECRATION: THE FEASTS

The feasts of Jehovah were the national signs and symbols of the fact that the people, dedicated to God as the offerings witnessed, permitted to approach through the mediation of the priestly service, separated in all the details of life, were by God consecrated to Himself.

The foremost place was given to the Sabbath. It was a perpetually recurring feast, to be observed throughout all the year, on every seventh day.

Following this we have the appointment of the set feasts in their relation to times and seasons and the passing of the year. Thus all time-measurements were related to eternal truth. The first feast was the Passover, which merged into that of unleavened bread. With these the year commenced. The Feast of First-fruits was appointed for the land into which God would bring them. Marking the beginning of possession, it served as a constant reminder of the truth that all they had was the result of His giving rather than of their getting.

After a lapse of seven full weeks, during which the whole harvest was gathered, the Feast of Harvest was observed, and Pentecost reminded them that all they needed was provided by Jehovah. The seventh month was the most sacred of all. Therein two great ordinances were observed: the Day of Atonement, and the Feast of Tabernacles. Preceding these, and preparing for them, came the Feast of Trumpets. This was held on the first day of the month. Its characteristic notes were rest, and proclamation of the will of God. The tenth day of the month was the great Day of Atonement, which has already been described. The last Feast of the year was that of Tabernacles. It was observed after all the work was completed, and the results thereof gathered. For seven days the people dwelt in booths, and heard the reading of the law. The section ends with instructions concerning the symbols of consecration, those namely of the oil and the shewbread.

E. RATIFICATION: THE SIGNS

The laws of ratification consisted of the outward signs of the principle of possession to be observed in the land, together with solemn promises and warnings. The first sign was of the Sabbath of the land. In the seventh year of rest the original Ownership of God was recognized. The second sign was that of the jubilee, wherein great human inter-relationships, dependent upon the fact of Divine possession, were insisted upon.

The laws of the year of jubilee affected the land, dwelling-houses, and persons. In these the foundations of the social order were firmly laid. All inter-human relationships, both of person and property, were conditioned in the fundamental relationship of the people to God.

The book ends with a section dealing with vows. The principle laid down is that it is not necessary that vows should be made, but that if they are made they must be religiously observed.

NUMBERS—*The Book of Wandering*

A ON THE MARGIN OF THE LAND *i.—x.*	B EXCLUSION AND WANDERING *xi.—xxv.*	C ON THE MARGIN OF THE LAND *xxv.—xxxvi.*
I. The Order of the Camp i.—iv.	**I. Discontent** xi., xii.	**I. The Census** xxvi.

i. The Census.   i.
ii. The Encampment.   ii.
iii. The Levites.   iii., iv.
	i. Against God xi. 1-3
	   The People.
	ii. Against Circumstances
	   xi. 4-35
	   The Mixed Multitude.
	iii. Against Moses xii.
	   Miriam and Aaron.
		II. The Inheritance of Women xxvii. 1-11

II. The Purity of the Camp v., vi.		**III. The Summons to Moses** xxvii. 12-23
i. Purification from Pollution. v. ii. Special Dedication. vi.	**II. Disaster** xiii., xiv.	(Sequel. Deut. xxxiv.)
	i. Fear. Sending of Spies. xiii. ii. Rebellion. xiv. 1-35 iii. Presumption. xiv. 36-45	**IV. Repetition of Laws** xxviii.—xxx.
III. The Worship of the Camp vii.—ix. 14		**V. War with Midian** xxxi.

i. Offerings of the Princes.   vii.
ii. Order of Worship.   viii.
iii. Passover and Purification.   ix. 1-14
	III. Discipline xv.—xxv.
	
	i. Domestic. xv.—xx. 13
	   a. The Sabbath-breaker.
	     xv.
		VI. Settlement of Reuben, Gad, and half-tribe of Manasseh xxxii.

IV. The Movement of the Camp ix. 15—x.	*b.* Korah, Dathan, and Abiram. xvi.
	   c. Laws. xvii.—xix.
	   d. Death of Miriam. xx. 1
	   e. Failure of Moses and
	     Aaron. xx. 2-13
		VII. List of Journeyings xxxiii. 1-40

i. Determined by the Cloud.   ix. 15-23
ii. The Method of Summons, and Order of March.   x.
	ii. Foreign. xx. 14—xxv.
	   a. Edom. xx. 14-21
	   b. Death of Aaron.
	     xx. 22-29
	   c. Victory over
	     Canaanites. xxi. 1-3
	   d. Murmuring. xxi. 4-9
	   e. Sihon and Og.
	     xxi. 1-35
	   f. Balaam. xxii.—xxv.
		VIII. Repetition of Laws xxxiii. 50—xxxvi.

NUMBERS * * * *

THE BOOK OF numbers deals with the wilderness. It is principally the story of a long discipline due to disobedience. The national idea moves forward, for God ever protects His own purposes against the failure of His chosen instruments. In the book of Exodus we saw the emergence and consolidation of the nation which God had chosen to be the channel of communication between Himself and the world at large. In Leviticus we considered the laws of its worship. In Numbers the movement toward actual possession of the land commences. This movement, however, was hindered for nearly forty years, and the book is principally occupied with matters relating to that period. It closes with the account of the return of the people to the borders of the land.

Thus it naturally falls into three parts, the first dealing with the Preparation for Entrance (i.-x.); the second giving the story of the Exclusion and Wandering (xi.-xxv.); while the last gives the account of how, after the long discipline, they were brought back and prepared for actual Possession (xxvi.-xxxvi.).

A. ON THE MARGIN OF THE LAND

In this division we watch the final movement of the chosen people in preparation for coming into the land, and in doing so observe the order of the camp, the purity of the camp, the worship of the camp, the movement of the camp.

By the command of Jehovah the men from twenty years

and upwards were numbered. This was the first movement in preparation not merely for their entrance to the land, but for their carrying out of the Divine purpose. That purpose was first punitive. In the interests of purity corrupt peoples were to be swept out.

Definite instructions were given concerning the relative positions to be occupied by the tribes, both in the time of encampment and on the march. At the center of everything was the Tabernacle. The Levites were encamped round the two sides and at the back thereof. Moses and the priests occupied the fourth side, close to the courts of worship. Outside the enclosure the tribes of the nation were grouped under their standards according to the Divine command. The service of the Levites was described in detail. Their sacred work was carefully apportioned both for the march and for places of encampment. All these provisions solemnly impressed upon the people the supreme importance of worship, and revealed to them the orderliness of Jehovah.

On the eve of the coming of the people into the land, the necessity for the purity of the camp was emphasized. All who were unclean were put outside. This, of course, does not mean that they were left to perish, but that they were not allowed to march in their proper place with the tribes of the people. For the time being they were camp-followers only. Moreover, the necessity for moral rectitude was insisted upon, and such as had in any way sinned against others made restitution.

Having provided for the purity of the camp by the exclusion of the unclean, special instructions were given concerning cases of peculiar and special devotion to a life of separation to God. There is absolutely nothing monastic in the order of the Nazarites. These men did not separate themselves from their fellow men, or from their ordinary avocations, but remained in the midst of their fellows, and prosecuted their daily calling, though yet maintaining an attitude of special consecration. At the close of this section dealing with the purity of the camp, we find the specific form in which the priestly blessing was to be pronounced upon the people.

Immediately following are the arrangements concerning the worship of the camp. This section opens with an account of the voluntary offerings on the part of the princes. It is first to be noticed that the giving was voluntary, and next that it was equal, thus precluding the possibility of a spirit of rivalry, and indicating a great unity of purpose. While all the story might have been told in a few words, it is set forth with elaborate detail. Every man is named, and every gift is chronicled.

In the final arrangements concerning worship, before the moving forward of the people, the one symbol referred to is that of the light, which was the type of the witness-bearing of the nation. In the consecration of the Levites, no anointing oil or blood was used, neither was any specific dress provided. The sign of their cleansing was the simple one of water. Finally, the great Passover feast was observed. A month later a special observance of the same feast was arranged for such as, through defilement, had been precluded from taking part in the first.

At last everything was ready for the march, and the hosts waited only the Divine will. The people were to follow the moving of the cloud, and to answer the blast of the trumpet. Careful instructions were given concerning the use of these trumpets. Different notes suggested different meanings to those who listened. On the twentieth day of the second month the actual movement of the camp commenced. The division ends with the suggestive words which Moses used at the commencement and close of each successive movement of the hosts. They indicated the profound recognition on his part, and on that of the people, that everything centred around the presence and government of God, both in regard to the victory of Israel over her enemies, and her own safety and well-being.

B. EXCLUSION AND WANDERING

In this second divison of the book is revealed the failure of man. Its general movement may be indicated by the words, Discontent, Disaster, Discipline.

The discontent manifested itself first against God. At the beginning there was no open revolt against authority. The people were, however, in all probability, conscious of the irksomeness of restraint. They were learning that liberty was not license, and so throughout the camp the Lord heard the tone of murmuring and discontent. His judgment was sudden and swift. Moses became an intercessor, and the fire abated.

A second time discontent manifested itself, and this time is was expressed against circumstances. Influenced by the mixed multitude which had accompanied them, the people hungered after the things of Egypt, apparently forgetting the cruelty of its bondage. Moses was perplexed and perturbed, and he poured out his complaint into the ear of God. In infinite patience God talked with him, and to the murmuring people He sent quails, and through them the

B. Exclusion and Wandering

punishing plague. As the psalmist afterwards sang, "He gave them their request; but sent leanness into their souls." A third time there was a manifestation of rebellion. Miriam and Aaron, in whose hearts there was evidently an undercurrent of jealousy, made the marriage of Moses to a Cushite woman the occasion of protesting against his exercise of authority. They were punished immediately, and pardoned in answer to the earnest cry of Moses.

The hour had now arrived when the people should have gone forward. The story of the sending of the spies, as told in Numbers, indicates that it was done in obedience to a Divine command. The comparison of this, however, with Moses' account of it in Deuteronomy will show that this command of the Lord was the sequel to a determination on the part of the people to do so. This was in itself an act of suspicion and unbelief. The spies were sent, and in forty days returned, bringing with them a majority report and a minority report. All were agreed as to the desirability of the land. The majority, however, had seen the difficulties of possessing, and beyond this had seen nothing. The minority had seen first Jehovah, then the excellencies of the land, and finally the difficulties. The essential difference was that of the vision of God. The people were influenced, as, alas! men too often are, by the majority, and in unutterable folly they declared that it was preferable to return to Egypt. One of the most magnificent pictures in the Old Testament is presented to us as Moses interceded with God on behalf of the people. His plea, however, was not based upon pity in his heart for the sinning people, but upon that deeper passion for the honor of the name of God. The people were pardoned, but they must be excluded from the land. They had themselves rejected the land toward which God had brought them, and their punishment was that they should not enter it.

This decree of Jehovah was followed by an instance of false repentance. The men came to the consciousness of their unutterable folly, and then resolved to go up and possess the land in their own strength. The result was defeat and disaster.

Then began the long years of discipline. It is a story full of sadness. At first we follow the people through a period in which the results of their failure were manifest in their internal life. The Sabbath was violated, and the guilty one was punished. Korah, Dathan, and Abiram led an organized opposition against Moses, and were summarily dealt with. After this new arrangements were made, and old laws repealed. Then as the people, toward the close of the forty years, were led back into the neighborhood of Kadesh-barnea, Miriam died, and was buried. In this neighborhood, moreover, Moses and Aaron both failed in simple allegiance to God, and they also were excluded from the land.

It would seem as though the people were moving, on their own part, in an attempt to find their way into the land. Their endeavor to go in one direction, changed through the opposition of Edom, would seem to indicate the absence of the guiding pillar of cloud and fire. During this time Aaron died. His death was a solemn and impressive ceremony. The robes of his office were transferred to his son. He then died, and was buried amidst the lamentations of the people. The transference of the outward symbols of the priestly office taught the truth that the priesthood was greater than the man. In these final days of exclusion Balaam was hired to prophesy against the people of Jehovah.

C. ON THE MARGIN OF THE LAND

The third and last section of the book of Numbers is devoted to the second numbering of the people, and their preparation for coming into possession of the land from which they had been excluded for forty years. In a study of this division there are discoverable two movements. The first chronicles historic facts in their sequence, and the other is an insistence upon the Divine government by the repetition of certain laws with new emphasis and applications. There is a marked continuity of purpose, notwithstanding the change of persons. Two men only of those who had come to the margin were allowed to pass into the land. The time for the passing of Moses had come, and in all God's dealings with him there is manifest a great tenderness. The final account of his death is reserved for the ending of the next book. In this, however, we have the story how he publicly appointed his successor. When the call of God came to him to ascend the mountain and view the land, and to be gathered to his people, the final passion of his heart was that which had so long sustained him in the midst of all the trying circumstances of his work as leader. He thought of the great congregation as the congregation of Jehovah, and prayed for the appointment of a successor. Thus there was granted to him the satisfaction of knowing that the one who succeeded him in leading the people was the man of God's own choice.

After a repetition of the laws concerning the great religious observances of the people, we have the account of a war directly connected with the sin of the people, resulting from the influence of Balaam. In the battle Balaam was slain. Even here the imperfection of the people was manifest in the desire on the part of Reuben, Gad, and the half-tribe of Manasseh to settle on the wrong side of the Jordan. Moses failed in judgment in allowing them to do so, out of which failure trouble arose in after-years.

The book ends with a list of the journeyings of the people during the period of their exclusion, and a repetition of laws with special reference to settlement in the land. Through all the book there is manifest the forward movement, not of men, but of Jehovah. It is a revelation of the sure procedure of God toward the final working out into human history of His purposes for the world.

DEUTERONOMY—*The Book of Reviews*

A RETROSPECT	B RÉSUMÉ OF LAWS	C WARNINGS	D THE COVENANT	E THE SONG	F THE BLESSING
		xxvii. 11— *xxviii.*	*xxix.—* *xxxi. 13*	*xxxi. 14—* *xxxii. 47*	*xxxii. 48—* *xxxiii.*
i.—iv. 43	*iv. 44—xxvii. 10*				
I. Introduction i. 1-5	Introduction iv. 44-49	I. Introduction xxvii. 11-26	I. Introduction xxix. 1-2a	I. Introduction xxxi. 14-30	I. Introduction xxxii. 48-52
The Place	Character and Place	The Curses			
II. The Discourse i. 6— iv. 40	II. The Discourse v.—xxvi.	II. The Discourse xxviii.	II. The Discourse xxix. 2b xxx.	II. The Song xxxii. 1-43	II. The Blessing xxxiii.
i. Review of the forty years. i. 6—iii. ı̈. Exhortation to Obedience. iv. 1-40 a. Retrospective. 1-24 b. Prospective 25-31 c. Introspective. 32-40	i. "Testimonies." v.—xi. 31 a. The Decalogue. v.—vi. b. Obedience. vii.—xi. 31 ii. "Statutes." xi. 32—xvi. 17 a. Worship. xii.—xiv. 2 b. Some effects of Worship on Conduct. xiv. 3—xvi. 17 iii. "Judgments." xvi. 18—xxvi. a. Principles of Law. xvi. 18-20 b. Administration of Law. xvi. 21—xxvi. 19	i. The Blessing of Obedience. 1-14 ii. The Cursing of Disobedience. 15-68	i. The Appeal to the past. xxix. 2b-9 ii. The Terms of the Covenant. 10-29 iii. The Appeal to the future. xxx.	i. Introduction. 1-3a ii. A Contrast. 3b-5 iii. An Appeal. 6a iv. A Contrast. 6b-18 v. Judgment. 19-28 vi. Lament. 29-30 vii. Final Deliverance. 31-43	
III. Sequel iv. 41-43 Cities of Refuge	III. Sequel xxvii. 1-10 Provision for the Land		III. Sequel xxxi. 1-13	III. Sequel xxxii. 44-47	

Historic Conclusion   xxxiv.

DEUTERONOMY ✳ ✳ ✳ ✳

DEUTERONOMY IS THE last of the books of the Pentateuch. It is didactic rather than historic. Its actual history covers a very brief period, probably not many days. It consists of a collection of the final public utterances of Moses. The form in which we possess it is in all likelihood the result of the work of an editor, who collected these great discourses, and connected them by such information concerning the occasion of their utterance as should make them a consecutive series, and thus give them value in their relation to the earlier books. It has been surmised that this work was done by Joshua, and this, to say the least, is quite probable.

The book is, therefore, essentially a book of Moses, for it consists of his final words to the people whom he had led, first out of Egypt, and then for forty years of wandering in the wilderness. It may therefore be most simply divided by the six discourses which it chronicles. Of these discourses the first was a Retrospect (i.-iv. 43); the second, a Résumé of Laws (iv. 44-xxvii. 10); the third, the uttering of Warnings (xxvii. 11-xxviii.); the fourth, concerned the Covenant (xxix.-xxxi. 13); the fifth was a great farewell Song (xxxi. 14-xxxii. 47); and the sixth, a final Benediction (xxxii. 48-xxxiii.).

A. FIRST DISCOURSE: RETROSPECT

In reviewing the forty years of wandering Moses dealt with the three great movements: first, from Horeb to

Kadesh-barnea; secondly, from Kadesh-barnea to Heshbon; and finally, from Heshbon to Beth-peor. In looking back he was careful to state all the facts in the light of God's government. Their disturbance at Horeb was due to the direct commandment of God, and even though the path of the wilderness was a terrible one, they had not been left to grope their way through it alone. God had ever moved before them, choosing them out a place in which to pitch their tents. Moreover, he reminded them that they had not only been the objects of God's love, but that His power had wrought on their behalf.

Having surveyed the history from Horeb to Beth-peor, he exhorted them to obedience. Reminding them of the importance of the commandments, he based his appeal upon the greatness of God and the perfection of His law, insisting upon it that their whole existence and history centered around a spiritual ideal. There had been granted to them no visible form of God, even amid the majestic manifestations of Sinai, and therefore he warned them against making any graven image.

Continuing this exhortation to obedience, he looked into the future, and in the light of subsequent history his words were indeed prophetic. At the close of the first discourse we have a brief account of his appointment of three cities of refuge.

B. SECOND DISCOURSE: RÉSUMÉ OF LAWS

A general introduction indicates the place, time, and subject of this second discourse, which deals with testimonies, statutes, and judgments. The testimonies were the actual words of the law given. and these were first dealt with. The statutes were the provisions for worship, and the conduct harmonizing therewith. The judgments dealt with the arrangements for civil and religious authority, and the administration of justice.

A study of the testimonies, or uttered words of the law, reveals the fact that no vital change was made at any point in the nature or binding force of the commandments. There were slight verbal alterations, but these were due to the circumstances in which they were uttered. One striking difference is that in connection with the law concerning the Sabbath: the ground of appeal was no longer the rest of God in creation, but their position as redeemed from Egypt's bondage. Having referred to the ten words, a great statement was made as to the deepest value thereof, and as to the peoples' corresponding responsibility. "Jehovah, our God, is one Jehovah." The true response of the people to this truth was that of fear issuing in obedience, and resulting in well-being. The discourse then proceeded to deal with the responsibilities in detail.

Dealing with the statutes, he carefully warned them against idolatry, and commanded that all idols and false places of worship were to be destroyed as they entered the land. Nothing was to be allowed to seduce them from their loyalty to Jehovah in worship. He then passed to injunctions, which revealed his consciousness of the effect of worship on conduct; and, finally, restated the arrangements for the observation of the great feasts.

In dealing with judgments, he first commanded the appointment of judges and officers, and then declared the principles upon which they were to act. The threefold medium through which the will of God would be interpreted

to the people—that, namely, of king, priest, and prophet—
he then described. The laws of peace and of war were set
out in great detail, and finally provision was made for a ceremony of blessing and cursing on the mountains of Ebal and
Gerizim when the land was entered.

C. THE THIRD DISCOURSE: WARNINGS

In this third discourse Moses devoted himself to solemnly
warning the people. Before proceeding to this more specific
purpose of his discourse, he spoke of the blessings which
would follow obedience. He described first the effect of disobedience in their own borders. Adversity of every kind
would overtake them in trade, agriculture, and in matters
of health; and in every way there would be suffering if there
were disobedience. In all this he really uttered prophetic
words, for we find here a detailed description of the Roman
victories, which came so long after, and the ultimate
destruction of the city and the driving out of the people.

D. FOURTH DISCOURSE: THE COVENANT

The terms of the covenant had been already given. In
urging the people to be true to it, Moses first of all referred
to the Lord's deliverances wrought in the past, from Egypt,
through the wilderness experience, and in the day of battle
on the eve of their coming into possession. His appeal was
made to all classes. In prophetic and burning words he described what would be the result of their breaking the
covenant. Recognizing their imperfection, and their inability to appreciate the methods of the Divine government,
he enunciated a principle of far-reaching importance and

perpetual application. He declared that the secret or hidden or mysterious things belong to God, while the things revealed belong to us and to our children. Continuing his discourse, he uttered words thrilling at once with all tenderness and urgency of appeal. We have here a great prophetic evangel, the value of which Israel has perhaps not learned even unto today.

After the conclusion of the formal discourse, Moses spoke to the people of his own departure, and encouraged their heart in view of their coming into the land by reassuring them of the presence and power of God.

E. FIFTH DISCOURSE: THE SONG OF MOSES

Preceding the public uttering of the great Song, Moses and Joshua appeared before the Lord in order that the latter might be officially appointed to succeed in the administration of affairs. Jehovah then solemnly spoke to His servant, telling him that his time had come to sleep with his fathers, but that the people he had so long loved and cared for would indeed fulfill his predictions concerning failure, and would be visited with punishment. Gloomy enough was the outlook for the great leader, but it was the occasion of one of those manifestations of the Divine love which are so full of beauty.

It was in face of this foreknown fact of failure that he was commanded to write the song. The purpose of it was distinctly stated. A song embodied in the nation's life remains from generation to generation, and in days of disaster will constitute a haunting memory, testifying to truth concerning God. Songs often remain after commandments are forgotten. The law was written and committed to the priests;

the song was written and taught to the people. The first part of the song consisted of a call to attention, and a statement concerning its nature. Heaven and earth were called to listen while the servant of God proclaimed the name of God. Moses sang of God as to His greatness, His perfection, His justice, His faithfulness. Then in a description equally brief, he referred to the people. It was a sad contrast. There is nothing said of them which is good. There follows a description of the tender government of God which is full of exquisite beauty. It is a revelation of the love which lies behind all law. The figure of the eagle and its method with its young is one of the most superb in the whole Bible, as a revelation of the truth that through methods which may appear almost unkind, love is working perpetually toward the higher development of those upon whom it is set. In strange contrast the song now became a wail as the unfaithfulness of the loved people was described. Such unfaithfulness had resulted in discipline necessarily severe. The people who had turned to the false were abandoned to the false. The face which had been as the sunlight was hidden from the people who had turned their back upon it. The very tenderness of love had become the burning of a fierce anger, and the benefits had been replaced by chastisement. The song then broke out into lament, "Oh, that they were wise," and celebrated God's ultimate deliverance of His people. Finally Moses appealed to the people to be obedient.

F. SIXTH DISCOURSE: THE BLESSING

These were the final words of the man of God. Often had he set before his people blessing and cursing. His last words were of blessing only. In stately and majestic language he affirmed anew the majesty of Jehovah. The great words of blessing were pronounced upon the tribes, Simeon only being omitted. Reuben and Judah were referred to in terms which suggested that they were to be saved, yet so as by fire. Levi, having lost all earthly things for the special honor of bearing the word of God, would receive the reward of such sacrifice. Benjamin was to have the special protection needed by frailty. The choicest things were said concerning Joseph. His were all precious things, and the good will of Him Who dwelt in the bush. His, therefore, was the portion of government. In Issachar and Zebulun there was to be triumph over disability. Gad, overcoming at last, was to be a judge; and Dan was the type of conquest. Naphtali was to be satisfied, and Asher sustained. Thus in his final benediction Moses made the peculiar realization of blessing by the tribes unfold the all-sufficiency of God.

The last chapter of Deuteronomy is in all probability the writing of another hand. It contains the story of the death of Moses, the equipment of Joshua for his work, and a last tender reference to the great leader and lawgiver. The passing of Moses was full of beauty. In the fact of his exclusion from the land toward which his face had so long been set was his punishment. Yet it was tempered with mercy. There had been no weakening of his force. His career ended in full strength. He went up into the mount to die, and Jehovah gave him a vision of the land, and buried him in the valley.

The last words are almost a wail of sorrow: "There hath not arisen a prophet . . . like unto Moses." Thus ends the last book of the Pentateuch. The nation created for regeneration among the nations was on the margin of possession. The great story will now move on through the history of these people to the coming of the promised One.

JOSHUA—*The Book of Possession*

A THE CONQUEST OF THE LAND *i.—xii.*	B THE SETTLEMENT OF THE PEOPLE *xiii.—xxi.*	C JOSHUA'S FAREWELL *xxii.—xxiv.*

I. Mobilization   **i., ii.**
 	
i. The Call to Arms.   i.
   a. God's Call to Joshua.
                1-9
   b. Joshua's Call to the
       People.   10-18
ii. The Mission of the
     Spies.   ii.
	**I. Settlement According
	to Mosaic Promise
	xiii., xiv.**
	
	i. The two-and-a-half
	    Tribes. xiii.
	ii. The Possession of Caleb.
	               xiv.
		**I. The Two-and-a-half
		Tribes xxii.**

II. Advance   **iii.—v.**
 	
i. Crossing of the Jordan.
            iii., iv.
   a. The Crossing.   iii.
   b. The Final Movements.
               iv.
ii. Ceremonies of Con-
    secration.   v.
	**II. Settlement of Nine-
	and-a-half Tribes
	xv.—xix.**
	
	i. Judah. xv.
	ii. Ephraim. xvi.
	iii. Manasseh. xvii.
	iv. Benjamin. xviii.
	v. The Rest. xix.
		**II. Farewell Addresses
		xxiii.—xxiv. 15**
		
		i. First Address. xxiii.
		ii. Second Address.
		         xxiv., 1-15

III. War   **vi.—xi.**
 	
i. Jericho.   vi.
ii. Ai.   vii., viii.
   a. Defeat. "But."   vii.
   b. Victory.   viii.
iii. Beth-horon.   ix., x.
   a. The Deceit of the
       Gibeonites.   ix.
   b. The Defeat of five
       Kings.   x. 1-27
   c. The following
       Conquests.   28-43
iv. The Northern Kings.   xi.
	**III. Settlement of Cities
	of Refuge and
	Levites xx., xxi.**
	
	i. Cities of Refuge. xx.
	ii. The Levites. xxi.
		**III. Final Things
		xxiv. 16-33**

IV. Extent of the Conquest xii.		

JOSHUA ✳ ✳ ✳ ✳

IN THE ANCIENT Hebrew Scriptures the second division was known as "The Prophets." In this division the first section included Joshua, Judges, First and Second Samuel, and First and Second Kings, and was called "The earlier Prophets." Of this division Joshua was the first book. It derives its name from the great leader, the story of whose work is chronicled therein.

Of its authorship nothing definitely is known. In all likelihood it was largely the work of Joshua himself, subsequently added to, and completed, by some one or more of the elders of Israel. Its content is a continuation of the history of the chosen people. The nation led out by Moses is led in by his successor. This book tells the story. It is the book of possession, and may be broadly divided into three parts: The Conquest of the Land (i.-xii.); the Settlement of the People (xiii.-xxi.); Joshua's Farewell (xxii.-xxiv.).

A. THE CONQUEST OF THE LAND

In this first division there are four sections dealing with mobilization, advance, war, and the extent of conquest.

The first fact chronicled is that of the call to arms, and therein God's call to Joshua. His right of entrance to the land was that God had given it to His people. His power of entrance was that of the Divine presence. The conditions of his success were that he should be strong and courageous, and in order to this he was charged to be obedient to the law. Thus commissioned, Joshua issued his call to the people. It was characterized by urgency and despatch. Within three days the hosts were to move forward. Forty years before, spies had been sent. Of these Joshua had been one of the few who had brought back a report true to God. He now sent them again. The principle of sending was, however, quite different. It was now the action of that faith which was characterized by caution. The spies, returning, made it evident that the promise of God that no man should be able to stand before Joshua was being fulfilled, for according to Rahab, "their terror was fallen upon the people." Rahab's action was that of faith. The men of Jericho shared her conviction, but rebelled against it. She recognized the activity of God, and yielded.

The first movement of the people forward was of such a nature as to impress them with the truth of their positive relation to God. They came on to the actual soil of Canaan, not by deflecting the course of the river, nor by bridging it, but by direct Divine intervention. While obedience demanded haste, haste was not allowed to cause neglect of religious observance. Safely over Jordan, the hosts paused while stones were gathered out of the river bed, and a ceremony of worship was observed. This miraculous crossing of the river produced a remarkable effect upon the surrounding people. "Their heart melted, neither was there any spirit in them any more." Before the actual march commenced, the Captain of the hosts of the Lord appeared to Joshua, and he was thus made to recognize that his authority and leadership depended upon his submission and obedience.

Preparation thus being complete, the hosts of Israel became the scourge of God, moving forward in judgment upon the corrupt peoples of the land. It is impossible to imagine anything more calculated to impress upon them their absolute weakness than the method of their victory. Marching priests and blatant horns are utterly inadequate to the capture of a city, and represent foolishness, judged by all ordinary methods of human warfare. The victory was theirs, but they were taught that it came not by might, and not by power, but by their being obedient to the government of God. Suddenly the triumphant people were defeated. The reason was the sin of a man, which was also the sin of a nation. Israel had now become a nation, and no one person could act alone. Thus individualism is seen to become a far greater responsibility when it has ceased to be isolation. The sin of the one became the sin of the community. The evil thing was judged and punished, and through this return to obedience on the part of the nation the campaign moved victoriously forward. The story of the taking of Ai is one of acute military strategy. Thus the truth is brought into prominence that in prosecuting the work of Jehovah there must ever be a recognition of the value of the use of the best in human reason. Strategy without obedience is useless. Obedience includes the use of reason, the employment of common sense. The fame and dread of the people were spreading far and wide. The kings of Canaan formed a league against the oncoming hosts. Before they had time to take action a new peril threatened Israel in the strategy of the Gibeonites. The deceit being discovered, the action of Joshua was immediate and decisive. He felt bound by the letter of his covenant, but condemned the Gibeonites to perpetual servitude, making them hewers of wood and drawers of water. This action of the Gibeonites aroused the anger of the confederate kings. In their peril the men of Gibeon appealed to Joshua. By forced marches he reached the scene of action, and the rout of the kings was complete.

Joshua followed up his advantage, immediately moving forward until the whole of Southern Canaan was in possession of Israel. A new confederacy had now to be faced and fought. The northern kings joined in an attempt to break the power of the conquering hosts. Turning swiftly north, Joshua routed them, and then turned back to Hazor, where victory still attended him. All this did not happen immediately. Indeed we are told that it had occupied "a long time." The division ends with a detailed summary of the extent of the conquest.

B. THE SETTLEMENT OF THE PEOPLE

Dean Stanley says, "In the book of Joshua we have what may without offense be termed 'The Doomsday Book of the Conquest of Canaan.' Ten chapters of that book are devoted to a description of the country, in which not only are its general features and boundaries carefully laid down, but the names and situations of its towns and villages enumerated with the precision of geographical terms which encourages, and almost compels, a minute investigation." Joshua was now about ninety years old, and was reminded that the conquest was by no means complete. There remained "much land to be possessed." In order that the chosen people might be able to complete the conquest and perfectly possess the land, it was now to be divided amongst them. Toward this end the provision made for the two and a half tribes on the east of Jordan was ratified.

–66

B. The Settlement of the People

Then followed provision for Caleb, who after forty-five years of waiting, claimed a definite possession in the land. Joshua's recognition of his friend, and of his right to a choice of possession, was quick and generous. He granted him the mountain which he asked, and blessed him.

In the settlement of the nine and a half tribes Judah stood first, as being the kingly and imperial tribe. The possession allotted to it was that of the fighting front. It remained loyal longer than the rest, but subsequently became contaminated with the abominations of the heathen. God's hosts are never overcome in fair and open fighting with His foes. It is the friendship of the world which is enmity against God. The inheritance of Joseph was divided between Ephraim and Manasseh. To Ephraim was allotted a fertile and beautiful district, nevertheless a place of difficulty because it still lay in the power of the Canaanites. The territory of Manasseh was indicated, and then Ephraim and Manasseh, being discontented, complained to Joshua. His answer was characteristic. He knew the weakness of these tribes, and that they would become strong only by conflict. He instructed them to go up to the mountain and cut down the trees, and drive out the foes, and so enlarge their borders by cultivating their possession, rather than by seeking new ground. After rebuking the seven tribes for being slow to possess the land, Joshua erected the tabernacle at Shiloh. He then appointed three men from every tribe to divide the land into seven parts. One of these portions was allotted to each of the remaining tribes. The first of the seven fell to Benjamin. Then follows an account of the portions of the rest—Simeon, Zebulun, Issachar, Asher, Naphtali, Dan. When all had been provided Joshua asked and obtained his portion.

Having thus come into possession of the land, the cities of refuge were provided according to the arrangements already made. Following these, the Levites made application for their cities and pasturage, and the rulers and the people made ready response. Jacob's prophecy concerning Simeon and Levi, "I will divide them in Jacob, and scatter them in Israel," was fulfilled in the case of Levi, in the scattering of the tribe through all the others. This second division of the book ends with the statement that the Lord gave, and they possessed the land. His promise to them was fulfilled. No man had been able to stand before them. Their enemies had been wholly delivered into their hands. They never completely realized the purpose of God in these matters. The failure, however, was wholly due to their own disobedience, and the record at this point fittingly closes with the declaration of the fidelity of God: "There failed not aught of any good thing which the Lord had spoken unto the house of Israel; all came to pass." Failure to possess what God gives is always that of His people, and never the result of unwillingness or weakness on His part.

C. JOSHUA'S FAREWELL

At the close of the war the two and a half tribes returned to their possession on the other side of the Jordan. As they departed Joshua commanded them for their fulfillment of their promise, and charged them to be loyal to Jehovah. As the time for Joshua's passing approached, he twice gathered the people together, and delivered farewell messages. The burden of the first was that of the power and faithfulness of God, with an earnest desire for the faithfulness of the people to Him. His warnings were perhaps more fiery and

C. Joshua's Farewell

searching than those of Moses. The address was a wonderful revelation of the strength of that man, and of that strength as consisting in his acute consciousness of the relationship of the people to Jehovah, and his consequent passion for their loyalty to His law. The second time he gathered them to Shechem. In his final address he traced their history from the call of Abraham to the then present time, emphasizing the fact that everything of greatness in their history was of God. He finally charged them, "Now, therefore, fear the Lord, and serve him." There was a fine touch of courageous irony in the appeal which followed. If they would not serve God he called them to choose whom they would serve. Would they go back to the gods of their fathers beyond the river, or would they turn to the gods of the Amorites, in whose land they dwelt? He ended by declaring, "As for me and my house, we shall serve the Lord."

The book closes with death—the death of Joshua, the second great leader, and the death of Eleazar, the second priest. Yet in the midst of the darkness of death there is something almost weird and yet full of the suggestion of hope—the bones of Joseph were buried in the land.

JUDGES—*Deliverances*

A AFTER JOSHUA *i.—iii. 6*	B THE JUDGES *iii. 7—xvi.*	C APPENDIX *xvii.—xxi.*
I. Israel and the Canaanites i. i. Judah. 1-21 ii. Joseph. 22-29 iii. The Rest. 30-36 **II. Israel's Failure ii.—iii. 6** i. Jehovah's Messenger. ii. 1-5 ii. The People under Joshua. 6-10 iii. Synopsis of History. 11-23 iv. The Enemies. iii. 1-6	**I. First Declension iii. 7-11** i. Sin. Idolatry. ii. Punishment. 8 years' oppression. iii. Deliverance. OTHNIEL. **II. Second Declension iii. 12-31** i. Sin. ii. Punishment. Eglon. 18 years. iii. Deliverance. EHUD (SHAMGAR) **III. Third Declension iv.—v.** i. Sin. ii. Punishment. Jabin. 20 years. iii. Deliverance. DEBORAH. BARAK. **IV. Fourth Declension vi.—viii. 32** i. Sin. ii. Punishment. iii. Deliverance. GIDEON. **V. Fifth Declension viii. 33—x. 5** i. Sin. Baalim. ii. Punishment. Abimelech. iii. Deliverance. TOLA. JAIR. **VI. Sixth Declension x. 6—xii.** i. Sin. Idolatry multiplied. ii. Punishment. Philistines. Ammon. 18 years. iii. Deliverance. JEPHTHAH (Successors) **VII. The Seventh Declension xiii.—xvi.** i. Sin. ii. Punishment. Philistines. 40 years. iii. Deliverance. SAMSON.	**I. Micah xvii., xviii.** i. Micah's Idolatry. xvii. ii. Its Punishment by Danites. xviii. **II. The Levite xix.—xxi.** i. The Outrage. xix. ii. War between Israel and Benjamin. xx. iii. Preservation of Benjamin. xxi.

JUDGES * * * *

THE BOOK OF Judges historically covers the period from the conquest of the land and the death of Joshua to the judgeship of Samuel and the introduction of the monarchy. It is a story, on the human side, of disobedience and disaster, and on the Divine of direction and deliverance. It is, as its name signifies, the book which gives us the account of the judges. These men were dictators raised up in times of special need for the deliverance of the people. The chronological history of the book ends with chapter xvi., which connects naturally with the first book of Samuel. That history properly begins in chapter iii. So that we may consider the book in three divisions: Conditions after Joshua (i.-iii. 6); the Period of the Judges (iii. 7-xvi.); Appendix (xvii.-xxi.).

A. CONDITIONS AFTER JOSHUA

The first act of the people after the death of Joshua was that of seeking to know the will of God as to who should commence the final work of conquest. Judah, the kingly tribe, was appointed. It is evident that this work, begun in earnest, eventually weakened. A false toleration toward a people utterly corrupt, who ought to have been exterminated, resulted in the ultimate undoing of the chosen nation.

The story is told of the coming of the messenger from Gilgal, who called them back to loyalty to God. A brief retrospect follows of the condition of affairs under

Joshua, and then a synopsis of the history which is to be set out in greater detail. In this synopsis the rotation of sin, punishment, and deliverance is the keynote to the historical portion of the book.

B. THE PERIOD OF THE JUDGES

This division of the book contains the story of seven consecutive failures, punishments, and deliverances.

The first declension was that of neglect of God and turning to idols. The punishment consisted of eight years of oppression. When under this affliction they cried to God, and the first of the judges appeared in the person of Othniel. Forty years of rest followed.

The second declension occurred after the death of Othniel, when the people sinned again. Punishment came from Eglon, and lasted for eighteen years. Then they cried to the Lord again, and Ehud, with whom Shamgar was associated, was the deliverer. Eighty years of rest followed.

The third declension then followed, and they were delivered into the hands of Jabin. Twenty years of oppression resulted, which became most terrible under Sisera. Again they cried, and were heard. The story of deliverance is full of romance and poetry, being associated with the name of Deborah. This daughter of the people, true child of faith, had suffered under the intolerable consciousness of the degradation of her people. She gained the ear of many to such a degree that she was appointed to judge the people, and at last she called Barak to her aid. He, inspired by her teaching, and she, helped by his consecration, went forward, and Israel was delivered from oppression. The great song of Deborah is full of fire and passion, and a remarkable index to the character of the woman herself. It may be divided into two parts. The first was a great chant of confidence, telling the story of the deepest secret of the victories won. The second part celebrated the victory. Everything ended with a cry: "So let all thine enemies perish, O Lord." Following this deliverance the land had rest for forty years.

The fourth declension issued in the victory of Midian, under whose oppression the people groaned for seven years. So terrible was it that the people hid themselves in dens and caves and strongholds. At last, in answer to their cry, the movement of deliverance began, and associated with this was the name and story of Gideon. He is seen first at his work, with the bitterness of the whole situation burning like a fire in his bones. When there came to him the supernatural visitor his double consciousness was confessed. "Did not the Lord bring us up?" "The Lord hath cast us off." He was conscious of the true relation of the people to Jehovah, and also that on account of their sin they had been judged. Called to act as deliverer, we follow him in his work of preparation. This proceeded in three stages. It began at home. He broke down the altar of Baal in connection with his father's house, and restored the worship of God. The second movement was that of the sending out of the call. The final one was his fellowship with God, in which signs were granted to him. The story of the conflict is one of the most remarkable on record. In response to his call to all the hosts of the people only thirty-two thousand gathered. Of these such as were faint-hearted and afraid were bidden to return, and twenty-two thousand went back. Those remaining were subjected to a further test, with the result that only three hundred were left. The victory was perfect; but it was so won as to teach the people that the one and only condition was that of dependence upon God and implicit obedience to His command. Following the deliverance from the oppression of Midian, Gideon had to deal with troubles among his own people. This section ends with an account of the last things concerning Gideon. One of them was characterized by great nobility, and the other revealed a weakness which issued in trouble. They sought to make him king. He absolutely refused, and thus indicated his disinterestedness and his loyalty to God. The story of the making of the ephod is somewhat difficult of interpretation. In any case, the effect produced was evil, for the people were thereby seduced from their loyalty, and Gideon himself suffered deterioration.

The fifth declension followed immediately upon the death of Gideon. They fell into the sin of worshipping the Baalim. Judgment this time came from within rather than from without. Abimelech, a natural son of Gideon, a man unprincipled and brutal, but of great personal force, secured to himself the allegiance of the men of Shechem, and practically usurped the position of king. In order to make his position secure, he encompassed the massacre of all the sons of Gideon, except Jotham. His parabolic prophecy from the height of Mount Gerizim indicated the line along which judgment would fall upon the sinning people. The tyranny of Abimelech's rule lasted for three years. He was then slain by the hand of a woman, and a period of forty-five years' quietness followed under the dictatorship of Tola and Jair.

The sixth declension was characterized by an almost utter abandonment of the people to idolatry. The list of the forms which this idolatry took is appalling. Judgment came this time from the Philistines and the men of Ammon, and continued for eighteen years. At last, sore distressed, they cried to God, and for the first time it is recorded that He refused to hear them, and reminded them of how repeatedly He had delivered them. The true attitude of Jehovah toward them, however, flamed out in a remarkable statement, ". . . his soul was grieved for the misery of Israel." Deliverance came at length through Jephthah, a study of whose history is full of interest. He was the son of a harlot, and had been thrust out from his inheritance by the legitimate sons of his father. The iron had entered his soul, and he had gathered to himself a band of men, and had become a kind of outlaw free-booter. He was a man of heroic daring, having certain excellencies of character which marked him out as capable in a crisis of need. The story of his victory and his vow follows. After his victory the men of Ephraim complained that they had not been called to help, as they had already done in the case of Gideon. The quarrel reveals the sad disintegration of the nation. The consciousness of its unity seems to have been largely lost.

The seventh declension opens with the declaration, "Israel again did that which was evil," and they were again delivered to discipline at the hands of the Philistines, under whose oppression they lived for forty years. Here occurs one of the strangest stories of the Old Testament, that of Samson. It is the story of a great opportunity and disastrous failure. Everything would seem to have been in his favor. His birth was foretold by an angel visitor. This foretelling led to his special training, and finally he was moved in his early years by the Spirit of the Lord. Grown to manhood's estate, he went to Timnath, and there was swept away by his passions into an unholy alliance. The story of his exploits is most remarkable. The circumstances of them are not to his credit. The overruling hand of God is seen checking the power of the Philistines through him, but through all, his deterioration is manifest. His final fall occurred at Gaza. There is nothing, perhaps, in the sacred writings at once more pathetic and tragic than Samson, with his eyes put out, grinding in the house of the Philistines. At last, out of his degradation he cried to God, and in his death struck the heaviest blow at the people from whose oppression he ought to have delivered his own nation.

Here ends the history of our book. It is taken up again in the first book of Samuel. The remaining chapters and the book of Ruth have their chronological place in the period already dealt with.

C. APPENDIX

The events here chronicled may have taken place closely following the death of Joshua. They give us a picture of the internal condition of the people, and it is most probably that they were added with that intention. Micah's act was a violation of the second commandment. His action was not that of adopting the idolatries of the heathen. His mother's language showed her recognition of Jehovah. "Blessed be my son of the Lord." Moreover, Micah's words when he persuaded the Levite to be his priest showed the same thing. "Now know I that the Lord will be my God." The images were intended to aid him in his worship of Jehovah. The whole story is a revelation of a degenerate condition. Micah had robbed his mother. On making restitution he accompanied the act, at her instigation, with this religious movement. The consent of the Levite to become a priest in the house of Micah for the sake of a living was a further revelation of the same degeneracy.

The story of the backsliding of individuals is followed by an illustration of its widespread existence among the people. The Danites, in the course of seeking new territory, found Micah and the condition of things established in his house. When presently they moved forward to possess, they did not hesitate to seize his images and capture his priest.

The story of the Levite follows, and is a clear revelation of the startling moral conditions. Resulting from it, the nation was stirred to its center, and a great moral passion flamed out. Israel went to war with Benjamin. Uninstructed zeal will, even in the cause of righteousness, often go beyond its proper limits. The carnage continued until not above six hundred men of the tribe of Benjamin were left. Then followed a sudden revulsion, and pity operated to the saving of Benjamin.

RUTH—*Faith Amid Faithlessness*

A THE CHOICE OF FAITH *i.–ii.*	B THE VENTURE OF FAITH *iii.*	C THE REWARD OF FAITH *iv.*
I. Naomi's Sorrows **i. 1-13** i. Elimelech to Moab. 1-2 ii. The Sorrows. 3-13	**I. Naomi** 1-5 Doubtful Yet in light of times	**I. The Redemption** 1-12
II. Ruth's Choice **i. 14-22** i. Orpah. 14 ii. Ruth. 15-18 iii. The Home-Coming of Bitterness. 19-22	**II. Ruth** 6-9 The Claims of Kinsman Rights	**II. The Marriage** 13a
III. Boaz' Field **ii.** i. Ruth's Purpose. 1-3 ii. Boaz. 4-16 iii. The means of Support. 17-23	**III. Boaz** 10-18 i. The Appeal to the next. of Kin. ii. The Tender Love.	**III. The Issue** 13b-22

RUTH * * * *

THE BOOK OF Ruth stands in striking contrast to the book of Judges, and yet is closely connected with it. In that book the national outlook has been presented, and so dark has it been as to create the impression of universal pollution. The story of Ruth illustrates the truth that God has never left Himself absolutely without witness. Throughout all the period of degeneracy there had been loyal and beautiful souls: children of faith, living, in the midst of the conflict and strife, the life of loyalty to God, simple, trustful, and triumphant.

This book is the story of a few such. Some incidents in their history are grouped together with fine poetic beauty. It is indeed an idyll of faithfulness amid infidelity. It has, moreover, the value of being a link in the history, showing how God led on to the next stage. All the interest of the book centers around the persons whose names are on every page. It may be divided into three divisions: the Choice of Faith (i.–ii.); the Venture of Faith (iii.); The Reward of Faith (iv.).

A. ᴛ ᴇ CHOICE OF FAITH

During a time of famine Elimelech, his wife, and two sons, went into the country of Moab to find bread and escape trouble. It is questionable whether their action was justified, and the sorrows which followed would seem to be of the nature of chastisement. To begin with, their sons married Moabitish women. Then Elimelech died, and his sons also, so that sorrow on sorrow came to the heart of Naomi. It is perfectly evident, however, that their action was rather that of foolish blundering than of willful rebellion. Through all they maintained their faith in the one God. Perhaps it would be nearer the actual facts of the case to say that Naomi, through all her suffering, was loyal. When the heart at its deepest is true to God, grace finds an opportunity to work through chastisement to best results, notwithstanding the follies of a faltering faith.

When at last Naomi turned her face again to her own country, with great generosity she urged her daughters-in-law to leave her, and settle among their own people. This was the occasion of that choice of Ruth which in its devotion, and in the manner in which she expressed it, has become enshrined in the admiration of the world. With constant recurrence Ruth's language has been used to express the fidelity of love. It was the choice of a strong affection. The young woman found her heart closely knit to the older one, and she declined to be severed from her in the pathway that lay before her, choosing to share whatever the future might have in store for the one upon whom her love was set. This hardly touches the deepest note, for it is impossible to read her language without seeing that the very reason of her love for Naomi was the new faith which she had learned from her. The deepest note in her expression of devotion was "thy God my God," and it was to Jehovah she appealed. She announced her devotion to Naomi even to death. The language of Naomi at the home-coming showed that she looked upon the sorrows that had come to her as God's testimony against her and His affliction of her. There was no

touch of rebellion in what she said, but that gracious recognition of chastisement which always indicates that the
lessons have been learned.

The home-coming was to poverty, and the practical problem of life faced the two women. This was rendered more
difficult by the fact that Ruth was a Moabitess. Yet she it was
who faced the fight, and went forth as a gleaner to gather
what would suffice for present sustenance. The human side
of things is beautifully expressed in the words, "Her hap
was to light on the portion of the field belonging unto Boaz."
The lines of the picture are few, but they are strong, and a
man of fine quality is revealed to us. His greeting to his
laborers, "The Lord be with you," and their ready
response, "The Lord bless thee," reveal a man of strong and
yet natural religious life. His presence in the field, oversee-
ing the affairs of harvest, and his quick recognition of the
strange girl gleaning, show a man of business capacity. Then
all the rest of the story evidences the graciousness of his
temper and the greatness of his heart. He knew that in all
probability a Moabitish woman would not be very earnestly
welcomed among his people; and he therefore, with as-
siduous care, provided for her. His influence is at once seen
in the absence of objection among the people, and their
readiness to co-operate with him. In short, Boaz stands out
as a man of finest fiber, living simply and strongly in a
degenerate age.

B. THE VENTURE OF FAITH

Gleaning as a means of livelihood could only last through
harvest, and Naomi was anxious about the future, especially
that of Ruth. As the outcome of her anxiety we have the

story of her venture to interest Boaz more fully, and bring about a marriage between him and Ruth. Of course the expedient to which she resorted must be judged in the light of her own age, as we have so constantly to remember. Yet, notwithstanding this, it can hardly be characterized as other than doubtful, and on the basis of faith it is difficult to justify it.

Yet again, it was rather an error of judgment than willful disobedience, and the overruling love of God moved on to beneficent issue. One element, and perhaps the strongest, was the confidence in Boaz which this venture revealed. In order to provide for the future, Naomi's appeal should have been made to one nearer of kin, but the whole attitude of Boaz toward Ruth had inspired such confidence in him that it was through him she hoped for succor. The story of her venture was on the whole to his honor rather than to theirs.

C. THE REWARD OF FAITH

The nobility and faithfulness of Boaz are manifest in this story. It is hardly possible to read this book naturally without believing that Boaz had already found himself in love with Ruth, and there is no doubt that he was perfectly ready to take the responsibility of the next-of-kin, but there was one who had a prior right, and in loyalty to the law of his people he gave him the opportunity. It is an interesting picture presented to us of the gathering of the elders in the gate, and the legal statement of the case. The next-of-kin had a perfect right to abandon his claim, seeing that another was ready to assume it; and moreover, it can hardly be denied that he was justified on the ground of not desiring to run the risk of impoverishing his own family, seeing that

C. *The Reward of Faith*

Boaz was well able to fullfil all the obligations of the case.

The story ends with poetic simplicity and beauty. "Boaz took Ruth, and she became his wife." Nothing need be added to this to indicate the joy and reward of two faithful souls, Naomi was at last comforted. The women of her own people spoke words of cheer to her, which unquestionably were full of comfort as they sang the praise of the one who had chosen to share her affliction, and had become the medium of her succor.

There is a stately simplicity in the story of the issue. "They called his name Obed: he is the father of Jesse, the father of David." In this final word of the book there is manifest the Divine movement in the history of the chosen people. Thus the kingly line was ordered in the midst of infidelity, through faithful souls. Presently the people clamored for a king, and one was appointed for a time, through whom they learned the difference between earthly rule and the direct government of God. The man after God's own heart succeeded him, and his coming was from those who had realized the Divine ideal, and walked humbly with God. Yet a larger issue followed as the centuries passed. From this union came at last, as to the flesh, Jesus the Christ.

I SAMUEL—*Transition*

A SAMUEL *i.—vii.*	B SAUL *viii.—xv.*	C DAVID *xvi.—xxxi.*
I. Preparation i.—iv. 1a	**I. Appointment viii.—x.**	**I. Preparation xvi.—xx.**
i. Birth and Childhood. i.—ii. 11 ii. Life at Shiloh. ii. 12–36 iii. Call. iii.—iv. 1a	i. The people's demand. viii. ii. Samuel's Search. ix. iii. Anointing and Coronation. x.	i. Anointed. xvi. ii. Progress. xvii.—xviii. 5 iii. Difficulties. xviii. 6—xx.
II. Crisis iv. 1b—vii. 1	**II. Reign xi.—xiv.**	**II. In Exile xxi.—xxvii.**
i. Eli. iv. 1b–22 ii. The Ark. v.—vii. 1	i. Kingdom established. xi., xii. ii. Wars. xiii., xiv.	i. Flight. xxi. ii. Varied experiences. xxii.—xxvii.
III. Judgeship vii. 2-17	**III. Rejection xv.**	**III. Returning xxviii.—xxxi.**
i. Twenty years. ii. Ebenezer. iii. Samuel, governing on Circuit.	i. War with Amalek. ii. Disobedience. iii. Rejection. iv. "Samuel mourned for Saul."	i. Saul and the Witch. xxviii. ii. David. xxix., xxx. iii. Death of Saul. xxxi.

I SAMUEL * * * *

THE FIRST BOOK of Samuel covers a period of transition in the history of the nation. It deals with the process from the judges to the kings. The condition of the chosen people under the judges we have seen to have been one of terrible degeneracy. It was during this period that they practically rejected God from being King. The clamor for an earthly king which followed was the natural outcome of this practical rejection.

In this book we have the history of the people from the last of the judges, Samuel, through the troublous times of Saul, in which they learned what government by man really meant, to the beginning of the reign of the king chosen by God, David.

The book naturally falls into three sections around the names of these three men. The periods of their influence overlap, but there is sufficient definiteness in the changes to create the possibility of the following analysis: Samuel (i.-vii.); Saul (viii.-xv.); David (xvi.-xxxi.).

A. SAMUEL

In the dark and troublous times Jehovah is seen working toward deliverance by answering the prayer of faith as it operated in the heart of a simple and trusting woman. There was much of human passion manifest in her desire, but the fact that she turned to Jehovah is evidence of her trust in Him; and upon the basis of that evidence He prepared a way for the future guidance of the people. Her boy Samuel was dedicated for life to the service of God.

The story of the life at Shiloh reveals two movements going forward simultaneously in Israel, those namely of degeneration and regeneration. The corruption of the priesthood was appalling. Within the precincts of the Tabernacle Samuel was preserved from pollution, and grew in the fear of the Lord.

At last, while yet a boy, Samuel was distinctly called, and the first message entrusted to him was a terrible one. A further period of training and growth followed before he was ready to assume the work of leadership. During that period the Lord vindicated him by permitting no word he spoke to fall to the ground, that is, to fail of fulfillment.

The crisis of judgment foretold by Samuel came in connection with the Philistine attack upon the people. In the midst of the disaster, hoping to save themselves, the men of Israel carried the ark of God into the fray. It was an entirely superstitious use thereof, and was utterly unavailing. The Philistines captured the ark itself.

The history of their possession of it is a most interesting one, in that it reveals how, when a people of God fail to bear testimony for Him among the nations, He becomes His own Witness. They first lodged it at Ashdod, in the house of the fish god, Dagon, with disastrous results to the idol. With speed and in fear they carried it to Gath, and a plague fell upon the people. They moved it hastily to Ekron, and painful and troublesome tumors broke out upon the people. At each move judgment became more severe, and Philistia found that, if she had been able to conquer and break the power of Israel, it was a different thing when she had to deal with Israel's God. At last they decided to send the ark back, accompanied by offerings which indicated their recognition of the fact that their plagues had been the visitation of God. Joshua of Beth-shemesh received the ark in a way worthy of an Israelite.

A dark period of twenty years is now passed over without detailed record. It would seem that during that time Israel was under Philistine rule without any definite center of worship. During this period Samuel was advancing from youth to manhood, and approaching the hour of his leadership. This was ushered in by the lamenting of the people after God. Of this he took advantage, calling them to return to Him, and put away all strange gods. They obeyed, and were summoned to Mizpeh. Here, by a direct Divine intervention, the power of Philistia was broken, and her cities restored to Israel. Samuel erected an altar, and called it Ebenezer. This man of clear vision recognized both the government of God and its beneficent method. The Lord had helped them, through chastisement, to sorrow for sin, and through such sorrow to freedom from oppression.

In a brief paragraph the story of his actual judgeship is told. At Ramah was his home, and from there he journeyed in circuit once a year to Bethel, Gilgal, and Mizpeh, thus maintaining oversight, and administering the affairs of the people.

B. SAUL

The book now merges into its second division, which has to do with Saul. The people clamored for a king. The occasion of their request was the maladministration of the sons of Samuel and their sinful practices. The real principle underlying it was a desire on their part to be, as they said, "like all the nations." They had been chosen to be unlike the nations, a people directly governed by Jehovah. Samuel declared to them what the issue of their wish would be if it were granted.

Saul was in every way a remarkable man. In the pursuit of his filial duty he was led into contact with Samuel. While they were alone, he communicated to him his Divine appointment. How long elapsed between this and his formal presentation to the people we do not know. This took place at Mizpeh. Here Saul manifested the first sign of weakness of character which eventuated in his failure. His hiding behind the stuff is often quoted as evidence of his modesty. Modesty, however, becomes sin when it prevents any man from stepping at once into the place to which God is calling him.

Returning to his house at Gibeah Saul did not take up the responsibilities of the kingship until the Ammonite invasion stirred him, and he gained a complete victory over them. Samuel immediately gathered the people to Gilgal, and Saul was confirmed in the kingship. On that occasion Samuel delivered what was practically his last great address to the nation. A study of that address will show how clearly Samuel understood that these people could only be great as they remained loyal to the throne of God. Two chapters give an account of the wars Saul waged. The Philistines gathered themselves together with the express intention of destroying the power of the chosen people. It was in the midst of the fear which possessed the Israelites that Saul manifested his self-independence by offering sacrifice in the absence, and without the instruction, of Samuel. The king's deterioration in character is manifest, moreover, in the fact that he remained idle in Gibeah with his army, and it was at this time that Jonathan made his great strategic attack upon the Philistines, which resulted in their rout.

Saul was commissioned by Jehovah through Samuel to smite Amalek, and in connection with that campaign occurred the sin which filled his cup to the brim, and caused him to be rejected.

While he was victorious, he was disobedient in that he spared Agag and part of the spoil. The two men are seen in striking contrast at this point. Saul, the man of great opportunity, miserably failing, and passing along the pathway of disobedience to ruin. Samuel, rejected long ago of the people, still mighty in his allegiance to God, burning in anger, denouncing in force, and finally, in a white heat of loyalty, himself hewing Agag in pieces. It was the last interview between the king and the prophet prior to the latter's death. Very touching is the statement, "Samuel mourned for Saul." When he failed, Samuel denounced him without sparing, and then in loneliness mourned over him.

C. DAVID

We now come to the third section of the book, in which David is the principal figure. Samuel was rebuked for his prolonged mourning, and was commissioned to arise and anoint the new king. Through the melancholy of Saul, David found his way to the court. Then immediately the two men are seen in the presence of a national danger. Saul, notwithstanding his position and his army, was utterly incompetent. David, without human resource, but conscious of the true greatness of his people, and sure of the strength of God, gained his victory over Goliath. One of the most charming love stories of the Bible is that of the friendship between Jonathan and David. Coincident with the commencement thereof, the hatred of Saul against David deepened, and manifested itself in deeply laid schemes and unworthy methods, in which he attempted to rid himself of his rival. These were trying days for the young man anointed to the kingly office, and it was natural that he should flee to Samuel for protection. Saul fast became an irresponsible madman, while David, through all the painful discipline, was being prepared for the work that lay before him.

At last the land itself seemed too hot to hold him, and he took refuge in flight. The period of his exile was character-ized by varied experiences. Once he found refuge at Achish among the Philistines, and there had to feign madness. Com-ing at last to Adullam, he gathered around him a band of the outcasts of his own people. During this period Samuel died. Twice the life of Saul was in David's hands, and on each occasion he spared it. So terrible was the pressure of these dark days that David himself became pessimistic. "He said in his heart, I shall now perish one day by the hand of Saul," and he passed into Gath, thus taking refuge among the Philistines.

Perhaps there is no chapter in Old Testament history more tragic than that of Saul's end. The last manifestation of his degradation was that of his visit to the witch of Endor. The men of Philistia became afraid of David, and he was dismissed from their midst. He returned to Ziklag, and found that it had been sacked by the Amalekites.

The closing chapter of our book is draped in sackcloth and ashes. It tells the story of the end of the career of one

C. David

of the most disastrous failures. Saul died upon the field of battle by his own hand. The chief spiritual value of this whole book lies in the solemn lessons it teaches by the life and failure and death of this man. Forevermore his story proclaims the fact that great advantages and remarkable opportunities are no guarantees of success, unless the heart be firm and steady in its allegiance to principle and its loyalty to God.

II SAMUEL—*Theocratic Monarchy*

A DAVID'S RISE *i.—x.*	B DAVID'S FALL *xi.—xx.*	C APPENDIX *xxi.—xxiv.*
I. The Reign over Judah i.—iv.	**I. The Sin xi., xii.**	**I. The Government of God xxi. & xxiv.**
i. His lamentation for Saul and Jonathan. i. ii. His anointing as King of Judah. ii. 1-4 iii. War between Judah and Israel. ii. 5—iv.	i. War. xi. 1 ii. Sin. 2-27 iii. Repentance. xii.	i. Famine. xxi. ii. The Census. xxiv.
II. The Reign over the whole Nation v.—x.	**II. The Punishment xiii.—xviii.**	**II. The Character of David xxii.—xxiii. 7**
i. Crowning. v. 1-5 ii. First Victories. 6-25 iii. The provision for the Ark. vi. iv. Concerning the Temple. vii. v. Conquests. viii. 1-14 vi. The appointment of Officers. 15-18 vii. Kingly kindness (Mephibosheth). ix. viii. Victories over Ammon and Syria. x.	i. In the Family. xiii.—xiv. 24 Amnon and Tamar. Absalom. ii. In the Kingdom. xiv. 25—xviii. Absalom. **III. The Restoration xix.—xx.** i. The King's return. xix. ii. Insurrection quelled. xx.	i. Psalm. xxii. God's Government. ii. Psalm. xxiii. 1-7 David's Failure. God's Faithfulness. **III. The Heroic Age xxiii. 8-39** The mighty men. Here, as at the close of the First Book, several matters are dealt with, not chronologically, but as illustrating the times under consideration.

II SAMUEL * * * *

THIS BOOK DEALS almost exclusively with the history of David. Not with the whole of it, for it begins in I. Samuel, and runs on into I. Kings, and is dealt with from another standpoint in I. Chronicles. It is, however, the principal history of his kingship, and presents to us the picture of the theocratic monarchy. The people had clamored for a king. God first gave them one after their own heart; He then gave them one after His own heart. By him also the failure of mediation in government was manifested. Yet he, by relation to God maintained even through times of sinning, contributed to the movement of history toward the one true King. There are three main divisions: David's Rise (i.-x); David's Fall (xi.-xx.); Illustrative Appendix (xxi.-xxiv.).

A. DAVID'S RISE

In this first division of the book there are two movements, the one dealing with David's reign over Judah, and the other with his reign over the whole nation.

The book opens with the story of the bringing to David by an Amalekite of the news of the death of Saul. The story was evidently a fabrication. David dealt with him severely, and then sang his great lamentation over the death of Saul and Jonathan. Over Saul and Jonathan it is stately and dignified, but it merges into extreme tenderness when it deals with his friend Jonathan only.

Anointed king of Judah, David's first act was that of inquiring of God as to what he should do. The spirit of Saul, which was that of antagonism to David, was perpetuated in Abner, who set himself to consolidate the kingdom of Israel around the house of Saul. Joab, a strange and rugged character, at once fierce and faithful, was nevertheless unswerving in his loyalty to David. In the first battle between Israel and Judah under these respective leaders, Asahel was slain. His death entered like iron into the soul of Joab, who never rested until his vengeance was satisfied on Abner. The struggle was a long and weary one, but, as the chronicler declares, "David waxed stronger and stronger, but the house of Saul waxed weaker and weaker."

David had won the heart of all Israel by his consistent justice and his manifestation of magnanimity toward those who stood in his way. The people recognized the kingly qualities of the man, and he was at last crowned king of the whole nation. His first victory was that of the taking of Jebus. An element of weakness manifested itself at this point, when, having come into possession of the kingdom, he multiplied his concubines and wives.

Victorious in war, the king was not unmindful of the central truth of that national life over which he was called to preside. He brought the ark into the capital. In close connection with the account of his doing so, the story of his desire to build the Temple is told. It was a perfectly natural and, indeed, a proper desire. So much was this the case that it appealed to Nathan, who advised him to do all that was in his heart. It was not, however, in the will of God that he should carry out this work, and the prophet was sent to deliver the message which was neither in agreement with David's desire nor with his own opinion. The story reveals the triumph of both Nathan and David in their ready submission to the declaration of the will of God. The prophet unhesitatingly delivered his message, even though it contradicted his own expressed opinion. David immediately acquiesced in the will of God, and worshipped.

The story of David's victories has a closer connection with his desire to build the Temple than appears upon the surface. By these victories he not only strengthened his position, but he gathered treasure. The house of the Lord was still in his mind, and although he knew that he would not be permitted to build, he was yet gathering in preparation for the work of his son.

There is an exquisite tenderness about the story of David and Mephibosheth. The king's love for Jonathan was still fresh. One can easily imagine how, in the days of his growing prosperity, he would think of the old strenuous times, and his friend's loyalty to him under circumstances so full of stress and peril. For David, the house of Saul, which had done him so much harm, was redeemed by his love for Jonathan, and he instituted inquiry as to whether there were any left of that house to whom he might show kindness for the sake of his friend. This inquiry was rewarded by the finding of Mephibosheth, whose very lameness was tragic and pathetic, in that it had been caused by the flight of his nurse on the awful day of Jezreel, when his father and grandfather had fallen together. To him the king restored the lands of Saul, and set him as an honored guest at his own table.

The record proceeds to give an account of victories gained over Ammon and Syria. Joab is revealed in all the rugged and terrible strength of his nature. It is interesting to note that he made no allowance for the possibility of ultimate defeat in his conflict with Ammon. When arranging for the battle, he divided his forces, but did so in order that if the Syrians on the one side should be too strong for him, the people under Abishai, his brother, should help him; or if, on the other hand, the children of Ammon should be too strong for Abishai, he would help him. It does not seem to have occurred to him that the combination may have been too much for them both. This is the true quality of the soldier. We are not surprised that the issue was victory for Joab. This story constitutes the culmination of the account of David's rise to power, and prepares for the terrible story of his fall, by showing us the general circumstances under which that fall occurred.

B. DAVID'S FALL

In all the Bible there is no chapter more tragic or more full of solemn and searching warning than that which tells the story of David's fall. Carefully pondering it, we notice the logical steps downward, following in rapid succession. First David tarried at Jerusalem. It was the time of war, and his place was with the army, but he remained behind in the sphere of temptation. In briefest quotations we may indicate the downward movement. "He saw," "he sent and inquired," "he took." The king is fallen, in answer to that inner weakness which has already been manifested as existing, from the high level of purity to that of terrible sin. His sin against Uriah, one of the bravest of his soldiers, was even more dastardly than that against Bathsheba. From the merely human standpoint the unutterable folly of the whole thing is evident, as it is seen how he put himself into the power of Joab by sharing with him his guilty secret. In a year the prophet Nathan visited him and charged him with his sin. One can almost imagine that after the year of untold misery this visit of Nathan came as a relief to the guilty man. His repentance was genuine and immediate.

The sincerity of David's repentance was manifested in his attitude in the presence of the punishment which now commenced to fall upon his head. When the child died, David worshipped. The sin of Amnon afflicted him grievously, but because it was after the pattern of his own, his arm was nerveless. Perhaps the severest suffering of all came to him through the rebellion of Absalom. The story is indeed full of tragedy. The heartlessness and cruelty of Absalom fell like an avalanche of pain upon the heart of David, and it is a question whether he suffered more in the day of Absalom's short-lived victory or in the dark and dreadful hour of his defeat and slaying. His lament over Absalom is a perfect revelation of grief.

At last, the rebellion being quelled, the king was brought back to the kingdom, and there was a reconstruction, new officers being appointed in the different departments of state.

C. APPENDIX

As at the close of the first book, so here several matters are dealt with, not in chronological order or relation, but as illustrating the times which have been under consideration. This appendix contains matter which reveals the direct government of God, two utterances of David which are a revelation of his real character, and an account of some of the deeds of the mighty men, which shows the heroic spirit of the period.

The account of the famine was one written to give a purely national lesson. Saul had broken faith with the Gibeonites, and the guilt of his action had neither been recognized nor expiated. The sin of the ruling house was the sin of the people, and it is noted by God, and must be accounted for. Hence the famine, which was only stayed when, by the sacrifice of the sons of Saul, the nation had come to consciousness of its guilt, and repented thereof.

The character of David is revealed in two psalms. In the first we find the deepest things. Such convictions as those of the absolute sovereignty of Jehovah, of His omnipotent power to deliver, of the necessity for obedience to His law, and of assurance that in the case of such obedience He ever acts for His people, constituted the underlying strength of David's character. In all likelihood the psalm was written before his sin, and if so it will readily be understood how terrible was his sorrow as he subsequently recognized his failure.

The second contains the last words of the great king. They breathe the consciousness of his own failure, and yet sing the song of the Divine faithfulness.

The reign of David was pre-eminently the heroic age in Israel's history. This is demonstrated in the whole list of the mighty men and the illustrations of their exploits which are given. It is interesting to remember that these were men who had gathered to him in Adullam, men who elsewhere are described as in debt, in danger, and discontented. They were men possessed of natural powers which had been spoiled, but in whom such powers had been redeemed and realized.

The book closes with one other picture, reminding us of the direct government of the people by God in that He visited king and nation with punishment for the numbering of the people. It has been objected that there was nothing sinful in this taking of a census, seeing that it had been done before in the history of the people by the direct command of God. But therein lay the contrast between previous numberings and this. *They* were by the commandment of God. *This* was done from some different motive. That the act was sinful is evident from David's consciousness that it was so, and in the presence of his confession it is not for us to criticize. As we have said, the motive undoubtedly explains the sin. Perhaps, while that motive is not explicitly stated, we may gain some idea of it from the protest of Joab, "Now the Lord thy God add unto the people, how many soever they be, an hundredfold, and may the eyes of my lord the king see it: but why doth my lord the king delight in this thing?" A spirit of vainglory in numbers had taken possession of the people and the king, and there was a tendency to trust in numbers to the forgetfulness of God. The choice of David as to punishment again revealed his recognition of both the righteousness and tenderness of Jehovah. He willed that the stroke which was to fall should come directly from the Divine hand rather than through any intermediary.

The book ends with the story of the erection of the altar in the threshing floor of Araunah the Jebusite, and in that we see finally the man after God's own heart turning the occasion of his sin and its punishment into one of worship.

I KINGS—*Disruption*

A THE PASSING OF DAVID *i.—ii. 11*	B SOLOMON *ii. 12—xi.*	C DIVISION *xii.—xvi.*	D ELIJAH *xvii.—xxii.*
I. The Rebellion of Adonijah i. 1-37 II. The Crowning of Solomon i. 38-53 III. The Last Charge and Death of David ii. 1-11	I. "In all his Glory" ii. 12—x. 　i. Solomon and the Traitors. ii. 12-46 　ii. The first Divine appearing. iii. 1-15 　iii. The Greatness of Solomon. iii. 16—iv. 　iv. His Life Work: The Temple. v.—viii. 　v. The second Divine appearing. ix. 1-9 　vi. Material Magnificence ix. 10—x. II. The Passing of the Glory xi. 　i. Degeneracy and Doom. 1-13 　ii. Execution of Judgment. 14-43	I. Rehoboam & Jeroboam xii.—xiv. 　i. The Revolt of the ten Tribes. xii. 　ii. Warning to Jeroboam. xiii.–xiv. 20 　iii. Rehoboam's reign. 21-31 II. Kings of Judah xv. 1-24 　i. Abijam 　ii. Asa III. Kings of Israel xv. 25—xvi. 　i. Nadab 　ii. Baasha 　iii. Ela 　iv. Zimri 　v. Omri 　vi. Ahab	I. The Curse Pronounced xvii. II. The Judgment of Carmel xviii. III. Elijah in the Wilderness xix. IV. The Downfall of Ahab xx.—xxi. 　i. Benhadad. xx. 　ii. Ahab and Naboth. xxi. 1-16 　iii. Elijah pronouncing judgment. 17-29 　iv. Micaiah's prediction and Ahab's death. xxii. 1-40 　v. The Kings of Israel and Judah. 41-53

I KINGS * * * *

THE TWO BOOKS of Kings appear in the Hebrew Bible
as one. They practically cover the whole period of kingly
rule over the ancient people. In the reign of Solomon the
kingdom reached the height of its material magnificence.
With his passing the kingship really ceased to be the medium
of Divine government. The prophetic period was introduced with the appearance of Elijah. The first book may be
divided thus: the Passing of David (i.-ii. 11); Solomon (ii.
12-xi.); Division (xii-xvi.); Elijah (xvii-xxii.).

A. THE PASSING OF DAVID

The days of David's feebleness created the opportunity
for rebellion against him under Adonijah, in which Joab
and Abiathar took part. In consequence of this rebellion
Solomon was crowned before the passing of David. The
action of Solomon toward Adonijah was characteristic of
the best side of his nature. It was one in which clemency and
dignified authority were blended. The last charge of David
was one in which he indicated the path of safety for Solomon.
It was that of absolute loyalty to God. That part of it
in which David referred to Joab and Shimei has been very
severely criticized. Much of this criticism would be impossible if some very simple things were borne in mind. First,
David knew these men by experience, and appreciated their
danger to the state. Second, he had kept his covenant with
them, and spared their lives. Third, in each case he left the

matter of how to deal with them in the hands of Solomon, assured of his wisdom. Finally, his words concerning the death of each are prophetic rather than vindictive.

B. SOLOMON

This division falls into two parts, first that which reveals Solomon in all his glory, and secondly that which tells of the passing of that glory.

Among the first acts of the new king were those in which he dealt with the leading men of the kingdom in whose hearts were the impulses of treachery. There was no vindictive vengeance, but there was no vacillating weakness.

Early in his reign Jehovah appeared to Solomon in a dream. With that appearance came Solomon's great opportunity, both to manifest himself, and to obtain the best. His choice was characterized by great wisdom, as it revealed his consciousness of personal inability for all the work devolving upon him. God gave him what he asked, and added thereto the things he might have chosen, yet showed his wisdom in passing by. The account of his choice is followed by a picture in which he is seen exercising the gift for which he had asked, and which God had granted to him.

He gave himself to a careful organization of his kingdom, gathering around him a company of officers of state, each having his own department, for which he was held responsible. These were the days of the nation's greatest material prosperity. The people lived in merriment, and dwelt safely beneath their own vines and fig trees.

Directly he had set his kingdom in order, Solomon turned his attention to the building of the Temple. It is evident that he appreciated the real purpose of his coming to the throne.

B. Solomon

The greatness of the work may be gathered from the account of the enormous amount of labor employed. Like the Tabernacle of old, its chief splendor was within, where everything was encased in gold, neither wood nor stone being visible.

The Temple being finished, it was solemnly dedicated. With great care, and impressive ceremony, they carried the ark into the holy of holies, and the glory of the Lord filled the house. The king offered the dedicatory prayer standing by the altar of burnt offering. Following the prayer, offerings were presented. At the close of the ceremonies the joyful people returned to their tents. It was the most perfect moment of national realization in the land. The Temple was erected, and the presence of God visibly manifested.

Jehovah now appeared to Solomon for the second time, declaring to him that his prayer was heard and answered, and urging the conditions which the people must fulfill. The material magnificence of the kingdom was marred by the admixture of failure. Cities were presented to Hiram, but he was dissatisfied with them. Cities were built within the kingdom, but they became hotbeds of evil. A commerce with other lands was established, but it became the medium of bringing into the land things which in their effect were evil. The coming of the queen of Sheba reveals how far the fame of Solomon had spread abroad. An account of the king's wealth cannot be read without the consciousness that the weaker, if not the baser, side of his nature is manifested in the abounding luxury with which he surrounded himself.

Suddenly the glory passed away, and in the rapid movements we behold his degeneracy and doom. His alliance with commercial enterprises led him into contact with surrounding peoples, and, giving himself over to Oriental custom, he allowed his heart to go after strange women. The wrong thus begun invaded higher realms. He built temples for the strange women who crowded his harem, and gradually but surely there followed the demoralization both of the king and his people, until at last the terrible words are written, "The Lord was angry with Solomon." The judgment of God began to operate immediately. Adversaries were raised up against him. At last there ended in gloom and failure a life full of promise, and that because the heart of the man turned from its loyalty to God in response to the seductions of his own sensual nature.

C. DIVISION

Following the death of Solomon we have an appalling story of the break-up and degradation of the people covering a period of about sixty years. The kingdom was rent in twain. Jeroboam's sin cursed the whole after-history of the people. The judgment of God proceeded immediately. Its first stroke was that of the sickness of Jeroboam's son, and in connection therewith the prophet Ahijah uttered the doom of the man, declaring that because of his sin he and all his were to be swept away. In the meantime Judah was also sinning. Thus so quickly after David, the nation was steeped in idolatry, and utterly failed to bear to the surrounding peoples the testimony to the purity of the Divine government which was the purpose for which they had been created. In Judah under Abijam the process of deterioration went forward. The corruption was not universal, for God maintained a lamp in the midst of His people. With the accession and long rein of Asa there was a halt in the downward progress.

D. *Elijah*

In the history of Israel the government of God can be traced, proceeding in a series of judgments against the continuity of sin which characterized the reigns of successive kings. Nadab the son of Jeroboam reigned for two years, and his influence was wholly evil. At last he was slain by Baasha, who succeeded him. He carried out the judgment of God on the house of Jeroboam by the destruction of all his sons, but for twenty-four years continued in the same line of evil. He was succeeded by Ela, a man utterly corrupt, who in turn was slain by Zimri. He carried out the judgment of God upon the house of Baasha, and after four years of civil war died by his own hand. All this is indeed appalling. The throne of the chosen people was possessed by men of depraved character who came into power by conspiracy and murder. After the death of Zimri there was division even in the house of Israel, half of the people following Tibni, and half gathering to Omri. Victory, however, was with Omri, who for six years continued in courses of evil. He was succeeded by Ahab, who was a veritable incarnation of the forces of sin. He united Jezebel with himself in the actual throne of power. She was a woman of great strength of character, an appalling instance of the fact that a strong woman fallen is the most terrible thing in human failure. During this period there was hardly a ray of light, for although, as subsequent declarations reveal, a remnant still existed loyal to God, their testimony was overwhelmed by abounding wickedness.

D. ELIJAH

With the appearance of Elijah the voice of the prophet was raised to that of national importance. From this point onward in the economy of the Divine government the prophet was superior to the king. Elijah appeared with startling and dramatic suddenness. Without apology, he declared himself the messenger of Jehovah, and at his word judgment fell upon the people. The story of the trial by fire on Carmel is full of majesty, and needs no comment. The lonely figure of Elijah is the center of observation as with calm dignity he stood against the combined evils of a corrupt court and priesthood. His vindication by the answering fire of God was perfect. The slaughter of the prophets of Baal aroused the ire of Jezebel to such a degree that she sent a message full of fury to Elijah. The man who stood erect in the presence of such tremendous odds now fled for his life. Full of tenderness was the method of God with His overwrought and fearful servant. Attending first to his physical needs, He then granted him a revelation of Himself. It was a new revelation by which Elijah found that God was in "the sound of gentle stillness." It is evident that from this time of the failure of his faith he was largely set aside. Once or twice only does he appear again in the narrative.

The rest of the book is occupied with the story of the downfall of Ahab. The first phase of it was public. Benhadad came in the pride of his arms against Samaria. By the voices of prophets Jehovah spoke to Ahab, who, acting under their direction, gained a complete victory over his enemies. In the very moment of triumph he failed by making a covenant with a man whom God had devoted to destruction. The next step was that of his sin in connection with the vineyard of Naboth. Elijah suddenly presented himself before the king, and in words that must have scorched his inner soul he pronounced upon him the terrible doom of his wrongdoing. The third and final movement in the downfall was that of his disobedience of the message of Micaiah. The arrow, shot at a venture so far as man was concerned, found its true mark. Thus ended the personal career of the worst man that ever occupied the throne of the chosen people.

II KINGS—*Corruption*

A ELISHA *i.—ix.*	B CORRUPTION *x.—xvii.*	C HEZEKIAH AND JOSIAH *xviii.—xxiii. 30*	D CAPTIV- ITY *xxiii. 31—xxv.*
I. Elijah **i.**	**I. Israel** **x.**	**I. Hezekiah** **xviii.—xx.**	**I. Tributary** **xxiii. 31—** **xxiv. 7**
i. The sin and sick- ness of Ahaziah ii. Elijah on behalf of God iii. The judgment of fire	i. The zeal of Jehu. 1-28 ii. The failure of Jehu. 29-36 **II. Judah** **xi., xii.**	i. His Accession and Character. xviii. 1-12 ii. The coming of Sennacherib. xviii. 13-37	Egypt. Babylon.
II. Elijah and **Elisha** **ii. 1-18**	i. Athaliah and Jehoash. xi. ii. Jehoash. xii. **III. Israel** **xiii.**	iii. Hezekiah–Isaiah Victory. xix. iv. The last things. xx.	**II. Begin-** **ning of** **Captivity**
i. The translation of Elijah ii. The succession of Elisha	i. Jehoahaz. Jehoash ii. Death of Elisha	**II. The Reaction** **xxi.**	**xxiv. 8-20**
III. Elisha **ii. 19—ix.**	**IV. Judah** **xiv. 1-22**	i. Manasseh. 1-18 ii. Amon. 19-26	
i. Healing of the waters of Jericho. ii. 19-22 ii. Punishment of mocking Children. 23-25 iii. The sign at the war with Moab. iii. iv. Wonders. iv.—vii. v. The restoration of the Shunammite's Land. viii. 1-6 vi. Foretells Benha- dad's death. 7-15 vii. Final Events. viii. 16—ix.	i. Amaziah ii. Azariah **V. Israel** **xiv. 23—xv. 12** i. Jeroboam II. xiv. 23-28 ii. Zechariah. xiv. 29—xv. 12	**III. Josiah** **xxii.—xxiii. 30** i. The finding of the Law. xxii. ii. Reform and death. xxiii. 1-30	**III. Carried** **Away** **xxv.**
	VI. Israel and Judah **xv. 13—xvi. 20** i. Israel's throne. xv. 13-31 ii. Judah's troubles. xv. 32—xvi. 20		
	VII. Passing of Israel **xvii.** i. Victory of Assyria. 1-23 ii. Samaria colonized. 24-41		

II KINGS * * * *

THE FIRST BOOK of Kings ended with the dark days
immediately following the death of Ahab, and the passing
into comparative obscurity of Elijah. This book centers first
around Elisha. The course from corruption to captivity is
then traced in sections alternating between Israel and Judah.
Conspicuous breaks in the history are caused by the reigns of
Hezekiah and Josiah. For purposes of survey we may divide
the book into four sections: Elisha (i.-ix.); Corruption
(x.-xvii.); Hezekiah and Josiah (xvii.-xxiii. 30); Captivity
(xxiii. 31-xxv.).

A. ELISHA

The book opens with the story of the sin and sickness of
Ahaziah, who sought counsel from Baal-zebub, the god of
Ekron. Elijah, who had been in seclusion, suddenly appeared, and protested against the action of the king. Twice
Ahaziah attempted to capture him, and in each case the answer of God on behalf of His servant was the swift judgment
of fire.

There is something pathetic and almost weird in the last
stories of Elijah. It would seem as though he tries to escape
into loneliness for that passing which he knew was at hand.
Elisha, upon whom his mantle had already been cast, followed him loyally, determined to stand by him. Having witnessed his translation, he at once commenced his own ministry, and two incidents are recorded, one beneficent, the heal-

ing of the waters, and the other punitive, the destruction of
the children. The last is misinterpreted if looked upon as an
act of personal vengeance. It was rather an evidence of the
sacredness of his office, and of the sin of refusing him as the
messenger of God.

The ministry of Elisha stands in many respects in vivid
contrast to that of Elijah. There is a gentleness about it
which, in spite of ourselves, reminds us of the Messiah in His
day. Instead of suddenly appearing at critical moments with
thunder and a flame, he seems to have moved about amongst
the people doing good wherever he came. Incidents follow
each other in quick succession. He made provision for the
need of the widow whose creditors were threatening her. He
showed kindness to the Shunammite woman who had
showed him hospitality. At Gilgal he purified the pottage,
and fed a hundred men with twenty loaves. During all this
time he was at the head of the prophetic school; and journeying from place to place, became known everywhere as the
messenger of God. The simplicity of his life is suggested by
the provision which the Shunammite woman, wealthy though
she was, made for his evident requirements. His apartment
was a little chamber on the wall, containing a bed and a table,
a stool and a candlestick. His dignity is manifest in the attitude toward him, especially of this woman, who in her converse with him, stood ever in the doorway, recognizing the
sacredness of his office.

The account of the healing of Naaman reveals Elisha's
perpetual attitude of dignified loyalty to God. He rebuked
the king, who was filled with fear at the coming of Naaman.
He demanded on the part of Naaman absolute obedience,
while he refused to take anything in the nature of personal

B. *Corruption*

reward for that which had been wrought by the hand of God. The incident of the swimming of the iron axhead is interesting, but quite secondary. In the hour of national peril Elisha rose above the gentler works which chiefly characterized his ministry. Revealing the plans of the Syrians, he saved his people from peril, and finally foretold the relief of Samaria. The influence of Elisha is incidentally seen in the converse of the king with Gehazi, and the restoration of the lands of the Shunammite woman for the sake of the prophet. Visiting Damascus, he foretold the death of Benhadad, and Hazael's share in the future suffering of Israel.

The story of Judah's corruption is then told, and that of the anointing of Jehu, and his carrying out of the purpose of Divine judgment in the case of the house of Ahab.

B. CORRUPTION

The story of the rapid and fearful corruption of the whole nation alternates between Israel and Judah. Both sections of the nation are seen sinking deeper and ever deeper into sin and decay. Jehu was used as the scourge of God in sweeping out Ahab's posterity, and in breaking and destroying the power of Baalism. His own story was, however, one of personal failure. The reign of Jehoash in Judah lasted for forty years. All that was beneficent in it would seem to have been due directly to the influence of Jehoiada the priest, for "he did that which was right in the eyes of the Lord all his days wherein Jehoiada the priest instructed him."

In Israel the story of the process of corruption continued under Jehoahaz. He was succeeded by Jehoash, in whose reign Elisha died.

Turning back to Judah we find Amaziah on the throne.

Success attended his arms, but issued in the lifting up of his heart, and his foolish challenge of Jehoash, king of Israel. Defeated, he seems to have been kept a prisoner until the death of Jehoash, and was then succeeded by Azariah, the Uzziah of Isaiah's prophecy.

There follows a section in which Israel and Judah are both seen. Jeroboam the Second occupied the throne of Israel, and in his reign Jonah, the son of Amittai, exercised his ministry. The throne of Judah was occupied by Uzziah, whose reign was in the main characterized by obedience to the Divine will. Yet the people continued to sin, and the king was smitten with leprosy. Turning to Israel, we have the chronicle of a period the most terrible in all its history. To the throne man succeeded man by the way of murder. Zechariah was slain by Shallum. After a month's occupancy of the throne, Shallum was slain by Menahem, who reigned for ten years in evil courses. He was at last succeeded by Pekahiah, his son, who, after reigning for two years in persistent evil, was slain by Pekah. He occupied the throne for twenty years, but at last was slain by Hoshea. Israel was practically under a military despotism, downtrodden and oppressed, and sinning with high hand against God.

The state of affairs was very little better in Judah. Jotham followed Uzziah, and was in turn succeeded by Ahaz, during whose reign the sin of Judah had its most terrible expression. Isaiah was uttering his message, and Micah also, but so far as the nation or its kings were concerned the testimony of truth was lost, and the name of God was being blasphemed among the heathen.

In Israel Hoshea was the last of the kings. The stroke of Divine judgment, long hanging over the guilty people, fell.

C. Hezekiah and Josiah

Shalmaneser first made them tributary, and after three years carried them away captive.

C. HEZEKIAH AND JOSIAH

The third division of the book includes the story of the reigns of Hezekiah and Josiah, with a period of reaction and sin between the two. Hezekiah did right in the sight of the Lord, and instituted reforms more widespread and drastic than had been attempted by any of his predecessors. It was during his reign, in the sixth year, that Israel was carried away into captivity. This in itself would have an influence upon Judah for a time at least, as there is no doubt that the prophets would carefully point out the real reason of this judgment.

When he had occupied the throne for fourteen years a most formidable foe appeared in the person of Sennacherib. In the hour of peril he turned to his old and trusted friend, Isaiah, who charged him to pray for that remnant of God's people which still remained. He also foretold the judgment which would fall upon Assyria, which prophecy was fulfilled in the destruction of the army, while Sennacherib escaped to Nineveh, only to be slain at the house of his own god. The last things in the life of Hezekiah were manifestations of his weakness. Yet his reign was in many respects a most remarkable one. Everything seemed to be against him, and yet the story reveals how much one man seriously loyal to truth may accomplish in the midst of most adverse and difficult circumstances.

Then comes the account of reaction, which was manifested in two reigns, both utterly evil, that of Manasseh lasting for fifty-five years, and that of Amon lasting for two. Manasseh's sin was not merely one of personal wrongdoing, but also of the deliberate undoing of what his father had been at such pains to accomplish. After a brief reign of two years Amon was slain by his servants.

With the accession of Josiah there came the last attempt at reformation before the final sweeping away into captivity. His first act was that of the restoration of the Temple. In connection with it came the discovery of the book of the law. The condition of affairs in Judah may be gathered from the fact of such a finding. So sadly was the Temple neglected and deserted that it would seem as though neither king nor priest knew of the whereabouts of this book. The reformation proceeded along deeper lines as the result of its discovery. So far as Josiah was concerned the whole procedure was the outcome of sincerity and loyalty. The people, however, were following the lead of the king. There was no turning on their part to God; and consequently there was no turning on the part of God from His purpose of judgment. Josiah was gathered to rest before the falling of the final stroke.

D. CAPTIVITY

The judgments fell at last in rapid succession. Jehoahaz succeeded to the throne, and, notwithstanding all that had been done during the reign of Josiah, returned immediately to evil courses in his brief reign of three months. He was deposed by the king of Egypt, and Jehoiakim was set upon the throne as tributary to Pharaoh. For eleven years, as the vassal of Egypt, he continued in evil courses. He became tributary to Babylon under Nebuchadnezzar. Finally Jehoiachin, who succeeded Jehoiakim, was carried away by Nebuchadnezzar, and in his place Zedekiah was made ruler as the repre-

D. Captivity

sentative and vassal of Nebuchadnezzar. His occupancy of the position lasted for eleven years, during which he also continued in evil courses. In process of time he rebelled against the king of Babylon, and was captured. The picture of this man is tragic and awful. With eyes put out, and bound in fetters, he was carried to the court of his conqueror, the type and symbol of the condition of the people who had rebelled against God, and had been broken in pieces.

Thus on the human side the record ends in tragic and disastrous failure. To those whose eyes are fixed upon the eternal throne it is certain that the Divine purpose must be accomplished. The people had passed into a period of long years of servitude and suffering, during which they were still watched over by their one and only King, and by these very conditions prepared for co-operation according to the covenant of grace in the ultimate movements of the overruling God.

I CHRONICLES—*The Temple,*
Desired and Approached

I CHRONICLES * * * *

THE TWO BOOKS of Chronicles cover the period of history already studied in I. and II. Kings. They record this history, however, from an entirely different standpoint. The outlook is almost exclusively confined to Judah, the chronicler never referring to Israel save in cases of absolute necessity. Within the tribe of Judah, moreover, the history is that of the house of David, all other matters being referred to only as they affect, or are affected by, the Davidic line. Moreover, the story of these two books centers around the Temple. The chief matter in David's reign is his interest in preparing for it, while in Solomon's the chief interest is in the building thereof. The distinctive note of the books is that of religion and its bearing on the national life. In the first certain genealogies are given, which lead up to David, and proceed from him. Then the story of his time is told in its relation, pre-eminently, to the religious life. It has been truly said that while the Kings describe the history from the prophetic standpoint, the Chronicles describe it from the priestly. The book may be divided into two parts: Genealogies (i.-x.), David (xi.-xxix.).

A. GENEALOGIES

The period included in these genealogical tables is that from Adam to the restoration under Nehemiah. The tables are not exhaustive, but serve a clearly defined purpose in that they indicate the Divine choice of the channels through which God moved to the accomplishment of His purpose. Side issues are traced in certain directions, but only as they touch upon the line of the Divine progress. This fact is illustrated at the very beginning. The only son of Adam mentioned is Seth. Through him the line is traced through Enoch to Noah. Then the genealogies of Japheth and Ham are given because of the relationship of their descendants to the chosen people of God. The direct line of the Divine movement is taken up through Shem, and finds a new departure in Abram. There is another digression from Abram in the tracing of the descent through Ishmael, and also that through the sons of Keturah. The direct procession continues through Isaac. A third excursion traces the descendants of Esau. Through Israel the program is carried forward. His twelve sons are mentioned, and all of them are subsequently referred to except Dan and Zebulun. The direct line of interest in tracing the Divine method passes through Judah, and so on through Jesse to David. Of his sons nineteen are named, but further descent is traced through Solomon and the kings of Judah on to the period of captivity. In tracing these genealogies it is interesting to notice how choice is based upon character; and moreover, how in the Divine progress there is constant deviation from the line of merely natural descent. The actual firstborn of the sons of Israel was Reuben, but he through sin forfeited the birthright, which passed to Joseph. And yet again, the Prince foretold was to come, not through Joseph, though to him had been given the birthright, but through Judah.

A long section is devoted to the priestly tribe. In the final movement the genealogies of each of the sons of Levi culminated in the person of one man, that of Kohath in He-

-118

man, that of Gershom in Asaph, that of Merari in Ethan. This division ends with the story of the death of the king chosen by men. It is a terrible picture of a man of magnificent capability going down in utter ruin. Routed by his enemies, he died by his own hand in the midst of the field of defeat. The reason of such failure is clearly declared. He trespassed against God, and then sought counsel of one who had a familiar spirit. Magnificent indeed was the ruin, but it was ruin. Saul was a man than whom no other had greater opportunities, but his failure was disastrous. Of good standing in the nation, distinctly called and commissioned by God, honored with the friendship of Samuel, surrounded by a band of men whose hearts God had touched, everything was in his favor. From the beginning he failed, and step by step declined in conduct and character, until he passed away, having failed himself, and dragged his nation to such confusion as threatened its very existence.

B. DAVID

In this division of the book there are four movements: the story of David's crowning, events connected with the ark of God, the account of his reign, and matters concerning the building of the Temple.

The chronicler passes over in silence the story of the seven years in which David reigned over Judah, and commences with the crowning at Hebron. Immediately after he had been recognized as king of the whole nation he captured Jebus, which became the city of his heart, and the metropolis of the nation. The account of the mighty men and their deeds is full of color. It is particularly interesting in view of what these men were in the days of David's exile. From being a company in debt, in danger, and discontented, they became "mighty men of valour . . . trained for war," their one unifying inspiration being their loyalty to David. They "came with a perfect heart to Hebron, to make David king." Thus he entered upon his kingdom under the most auspicious circumstances.

The king's consciousness of the true strength of his kingdom is manifest in his anxiety concerning the ark of God. It had been at Kiriath-jearim, and neglected for long years. He now set himself to bring it into the midst of the people as a recognition of the nation's relationship to Jehovah. The long neglect of the ark would seem to have rendered the people unfamiliar with all the particular regulations for its removal, which they attempted by a device of their own. The swift judgment on the man who stretched out a hand to save the ark is evidence at once of the presence of God among His people, and of the necessity for perfect conformity to His minutest instructions.

At this time there commenced a commercial friendship with Hiram, which continued into the reign of Solomon. The statement is now made of David's multiplication of wives. The silence of the chronicler concerning his sin is remarkable throughout this book. Two victories over the Philistines are described.

Again David turned his attention to the ark, bringing it up from the house of Obed-edom to Jerusalem. Companies of instrumentalists and singers accompanied the ark, and with high jubilation it was borne by the priests into the tent prepared. One shadow fell across the brightness of the day. It was that of the mockery of Michal, Saul's daughter. The incident illustrates the perpetual inability of the worldly-minded to appreciate the gladness of the spiritual. The chronicler gives us the psalm sung by the trained musicians on this occasion. It is a compilation of parts of three to be found in our Psalter, and is a general ascription of praise, merging into a call to remember the works of God, and His government covenant with the people.

The presence of the ark in the city seems to have created the desire in the heart of David to provide for it a permanent and more worthy resting-place. Of this desire he spoke to Nathan, who, acting without Divine consultation, charged him to go forward. Both prophet and king, however, had to learn that God's way are not man's ways. While David's desire was not granted, yet, when in communion with God, he had been brought to the place of a resting worshipper, he was permitted to make great preparation for the building of the Temple by his son.

The next section tells the story of David's reign, and first gives the account of his victories over surrounding foes. In view of his desire to build the Temple of God, it is of special interest to notice how in all these wars he was amassing treasure with that end in view. The victories of David were the direct result of God's blessing upon him. Yet in the midst of them he sinned his greatest sin, and that notwithstanding the fact that in his deepest heart he desired to build God's house. One statement in this book is all that in any sense can be construed into a reference to that sin. "But David tarried at Jerusalem."

The cause of David's action in numbering the people is distinctly stated to be Satan. Therein lies a revelation of its nature. The one sin of Satan is that of pride and ambition, and this was the sin of David. In the place where the mercy of God operated in staying the plague resulting from his sin,

David chose to build the house of his God. The threshing floor of Ornan the Jebusite was chosen as the site of the Temple.

During the latter days of David's life the deep underlying desire became again the supreme matter. In perfect acquiescence with the will of God, he gave up all thought of building, and set himself to preparing everything for another hand to carry out the work. His charge to his son is full of beauty. He frankly told him how God refused to permit him to build, and named the reason. He was careful, moreover, to teach Solomon that his appointment to build was of God, and thereby created a solemn sense of responsibility in the matter.

His interest in the Temple was not only manifested in his material preparation. He practically abdicated the throne to Solomon in order to supervise the setting in order of the worship. Arrangements were made for the work of the Levites, and with great care and remarkable democracy of choice the courses of the priests were next set in order.

It is easy to imagine what delight the poet-king took in arranging the song service of the new Temple. Music had played a very important part in his career. His skill therein had been his first introduction to Saul. His psalms breathe the spirit of the varied experiences through which he passed. The days of his simple life as a shepherd, the period of his exile and suffering, the hours of battle and weariness, the triumph of his crowning, the agony of his sin, the joy of pardon—these and many other experiences are reflected in the great collection. And now at the end he gave himself to arranging the service of song in the Temple which was to be built. Finally he arranged the courses of the porters, and the duties of such as had charge of all the stores set apart for the sacred work.

Before coming to the last charges of David, in a parenthetical section (chapter xxvii.), we have an idea of the internal order of the kingdom under the government of David. This chapter is a striking revelation of the fact that the greatness of David as a king was not confined to his victories in war. He was no less great in the arts of peaceful administration. The tilling of the ground, and its careful cultivation, the rearing of cattle, and all matters pertaining to the internal welfare of his people were arranged for under duly qualified and appointed oversight. There is no doubt that under the reign of David the Hebrew people realized their greatest strength, even though they did not reach the height of their material magnificence. Fundamentally a man of God, David was also a warrior, a poet, and an administrator, and with his passing the day of Hebrew greatness passed its meridian.

The book ends with an account of the solemn charge he gave to Solomon, and of the ceremony in which he gave to the Lord all that he had gathered for the carrying out of the work of the Temple. Finally the chronicler declares that David "died in a good old age, full of days, riches, and honour." It had been in very truth a great reign. Through varied experiences the king had come at last to the highest that was in him, and, as Paul declared, "after he had in his own generation served the counsel of God, he fell on sleep."

II CHRONICLES—*The Temple,*
Possessed and Abandoned

A SOLOMON *i.—ix.*	B THE KINGS OF JUDAH *x.—xxxvi.*	
I. First Vision and Things Following i.—vii. 10	**I. The Revolt of the Ten Tribes** x.—xi. 4	
i. The Vision. i. 1-13 ii. National Prosperity. i. 14—ii. 18 iii. The Temple. iii.—v. 1 iv. Ceremonies of Consecration. v. 2—vii. 10	**II. Period of Degeneracy** xi. 5—xvi.	i. Rehoboam. xi. 5—xii. ii. Abijah. xiii. iii. Asa. xiv.—xvi.
	III. Reform under Jehoshaphat xvii.—xx.	i. Reform. xvii. ii. Lapse and Restoration. xviii., xix. iii. Prevailing Prayer. xx.
II. Second Vision and Things Following vii. 11—ix.	**IV. Period of Degeneracy** xxi.—xxiii.	i. Jehoram. xxi. ii. Ahaziah. xxii. 1-9 iii. Athaliah. xxii. 10—xxiii.
i. The Second Vision. vii. 11-22 ii. Various Acts of the King. viii. iii. The Queen of Sheba. ix. 1-28 iv. Epilogue. 29-31	**V. Reform under Joash** xxiv.	i. Influence of Jehoida ii. Failure of Joash
	VI. Period of Degeneracy xxv.—xxviii.	i. Amaziah. xxv. ii. Uzziah. xxvi. iii. Jotham. xxvii. iv. Ahaz. xxviii.
	VII. Reform under Hezekiah xxix.—xxxii.	i. Consciousness of Sin and consequent Cleansing. xxix. ii. The Passover. xxx. iii. Practical Reforms. xxxi. iv. The Trial of Faith. Sennacherib. xxxii.
	VIII. Period of Degeneracy xxxiii.	i. Manasseh. 1-20 ii. Amon. 21-25
	IX. Reform under Josiah xxxiv., xxxv.	i. Josiah's first Reforms. ii. The Finding of the Book of the Law. iii. The Passover.
	X. Period of Degeneracy xxxvi. 1-10	i. Jehoahaz. 1-4 ii. Jehoiakim. 5-8 iii. Jehoiachin. 9-10
	XI. Captivity xxxvi. 11-23	

II CHRONICLES * * * *

THIS IS REALLY the second half of the one Book of Chronicles. The essential values are the same as those in I. Chronicles. The history centers round the religious life of the people, and is confined to Judah and the Davidic line of kings. Degeneracy resulted from neglect of the house of God, and each reform was associated with return thereto. The story is a very sad one, opening with all the glory of Solomon's reign, and ending with captivity and the patronage of Cyrus. Its broad divisions are Solomon (i.-ix.); the Kings of Judah (x.-xxxvi.).

A. SOLOMON

This book opens with the story of Solomon's entering upon full possession of his kingdom, and taking up the great work entrusted to him of building the Temple. He commenced by gathering the people with him to a sacred act of worship. God met him in a special vision of the night, as a result of which wisdom was granted to him, and the promise was made of great material prosperity. Then followed the days of Israel's greatest glory so far as material things were concerned. Prosperity is always a more insidious danger than adversity to the man of faith.

Solomon devoted himself to his great work of building the Temple. In all fundamental essentials it was on the pattern of the Tabernacle which Moses had made. Its proportions and relations were identical, but it was larger. The period occupied in building was seven years. The work being completed, with filial and godly care the king carried into the sacred enclosure all that his father had collected and dedicated to the purpose. Thus, nearly half a millennium after the Exodus, the chosen people were found in the land, having a king on the throne, and a Temple in the midst of the chief city at the center of the national life. The only principles of permanence, however, are faithfulness and purity, and already the elements of decay were at work in the heart of the king and among the people.

The work of construction being completed, there followed the glad and solemn ceremony of dedication by the people, and consecration by God. With awe-inspiring dignity the ark of God was carried to its resting-place. As at the erection of the Tabernacle of old, so now in the new Tabernacle God answered the work of man as the cloud of glory possessed and filled the sacred place, so that the ministrations of the priests had to cease. In the presence of that manifestation the king pronounced a blessing on the people, which merged into a blessing offered to God. After praise the king offered his prayer, which was great in its comprehensiveness and in its understanding of the heart of God. As the ceremonies had begun with sacrifice and song, so they closed, and it is quite easy to realize how joyful and glad of heart the people were as they dispersed.

The greatest work of Solomon's life being now completed, God appeared to him in a second vision, in which He first declared that the work done was accepted, and the prayer offered heard and answered. Then, with the tenderness and faithfulness of infinite love, He restated for the king the conditions of his safety.

–126

B. *The Kings of Judah*

Then follows the record of certain doings of the king in matters of administration. He consolidated the internal strength of the nation by building cities. He organized the labor of the conquered peoples within his dominions. He set in order the Temple worship. He enlarged his commercial activities.

The fame of Solomon's wisdom attracted the queen of Sheba, who came principally to discuss with him certain problems on her mind. He welcomed her with fine courtesy, and answered her questions to her satisfaction. The chronicler ends the story with the account of the wealth Solomon gathered, and the magnificence which characterized his reign. No account of his failure and fall is given. The purpose of the writer was served when he had made clear the relationship existing between loyalty to the Temple of God, with its worship and success, and the greatness of king and people.

B. THE KINGS OF JUDAH

Despotism is seldom transmissible. That Solomon had been an autocrat, and had ruled with a hand of iron under the glove of velvet, is evidenced by the words of the men of Israel: "Thy father made our yoke grievous." With his death men breathed anew, and discovered their chains. As a result of the quarrel between Jeroboam and Rehoboam, the nation was rent in twain. Ten tribes revolted, and the history of the book gathers round the kings of Judah, beginning with Rehoboam. Throughout his reign, and that of Abijah, there was war between Israel and Judah, and a process of corruption in the kingdom. Asa reigned for a long period, and in the earlier years gave the nation some gleams of a better order. In the latter years, however, he sadly failed, turning to Syria for help.

With the accession of Jehoshaphat, a period of definite reformation opened for Judah. He commenced by organizing what in these days would be called special missions conducted through the cities of Judah by representative princes, the Levites, and the priests. Coincident with this activity within, a remarkable fear of the Lord fell upon the peoples without, so that they ceased to make war upon Jehoshaphat. Economically he strengthened his kingdom by the building of castles and cities, by commerce, and by the carrying out of many works. After a while he had a strange lapse in his loyalty to God, in that he made affinity with Ahab, perhaps the most evil king that ever sat upon the throne of Israel. His repentance, however, was manifest in the new mission which he presently undertook throughout the land, to bring his people back to the Lord, and to consolidate the internal administration in righteousness.

He was undoubtedly a man of simple and yet splendid faith. This is seen in the story of how, when his kingdom was threatened with powerful and terrible invasion, he gathered his people about him and prayed. The answer was not delayed. It was a moment bright with light amid the darkness. Once more in the history of His own people the arm of the Lord was seen acting in strength, as when in the ancient days it broke the power of Egypt. The story of Jehoshaphat's life and reign concludes with a brief statement of yet another lapse, in that he made commercial alliances with Ahaziah, the king of Israel. His enterprises were unsuccessful, because God broke his ships in pieces.

With the passing of Jehoshaphat another period of

B. The Kings of Judah

degeneracy and darkness set in over the kingdom of Judah. He was succeeded by his firstborn, Jehoram, a man of utterly evil nature, who attempted to make his throne secure by the murder of his brothers. In the midst of his wickedness a message came to him by writing from Elijah. It was a terrible sentence of judgment, which was fully carried out after eight years of reign. He was immediately succeeded by Ahaziah, his youngest son, whose brief reign of one year was influenced for evil by Athaliah, his mother. Dark and terrible days followed his death, during which this woman, Athaliah, reigned over the land. Her first act was that of the destruction of all the seed royal of the house of Judah, except Joash, who was rescued, and for six years preserved within the temple by Jehoshabeath, and the high priest, Jehoiada.

The reform under Joash was really due to the influence of this man Jehoiada. It centers, as always in this book, around the Temple. While Jehoiada lived, worship was maintained, but after his death the king who had been zealous in reform became determined in wickedness.

The account of the reign of Amaziah opens with a remarkable statement: "He did that which was right in the eyes of the Lord, but not with a perfect heart." Notwithstanding the general direction of his life, either through personal indulgence or ambition or carelessness, the whole heart was not set upon doing the will of God, and consequently the reign was characterized by failure. Uzziah, who succeeded him, and reigned fifty-two years, was a man of strong character, and the early part of his occupancy of the throne was characterized by true prosperity. The last years of his reign were full of suffering and sadness. In an evil moment of pride he entered into the sacred courts, and violated the ancient order of God concerning the offering of sacrifices. He was smitten with leprosy, and lived for the latter part of his life a prisoner, isolated from his fellow-men. He was succeeded by Jotham, who reigned in equity, and refrained from his father's sin. During the whole of this period, however, the corruption of Judah went forward, and the great ministry of Isaiah commenced. The reign of Ahaz was marked by terrible and rapid degeneracy. With appalling fearlessness he restored all the evils of idolatry, even including the terrible offering of children to Moloch. The evil of his character is manifest in the fact that calamities did not seem to have the effect of rousing him to consciousness of his sin. "In the time of his distress did he trespass yet more against the Lord, this same king Ahaz."

With the accession of Hezekiah a great change came over the life of Judah. Among all the reforming kings he was undoubtedly the most remarkable. This was in all probability due to the influence of Isaiah. His reformation commenced in his own deep consciousness of the wretched condition of the people, and the reason thereof. His first reforming act was that of cleansing the house of God, and restoring it as the place of worship. He then made arrangements for the keeping of the Passover, and with a largeness of heart sent messengers throughout Israel, inviting them to come and take part therein. Only a remnant responded. The observance of the feast was followed by the work of reorganization in the nation. The story is told in general terms, and special note is made of the thoroughness with which the king carried out the work. "In every work that he began to do in the service of the house of God, and in the law, and in the commandments, to seek his God, he did it with all his heart, and prospered." Then came a trial of his faith in the invasion of Sennacherib. In the presence of the peril his heart did not fail. He acted with promptitude by stopping the supply of water, by strengthening the fortifications, by mobilizing his army, and then sought refuge in prayer and in fellowship with the prophet Isaiah. The chronicler then briefly relates the story of his illness, and of that failure which characterized his last days.

Manasseh the son of Hezekiah seems to have set himself to the most willful and persistent form of every abomination. The strong hand of God was stretched out against him, and he was carried away in irons, broken and defeated. In his distress he cried out for help to God. His repentance was evidently the chief subject in the mind of the chronicler, and constitutes a wonderful picture of the readiness of God to pardon. Amon, on coming to the throne, followed the earlier example of his father, and was so utterly corrupt that his own servants conspired against him and slew him.

The story of the reign of Josiah is full of brightness. Ascending the throne when eight years old, at the age of sixteen he began to seek after God. Four years later he set himself to the actual work of reformation. It was during the cleansing of the Temple that the book of the law was discovered, the result of which was a still greater determination on his part to reform the nation. He observed the Passover. Following the story of his death, we read of the lamentation of the people. The reformation under him was due entirely to their love for him, and not to any return on their part to God.

The story of final movements in the downward course of the nation concludes the book. Jehoahaz reigned for three months. He was deposed by the king of Egypt, who appointed Jehoiakim. After eleven years of evil courses he was carried away by Nebuchadnezzar to Babylon. He was succeeded by Jehoiachin, who also was carried away by Nebuchadnezzar. Zedekiah, appointed by Nebuchadnezzar to the succession, rebelled against him, and continued his evil courses for eleven years. The Chaldeans carried the remnant away to Babylon. The book closes with the statement of the proclamation of Cyrus, which also opens the book of Ezra.

EZRA—*A Returning Remnant*

A **ZERUBBABEL** *i.—vi.*		**B** **EZRA** *vii.—x.*	
I. Return	**i., ii.**	**I. Return**	**vii., viii.**
i. The Edict of Cyrus.	i.		
ii. The Returning Exiles.	ii.	Interval of Sixty Years.	
Note:		i. The Coming of Ezra.	vii.
The Small Number of Levites.		ii. The Returning Exiles.	viii. 1-14
The Nethinim.		iii. The Preliminary Convention.	15-30
The Totals.		iv. The Return.	31-36
II. Reorganization	**iii.—vi.**	**II. Reformation**	**ix., x.**
i. Resumption of Worship.	iii.	i. The Conditions in Jerusalem.	ix. 1, 2
ii. Opposition.	iv.	ii. Ezra's Intercession.	3-15
a. General Statement.	1-6	iii. The Reformation.	x.
b. Particular Account.	7-42		
iii. Resumption of Building.	v.		
iv. Darius.	vi.		

EZRA * * * *

THE BOOK OF Ezra contains an account of a most important epoch in the history of the people of God. After seventy years of captivity, through the decree of a Gentile king, a return was made possible. This book gives us the story of that return, and of the rebuilding of the Temple. It is not consecutive history, for, while in conjunction with the book of Nehemiah it covers a period of about one hundred years, there is in the midst of this book a gap of sixty years. There are two main divisions: first, the story of the return under Zerubbabel and the rebuilding of the Temple (i.-vi.); then, after sixty years, that of the coming of Ezra, and the work he undertook (vii.-x.). It may therefore be simply divided around the names of these two men.

A. ZERUBBABEL

The story which centers around Zerubbabel is that of the return of a remnant of the people to Jerusalem, and their reorganization.

The purposes of God may seem to tarry; they are never abandoned. Indeed, there is a very true sense in which they never even tarry for a moment. The chosen nation had become a people scattered and peeled, having lost national position and power, and to a large extent national consciousness. Through the seventy years God prepared a remnant, through processes of suffering, to return and rebuild, and hold the fort until He, the true Seed and Servant, should come. The history of the return sets forth clearly the truth concerning this overruling of God. Through a most unlikely instrument, Cyrus, the way was made plain.

The list of those returning is principally remarkable from the small number of the Levites it contains. Nearly ten times as many priests as Levites went back to the land. Another point is that of the Nethinim. They seem to have been prominent in these times, for they are only once mentioned elsewhere. It is almost impossible to determine their origin.

The leaders in this return were evidently conscious of the matters of real importance in the life of the people. Directly they were settled in their cities, the altar of God was established at Jerusalem. As far as possible they restored the Divinely appointed order of worship, and immediately commenced the work of rebuilding the Temple. The foundations were laid, and in the second year of the return, with fitting ceremonies of praise, they rejoiced.

This work stirred up the opposition of the Samaritans. This was first manifested in an attempt to induce Zerubbabel and those associated with him to admit into partnership such as were really enemies of the work. This being definitely refused, these enemies set themselves in every way to harass the work and hinder it, until at last they were successful in obtaining letters from the reigning monarch which interdicted the work. Thus for a long period the rebuilding of the house of God ceased, while the building of the houses of the people went forward unchecked.

A study of the prophecies of Haggai and Zechariah makes it perfectly evident that the cessation of the work of building was unworthy of the men who had commenced. Judged by all human standards, they could fairly urge the difficulties of the situation, and the necessity for obedience to the edict of the reigning king. Judged by the Divine standard, as the burning words of the prophets made perfectly clear, they had no right to cease.

Under the inspiration of these prophetic messages, governor and priest, Zerubbabel and Jeshua, commenced the work again. Again opposition was raised. To this they gave no heed, and Tattenai sent a letter to Darius concerning the edict of Cyrus.

There can be no doubt that Tattenai felt that the finding of such a decree was unlikely, if not impossible. That the search was a thorough one is indicated by the statement of where the roll was found. The searchers naturally commenced in the house of the archives in Babylon. It was not there, but at Achmetha, in the royal palace, that it was discovered. In consequence of this the edict of Darius not only gave them permission to carry forward their work, but compelled Tattenai to help them with great gifts. At last the Temple was finished, and solemnly dedicated to God with sacrificial offerings and songs of thanksgiving.

B. EZRA

Between chapters vi. and vii. there was an interval of at least sixty years, uneventful in the history of the people settled in Jerusalem. That they had largely failed in the purposes of Zerubbabel is evident from the work done by Ezra, and subsequently by Nehemiah. Again the wonderful overruling of God is seen in the working of the minds of two men in Babylon. Ezra was stirred with desire to help his people in Jerusalem. Artaxerxes was moved with fear lest there should be "wrath against the realm of the king and his sons."

It is perfectly evident that he had some clear consciousness of the power of God. Thus by the creation of different emotions in the hearts of two men, which brought them into co-operation with each other, and thus with His purpose, He moved forward.

Ezra gathered together members of the priestly and royal houses, and a further contingent of the people at Ahava, in order that he might review them, and prepare for the journey. Finding that there were no Levites in the company, he sent to Iddo, and in response to his appeal certain of their number joined him. The character of Ezra is remarkably revealed in his refusing to seek help from an earthly king. It is a fine illustration of the independence and dependence of such as follow the Lord. The king's voluntary gifts were gladly accepted; but to ask for soldiers would have been to make a tacit confession of questioning in his heart as to the ability or willingness of God to help. After a long journey they arrived in safety at Jerusalem, and made their offerings.

Ezra found a condition of affairs at Jerusalem which was a sad revelation of the deterioration of the people. There had been no return to idolatry, but there had been an intermixture with the people of the land, and the chief offenders had been the princes and the rulers. He was moved with righteous indignation, and sank into silent astonishment until the time of the evening oblation. Then before God he poured out his soul in prayer.

The sincerity of Ezra's vicarious repentance produced immediate result. The people who had gathered about him through the long hours of the day came to a consciousness of the enormity of their sin as they saw how he was affected thereby. At last one of their number spoke to him, acknowledging the sin, and suggesting a remedy. He at once became a man of action, first calling them to a sacred covenant that they would put away the evil thing from amongst them; and then leading them in the carrying out of their covenant.

NEHEMIAH—*Consolidation*

A THE BUILDING OF THE WALL *i.—vii. 73a*	B THE READING OF THE LAW *vii. 73b—x.*	C THE SETTLEMENT OF THE CITIES *xi.—xiii.*
I. Initiation　　i., ii. i. Nehemiah's Grief concerning Jerusalem.　i. ii. Nehemiah's Coming to Jerusalem.　ii.	**I. The Reading of the Law and Feast of Tabernacles** 　　vii. 73b—viii. i. The Reading of the Law. 　　vii. 73b—viii. 12 ii. The Feast of Tabernacles. 　　13-18	**I. The People in Jerusalem**　　xi.—xii. 26 i. The princes and ten per cent compulsorily, and some voluntarily.　xi. 1, 2 ii. Lists.　　xi. 3—xii. 26
II. Process　　iii.—v. i. The Building of the Wall. 　　iii. ii. Opposition and Persistence. 　　iv. iii. Internal Difficulties.　v.	**II. The Great Prayer of the Levites**　　xi. i. The Day of Humiliation. 　　1-4 ii. The Offering of Praise. 　　5-29 iii. Prayer.　　30-38	**II. The Dedication of the Wall**　xii. 27—xiii. 3 i. Dating Difficult ii. Ceremony 　a. Two Processions of Singers.　xii. 27-47 　b. The Reading of the Law.　xiii. 1-2 　c. Separation.　　3
III. Completion 　　vi.—vii. 73a i. Opposition and Victory. vi. ii. The People.　vii. 1-73a	**III. The Re-establishment of a Covenant**　x. i. The Sealing.　　1-28 ii. The Covenant.　29-39	**III. Nehemiah's final Reformation** 　　xiii. 4-31 i. Twelve years later. ii. Correction of four Abuses. iii. His Method (ver. 25).

NEHEMIAH * * * *

THIS IS THE last book of Old Testament history. An interval of about twelve years occurred between the reformation under Ezra and the coming of Nehemiah. The story is that of the continuation of the work commenced by Zerubbabel in the matter of the rebuilding of the wall. The book is intensely interesting, among other reasons because in large measure it is autobiographical. Nehemiah tells his own story, and with a freshness and vigor and transparent honesty which make it for evermore one full of interest. Beyond the account of the building of the wall we have that of a further reformation in which Nehemiah and Ezra were united as leaders, and finally an account of the settlement of the cities.

The book may therefore be divided broadly thus: The Building of the Wall (i.-vii. 73a); The Reading of the Law (vii. 73b-x.); The Settlement of the Cities (xi.-xiii.).

A. THE BUILDING OF THE WALL

Nehemiah's position as cupbearer at the court of the Gentile king was one of honour, and admitted him into relationship of some nearness and familiarity. In the midst of these circumstances he had not forgotten his relationship to the chosen people, but on the contrary was interested in them, and made inquiry of those who came to the court concerning Jerusalem. The news they brought was full of sadness, and grief possessed his heart. He carried his burden to God in prayer, asking that He would give him favour in the eyes of the king he served. There was thus evidently in his heart a resolution to do more than pity, if the door of opportunity offered.

The sadness in his heart could not wholly be hidden, and when the king detected it Nehemiah was filled with fear. Through the fear a splendid courage manifested itself, and he asked that he might be allowed to go and help his brethren. The request was granted, and he departed for Jerusalem. Having arrived, he carefully ascertained the true state of affairs, and then called the elders to arise and build. Opposition was at once manifested on the part of surrounding enemies, and with strong determination Nehemiah made it perfectly clear that no co-operation would be permitted with those who were derisive of the effort.

The account of the method of arrangement for the building of the wall shows how system characterized Nehemiah's procedure. The description given takes in the whole city's circumference. The arrangements made indicated the necessity for speedy work, and were characterized by a sense of the importance of division of labor, and a fitting apportionment thereof in the matter of persons and neighborhoods.

As the work proceeded the opposition of outsiders turned from derision to anger, but rose no higher at the moment than that of contempt. An illuminative sentence, "the people had a mind to work," shows how completely Nehemiah had captured and inspired them, and we are not surprised when we read that the wall was half finished. At this point opposition became more severe, and a positive attempt was made by conspiracy to hinder the progress of the work. In

A. The Building of the Wall

Nehemiah's method there was neither foolish independence of God nor foolhardy neglect of human responsibility. "We made our prayer and set a watch."

A new difficulty arose among the people themselves. The rich had exacted usury from their poorer brethren to such an extent as to oppress and impoverish them. Nehemiah again acted with promptitude. There is a fine touch in his declaration, "I consulted with myself, and contended with the nobles." Setting an example of self-denial, in that he took no usury, nor even the things which were his right as the appointed governor of the people, he produced immediate results in that all the nobles did the same. Thus the people were relieved, and went forward with their work with new enthusiasm.

Opposition now moved on to a new plane. Having begun in contempt, and proceeded through conspiracy, it now adopted a method of cunning. Affecting friendship, the enemies of Nehemiah four times proposed conference with him, which he resolutely declined. This was followed by an open letter containing a slander. With singular directness he denied the slander, and carried on his building. Finding that he was not to be seduced, they attempted to fill him with fear. This attempt he scorned, and hastened the workers. Through the whole period he was harassed by the complicity of certain nobles with Tobiah.

At last the wall was finished by the setting up of the doors, and the placing in order of porters, singers, and Levites. Arrangements were made for the safety of the city in the presence of surrounding enemies by careful provision as to the hour for opening and closing the city gates, and by an arrangement of watchers.

B. THE READING OF THE LAW

In this section of the book, Ezra appears upon the scene. A most remarkable religious convention was held. The first day witnessed the assembling of the people, and was given to the reading of the law. This was not merely the reading aloud of passages therefrom, but was reading accompanied by exposition undertaken by men specially appointed to act in conjunction with Ezra. It was a day of conviction, resulting in great sadness in the heart of the people. On the second day a smaller gathering of the rulers was held, who came in order more perfectly to understand the law of God. An immediate application was made by the observance of the feast of tabernacles.

Following the feast, after a brief interval, came the great day of humiliation. The people separated themselves entirely from all that were not actually within the covenant, and gave themselves to confession and humbling before God. In all this they were led by the Levites, and the great prayer they offered is given in full. Its first section was an ascription of praise; its second set forth Jehovah's grace in contrast with the repeated failure of the people; and the last movement was that of definite seeking for His continued goodness and help.

Following upon the humiliation of the people they entered into new covenant relationships with God. This covenant was sealed representatively by priests, Levites, and rulers. To its terms all the people agreed. They were set forth in general phrases and in particular application. Generally the people promised "to walk in God's law . . . to observe and do all the commandments." Particularly the covenant re-

C. *The Settlement of the Cities*

ferred to matters in which the people had been in danger c f failure, those namely of intermarriage with the heathen, of neglect of the Sabbath, of Temple maintenance and arrangement, and of the offering of first-fruits and tithes.

C. THE SETTLEMENT OF THE CITIES

In this third and final division of the book the arrangements made for the settlement of the cities are given. In the first section we have the account particularly of the settlement of Jerusalem. Perhaps not more than fifty thousand had returned from captivity. By no means all of these had come to Jerusalem. Many of them were scattered through the surrounding cities. Jerusalem was peculiarly difficult of settlement, in that it was the center of danger and of possible attack. It was therefore arranged that the princes should dwell in the city, and ten per cent. of the people, selected by lot, must take up their abode there. In addition to these there were certain who voluntarily came forward to dwell in the place of danger.

It would seem as though the dedication of the wall had been postponed for some considerable time. The actual time is of no moment. The ceremony of dedication proceeded in three stages—first, two processions of singers who chanted the praises of God; secondly, the reading of the law; and finally, the separation of the mixed multitude from the people of God.

After the building of the wall Nehemiah had evidently gone back to the court of the king. Twelve years later he returned, and the last deeds recorded were such as reveal the continued strength and loyalty of the man. There were four abuses which confronted him. Eliashib the priest had given place within the very Temple of God to Tobiah. Nehemiah flung out occupant and furniture, and restored the chamber to its proper use. In the second place he found that the Levites, instead of being able to devote their whole time to the service of the Temple, had to earn their living, because the people neglected the bringing in of the tithe. He corrected this abuse. In the third place he found that the Sabbath was violated, and he restored the Divine order. Finally, the people had again made mixed marriages, and with characteristic roughness and force he dealt with the matter.

ESTHER—*God Amid the Shadows*

A THE KING'S COURT *i.—iii.*	B THE COUNTRY *iv. 1-3*	C THE KING'S COURT *iv. 4—viii.*	D THE COUNTRY *ix.*	CONCLU- SION *x.*
I. The Feast at Shushan i.	I. Mordecai 1-2	I. Esther and Mordecai iv. 4-17	I. Poetic Retribution 1-19	Ahasuerus and Mordecai
II. The New Queen ii.	II. The Jews	II. Esther and the King v. 1-8	II. The Feast of Purim 20-32	
III. Haman iii.		III. Haman 9-14		
		IV. The Sleepless King vi.		
		V. The Queen's Banquet vii.		
		VI. Mordecai viii.		

ESTHER * * * *

THE EVENTS RECORDED in the book of Esther occurred between the completion of the Temple and the mission of Ezra (between Ezra vi. and vii.). In all likelihood
the narrative, as we have it, was taken directly from the
Persian records. This would account for much that has
created difficulty in the minds of some as to the presence
of this book in the canon of Scripture. The fact that the name
of God is not mentioned would be perfectly natural if the
historian were a Persian. That many things are chronicled
without apology, which are the customs of a godless nation,
would also be explained thereby.

All this, however, makes the persons and teaching of the
book more valuable. It is a fragment of profane history captured for sacred purposes. The story reveals, to such as have
eyes to see, that same principle of the overruling of God
on behalf of His people which marks all their history. Here,
however, it is seen operating on their behalf in a foreign
land.

The principal value of the book is not its revelation of His
care for individuals, though, of course, that also is present.
It is rather that of His preservation of the people as a whole,
in an hour when they were threatened with wholesale slaughter; and moreover it emphasizes His care even for those who
had not returned with Zerubbabel. The feast of Purim,
observed even to-day, is the living link to the events
recorded, and historically sets the seal upon the accuracy

of the story. That feast celebrates, not so much the defeat of
Haman, or the advancement of Mordecai, as the deliverance
of the people. The book is pre-eminently dramatic, and is
best analyzed around the scenes: The King's Court, Ahasuerus (i.-iii.); the Country, Mordecai, and the Mourning
Jews (iii.-iv. 3); the King's Court, the unnamed God (iv.
4-viii.); the Country, Purim, the Rejoicing Jews (ix.); Conclusion (x.).

A. THE KING'S COURT, AHASUERUS

The first scene presented to us is that of a great feast in
the palace of the king. In the midst of it the king commanded his queen, Vashti, to his presence. The one
redeeming feature in the revelation of the conditions at the
court of Ahasuerus was that of Vashti's refusal to obey the
command of the king. She paid the price of her loyalty to
her womanhood in being deposed.

Mordecai's action in the case of Esther is open to question. His love for her was evident, and the picture of him
walking before the court of the women's house into which
she had been taken indicated his continued interest in her.
His advice that she should not betray her nationality was
questionable, as her position at the court of the king was one
of peril for a daughter of the covenant. Her presence in the
palace was part of that process by which the overruling of
God preserved His people, and frustrated their foe.

Haman is now introduced, a man haughty and imperious,
proud and cruel. His malice was stirred against Mordecai,
and also, therefore, against all his people, and he made use
of his influence with the king to obtain authority practically
to exterminate the whole of them.

B. THE COUNTRY, MORDECAI, AND THE MOURNING JEWS

The intention of Haman became known to Mordecai, who at once took up his position outside the king's gate, and there raised a loud and bitter cry. The royal proclamation filled the people through the provinces with sorrow, and they mourned with fasting and weeping and wailing.

C. THE KING'S COURT, THE UNNAMED GOD

The news of this mourning reached Esther in the royal palace, and she sent to make inquiries. Thus between the extreme need of her people and the king she became a direct link. The custom and law of the court forbade her approach to her lord save at his command. The urgency of the case appealed to her, however, and with splendid heroism she ventured. Conscious of her need of moral support, she asked that the people would fast with her. There was a note of sacrifice and abandonment in her words, "If I perish, I perish."

Her venture was crowned with success. It might have been quite otherwise, and the graciousness of the king, notwithstanding Esther's violation of the law of the palace, was undoubtedly due to the disposition of that God in Whose hand are the ways of kings, whether they will or not. Her request was at first of the simplest. She invited the king and Haman to a banquet. The overwhelming pride of Haman was manifest in his gathering of his friends, to whom he boasted of his riches, of his advancement, and now of this last favor, that he alone was invited to accompany the king to the banquet of Esther. Acting upon the advice of wife and friends, he committed the folly of making the time of the banquet merry for himself by first erecting a gallows for Mordecai.

In the economy of God vast issues follow apparently trivial things. In the case of Ahasuerus a sleepless night was the means through which God moved forward for the preservation of His people. To while away its hours, the records were read to the king, and a deed of Mordecai therein recorded led to the hasty and strange happenings which filled the heart of Haman with anger and terror. Mordecai was lifted from obscurity to the most conspicuous position in the kingdom. Events moved rapidly forward. By the way of the banquet Haman passed the gallows. It was a fierce and terrible judgment, and yet characterized by poetic justice.

D. THE COUNTRY, PURIM, THE REJOICING JEWS

The peril of the Hebrew people was not yet, however, averted. The royal proclamation had gone forth that on the thirteenth day of the twelfth month they should be exterminated. By the constitution no royal proclamation could be reversed. The king granted Mordecai to write and sign letters to his people, permitting them to arm and defend themselves. The fateful day arrived, but it was one on which the changed conditions in the case of Haman and Mordecai were repeated throughout the whole of the provinces.

In memory of the deliverance the feast of Purim was established. According to Jewish tradition "all the feasts shall cease in the days of the Messiah, except the feast of Purim." It is a remarkable thing that while there have been breaks in the observance of the other great feasts, and some of them have been practically discontinued, this has been maintained.

CONCLUSION

Whatever view we may hold of this book of Esther, it is certain that Jewish leaders have treated it as an exposition of the method by which God wrought deliverance for His people in a time of peril, even while they were in exile.

JOB—*The Problem of Pain*

| Prologue. | The Man Before the Process | i. 1-5 |

| | THE DRAMA | i. 6—xlii. 6 |

A CONTROVERSY BETWEEN HEAVEN AND HELL *i. 6—ii. 10*	B CONTROVERSY BETWEEN JOB AND HIS FRIENDS *ii. 11—xxxvii.*	C CONTROVERSY BETWEEN JEHOVAH AND JOB *xxxviii.—xlii. 6*
I. The First Cycle i. 6-22	**I. Their Coming** **ii. 11—iii.**	**I. Jehovah, the First Unveiling** **xxxviii.—xxxix.**
i. Council in Heaven. 6-12 ii. Conflict on Earth. 13-22	i. Their sympathy. ii. 11-13 ii. Job's lament. iii.	The Creation and Sustenance of the material Universe. A challenge to Job.
II. The Second Cycle ii. 1-10	**II. The Controversy** **iv.—xxxi.**	**II. Interlude** **xl. 1-5**

i. Council in Heaven.   1-6
 ii. Conflict on Earth.   7-10
	i. First Cycle. iv.—xiv.
	    a. The argument. God is righteous. He punishes the wicked. He blesses the good.
	    b. The answer of Job. He is not wicked, but just, and yet he is afflicted.
	 ii. Second Cycle. xv.—xxi.
	    a. The argument. It is the wicked who are afflicted.
	    b. The answer of Job. The righteous also are afflicted. The wicked are not always afflicted.
	 iii. Third Cycle. xxii.—xxxi.
	    a. The argument. Job has sinned, therefore he suffers.
	    b. The answer of Job. Solemn protestation of innocence.
		i. Jehovah's challenge. 1-2
		 ii. Job's answer. 3-5
		
		 III. Jehovah, the Second Unveiling **xl. 6—xli.**
		
		 The Government of the material Universe. A challenge to Job.

	III. The Last Voice **xxxii.—xxxvii.** Suffering is educational.	**IV. Job's Answer** **xlii. 1-6**

| Epilogue. | The Man beyond the process. | xlii 7-17 |

JOB   ✳ ✳ ✳ ✳

IN MAGNIFICENCE OF argument and beauty of style this book is one of the grandest in the Divine Library. It is enshrouded in mystery, as to authorship, as to the characters presented, as to the geographical location of the scenes, and as to date. There are differences of opinion as to whether this story is historically true. Some look upon it as a dramatic poem intended to teach certain truths, but having no actual historic basis. I hold, upon the testimony of other parts of Scripture (Ezek. xiv. 14, 20; James v. 2), that the man Job actually lived, and that the story of his experiences as here set forth is a true one. This view does not for a moment interfere with the fact that the book is a dramatic poem, and therefore it is not necessary to suppose that either Job or his friends uttered their speeches in the exact form in which they are here presented to us; but the views they held, and the arguments they advanced, are accurately set forth.

There is every internal evidence that this is an ancient story, probably patriarchal. Its great problem is that of pain. Its relations are three-fold: first, of the relation of man to the spirit world—evil and good; second, of the inadequacy of human philosophies to account for human problems; third, of the purpose of God as gracious.

The analysis is an attempt to show the form and content of the book.

THE PROLOGUE

The book opens with a picture full of sunshine and beauty. Job is seen in a three-fold greatness. The first fact of that greatness is that of his wealth; the second is that of his family relationships; and the third is that of his relation to God. As to material wealth, he was "the greatest of all the children of the East." As to his family, he is seen rejoicing in the joy of his children, while caring for them in fatherly intercession. As to his God, he is declared to be "perfect and upright, and one that feared God, and eschewed evil."

A. THE CONTROVERSY BETWEEN HEAVEN AND HELL

This is a somewhat brief section, and yet absolutely necessary to a study of all that follows. In it, the veil is drawn aside, and we are given a view of councils in the spiritual world concerning man. The messengers of God are seen presenting themselves before Him. Among them comes one who is called Satan, or the adversary. He expresses his opinion concerning Job in the words, "Doth Job fear God for nought?" The question suggests that Job's confidence in God, his faith and loyalty, are due to the fact that God has cared for him. In other words, he declares that man's faith is based on selfishness, affirming that if the things he possesses be taken from him, his fear of God will cease. In answer to this challenge he is given permission to test Job within the limits of his own suggestion, "All that he hath is in thy power; only upon himself put not forth thine hand." Immediately we have the story of the calamities which overtake Job. The life which was seen in the prologue in calm and sunshine is merged in storm and strain, in agony and pain. Its strength, however, is proved in the fact that when stripped of everything Job is able to say, "The Lord gave and the Lord hath taken away; blessed be the name of the Lord." Thus the enemy is defeated and his slander disproved.

Again the council in the spiritual world assembles. Satan, compelled to admit his defeat so far, suggests new methods of attack, and again he is permitted to go forth to do all that he has suggested. He is strictly limited, however, by the fiat of God. Job is now seen plunged into yet deeper darkness, and more terrible circumstances of trial, and the first section ends with the picture of a man despoiled of earthly possessions, bereaved of children, and tempted to the uttermost by the suggestion of his wife that he should "curse God and die." He is still able to resist, and does not sin with his lips.

B. CONTROVERSY BETWEEN JOB AND HIS FRIENDS

In order to a true appreciation of all that is to follow, it is necessary that the condition of Job be clearly apprehended. With no knowledge of what has passed in the councils of the spiritual world, he sits in the midst of desolation and darkness, filled with physical, mental, and spiritual pain. His greatest anguish is that he cannot understand why these things have come to him. His life has been one of faith in God, and he has no consciousness of having committed sin. Why, then, has he been plunged into the midst of such circumstances?

While in the midst of this desolation, and on the

very verge of despair, his three friends come to him. Their coming is prompted by love of him, and sympathy for him. In the later movements of the book, Job, in keen disappointment, inquires what has become of all the people he had helped in the day of his prosperity, and the question is a pertinent one. The day of darkness had sifted the crowds of his professed friends. For the three who come we can have nothing but admiration. So terribly was Job changed by his experiences that these men are overwhelmed with astonishment as they behold him, and for seven days and seven nights they sit in silence in the presence of his grief.

Their silent sympathy appeals to him so that he pours out his great lamentation in their listening ears. It was a terrible cry pulsating with pain. He first curses the day of his birth, and the night of his conception. He then laments his preservation, and thinks of the quietness which would have been his if he could but have ceased to be. Finally he mourns his continued being, seeing that he is in circumstances of such unceasing and irremediable sorrow. So overwhelmed is he that he has lost his sense of the greatness of personality which he had affirmed at the close of the first attack of the adversary. He has, moreover, lost his clear sense of relation to God in his perplexity concerning the trial through which he has passed. The lamentation is a great cry for escape.

In answer to this lamentation the friends speak, and the controversy commences. It moves forward in three cycles, in the whole of which they speak from the standpoint of their own philosophy of life, and he answers out of the midst of his consciousness of the actual experiences through which he is passing.

B. *Controversy Between Job and His Friends*

In the first cycle the three friends speak to him in turn, he replying to each one in order. Their statement of the case may be briefly summarized thus. God is righteous: He punishes the wicked; He blesses the good. It is perfectly obvious that the deduction which they expect he will make is that they hold him guilty of some sin, of which sin all his sufferings constitute the Divine punishment. There is an evident method in their statement of the case, Eliphaz, in his speech, declares the principle in general terms. Bildad, in his turn, illustrates the principle, while Zophar applies it more directly to the case of Job. To each of these Job replies, with varying emphases, according to their differing methods, that he is not wicked but just, and yet he is afflicted, his main contention being that he is innocent, and yet God has afflicted him, and his principal desire being some explanation of this mystery.

In the second cycle again the three friends address Job in the same order, and he replies to each in turn. Their viewpoint is not changed, but throughout these addresses they state it within narrower limits. The whole argument in this case may thus be expressed: It is the wicked who are afflicted. Job answers by declaring that the righteous also are afflicted, and that the wicked are not always afflicted. On the part of the friends there is now evidence of some anger growing out of personal resentment. In his first reply Job has treated them with scorn and sarcasm, and their consideration for him is not as great as it was in the beginning. While they are profoundly convinced that such suffering can only be accounted for by the fact of definite sin having been committed, they look upon his attitude toward God as being impious, and therefore their words are less considerate and their method of attack more direct. Job, on the other hand, while treating them with scorn, seems throughout the movement to be more than ever determined to make his appeal directly to God, and thus is seen forcing his way to the point of direct dealing with Him.

In the third cycle we have a change. Eliphaz and Bildad are the only speakers. Their philosophy is still unchanged, only now they state it with more absolute directness of application to the case of Job. They charge him definitely with having sinned, and declare that this is the reason of his suffering. He replies to Eliphaz and Bildad, denying their affirmations concerning himself; and then, after a pause, in which he seems to have waited for Zophar, who does not speak, he makes a lengthy and solemn protestation of innocence. This takes a legal form, such as a man would adopt in some high court of justice, where upon oath he avows his innocence of the charges made against him.

The last voice of the earthly controversy is now heard. It is a new voice, and opportunity never comes to Job to answer it. Elihu introduces himself, with apologies to the ancient men, and yet expresses his disappointment that they have been unable to deal with Job.

The argument of Elihu moves forward in three sections. He first of all, at great length, declares that through suffering God is dealing with man to some higher issue. According to this argument suffering is educational. He closes this first movement by challenging Job to hear him while he speaks, and to answer him if he has anything to say.

Job gives no answer, and Elihu proceeds. He then makes two quotations from things which Job had said in the course of the previous controversy. The first may be summarized as a contention that he has been afflicted by God, notwithstanding his integrity. The second is one which suggests that nothing is gained by loyalty to God. In answer to the first, Elihu declares that God cannot do wickedness. In the case of the second, he affirms that when Job questions the advantage of serving God, he sets up his righteousness as being "more than God's."

After a pause, Elihu commences his last address, which is intended to be a defense of God against Job, and proceeds to illustrate it by reference to a storm. The dramatic setting of the story makes it probable that he described a storm which was actually gathering at the time, out of the midst of which presently the voice of God was heard.

C. CONTROVERSY BETWEEN JEHOVAH AND JOB

Out of the midst of the whirlwind speaks the Divine voice, for which Job has long been waiting. This speech of Jehovah is first of all a setting forth in language of inimitable splendor of the truth concerning the creation and sustenance of the material universe, at the close of which He challenges Job to answer. The answer is full of suggestiveness. The man who in mighty speech and strong defiance had been of unbroken spirit in the presence of the arguments of his friends now cries out, "Behold, I am of small account." He has yet to be taught that he is of much account to God.

Again Jehovah proceeds, and this time sets forth, in language equally sublime, the facts of His government of the material universe, ending with another challenge to Job. Job's answer is full of the stateliness of a great submission. This utterance of surrender is God's victory of vindication.

The great victory being won in the soul of Job, Jehovah

deals with his friends. His wrath is kindled against them, yet it is mingled with mercy. Their intention was right, but their words were wrong. Jehovah's vindication of Job is marked by the fact that He speaks of him as "my servant," and also by His appointment of Job as intercessor on behalf of his friends. They had attempted to restore Job to God by philosophy. He is to be the means of restoring them by prayer. As at the beginning there were things to be said in their favor, so at the close. Their sincerity is manifest in the fact that they submit. The rest is told in brief sentences. The latter days of Job on earth were characterized by greater prosperity than the earlier ones.

PSALMS—*The Book of Worship*

BOOK	PSALMS	DOXOL-OGY	DOMINANT NOTES OF WORSHIP	DIVINE TITLES			
				JEHOVAH	ELOHIM	ADONAHY	JAH
I.	i. to xli.	xli. 13	**Jehovah—The Becoming One. The Helper** Adoring Worship.	275	68	14	—
II.	xlii. to lxxii.	lxxii. 18-19	**Elohim—The Wonder-working God** Wondering Worship.	32	214	19	1
III.	lxxiii. to lxxxix.	lxxxix. 52	**Elohim-Jehovah. The Mighty Helper** Ceaseless Worship.	44	80	15	—
IV.	xc. to cvi.	cvi. 48	**Jehovah—The Governing King** Submissive Worship.	103	72	2	7
V.	cvii. to cl.	cl.	**Jehovah—The Redeemer** Perfected Worship.	236	40	12	32

PSALMS   ✳ ✳ ✳ ✳

THE WORD "PSALM" is the Anglicized form of a Greek word, which really means a poem set to music. The Hebrew title of the book was simply Praises, or Book of Praises. It is pre-eminently the worship book of the Hebrew people, and consists of a collection of songs which express the attitude of the soul in the presence of God, when contemplating past history, existing conditions, or prophetic hopes. The whole collection consists, in the Hebrew Bible, of five books. In the English and American Revisions this subdivision is shown.

We have no definite proof who the editor was. His method becomes evident by an examination of the grouping of the psalms. It is perfectly clear that neither authorship nor chronology was in his view. Eusebius declares that "the psalms are disposed according to a law of inward affinity," and Dr. Anderson says: "It must be remembered that every attempt to classify and arrange the psalms apart from the division of the whole Psalter into the five books as found in our Hebrew Bible, in the Septuagint, Syriac, and Vulgate Versions—every such attempt is confessedly imperfect, and more or less arbitrary."

The key to the method of the editor is to be found in the doxologies with which the books close. Each of the five has such a doxology, and an examination of these will reveal a certain conception of God, and an attitude of the soul in worship resulting from such conception. They may be grouped thus:

Book I. Psalm xli. 13.—Worship of Jehovah as the Becoming One, Who is the Helper.

Book II. Psalm lxxii. 18, 19.—Worship of Jehovah as the wonder-working God.

Book III. Psalm lxxxix. 52—Worship of Jehovah ceaseless.

Book IV. Psalm cvi. 48.—Worship of Jehovah rendered.

Book V. Psalm cl. 1-6.—Worship of Jehovah consummated.

The individual psalms are natural expressions by many authors, at various times, under differing circumstances, of the consciousness of God. The editing gathers these individual songs around the notes of truth dominant in each.

These notes are indicated in each book by the particular title of Jehovah which preponderates. The subject of the Divine titles is too great a one to be discussed at length now, but as an introduction to the study of the Psalter, recognition of difference is necessary. The proportion in which the four titles are used in the book of Psalms, as indicated in the diagram, is a somewhat rough one. That is to say, under *Elohim* are included *El* and *Eloah,* because while there is a minor difference of suggestion between the singular and the plural, the underlying thought is the same. So also with reference to *Adonahy* and *Adon.*

JEHOVAH. In the ancient Hebrew Scriptures this particular title was always written in the form of a tetragrammaton— YHVH—and there are differences of opinion as to what the actual form of the word should be. Without entering into any discussion of the varied interpretations, I adopt that of Mr. Joseph Bryant Rotherham in the "Emphasized Bible," both as to spelling and significance. He claims that the word thus abbreviated is Yahweh, and interprets it as meaning "the Becoming One." In his Bible he says, "Yahweh is almost always regarded as the third person singular, masculine, imperfect tense, from the root Hawah, an old form of the root Hayah. The one meaning of Hawah is 'become.' So that the force of Yahweh, thus derived as a verb, would be, 'He will become,' or, as expressive of use and wont as a noun it is, 'He who becometh,' 'The Becoming One.' " In a letter written to me in the course of correspondence on the subject, referring to this meaning, Mr. Rotherham says, " 'He becometh'; that is, 'He who becometh,' 'The Becoming One': becoming to His people whatever in His rich favor He pleases, in order to meet their need, and at last becoming Man." The truth therefore suggested by the use of this word is always that, first of the essential Being of God which enables Him to become; and by deduction, that God in infinite grace does become whatever man needs.

ELOHIM. This is a plural noun, but it is plural in a sense peculiar to the Hebrew language. Canon Girdlestone says: "It is well known that the Hebrews often expressed a word in the plural, so as to give it a special or technical meaning, as in the case of the words blood, water, wisdom, salvation, righteousness, life. . . . It is implied that the word in the singular number is not large enough to set forth all that is intended; and so, in the case of the Divine Name, the plural form expresses the truth that the finite word conveys an inadequate idea of the Being Whom it represents. Other names of God will be found to be plural also, and it is worthy of notice that in the well-known passage in Ecclesiastes (xii. 1) the Hebrew runs thus, 'Remember now thy Creators in the days of thy youth.' " The root idea of the word is that of strength or might; and the thought of God suggested by it is that of His strength as revealed in creation, and in all the operations of His power.

ADONAHY. This is again plural in form. Its simple signification is "Master" or "Lord"; and the thought it suggests is that of sovereign supremacy.

JAH. This is the shorter form of the name Jehovah, and is only found in Scripture; twice in Exodus, a few times in Isaiah, and in thirty-five passages in the book of Psalms.

These names reveal the doctrine of God, which creates the worship of man. Recognizing that Jehovah and Jah have the same essential significance, there are three lines of thought suggested. First, the essential Being of God, and the fact that He becomes in grace what man needs. Second, the essential Might of God, and the fact that it operates in power. Third, the essential Lordship of God, and His consequent sovereignty over man.

The analyses are intended to help in the study of the collection as to the conceptions impelling to worship.

BOOK I. PSALMS I.—XLI.

DOXOLOGY

"Blessed be the Lord, the God of Israel,
From everlasting and to everlasting. Amen, and Amen."   Psa. xli. 13.

A THE TITLE	B THE RELATION	C THE QUANTITY	D THE QUALITY
"Jehovah" The mysterious name, suggestive of essential Being, becoming whatever is needed by men, and therefore uniformly used as indicating God's relation to His people as Helper.	**"The God of Israel"** "God." Elohim. The idea of supremacy. "Of Israel." The Chosen People.	**"From everlasting to everlasting"** "The word 'everlasting' means the concealed or vanishing point; and suggests the mysterious past, and the unknown future. In its use here it reminds the heart of the eternity of God."	**"Blessed"** The root idea is that of prostration in the attitude of adoration. **"Amen, and Amen"** The consent of all to such adoration.

THE DIVINE NAME.

The Prevailing Name in this book is Jehovah. It occurs in every psalm at least twice, and in one (xxix) as many as 18 times.

"God" is found 18 times in the singular, 50 times in the plural; in all 68 times. From 13 psalms it is absent altogether.

The general title "Lord" (Adonahy) only occurs 14 times in all, and these occasions are all in 8 psalms.

THE DOMINANT THOUGHT.

The dominant thought in this book is that of God as Jehovah, the Helper of His people. The psalms are songs of varying emotion and differing condition, but all express themselves in harmony with this note.

TITLES

1. Jehovah's Law. A contrast. Obedience and disobedience.
2. Jehovah's King. Folly of rebellion. Wisdom of submission.
3. Jehovah's salvation. Confidence in peril.
4. Jehovah's countenance the cause of confidence.
5. Jehovah's leading in time of persecution.
6. Jehovah's deliverance in time of chastisement.
7. Jehovah's deliverance confidently hoped in.
8. Jehovah's excellence manifest in Nature and man.
9. Jehovah's righteous rule rejoiced in.
10. Jehovah's judgment besought.
11. Jehovah's throne the foundation.
12. Jehovah's rule in the midst of ungodliness.
13. Jehovah's succor sought by the afflicted.
14. Jehovah's knowledge of the godless.
15. Jehovah's friend described.
16. Jehovah the Portion of the trusting.
17. Jehovah appealed to, to exercise judgment.
18. Jehovah worshipped.
19. Jehovah revealed in Nature and Law.
20. Jehovah appealed to for help on behalf of the king.
21. Jehovah praised as the Strength of the king.
22. Jehovah the Succorer of the afflicted one.
23. Jehovah the Shepherd of His own.
24. Jehovah conquering through His King.
25. Jehovah besought for deliverance.
26. Jehovah worshipped. Conditions.
27. Jehovah worshipped. Experience.
28. Jehovah appealed to and worshipped.
29. Jehovah in the majesty of the storm.
30. Jehovah delivering from affliction.
31. Jehovah the Refuge of the afflicted.
32. Jehovah and the backsliding soul.
33. Jehovah the mighty Deliverer.
34. Jehovah the constant Succorer.
35. Jehovah besought for help against enemies.
36. Jehovah forgotten and recognised. A contrast.
37. Jehovah the Confidence of His people.
38. Jehovah appealed to in penitence.
39. Jehovah the Hope of the afflicted.
40. Jehovah worshipped in praise and prayer.
41. Jehovah recognised as rewarding compassion.

ANALYSIS

A AUTHORITY ESTABLISHED i.—viii.	B AUTHORITY DEFENDED ix.—xv.	C AUTHORITY ADMINISTERED xvi.—xli.
I. The Foundations i.—ii.	**I. The Need** ix.—x.	**I. The Person** xvi.—xxiv.
i. Obedience and disobedience. i. ii. The enthroned King. ii.	i. The Throne and the enemy. ix. ii. Appeal for action. x.	(See Titles.)
II. The Experiences iii.—vii.	**II. The Activity** xi.—xv.	**II. The Process** xxv.—xxxix.
(See Titles.)	(See Titles.)	i. Songs of Assurance. (See Titles.) xxv.—xxix. ii. Songs of Appropriation. (See Titles.) xxx.—xxxiv. iii. Songs of Aspiration. (See Titles.) xxxv.—xxxix.
III. The ultimate Purpose viii.		**III. The Person** xl.—xli.

BOOK II. PSALMS XLII.—LXXII.
DOXOLOGY

"Blessed be the Lord God, the God of Israel,
 Who only doeth wondrous things:
And blessed be his glorious name for ever;
And let the whole earth be filled with his glory. Amen, and Amen."   Psa. lxxii. 18-19.

A THE TITLE	B THE RELATION	C THE QUALITY	D THE QUANTITY	E THE EXTENT
"Jehovah Elohim"	"The God of Israel"	"Blessed"	"For Ever"	"The whole earth filled with His Glory"
The essential Helper Supreme.	"Who only doeth wondrous things."	The Person. His Name. "Amen, and Amen."		

THE DIVINE NAME.

The dominant name in this book is "God." It occurs in every psalm at least twice, and in one as many as 26 times. It is written in the singular (El) 16 times, and in the plural (Elohim) 198. "Jehovah" is found 32 times. From 15 psalms it is absent altogether.
The general title "Lord" (Adonahy) occurs 19 times scattered through 12 of the psalms.
In addition, the title "Jah" is used once.

THE DOMINANT THOUGHT.

In the second book the dominant thought is that of the might of God realized by His people, and manifest through them.
The worship is that of Jehovah as the wonder-working God.

TITLES

42. God remembered in exile.
43. God leading the exiled home.
44. God the Author of good and evil.
45. God gladdening the king and his bride.
46. God the Refuge of His people.
47. God reigning over the nations.
48. God reigning over His own.
49. God the Source of immortality.
50. God manifesting Himself through His people.
51. God the Saviour of the sinful.
52. God the Destroyer of the sinful.
53. God disappointed in man.
54. God the Helper of the oppressed.
55. God the Deliverer of the betrayed.
56. God the tender Friend of the oppressed.

57. God the Refuge in calamity.
58. God the God of vengeance.
59. God the High Tower of the oppressed.
60. God the Hope of His people.
61. God the Hope of man.
62. God the only Hope of man.
63. God the perfect Hope of man.
64. God the Defense of the persecuted.
65. God the God of harvest.
66. God the Object of worship.
67. God the perfect Governor of the nations.
68. God the Strength of His people.
69. God the Succorer of the sorrowful.
70. God the Hope of the despairing.
71. God the Confidence of old age.
72. God the King of the king.

ANALYSIS

A MIGHTY DELIVERANCE *xlii.—li.*	B MIGHTY DEFENSE *lii.—lx.*	C MIGHTY DOMINION *lxi.—lxxii.*
I. Exile xlii.—xliv.	**I. The Enemy** lii.—lv.	**I. The Need** lxi.—lxiv.

i. The Desire.   xlii.
ii. The Prayer.   xliii.
iii. The Despair.   xliv.
	i. The Godless One.
	        lii.—liii.
	ii. The Cry of Distress.
	        liv.—lv.
		i. Assurance. lxi.
		ii. Patience. lxii.
		iii. Confidence. lxiii.
		iv. Certainty. lxiv.

II. Hope xiv.—xlix.	**II. The Defender**
	        lvi.—lx.
		II. The Answer
		        lxv.—lxviii.

i. The King. xlv. ii. The Refuge. xlvi. iii. The Victor. xlvii. iv. The Defender. xlviii. v. The Life-Giver. xlix.	i. Hope. lvi.—lvii. ii. Prayer. lviii.—lx.	i. Praise for Might. lxv. ii. Praise for Deliverance. lxvi. iii. Universal Praise. lxvii. iv. The Arising of God. lxviii.
III. Restoration l.—li.		**III. The Process** lxix.—lxxii.

i. The Act of God.   l.
ii. The Attitude of Man.   li.
		i. The Suffering Witness.
		        lxix.
		ii. The Cry for Help. lxx.
		iii. The Cry of Confidence.
		        lxxi.
		iv. The King and the King-
		     dom. lxxii.

BOOK III. PSALMS LXXIII.—LXXXIX.

DOXOLOGY

"Blessed be the Lord for evermore. Amen, and Amen." Psa. lxxxix. 52.

A THE TITLE	B THE QUALITY	C THE QUANTITY
"Jehovah"	"Blessed"	"For evermore"
The Essential Helper. (See first Doxology.)	"Amen, and Amen."	

THE DIVINE NAME.

In the dominant name in this book is still "God." It occurs once at least in every psalm, and in one as many as 15 times. It is written in the singular (El) 20 times, and in the plural (Elohim) 60 times.

"Jehovah" is found in the book 44 times. It is only absent from two psalms, and occurs in one 10 times.

The general title "Lord" (Adonahy) occurs 15 times scattered through six psalms.

The title "Jah" is used twice.

THE DOMINANT THOUGHT.

In the third book the dominant thought is that of the worship of God under all circumstances. Both names are used throughout, although that of God predominates. While this is so, the final doxology speaks of Jehovah, showing that the thought is that of worship rendered to God because He is the essential Helper.

TITLES

73. God the God of His people.
74. God as silent and inactive.
75. God as speaking and active.
76. God the God of victory.
77. God the Healer of sorrow.
78. God the God of patience.
79. God the Hope of the distressed.
80. God the Restorer of His people.
81. God the Strength of the loyal.

82. God the Judge of the judges.
83. God vindicated as most High.
84. God the Strength of the pilgrim.
85. Jehovah the Restorer of the wanderer.
86. The Lord the mighty Helper of the needy.
87. Jehovah, His city and His peoples.
88. Jehovah the only Hope of the sorrowing.
89. Jehovah the God of Discipline.

ANALYSIS

A MIGHTY HELP— THE FACT lxxiii.—lxxvii.	B MIGHTY HELP— THE EXPERIENCE lxxviii.—lxxxiii.	C MIGHTY HELP— THE HOPE lxxxiv.—lxxxix.
I. The Viewpoint lxxiii. The Sanctuary. The Problem of the Prosperity of the Wicked. The Solution.	**I. History** lxxviii. Egypt to David. i. The Institution for children. ii. The Patience of God.	**I. Confidence** lxxxiv.—lxxxv. i. The pilgrimage contemplated. lxxxiv. ii. Salvation sought. lxxxv.
II. The Revelation lxxiv.—lxxvi. i. The Hope. lxxiv. ii. The Certainty. lxxv. iii. The Activity. lxxvi.	**II. Special Manifestation** lxxix.—lxxxi. i. The Devastation. lxxix. ii. The Appeal. lxxx. iii. The Deliverance. lxxxi.	**II. The Attitude** lxxxvi.—lxxxvii. i. Personal Submission. lxxxvi. ii. Relative Government. lxxxvii.
III. The Vision lxxvii. The Years of the Right Hand.	**III. Administration** lxxxii.—lxxxiii. i. Home. lxxxii. ii. Foreign. lxxxiii.	**III. The Summary** lxxxviii.—lxxxix. i. Human Need. lxxxviii. ii. Divine Resource. lxxxix.

BOOK IV. PSALMS XC.—CVI.

DOXOLOGY

"Blessed be the Lord, the God of Israel,
From everlasting even to everlasting,
And let all the people say, Amen,
Praise ye the Lord." Psa. cvi. 48.

A THE TITLE	B THE RELATION	C THE QUALITY	D THE QUANTITY	E THE EXTENT
"Jehovah" The essential Helper. (See first Doxology.)	"The God of Israel"	"Blessed" "Hallelujah."	"From everlasting to everlasting"	"And let all the people say, Amen"

THE DIVINE NAME.

The dominant name in this book is again "Jehovah." It occurs more than once in every psalm, and in two as many as 11 times.

The name "God" is absent altogether from five, and occurs only 27 times, 9 of them being singular (El), and 18 plural (Elohim).

The general title "Lord" (Adonahy) only occurs twice.

"Jah" is found 7 times.

THE DOMINANT THOUGHT.

In this book the worship of Jehovah is rendered by all people. They are songs of His government and administration, for which the heart is lifted in adoration.

TITLES

90. Jehovah the Eternal Dwelling-place of man.
91. Jehovah the Sanctuary of the perfect One.
92. Jehovah praised for His righteous dealing.
93. Jehovah the King—the Fact.
94. Jehovah the King—Faith's affirmation.
95. Jehovah the King—A warning.
96. Jehovah the King—Worship.
97. Jehovah the King—His Judgments.
98. Jehovah the King—Worship.
99. Jehovah the King—His Reign.
100. Jehovah the King—Worship.
101. Jehovah recognized in public and private life.
102. Jehovah the eternal God.
103. Jehovah the loving Father.
104. Jehovah the Creator and Sustainer.
105. Jehovah the true and mighty One.
106. Jehovah the faithful and patient One.

ANALYSIS

A THE PRINCIPLES xc.—xcii.	B THE PRACTICE xciii.—c.	C THE PRAISE ci.—cvi.
I. The Age-abiding Fact xc. Man's Failure.	**I. The Enthroned King** xciii.—xcvi. i. The Fact. xciii. ii. The Courage of Faith. xciv. iii. The Caution of Faith. xcv. iv. Worship. xcvi.	**I. The Attitude of Praise** ci. Submission.
II. The Unshaken One xci. Man's Hope.	**II. The Activity of the King** xcvii.—c. i. His Judgments. xcvii. ii. Worship. xcviii. iii. His Reign. xcix. iv. Worship. c.	**II. The Benefits** cii.—cvi. i. The Age-abiding God. cii. ii. The Loving Father. ciii. iii. The Creator and Sustainer. civ. iv. The True and Mighty One. cv. v. The Faithful and Patient One. cvi.
III. The New Realization xcii. Man's Restoration.		

BOOK V. PSALMS CVII.—CL.

DOXOLOGY

"Praise ye the Lord. Praise God in his sanctuary. Praise him in the firmament of his power.
Praise him for his mighty acts: Praise him according to his excellent greatness.
Praise him with the sound of the trumpet: Praise him with the psaltery and harp.
Praise him with the timbrel and dance: Praise him with stringed instruments and the pipe.
Praise him upon the loud cymbals: Praise him upon the high sounding cymbals.
Let everything that hath breath praise the Lord. Praise ye the Lord."   Psa. cl.

A THE TITLE	B THE QUAL-ITY	C THE PLACE	D THE REA-SON	E THE MEASURE	F THE MEANS	G THE CONDI-TION
In this Doxology which occupies the whole psalm the name of God only appears:— 1. As "Jah" in the perfect note of praise, "Halle-lujah" twice re-peated, "Jah" being in such case a contrac-tion of "Jeho-vah." 2. As God in the singular form "El," which is always signifi-cant of His might.	"Praise Him"	"In" "Sanc-tuary." Center. "Firma-ment." Circum-ference	"For" "His Mighty Acts."	"Accord-ing to" "His excellent greatness."	"With" "Instru-ments of music."	"Every-thing that hath breath"

The Divine Name.

Again in the final book, "Jehovah" is the predominant name. It occurs in every psalm but two, in some of them many times—236 in all.

The name "God" is absent from 22 of these psalms. It occurs 40 times, 10 in the singular and 30 in the plural.

The general title "Lord" (Adonahy) is found 12 times. "Jah" 32 times.

The Dominant Thought.

In this book, as an examination of the doxology will show, the worship of Jehovah is consummat-ed. It rises in volume and beauty until in the closing words of the doxology ultimate purpose is declared. "Let everything that hath breath praise the Lord. Hallelujah."

Still the songs are those arising out of various experiences. A large section is devoted to Songs of Ascent which are those of the pilgrims as they gathered by many ways and along different paths to the place of the Divine glory.

TITLES

ANALYSIS

A SONGS OF THE HOPE	B SONGS OF THE PROCESS	C SONGS OF THE WILL	D SONGS OF THE PILGRIMAGE	E SONGS OF THE EXPERIENCE	F SONGS OF THE PERFECTED PRAISE
cvii.—cxii.	*cxiii.—cxviii.*	*cxix.*	*cxx.—cxxxiv.*	*cxxxv.—cxliv.*	*cxlv.—cl.*
I. The Hope cvii.— cix.	I. Jehovah's Activity cxiii.— cxiv.	The Perfection of the Revealed Will	I. The Far Country cxx.—cxxi.	I. Sufficiency of Jehovah cxxxv.— cxxxix.	I. Introductory cxlv.
i. Assurance of faith. cvii.	i. His humility. cxiii.	Aleph. 1-8 The Perfect Law. Beth. 9-16 The Way of Cleansing.	i. Desire. cxx. ii. Assurance. cxxi.		
ii. Fixity of faith. cviii.	ii. His accomplishment. cxiv.	Gimel. 17-24 The Fountain of Joy. Daleth. 25-32	II. The Start cxxii.—cxxiii.		
iii. Triumph of faith. cix.	II. Jehovah's Servant cxv.— cxvi.	The Strength of Trial. He. 33-40 The Medium of Guidance. Vau. 41-48	i. Anticipation. cxxii. ii. Confidence. cxxiii.	II. Helplessness of Man cxl.— cxliii.	II. Jehovah cxlvi.— cxlvii.
II. The Reason cx.— cxii.	i. The Passion. The glory of His name. cxv.	The Inspiration of Testimony. Zain. 49-56 The Comfort of Sorrow. Cheth. 57-64	III. The Journey cxxiv.—cxxxi.		i. Grace. cxlvi. ii. Government. cxlvii.
i. The Coming One. cx.	ii. The Experience. Darkness and Deliverance. cxvi.	The Medium of Fellowship. Teth. 65-72 The Key of Affliction. Jod. 73-80	i. Escape. cxxiv. ii. First glimpse of City. cxxv. iii. Approach.		
ii. The Greatness and Grace of Jehovah. cxi.	III. Jehovah's Praise cxvii.— cxviii.	The Depths of Desire. Caph. 81-88 The Confidence of Darkness. Lamed. 89-96	cxxvi.—cxxxi. a. Laughter and penitence. cxxvi. b. The Family Strength. cxxvii.		III. The Worship cxlviii.— cxlix.
iii. The Blessedness of the Trusting Man. cxii.	i. The call of the Ideal Servant. cxvii.	The Foundation of Faith. Mem. 97-104 The Delight of Life. Nun. 105-112	c. The Family Responsibility. cxxviii. d. A backward look. cxxix.	III. Sufficiency answering Helplessness cxliv.	i. Creation. cxlviii. ii. The Saints. cxlix.
	ii. The Song of the Redeemed. cxviii.	The Light of Pilgrimage. Samech. 113-120 The Line of Rectitude. Ain. 121-128	e. Penitence and Confidence. cxxx. f. Rest in the Will of God. cxxxi.		IV. The Doxology cl.
		The Hope of Distress. Pe. 129-136 The Light of Life. Tzaddi. 137-144	IV. The Entrance cxxxii.		
		The Knowledge of God. Koph. 145-152 The Inspiration of Devotion. Resh. 153-160	V. The City and Worship cxxxiii.— cxxxiv.		
		The Principle of Life. Schin. 161-168 The true Wealth. Tau. 169-176 The perfect Law.	i. By Day. cxxxiii. ii. By Night. cxxxiv.		

PROVERBS—*Practical Wisdom*

INTRO-DUCTION i. 1-7	A INSTRUCTIONS ON WISDOM i. 8—ix.	B PROVERBS 1st COLLECTION x.—xxiv.	C PROVERBS 2nd COLLECTION xxv.—xxix.	APPEN-DIX xxx.—xxxi.
The Title. 1				
I. The Purpose 2-5	I. Parental Counsel i. 8-19 i. Wisdom—True Friends. 8-9 ii. Folly—False Friends. 10-19	I. Proverbs x.—xxii. 16 A collection of Proverbs which cannot be analysed.	I. Title xxv. 1	I. The Words of Agur xxx. Unknown. i. Title. ii. Human Incompleteness in Wisdom. 1-6 iii. Prayer. 7-9 iv. Conduct 10-33
II. The Method 6-7	II. Wisdom's Call i. 20-33 i. The Announcement. 20-21 ii. The Call. 22-33 III. Parental Counsels ii.—vii. i. On Wisdom. ii.—iii. ii. A Personal Testimony. iv. 1-9 iii. Exhortations. iv. 10—vii. IV. Wisdom's Call viii. i. The Announcement. 1-3 ii. The Call. 4-36 V. A Contrast ix. i. Wisdom. 1-12 ii. Folly. 13-18	II. A Series of Proverbial Discourses xxii. 17—xxiv. i. A Social Admonition. xxii. 17—xxiii. 14 ii. Parental Counsels. xxiii. 15—xxiv. 22 iii. Concerning Social Order. xxiv. 23-34	II. Proverbs xxv. 2—xxix. A posthumous collection. Another collection of Proverbs. These in some senses are more picturesque than the former. They were statements. These are pictures.	II. The Oracles of Lemuel xxxi. Unknown. i. His Mother's Counsel. 1-9 ii. His Mother's Picture. 10-31

PROVERBS ✳ ✳ ✳ ✳

THE BOOK OF Proverbs is one of the wisdom books of the Hebrew people. That is to say, its theme and purpose is wisdom. The word itself occurs frequently, and there are others which in some senses are synonymous with it—knowledge, understanding, discretion, subtlety. Each of these expresses some application of wisdom, the word wisdom itself being greater than any, because including all. In all its teaching this book takes for granted the wisdom of God, and seeks to instruct man concerning what His wisdom really is.

The underlying conception of all the wisdom books of the ancient writings is that of God Himself, the All-Wise. They also recognize that His wisdom is expressed in all His works and words. Man is wise in proportion as he recognizes these truths and answers them in the conduct of his life. The perfectly wise man is the one who in his whole being lives and thinks and acts in right relationship to the All-Wise God. His wisdom commences emotionally in the fear of God; is manifest intellectually in his acquaintance with the manifestations of the Divine nature in word and work; is active volitionally in obedience to the will of God, as revealed in word and work. The word translated *proverb* really means likeness, and we come nearest to the thought in our word *parable*. In this book we have the setting forth of the underlying wisdom by discourses on its value, and declarations of its practical application.

The book may be divided thus: Introduction (i. 1-7); Instructions on Wisdom (i. 8-ix.); First Collection of Proverbs (x.-xxiv.); Second Collection of Proverbs (xxv.-xxix.); Appendix (xxx., xxxi.).

INTRODUCTION

The first verse constitutes the title of the book, and the following six contain what we should to-day speak of as a preface. That preface first declares the purpose of the book in terms so simple as to need no comment. Then follows a statement of method which is necessary to the right use of the whole book. The beginning of wisdom is the fear of the Lord. The fact of God, and of man's relation to Him must be taken for granted and answered if there is to be any true wisdom.

A. INSTRUCTIONS ON WISDOM

These general instructions prepare the way for the proverbs proper. The first is a parental counsel, in which the wisdom of recognising true friends is set forth in words which urge the habit of loyalty to father and mother; and the folly of forming false friendships is set forth in a series of warnings.

Then Wisdom is personified, and her first call is stated. It is an appeal to turn from simplicity and scorning and hatred of knowledge, with the promise that she will reward such as search after her. This is succeeded by a warning that Wisdom neglected, at last refuses to answer.

Following the first call of Wisdom we have a series of parental counsels, all of which begin with the words "my son." They deal with the value of wisdom, and make practical ap-

A. Instructions on Wisdom

plication of the teaching. The first of these addresses deals with the search for wisdom, as to its method, and as to its value. In the search there must be willingness and desire to know, accompanied by devotion. The values of the search are the discerning and discreet heart, which enables man to understand his pathway; the consequent ability to refuse false friendships; and the resulting choice of the path of good, with all the benefits arising therefrom. The next address is an appeal to cultivate wisdom. It consists of a declaration of the essence of wisdom, a description of its excellences, and a declaration of the safety which it brings. In the next address the father urges his own experience. His father had given him advice, which he declares was good. This personal testimony lends urgency to his exhortations to his son. Then, conscious of the temptations which beset the path of the young, he urges to obedience. The attitude toward temptation is to be that of avoiding it completely. Wisdom in the heart, persistent looking straight ahead, and untiring caution, are the things necessary to fidelity. Then follows an exhortation against impurity, expressed in words of great delicacy and beauty. The allurement of evil is vividly described. It is put into immediate contrast with the issue of yielding thereto. It is a change from honey to wormwood, from the smoothness of oil to the sharpness of a sword, from the path of life to the highway of death. Impurity of conduct may seem to be of silken texture in its enticement; it becomes a hard and unyielding cable when it binds the life in slavery. The parental exhortations are continued against suretyship, indolence, the evil in man, and certain specific things which the Lord hates. These counsels close with two solemn warnings on the same subject. Each commences with tender and urgent entreaties to attend to what is said, because the advice is for the good of the son to whom it is addressed. In the hour of sin's glamor it is good for the soul to look through to the end, which is in Sheol and the chambers of death. When the voice of the siren is heard, it is good to pause and listen to the moan of the breakers on the shore of darkness and death, for to that shore the way of impurity assuredly leads.

The division containing the instructions on wisdom ends with two discourses, the first of which is a great call of Wisdom. This takes up and deals more minutely with the call in the earlier part of the book. It opens with an announcement that Wisdom is making her appeal everywhere amid the busy activities of human life. Then follows her call. This is, first, an appeal to men to attend. This they should do because Wisdom speaks excellent things, and speaks in righteousness. Moreover, they are plain words, and more valuable than all riches. The foundations of Wisdom are next declared. Essentially these are prudence, knowledge, discretion. As to man, the foundation is the fear of the Lord, which expresses itself in hatred of all He hates. In such Wisdom lie the secrets of strength. Then the values of Wisdom are described. All authority is based on it. She is the lover of such as love her. She yields all highest wealth to such as yield to her. Next, Wisdom claims age-abiding relation to Deity. Ere the beginnings of creation, Jehovah possessed Wisdom. Through all the processes Wisdom wrought with God, and God delighted in Wisdom, until man, the crowning glory of all, gave Wisdom chief delight. This passage may be set side by side with the prologue to John's Gospel for fuller understanding. The call ends with a final appeal. Those who attend to the call of Wisdom are blessed indeed, and those who sin against Wisdom wrong their own soul.

The last address is a contrast between Wisdom and Folly. Each is personified as a woman calling to youth. Wisdom has built her house and spread her feast in the high places of the city. She calls to a feast of life. Folly, in the garb of the evil woman, sits at the door of the house also in the high places of the city. She also calls to a feast, but it is a feast of death. Between the two descriptions there is a passage revealing the fact that the effect produced will depend upon the attitude of those who hear. The man who scorns gets shame, and it is useless to reprove him. The wise man is willing to be taught, and it is worth while reproving him. What, then, is this first Wisdom which expresses itself in willingness to learn, and gains yet greater Wisdom? It is the fear of the Lord and the knowledge of the Holy One. In every city, on every street, by every door of opportunity, these two voices of Wisdom and Folly are appealing to men. To obey the call of Wisdom is to live; to yield to the clamor of Folly is to die. How shall we discern between the voices? By making the fear of the Lord the central inspiration of the life; by yielding the being at its deepest to Him for correction and guidance.

B. FIRST COLLECTION OF PROVERBS

Here begin the proverbs proper. In this first collection they are antithetical. They present a sharp contrast between wisdom and folly in the outworking of each in practical life. Seeing that this is indeed a collection of proverbs, there is no direct connection or system save this underlying purpose of contrast. No exposition is possible save that of taking each proverb and considering it in its separate value. This in the majority of instances is unnecessary, because they are self-evident expositions of one abiding truth.

C. SECOND COLLECTION OF PROVERBS

These, as the title specifically declares, constitute a posthumous collection, having been gathered together in the days of Hezekiah. Speaking generally, the proverbs in this collection are more picturesque than the former. They were for the most part antithetical and logical. These are pictures, and are more perfectly parabolic.

APPENDIX

In this appendix we have the words of Agur and Lemuel. It is impossible to say who Agur was. In this selection from his writings, we have, first, an introduction, in which he affirms the fact of human incompleteness in wisdom, and then utters the memorable prayer, in which he reveals his faith in the Lord, and his desire for that balanced life which is one of safety. From the prayer to the end of the chapter we have his observations on various matters affecting conduct. In these observations we have, first, a proverb. This is followed by two groups of four things—four evil things and four things perpetually dissatisfied. Then follows another proverb, and four groups of four things. The first four are such as excite wonder. The second four cause terror. The third four are little things, but exceeding wise. The final four are things of stateliness. The whole movement ends with a proverb.

There have been many conjectures as to the identity of

King Lemuel, but nothing can be certainly affirmed. His words recorded here fall into two parts. The first of these consists of his mother's advice to him, wherein she urged him against becoming the slave of passion, warning him that while there may be some excuse for the man who is ready to perish if he takes strong drink, it must utterly be avoided by kings and princes. Finally, there is set before him the first duty of the kingly office—that of caring for all who are oppressed and needy. The second part consists of a beautiful picture of a virtuous woman, and may be supposed to be King Lemuel's picture of his mother. After a fine description of her beauty and her diligence, and the helpful influence she exerted in bringing her husband to places of power, he ends with the declaration:

> Many daughters have done virtuously,
> But thou excellest them all,

and with a blessing pronounced upon her.

THE BOOK OF ECCLESIASTES—*The Vanity*
of Materialism

A THEME *i. 1-11*	B THE EVIDENCE *i. 12—viii.*	C THE EFFECT *ix.—xi. 8*	D THE CORRECTION *xi. 9—xii.*
Title Page 1			

I. Inclusive Statement
   2-3
 	
Vapor of Vapors.
	I. Personal i. 12—ii.
	
	 i. Knowledge. 12-18
	 ii. Mirth. ii. 1-3
	iii. Wealth. 4-11
	iv. Life. 12-26
		I. Worldly Wisdom Extolled
		   ix. 1-16
		
		 i. One event to all.
		   1-6
		 ii. Enter into life.
		   7-10
		iii. Advantages are of little worth.
		   11-12
		iv. Wisdom under the Sun. 13-16
			I. Stated
			   xi. 9-10

II. Elaboration
   4-11
 	
Generation.
Sun.
Wind.
Rivers.
Man.
The consciousness of the grind of material forces.
	II. Relative iii.—viii.
	
	 i. The Mechanism of the Universe. iii.
	 ii. Sociological Oppressions.
	   iv.
	iii. Religion. v. 1-7
	   This is also wholly of fear.
	iv. Poverty and Prosperity.
	   v. 8—vi.
	 v. Indifference. vii.—viii.
		II. Worldly Wisdom Exemplified
		   ix. 17—xi. 8
		
		 i. Discretion.
		   ix. 17—x.
		 ii. Diligence. xi. 1-7
		iii. Darkness. 8
			II. Urged
			   xii. 1-12
			
			III. Summarized
			   xii. 13-14

ECCLESIASTES   * * * *

THE WORD ECCLESIASTES means preacher or teacher, and this book is, in matter of fact, one set and systematic discourse. The theme of the book is the "vanity" of everything "under the sun." This is first announced, then proved from the preacher's personal experience, and from his wide-reaching observation. Finally, by appeal and declaration, he shows that the whole of life is only found as there is recognition of things above the sun as well as of those under the sun—of things spiritual as well as material.

It is a living book because it still faithfully mirrors the experiences of such as dwell wholly in the material realm, and because it makes the one and only appeal which, being obeyed, issues in the correction of the despair. It may be thus divided: the Theme stated (i.1-11); the Evidence massed (i. 12-viii.); the Effect revealed (ix.-xi. 8); the Correction declared (xi. 9-xii. 14).

A. THE THEME STATED

In the statement of his theme the preacher employs phrases which recur through the whole of the book—"vanity," "what profit," "under the sun." The statement is a declaration of the emptiness of life when it is wholly conditioned in material things.

In this first division, beyond the preliminary declaration, there is a more particular statement in terms of general illustration. The generations come and go, while the earth abides. The sun rises and sets. The wind moves in a cease-less circuit. Rivers run into the sea only to return to the places from which they came. Man comes to the scene with desires which are never satisfied, and passes away into a land of forgetfulness. The intention of the whole passage is to impress upon the mind the fact of the constant grind of the mechanism of the universe in the midst of which man lives his day briefly, and passes out to forget and to be forgotten. This is still the consciousness to which men come who have lost their vision of the spiritual realities which constitute the upper half of human life.

B. THE EVIDENCE MASSED

The discourse now proceeds to state the ground upon which such conclusions have been arrived at. They are two-fold. First, the actual experiences of the king; and secondly, the widespread observation of other men, and of matters in general.

Commencing with his own experience, he states the vanity of knowledge, of mirth, of wealth. As to knowledge, he had applied his heart to seek and search out all works done under the sun, and had come to the conclusion that they were all vanity, and that knowledge of them was grief. Knowledge unilluminated by spiritual consciousness is utterly unsatisfying.

Turning from the pursuit of knowledge to the pathway of pleasure, the king had given himself up to mirth, seeking the false stimulus of wine. In this also he had been disappointed, finding that mirth was madness, and all pleasure imcompetent to satisfy.

He next turned to his great possessions, attempting to make such use of them as to bring satisfaction not found

B. *The Evidence Massed*

elsewhere. He surrounded himself with every kind of luxury, gathered large possessions, gave himself over to music and to women, allowing full rein to all his desires. All this he had found to be vanity, nothing but a striving after wind, and he had again been driven to the conclusion that there was no profit under the sun.

Once again he had tried a new pathway. He turned himself from the things that were almost exclusively physical to those of the mind. These were better, and he found that "wisdom excelleth folly." Yet he also perceived that "one event happeneth to all," both the fool and the wise pass on to death, so that this also ended in disappointment as keen as the others. He then summarizes the results of his own experience of life "under the sun" in the terrible words: "I hated life . . . I hated all my labour . . . under the sun." The very exercise of wisdom resulted in the gathering of results into which the toiler did not enter, but which he left to another. Everything was vanity. The ultimate conclusion of his own experience was that there was nothing better than to eat and drink. Materialism necessarily becomes fatalism.

Turning from his personal experience to the evidence gained by observation, he again, but in greater detail, describes the mechanism of the universe, referring to its ceaseless routine, deducing therefrom a conception of God as a Being Who is absolutely inexorable, and from Whom there is no escape. The issue of this is confusion rather than order. In the place of judgment and of righteousness, wickedness exists. After all man is no better than the beasts.

From this general survey the preacher returns to examine the condition of the beings whom he has described as being no better than the beasts. He sees everywhere the suffering of society, and even where men are successful enough to amass wealth, they find themselves in circumstances of pitiable loneliness. Kingship itself is empty and disappointing.

The observation of the religious life brings no truer satisfaction. The preacher expresses no contempt for religion; but there is in his outlook, no joy, no satisfaction. The recognition of God is irksome, and issues, at its best, in a caution based on fear. Turning again to a general survey of the conditions under which men live, the preacher appeals against surprise at oppression. Poverty is preferable to wealth. Wealth is disappointing. His advice, in view of his observations, may be summarized thus: Do not hoard anything, but enjoy it. It is the advice of utter selfishness.

Being experimentally far better acquainted with wealth than with poverty, he returns to a full declaration of the sorrows of the wealthy. His evident thought is that the more a man possesses under the sun, the more profoundly conscious does he become of the vanity and vexation of it all.

He then proceeds to the inculcation of indifference toward all the facts of life as the only attitude which is in the least likely to be satisfactory. He recommends that men should take things as they come. This general advice he emphasizes by particular illustrations. Righteousness does not always pay; wickedness sometimes does. Therefore morality is to be a thing of calculation. Men are urged to walk the middle way. The whole attitude of mind revealed is that of cynicism; but it is the attitude of a man who had lived his life "under the sun."

C. THE EFFECT REVEALED

In view of the evidences of the truth of his affirmation, "vanity . . . all is vanity," the preacher now turns to the

D. The Correction Declared

effect of this fact on the mind of the man living "under the sun." He extols worldly wisdom. It is to be granted that all things are in the hand of God, and this being so, men do not know them, nor can they. The only certain thing is that there is one event to all—righteous and wicked, clean and unclean, the worshipper and the man who fails in worship, the good and the sinner, the swearer and the man who fears an oath. All these are really evil, with madness in their heart during life, and move toward death. Therefore there is nothing for it other than to enjoy the present life, to eat and drink, and to dress; to enter into the experiences of the life of vanity. Everything is to be done in the present moment, and that with might, because there is cessation beyond. Wisdom under the sun is granted to be of some relative value, but in the long issue it is of little worth. How, then, does worldly wisdom work? The preacher shows that its first manifestation is that of discretion based upon selfishness. It is, moreover, that of diligence in the midst of the things of this life. Almost weirdly, this setting forth of the value and method of worldly wisdom ends in the same wail of disappointment which has characterized the whole discourse. "If a man live many years, let him rejoice in them all; but let him remember the days of darkness, for they shall be many. All that cometh is vanity."

D. THE CORRECTION DECLARED

The first word of the last division of the book, like the first word of the Manifesto of the King in later days, indicates the true thought and desire of God for man: "Rejoice." A statement of life which includes all of truth recognized in the discourse, and yet which far transcends the whole of it, is first made. A man is to enter life—his own life and his present life—with avidity; and he is constantly to do so in the sight of God, remembering his relationship to Him. Judgment here does not mean punishment, but verdict. Everything is to be tested first by the supremacy of God. To attempt to find Him through the medium of our self-pleasing use of life is utterly to fail. To enthrone Him first, and then to attempt to find life through Him, is to cancel forever the word "vanity."

The preacher proceeds in language full of poetic beauty to urge the young to remember the Creator. We then reach the epilogue of the sermon. It first repeats the theme as announced at the beginning, and tells how the preacher, through study and diligence, still attempted to teach the people knowledge; and finally, in the concluding two verses, a great statement of truth is made, understanding and acting upon which, the pessimistic views of life resulting from materialism will never be known.

At the center is this statement: "This is the whole of man." The word "duty" has no real place in the sentence. What is the whole of man? "To fear God and keep His commandments." To do this is to find life not merely under the sun, but over it as well, to pass from the imperfect hemisphere into the perfect sphere. To do this is to have light upon the facts and problems of life, which otherwise are dark and dismal.

SONG OF SOLOMON—*The Canticles of Love*

SONG OF SOLOMON ✳ ✳ ✳ ✳

NO BOOK HAS been more provocative of controversy than
this. The question at issue is as to its place and value in Holy
Scripture. Decision as to its right to be there depends ultimately upon the interpretation of it which is adopted. While
there are different varieties of each, the interpretations may
be divided into two main classes—the material and the mystical. Without staying to deal with the many interpretations
of either kind, may it not be true that the gravest mistake
has been that of imagining that either method in itself ex-
hausts the meaning? On the extreme left are those who
declare it to be simply a voluptuous Eastern love song.
On the extreme right are those who at once say it is a
portrayal of the love existing between Christ and His
Church. To take the second view first, for whatever value
the Holy Spirit may have caused this to be written, it is perfectly certain that Solomon did not see in it all that
such interpreters find there. I am not denying that these
things are there for us, but merely say Solomon did not write
to set forth these things, for the mystery of the Church was
a hidden one under the whole economy of Hebraism. On
the other hand, if some mystical value is recognized as lying within the purpose of the writer, the songs are at once
saved from the possibility of being charged with voluptuous-
ness.

In order to understand the value of the book, I think it
necessary to recognize, first, a basis in actual fact; and second,

an increasing understanding of the deepest values with the process of the centuries.

The basis of fact we shall find by recognizing that these songs are idyls, and that behind them is the actual story of the wooing and winning of a bride. As Dr. Moulton lucidly points out, the idyllic form does not proceed in consecutive order in its description, and it is necessary to construct the story by careful examination of the songs themselves.

They first set forth the love existing between bride and bridegroom. The thought of the relationship of bride and bridegroom, as setting forth that existing between Jehovah and Israel, is peculiarly Hebrew. In the prophets this is subsequently made clearly manifest. Moreover, Jewish expositors have so interpreted these songs, and it is certainly easily probable that Solomon had some such intention in mind.

In the New Dispensation, that of the Church, the same figure is the most glorious in setting forth the nature of the relation existing between Christ and His Church. Some of the most sainted writers of the Christian Church have interpreted these songs in the light of this New Testament truth; such, for instance, as Rutherford and McCheyne. Dr. Adeney, in the Expositor's Bible, while arguing against the mystical interpretation, yet says: "It may be maintained that the experience of Christians has demonstrated the aptness of the expression of the deepest spiritual truths in the imagery of the Song of Solomon." His later contention, that New Testament writers make no use of the poem in this way, is of no weight, for we believe in the ever-increasing light upon the deepest values of the earlier Scriptures. The fact that Solomon had no intention of setting forth the relation between Christ and His Church is of no moment. If through the songs of human love he did intend to set forth the spiritual idea of the love between Jehovah and His ideal people, the fulfillment of the thought of the songs would come with the working out into history of the realization of that purpose.

The songs should be treated then, first as simple and yet sublime songs of human affection. When they are thus understood, reverently the thoughts may be lifted into the higher value of setting forth the joys of the communion between the spirit of man and the Spirit of God, and ultimately between the Church and Christ.

No further exposition of these songs is necessary in an outline study. As songs of human love they need no other exposition. As songs of spiritual love they are better interpreted experimentally than in any other way.

ISAIAH—*The Prophet of the Theocracy*

A PROPHECIES OF JUDGMENT *i.—xxxv.*	B HISTORICAL INTERLUDE *xxxvi.—xxxix.*	C PROPHECIES OF PEACE *xl.—lxvi.*

ISAIAH ✳ ✳ ✳ ✳

ISAIAH WAS A prophet of Judah. He exercised his ministry wholly within her borders, and with a view to her correction and comfort. His burdens of the nations were uttered concerning those which surrounded Judah and had harassed her. His outlook was world-wide, and inclusive of the whole purpose of God. Profoundly conscious of the intention of God that through His people all peoples should be blessed, he saw through all the processes of judgment the ultimate blessing of the whole earth.

The book as a whole sets forth the two facts of Judgment and Peace, and shows their interrelation in the economy of God. Dealing first with Judgment, his messages show how it ever proceeds to Peace. Dealing finally with Peace, they show how it is always conditioned in Righteousness. Between these principal parts of the book is an historical section, the first part of which is related to the Judgment prophecies, and the second to those concerning Peace.

Isaiah's messages were delivered during a dark period in the history of the people. He lived and taught during the reigns of Uzziah, Jotham, Ahaz, and Hezekiah. Contemporary with him, Hosea was prophesying to Israel, and Micah to Judah.

The unity of the teaching is conspicuous, and is the chief argument in favor of the unity of authorship.

The book naturally falls into three parts: Prophecies of

Judgment (i.-xxxv.); Historical Interlude (xxxvi.-xxxix.);
Prophecies of Peace (xl.-lxvi.).

A. PROPHECIES OF JUDGMENT

The prophecies of judgment move in three circles, the
first of which deals with Judah and Jersualem, the second
with the nations and the world, the third with the chosen
and the world.

The prophecies dealing with the judgment of Judah and
Jerusalem were delivered during the reigns of Uzziah,
Jotham, and Ahaz. The first five chapters contain the messages delivered during the reign of Uzziah. The prophet first
impeached the whole nation. Having summoned the
heavens and the earth to attention, he uttered Jehovah's complaint that "Israel doth not know, my people doth not
consider," and made his appeal to them to learn wisdom
from their stricken condition. He then proceeded in the
name of Jehovah to correct their false notions of religion,
declaring that while they had been satisfied with things
external, He had sought righteousness and judgment. After
having uttered the call of Jehovah, which was full of grace
and tenderness, Isaiah described the corruption of the city
and the consequent judgment which was necessary for
restoration, declaring at the same time that there is a judgment which is reprobation in the case of persistent sin.

After the impeachment, the prophet uttered a great appeal, in which he first described the latter days in which the
Lord's house is to be established, the law is to proceed from
Zion, and the issue is to be peace. Then, calling them to walk
in the light of the Lord, he declared what that light revealed
of existing corruption and consequent judgment, appealing

to them to desist from evil. Following this he described in detail the judgment of a corrupt society, which must fall upon the unjust rulers and the people who had submitted to their rule. With a keen understanding of the corruption of society and its reason, he declared the judgment of Jehovah must fall upon the women who were haughty, who had lived in luxury, and whose influence had been evil in the life of the nation. The great appeal ends with another vision of the latter day, which he described as to its material prosperity, its moral purity, and its mighty protection.

Finally he denounced the nation, first by singing to them the song of the vineyard, in which he showed how utterly they had failed to fulfill the Divine purpose. Therefore he pronounced woes against monopoly, dissipation, unbelief, moral confusion, conceit, and the perversion of justice. It was because of these things that the anger of the Lord was kindled against the people, and the prophet foretold the coming of the scourge.

The second part of the first circle of prophecy contains the messages of Isaiah during the reigns of Jotham and Ahaz. When Uzziah died, Isaiah was called to the exercise of a larger ministry, and was prepared for the same by the special vision granted to him. It was a vision of the glory and the grace of Jehovah. He was revealed as One Who was at once the center of adoring worship, and Who heard the sigh of the sinner in his need, and stayed the song of the seraph in order that that cry of need might be answered.

Following the vision and the prophet's cleansing, he was commissioned to the ministry of judgment. Immediately following this new call, the prophet encountered Ahaz, and in consequence of his obstinacy, foretold the judgment

–201

which would fall upon Judah by the coming of the Assyrian hosts.

After this encounter the prophet turned from his more public ministry to devote himself to a small circle of believing souls. He was instructed to bind the testimony and seal the law, and his children were to be for signs and wonders to the people. Turning to the work of instructing this small group, the prophet described to them the false way of seeking familiar spirits and wizards, with the disastrous results of doing so; and then delivered to them the message of hope, which culminated in a glorious description of the coming Deliverer.

This is followed by a prophecy of judgment on Israel, which falls into four distinct parts, each ending with the words: "For all this his anger is not turned away, but his hand is stretched out still." Through all the methods of judgment the afflicted people manifested stubbornness of heart and persistence in wickedness, so that the anger of the Lord could not be turned away, but His afflicting hand continued to be outstretched.

The prophecy of judgment upon Assyria comes next in order. Assyria was the power which Jehovah was about to use for the punishment of His people, but because it failed to understand its true relation to God, it must in turn be judged. The prophet first indicated this contrast of intention. Jehovah's intention was that the Assyrian should be the rod in His hand. The Assyrian intention was to destroy the people of God. Therefore Assyria must also be judged. Nevertheless the purpose of God would be fulfilled, and the prophecy ends with a graphic description of the Assyrians' approach, and of the judgment which would fall upon the chosen people by their coming.

With judgment imminent, the prophet yet saw the ultimate issue of it all. He described the coming Deliverer, which description is followed by songs celebrating His victories.

The second circle of the first division contains Isaiah's prophecies concerning the nations of the world. He first described the doom of Babylon. Media was to be the instrument of the destruction, and the issue thereof was intended to be the restoration of Israel through the compassion of Jehovah. Anticipating the day of restoration, the prophet put into the mouth of Israel the parable or song which celebrates the downfall. This moves in five distinct strophes, the first of which describes the overthrow and the consequent rest of the whole earth. The second speaks of the consternation of the underworld at the fall of Babylon. The third declares the sin which culminates in such destruction. The completeness of destruction is the subject of the fourth. The final strophe announces the utter extermination of Babylon.

There follows a fragment concerning Assyria, in which the prophet reaffirmed Jehovah's intention to break its power.

That concerning Philistia is of the nature of a warning spoken to her. Although she oppressed the people of God, she was herself in peril. She was not to rejoice because the rod which smote her was broken, for there were other forces at the disposal of Jehovah, and they threatened her.

The prophecy concerning Moab commences by describing her desolation. A catastrophe would overtake her in a night, the result of which would be the mourning of her people, and their scattering far and wide. The prophet declared, moreover, that this visitation of Moab would be in fulfillment of an ancient prophecy, and that at last the time limit was actually set.

The burden of Damascus announces its doom. It is evident, however, that the prophet had in mind the alliance which had been entered into by Israel or Ephraim with Damascus. The doom of Damascus would mean the destruction of the fortress of Ephraim. The prophet then proceeded to describe the judgment of Ephraim which would issue from the destruction of Damascus, and he declared that the effect produced would be that of compelling men to look to Jehovah rather than to idols. The reason of this visitation was that Ephraim had forgotten God.

In the midst of these burdens of the nations we have a soliloquy of the prophet, which falls into two sections. The first reveals his consciousness of the opposing peoples, and of Jehovah as perfect defense. The second is of the nature of a proclamation to certain ambassadors, who were charged to return to their people, and to wait for Jehovah.

Immediately following this soliloquy we have the burden of Egypt. Jehovah's advent will result in the destruction of idols, in civil war, in failure in counsel, and in the government of the Egyptian people by a cruel lord and a false king. This day of visitation will be one of physical catastrophe. The waters of the Nile will fail, and consequently all industry—fishing, weaving, and building—will be paralyzed. Yet the prophet saw hope even for Egypt, and with the far-reaching vision of faith he saw both Egypt and Assyria joined in the worship of Jehovah, and ultimately a triple alliance of Israel, Egypt, and Assyria made a blessing in the midst of the earth.

Turning again to Babylon, the prophet described the whirlwind sweeping against it, and so terrible was the sight that he was filled with horror.

Very brief but very forceful is the burden of Dumah. The prophet had heard some inquiring voice demanding the hour of the night. In briefest words he answered that he saw morning and night, and invited further inquiry.

The burden of Arabia consists of a vision and an interpretation. The vision is that of a fugitive people. The interpretation announces the coming of judgment within a year upon the children of Kedar.

In the midst of the prophecies concerning the nations occurs one of protest against the indifference of Jerusalem to the things concerning which the prophet is speaking. He first described the joyous people as they stood in contrast to him with his sorrow and his broken heart. It was a day in which Jehovah had called to mourning, and they were full of merriment. This was an unpardonable sin, as it revealed their callousness. Immediately following this protest, the prophet uttered his denunciation of Shebna, declaring that he would be rejected from his office, and his place be taken by Eliakim.

The burden of Tyre is a graphic description of her desolation. Her harbors are closed. Her borders are desolate. The sea, which had been her highway, is abandoned, and Egypt her ally is affrighted at the report. This desolation is the act of Jehovah. After seventy years the prophet declared that she should be visited by Jehovah, and restored to a position of affluence. There is in the prophecy no hint of any turning to God on the part of Tyre. Her restoration was to be, in some way, of service to God's own people.

In the last chapters of the second circle the prophet takes a wider outlook, and the world is seen under the government of the throne of God. In consequence of widespread corruption, widespread desolation is determined upon. The earth is seen to mourn and fade away, devoured by a curse, while all mirth ceases. This prophecy of world-wide judgment ends with the declaration that it will be by the act of Jehovah, and will issue in perfect victory. There follows immediately a song of praise for judgment both in its procedure and in its results, which results are to be the spreading of a feast in the mountain of the Lord, and His illumination of the nations, followed by the ending of sorrow and the wiping away of tears. Naturally following this prophecy of praise is the great song which would be sung in the day of Jehovah's ultimate victory. The deep secret of the new condition will be that of the mind stayed on Jehovah. Remembering that he was still speaking in the midst of circumstances of judgment, and that its processes must proceed to consummation, the prophet uttered the final call to the people of God, urging them to quietness and patience until the indignation be overpassed. This circle ends with a message which describes the process toward ultimate restoration, and announces its certainty. The way is the way of judgment. The first issue of judgment would be the restoration of the chosen people, and to this he referred under the figure of the vineyard. The figure here stands in striking contrast to the way in which it appeared in chapter five.

The third and last circle consists of a series of prophecies concerning the chosen and the world. It opens with a graphic revelation of the difficulties with which Isaiah had to contend, and of his unswerving loyalty to the truth. In answer to his declaration that judgment was to fall upon Ephraim; priests and prophets, overcome by strong drink, taunted him with the slowness of his speech and its halting method. He answered them by declaring that there was another method of speech, and, moreover, that there was a purpose in the halting method which he had adopted. He then warned them of their folly, declaring that their false covenant with death should be disannulled, and urging them to cease their scorning.

A series of declamations follows this picture. The first sets forth the purpose of Jehovah in judgment. The prophet then denounced an alliance with Egypt, declaring the shame of it and its uselessness, and proceeded to foretell again the destruction of Assyria. A second time he denounced the alliance with Egypt, declaring it to be a false trust consequent upon the turning of their back upon Jehovah.

The prophet then described the reign of the coming King, which is to be characterized by the establishment of order, and the consequent creation of refuge and refreshment for all who are in distress. The beneficent effects of such a reign will be the restoration of sensibility, and of a true sense of values in which men will know violence and call it by its right name, recognizing true nobility. Evidently conscious of how different were the circumstances described, to those in the midst of which he was exercising his ministry, he made his appeal to the women. This recognition of the influence of women, for the second time in the course of this volume, is a

revelation of the prophet's keen insight and accurate apprehension of one of the most prolific causes of national disaster.
A degraded womanhood always creates a dissipated and ener-
vated manhood.

After the great message the prophet celebrated a victory,
and predicted the method of the final triumph. The presence of God is a fire filling the heart of the sinner with fear,
while the righteous dwell in safety in the midst of its burning.

The last two chapters of the first division reveal the
prophet's breadth of outlook. He saw, in the future, world-
wide desolation. From this wide outlook he passed to a description of the judgment of God upon Edom, which illustrates the larger truth already declared. The final word
stands in startling contrast. Following the picture of desolation, we have one of restoration. The whole earth was seen
in the former as brought into confusion and emptiness. Now
we observe the restoration of the natural order. Thus, at
the close, as throughout the whole of this great division, God
is seen moving through judgment toward peace.

B. HISTORICAL INTERLUDE

This interlude has to do wholly with events transpiring in
the reign of Hezekiah. The first was that of Sennacherib's
invasion. The hosts of Assyria were assembled in the neighborhood of Jerusalem, and Rabshakeh was sent as an ambassador of Sennacherib. With pride amounting to insolence
he taunted the rulers who came out to confer with him. Full
of fear, they requested him to speak in Aramaic, that the
Jews might not understand. To this he responded by address-

ing himself directly to the people still in the Hebrew tongue, bidding them trust neither Hezekiah nor Jehovah. Instructed by Hezekiah, the people maintained a dignified silence.

In this hour of trial Hezekiah sent messages to Isaiah, who returned to him an answer full of hope. Rabshakeh having returned to his master, an insolent and blasphemous letter was sent to Hezekiah, which he spread out before Jehovah. While he thus waited upon Jehovah, Isaiah sent him a message declaring the coming judgment of God upon Sennacherib on account of his sin of blasphemy. By the direct act of Jehovah the Assyrian army was destroyed, and Sennacherib, returning to Nineveh, was slain by his own sons.

We next have an account of Hezekiah's sickness and of his prayer that his life might be spared, with the answer vouchsafed. In connection with this story there is preserved for us the psalm which Hezekiah wrote. The first part of it is descriptive of the days of darkness and anguish through which he had passed, while the latter celebrates his deliverance by Jehovah. This psalm makes it evident that he recognized his affliction, as well as his deliverance, as within the method of God's discipline, for in the course of it he exclaimed, "O Lord, by these things men live."

The last event chronicled in this historical interlude is that of Hezekiah's folly. Flattered by the letters and present sent to him from the king of Babylon, he exposed all his wealth to the messengers. Isaiah visited him, and evidently understanding the sinister motive of the king of Babylon, predicted the coming of a day in which Babylon should carry away all the things which the spies had seen.

C. PROPHECIES OF PEACE

The prophecies of peace move in three circles. The first deals with the purpose of peace; the second with the Prince of peace; the third with the program of peace.

The prophecies dealing with the purpose of peace are introduced by a prologue, which declares their burden, "Comfort ye, comfort ye my people." A voice calls for the preparation of a highway in the wilderness for the march of God, and the prophet is commissioned to announce the advent of Jehovah God.

Immediately following the prologue, the majesty of Jehovah is celebrated, first, in its essentials of might, of wisdom, and of government; secondly, by the impossibility of comparison; thirdly, by the evidences in creation of the established government of the earth and of the heavens; and finally, by the grace which knows the way, and out of the inherent strength of Jehovah supplies the need of such as lack.

The great manifesto of Jehovah comes next in order. It declares the Divine choice of Cyrus as a servant of God. The presentation of the servant is preceded by an argument, in which Jehovah challenges all peoples as to the fact that He has made known beforehand things to come. In the midst of this argument Israel is addressed as the chosen servant of God, and Jehovah's purpose for them is declared to be that of peace, through which they will be able to fulfill their high and holy vocation. Yet the people are seen in such condition as to prove their inability to fulfill the Divine purpose in their own strength. There is neither man nor counselor who is able to answer when God calls. Therefore all His highest purposes are to be realized in one Man in order that ultimately they may be realized in the nation. While the eyes of the prophet in the whole vision were fixed upon Cyrus, it is evident that he was looking far beyond him to Another. The description of the Servant of Jehovah is full of stately beauty. He is presented in Person, His manifestation is announced, His commission declared, His method described, and His might foretold. This Servant of God was to be called, held, and given by Jehovah, and that for the glory of His name. In view of His coming the whole earth is called upon to sing, as Jehovah declares His purpose of moving through passion to peace. The prophet appealed to the people to hear, look, and understand the meaning of the Divine method.

Following the manifesto we have certain messages of Jehovah. The first declares His perpetual purpose for His people. He created, formed, and called them for His glory. The next declares His present purpose of deliverance, affirming His intention to destroy their foes, making an appeal to the people, promising the outpouring of the Spirit in blessing upon Israel, with resultant blessing to others. He then compares Himself with idols, claiming to be the first and the last, alone knowing and declaring, and describing with fine scorn the vanity of idol makers and the unprofitableness of idols made. In startling contrast, and in words full of beauty, He speaks of His own might.

Next in order we have His charge to Cyrus, consisting of the making of a promise, the declaration of a purpose, the claiming of power, and a protest against objections. Following this He announces His purpose for Israel, that all the peoples shall submit to them. Finally, He declares His purpose for the ends of the earth, calling upon the nations to compare Him with idols, and to submit to Him in order to find salvation. All these messages of Jehovah are introduced by the prophet by the same formula, "Thus saith the Lord."

The fall of Babylon is the subject of the next message, which is delivered to the house of Jacob, to the remnant of Israel, and first declares that the fall of Babylon is determined upon. This declaration is the occasion of a striking contrast between the false gods and Jehovah. They are seen bowing down and stooping, while men have to carry them in an attempt to place them in safety. He is the One Who has carried His people, and will continue so to do. The fall of Babylon is then described as degradation from high position, as disgrace amid the nations, as desolation after luxury and boastfulness, and as destruction utter and complete.

The section dealing with the Purpose of Peace ends with a final appeal, in which Jehovah declares that His method is that of prophecy and performance. Because of their obstinacy He had declared from of old what He would do. For His name's sake He would defer His anger. An illustration of the method is that of the calling of Cyrus. He finally declares again that His purpose is their peace and their redemption. The last word of the section is, "There is no peace, saith Jehovah, unto the wicked."

In the next section the Prince of Peace is presented to our view. In a series of remarkable messages we see Him first sustained through suffering, and then singing in triumph. The Servant is Himself the speaker, and He tells the story of His call by Jehovah. Conscious of His own call, He yet complains that His labor has been in vain. To that complaint Jehovah replies by speaking again of His first purpose for Him, and declaring that the purpose is enlarged. The despised and exalted One is yet to be the messenger of deliverance to the oppressed people. In answer to this, Zion declares that Jehovah has forgotten her. The reply is that He cannot forget, and that deliverance is certain. Jehovah challenges the complaining people to produce proof that He has cast them off, and declares the reason of all their suffering to be their own sin. In all this it is evident Jehovah is calling His Servant to a triumph which can only be won through suffering. The Servant answers by consecrating Himself to the processes, while His eyes are set upon the issue. He yields Himself to the smiters and to all the suffering and shame. Out of this consecration comes courage. The ministry of suffering is then described. An appeal is made to those who sit in darkness to trust in God. Then the faithful remnant is charged to be courageous and to rest in the assurance of the comfort of God, and in His promise of succor. Messages follow to such as are afflicted, which tell of the coming end of suffering, and the beginning of strength, as the result of the return of Jehovah. An account of the completion of the suffering of the Servant follows these messages. The pathway of suffering is described in the plaintive and wonderful language with which all are familiar. It is a pathway of rejection, of vicarious suffering, of atoning death. Yet it is the pathway which leads to triumph, and the Servant of God is seen as He passes through pain to prosperity, through travail to triumph, through humbling to exaltation.

Immediately after this description of the suffering Servant of God there follows a section which contains the story of triumph. First there is a song of assurance, which tells of restoration, and of the end of all forsaking. The glory of that restoration is described in its material magnificence, in its moral rectitude, and in its mighty defense. Upon the basis of the suffering and triumph, and immediately following the song, is a message containing a great appeal. The thirsty and the dissatisfied are called back to Jehovah in order that they may enter into the peace and prosperity which are the portion of those who hear His word and obey it. The section ends with a description of the administration of the kingdom. In view of the promise of salvation, and of the fact that salvation is near, the man is pronounced blessed who submits himself. Moreover, the strangers and all who have suffered loss through loyalty to Him are to have an assured place in the restoration. Evil is to be judged, and the judgment must first fall upon the spiritual leaders because of their pollution and their neglect of the righteous. It is also to fall upon all the apostate people. Judgment is, however, as always in the economy of Jehovah, to be discriminative. The high and lofty One will dwell in fellowship with such as are of contrite and humble spirit. This section presenting the Prince of Peace ends with the same declaration as does the first—"there is no peace, saith Jehovah, unto the wicked."

The last section deals with the Program of Peace, and declares, first, what are its conditions. The prophet condemns formalism which is punctilious in its observance of all external things, and yet complains that there has been no response on the part of God, declaring that the reason for this silence is that the fasting has been formal and not sincere. He then describes what true religion is, and declares what are its rewards. Recognizing the fact that God has not appeared on behalf of His people, the prophet breaks out into a great confession, in which he first describes the sin of the people, then their suffering, and finally confesses the sin.

C. Prophecies of Peace

Having thus declared the moral requirement, and confessed moral failure, he proceeds to speak of the moral victory, which is assured. This is based upon Jehovah's knowledge, and will result from Jehovah's judgment being carried out by Jehovah's Redeemer.

In messages full of beauty, the prophet next describes the ultimate realization of peace, first as to its material prosperity. In the midst of darkness light shines, and the exiles are seen returning from far and near, bearing wealth with them, and followed by the peoples. The city of God is established, and at last there comes a day of perfect government, perfect glory, perfect gladness. Beneath the material realization there is spiritual realization, which the prophet then describes. This is brought about by the anointed Messenger, through Whose work the people are restored to their true place in the economy of God. Thus, issuing from the material and spiritual realizations, the vocational fulfillment is described. The old names "Forsaken" and "Desolate" are changed for new ones—"Hephzi-bah" and "Beulah."

The last messages of the book reaffirm the Divine principle of discrimination. The glorious victories which have been described can only be won through processes of judgment. It would seem as though the prophet lifted his eyes and saw, in clear though distant outline, the last goings forth of God in judgment, with the things resulting therefrom. He saw the Warrior returning from the fight, stained with the conflict, but marching in the might and majesty of the victory won. The vision called forth his praise, his confession, and his prayer, which move in orderly sequence. He then described the sifting of the people. The rebellious are doomed, while such as are the servants of the Most High are led into the realization of all His high purpose of Peace. The great prophecy closes with the reaffirmation of the coming of Jehovah as a whirlwind, to plead by fire with men, and to bring in the new heavens and the new earth.

JEREMIAH—*The Prophet of Failure*

JEREMIAH * * * *

JEREMIAH WAS JEHOVAH'S spokesman in days of darkness and disaster. Through great personal suffering he delivered his messages of punishment and of promise with unswerving fidelity, notwithstanding the fact that the people refused to hear or to obey. He was the son of Hilkiah, of priestly family. Whether this was the Hilkiah who discovered the book of the law in the eighteenth year of Josiah's reign, that is, five years after Jeremiah's prophesying commenced, cannot be absolutely decided. It is possible, if not probable.

His ministry extended from the thirteenth year of Josiah to the eleventh of Zedekiah, that is, over a period of forty years. No prophet in all the long and honourable succession had a more thankless work. To stand, the lonely messenger of God, in the midst of the rebellious opposition of his own people, was a task needing the greatest courage. We wrong Jeremiah when we speak of him merely as the prophet of tears, or think of him only as a man haunted by fears. His tears were evidences of his compassion, but his compassion never made him unfaithful to the Divine message. All evidences of weakness were manifested in the presence of God, and never when he stood as God's messenger. Only once was there a momentary failure—in the case of the false word of Hananiah—and this was rather a mistake of judgment than a deflection from the clearly marked path of duty.

The first part of the book gives us the story of his Call and Commission, and the last the account of his Ministry. It may be that the messages in the first part were delivered as they were received, but it is evident throughout that he was being prepared for that more sorrowful and yet weighty ministry which was to follow.

The book thus falls into two parts: the Prophet's Call and Commission (i.-xiii.); the Prophet's Ministry (xiv.-li.); with an historical Appendix (lii.).

A. THE PROPHET'S CALL AND COMMISSION

The first three verses constitute a title page, naming the author, and giving the dates of the period during which he exercises his ministry.

The call of the prophet was first personal. Over against the "I" of Jeremiah's fear, Jehovah set the "I" of His own omnipotence. The call was then official, and was ratified by the two signs, of the almond-tree, and the seething caldron.

In the commissioning of Jeremiah for his ministry there are three distinctly marked movements, each of which ends with the account of how Jehovah strengthened His servant.

The first movement commences with the command to utter an impeachment of Israel. She was charged with forsaking Jehovah, and with obstinate sinfulness. The impeachment ended by a summary, describing Israel's infidelity and its issue.

Following the impeachment the prophet appealed to the people to return, pointing out the conditions upon which they might do so. This appeal was followed by the recitation of an ideal confession for the sinning people, and ended with the promise of Jehovah that if Israel would return she should be established.

Suddenly the prophet turned to the subject of judgment.

A. The Prophet's Call and Commission

He declared that it was determined on, described it, and affirmed its inevitableness. His own anguish was revealed in the course of this declaration. He proceeded to announce the reason of judgment as being their utter corruption of conduct, their unbelief of the prophetic message, and their revolting and rebellious heart. He then foretold, in graphic description, the taking of the city, and the suffering of the people consequent thereupon.

The movement ends with an account of the words spoken by Jehovah to Jeremiah, in order to strengthen him.

The second movement in the commissioning of the prophet deals first with the sins of worship. At the gate of the Temple the prophet rebuked the people for trusting in external forms. So terrible was the condition that he was charged at last not to pray for them. For this idolatry of formalism the sentence of judgment was again pronounced.

The sin of idolatry had been aggravated by their terrible persistence therein. If men fall, it is naturally expected that they will rise; if they wander, that they will return. In the case of Judah this had not been so. The backsliding had been perpetual, therefore the judgment must be complete.

The strain of the terrible messages upon the prophet now becomes evident as it is seen how he poured out his soul in lamentation. To this cry of His servant Jehovah replied in a fivefold declaration. He had no choice but to afflict, because of their sin. He also suffered. The reason of judgment was that of their persistent rebellion. He called the people to lamentation, but insisted that it should be for right causes. Finally He proclaimed the true ground of glorying for man to be, not his own wisdom or riches, but his understanding and knowledge of Jehovah.

In the third movement in the commissioning of the prophet the sin of idolatry is again dealt with. He revealed its unutterable folly in a powerful contrast between idols and Jehovah. On the sin of idolatry he then pronounced judgment.

There came to the prophet from the Lord a special word commissioning him to pronounce a curse upon "the man that heareth not the words of this covenant." He was to proclaim in the cities of Judah and the streets of Jerusalem the sin of the fathers, and the fact that it was being repeated by their sons. They were guilty of conspiracy against Jehovah in turning back to other gods. Therefore Jehovah visited with judgment.

The closing part of the third movement is occupied with an account of how Jehovah strengthened Jeremiah in view of the persecution which was already stirred against him, and of the yet severer troubles awaiting him. From the midst of peril in Anathoth, Jeremiah appealed to Jehovah to be his Defender, and was answered by the declaration of the Divine determination concerning his evil neighbors. Perplexed, the prophet poured out his soul to God in questions. The answer of Jehovah indicated the fact that the things he had seen, and the trials through which he had passed, were as nothing to those which awaited him.

The account of the commissioning of the prophet ends with the story of how Jehovah gave him two signs, one for himself and one for his people.

B. THE PROPHET'S MINISTRY

The second division of the book contains the account of the prophet's ministry. It falls into three sections: prophecies

B. The Prophet's Ministry

before the fall of Jerusalem, prophecies after the fall of Jerusalem, and prophecies concerning the Nations.

The prophecies before the fall of Jerusalem open with a declaration of God's determination to punish. This is introduced by a graphic parable of drought, in which the high and the low are alike affected, the whole ground is barren for lack of rain, and all animal life suffers.

Then follows the account of a remarkable controversy between Jeremiah and Jehovah. The prophet appealed to Jehovah repeatedly on behalf of the people. Jehovah replied by forbidding him to pray for them, and declaring His determination to punish them. On hearing this Jeremiah cried out in his anguish, and Jehovah replied by promising to strengthen him for the delivery of his message. This controversy was immediately followed by a new charge to the prophet. He was called to a life of personal asceticism, and commanded to abstain both from mourning and from mirth. He was to stand aloof from the people, in order to deliver to them the messages of God.

Once again Jehovah declared His determination to deal with the people in judgment, because of the defiant definiteness of their sin. This declaration was followed by a contrast between the man who trusts in men, and the man who trusteth in Jehovah. The first dwells in the midst of desert desolation. The second is rooted by the springs of fruitfulness. To these words the prophet replied in a great affirmation of faith, and an equally great appeal of need. He was then commissioned to stand in the gate of the people and offer them the test of the Sabbath, warning them of how their fathers failed in this respect, and declaring to them that if they refused to hearken, the judgment must fall.

The second series of messages before the fall of Jerusalem consists of declarations of God's absolute supremacy. In preparation, Jeremiah was sent to the house of the potter. Power was manifest in the potter's manipulation of the clay in his hand, and pity in his re-making of the marred vessel. The explanation was given by Jehovah Himself. The house of Israel was as clay in His hand, but His will must be accomplished, and they could not possibly escape from Him. The delivery of these messages stirred up new opposition to the prophet, and a conspiracy was formed against his life. He was then commissioned to go forth into the valley of the son of Hinnom, taking with him a potter's vessel, and there to deliver a message of judgment, symbolizing the same by breaking the vessel in the sight of the people. Returning from Topheth, having obeyed the command, he sat in the court of the Lord's House, and repeated the fact of coming judgment.

This action stirred up yet fiercer persecution against him. He was arrested and imprisoned. Out of the midst of these circumstances he poured out his soul in the presence of Jehovah, complaining that he had been the laughing-stock of the people, and had become a reproach and derision. He had declared that he would not speak the word, but it had become a burning fire, and he had been compelled to utter it. The tempest-tossed condition of his mind at this time is seen in his alternating declarations of faith and fear.

The final series before the fall of Jerusalem consists of messages delivered to Zedekiah. The scourge which Jeremiah had foretold seemed to be imminent. Nebuchadrezzar was approaching. Zedekiah sent to inquire whether he might hope for the interference and deliverance of Jehovah. There was nothing halting or unswerving in the prophet's answer. He foretold the disaster in detail.

The message of Jeremiah by the deputation was not enough. He was commanded to go to the house of the king. Arrived at the court, he repeated his call to repentance and his warning. He then reviewed the history of Zedekiah's three predecessors—Jehoahaz (Shallum), Jehoiakim, and Jehoiachin (Coniah), and proceeded to charge the failure of the people first upon the kings. In the Divine economy the king has always been a shepherd; but the men who had held the office had destroyed and scattered the sheep. He then turned to the prophets, and spoke of them out of a broken heart. Their judgment was consequent upon the falseness of the messages they had delivered. They had dreamed their own dreams rather than delivered the word of Jehovah. Jeremiah's acute understanding of the process of the nation's corruption is clearly revealed. False kings and prophets had led the people into courses of evil. The people, in their turn, had willingly listened and followed.

Still speaking to Zedekiah, Jeremiah repeated three prophecies from the past, the first being a vision in Jeconiah's captivity, the second a message delivered in the fourth year of Jehoiakim, and the last delivered in the beginning of Jehoiakim's reign. At this time false prophets were also speaking among the captives and in Jerusalem, and throughout the remainder of Jeremiah's message to Zedekiah he denied the authority and inspiration of these false teachers.

Still speaking to Zedekiah, Jeremiah reminded him of the word which came in the fourth year of Jehoiakim, announcing the judgment of God as determined against Judah, Babylon, the nations, the world. Thus the king would see how inevitable was the doom now threatening himself and Jerusalem.

He then repeated the message delivered in the beginning of the reign of Jehoiakim. The priests, the prophets, and the people seized Jeremiah, and condemned him to die. The princes rescued him, and Jeremiah again addressed himself to Zedekiah. Having shown, by his vision of the basket of figs, what was determined against Judah, he declared the attitude of Jehovah in the matter. Messengers representing a confederacy of kings for the purpose of resisting Nebuchadrezzar were answered by the declaration that all such attempts would be useless. He then directed his attention specially to Zedekiah, urging him to submit to the king of Babylon.

In the incident between Hananiah and Jeremiah we see the conflict with the false prophets clearly manifest. For the moment Jeremiah was deceived, and permitted Hananiah to take the bar from off his neck and break it. Immediately the word of the Lord came to Jeremiah contradicting all that Hananiah had said. It is evident that the exiles were disturbed by the false prophesying, and Jeremiah sent a letter to them on the subject. He warned them that it was better for them to settle in Babylon, and beware of false prophets. Deliverance was in the purpose of God for them, but it would not be accomplished until after seventy years.

At this point there occurs a series of prophecies whose dominant note is that of hope. These are remarkable from the fact that they were uttered during the time that Jeremiah was in prison, and the condition of affairs in the city was calculated to fill his mind with despair. In the midst of this darkness Jeremiah was granted visions of ultimate

B. The Prophet's Ministry

restoration, and his messages are therefore full of hope. The first of these may be described as a song, declaring that the people of God, now so overwhelmed with sorrow, should yet ultimately pass through trouble to triumph. In graphic language the prophet described the time of Jacob's trouble, and predicted deliverance. In words that still burn as we read them, he depicted the friendlessness of the forsaken people, and announced their restoration to favor, describing the tempest by which the change would be wrought. The song then merges into a description of the issues of restoration; the city rebuilt, and the people gathered back to it, so that sorrow passes away, and the new contentment with the Divine government and administration is manifest. In that day a new covenant will be made between Jehovah and His people, a covenant not external and material, but internal and spiritual, and universal in application. The song ends with a declaration of Jehovah in which He uses the signs in the heavens as the seal of His promise. The next of the prophecies of hope is introduced by the statement that Jeremiah is imprisoned, and the account of the charge given to him to purchase the field in Anathoth. This command he obeyed, and then in perplexity inquired of Jehovah what was the use of purchasing a field when the land was wholly given over to judgment. The answer of Jehovah announced the certainty of the judgment which Jeremiah anticipated, but also declared the equal certainty of ultimate restoration, so that the purchase of the field was intended as a sign of the ultimate repossession of the land. The last of the prophecies of hope is a song full of beauty, and full of confidence. It celebrates that ultimate restoration which Jehovah had promised, first as to the gathering of the people and the building of the city, describing a moral and consequent material restoration. This is all to be brought about in the days of the Branch, when the two functions of king and priest shall be restored in the person of one Deliverer. The song ends with the Divine affirmation, in which Jehovah again uses the sign of day and night, and declares His determination to accomplish His purpose in spite of unbelief.

Next in order we have three prophecies delivered while Nebuchadrezzar and his army were round about the city. In the first the prophet foretold the success of Nebuchadrezzar and the consequent fall of Jerusalem, and described the manner of Zedekiah's death. The next is a denunciation of Zedekiah for having broken his covenant with the Hebrew servants. The prophet delivered the message of Jehovah, describing the sin and pronouncing judgment. In the last Jeremiah told the story of how the Rechabites, when put to the test, were true to their vow, and refused to drink. The purpose of the telling of the story was that the prophet might put into contrast with it the sin of Judah. The sons of Rechab had been true to the command laid upon them by their father. Judah had been untrue to the perpetual messages of Jehovah. Upon Judah, therefore, evil should come, while a gracious promise was made to the Rechabites.

Chapter thirty-six constitutes a break in the historic method of the prophecy, and gives us the account of how the prophecies of Jeremiah against Judah and Jerusalem were committed to writing. In the fourth year of Jehoiakim Jehovah commanded Jeremiah to write. He obeyed by dictating to Baruch. In the following year, the fifth of Jehoiakim, Baruch read the writings in the hearing of all the people. He next read them by special invitation to the princes, who in

B. *The Prophet's Ministry*

alarm advised Baruch and Jeremiah to hide. Finally they were read by Jehudi to the king, who in anger mutilated the writings and destroyed the roll. It is possible to mutilate and burn a writing, but not to destroy the word of Jehovah. Jeremiah again dictated, and Baruch wrote, but this time many other words were added.

The final movement in the section of the book devoted to the prophecies before the fall of Jerusalem consists of a history of the siege. Jeremiah is first seen as free. The army of Pharaoh had come forth out of Egypt, and the king hoped that it might aid him against Nebuchadrezzar. Then Jeremiah declared that there was no hope in that quarter. For the moment events seemed to contradict his prophecy, as the army of the Chaldeans fell away. He left the city to go to Benjamin, and was arrested and imprisoned on the charge of falling away to the Chaldeans. After many days' imprisonment Zedekiah sent for him, and to him he delivered the same stern message, foretelling the victory of the king of Babylon. The issue of the interview was that Jeremiah was removed, still as a prisoner, into the court of the guard, and was there supplied with bread. He continued his foretelling of the doom about to fall upon the city, and as a result was cast into a loathsome dungeon. Through the intervention of Ebed-melech he was released from thence. Sadly perplexed, and almost distraught, Zedekiah again sent for him, and the prophet still insisted upon the truth of his declaration that the city should be taken by the Chaldeans. He therefore advised Zedekiah to surrender, and so save the city from burning, and himself from death, warning him that if he refused, even the women of his own household would heap reproaches upon him. The section ends with the story

of the fall of Jerusalem, which the prophet had so long foretold. Nebuchadrezzar and his princes forced an entrance, and
Zedekiah fled. He, however, was pursued and overtaken, his
sons were slain before his eyes, and then his own eyes were
put out, and he was bound in fetters and carried to Babylon.
This was followed by the sack of the city. In the midst of the
rout Jeremiah was protected, undoubtedly as the result of
the overruling of Jehovah, and he was commissioned specially to find Ebed-melech the Ethiopian, who had succoured
him, and to declare to him that he also was under Divine
protection.

Chapters forty to forty-four tell the story of Jeremiah and
his prophesying after the fall of Jerusalem. The first movement in this section gives an account of the events immediately following, and of Jeremiah's protest against going into
Egypt. The second chronicles the prophecies in Egypt. Released by Nebuzaradan, Jeremiah joined the remnant remaining in the land under the governorship of Gedaliah,
who sought to restore order, urging the people to avail themselves of the privilege granted to them to settle in the land,
he promising to abide at Mizpah in order to stand before the
Chaldeans. In response to this invitation, many of them
gathered from the distant places to which they had been
scattered. The governor was warned by Johanan of the plot
formed against his life by Ishmael, but he refused to believe
the report. Ishmael through the basest treachery carried out
his design, slaying Gedaliah and others, and leading captives
away to the children of Ammon, Johanan, who had warned
Gedaliah of his danger, rescued these captives, compelling
Ishmael to flee, and prepared to go into Egypt. Before going,
they sought counsel from Jeremiah, asking that he should

inquire the will of Jehovah, and promising implicit obedience to whatever might be revealed. After ten days he delivered his message, telling them distinctly that the will of God was that they should not go into Egypt, urging them not to be afraid of the king of Babylon, declaring that Jehovah was with them, and that His purpose was one of mercy, and that they should return to their own land. With great solemnity, he warned them that if they went into Egypt, the judgment of God would fall upon them. He moreover charged them with dishonesty in inquiring from him; and therefore, he foretold the certain judgment of God which would fall upon them.

As Jeremiah had foreseen, his word was not obeyed. They charged him with having spoken falsely under the influence of Baruch, and in rebellion passed over into Egypt. They compelled Jeremiah to accompany them, and his next messages were delivered there. The first of these consisted of a prophecy of the coming victory of Babylon over Egypt. The next was a fiery protest against the persistent rebellion of the people of God, in which he reminded them of the patience of God, of how His anger had already been poured out upon Jerusalem, and declared that the rebellious remnant which had found its way into Egypt should be wholly cut off. This message the men answered by a defiant and persistent word of rebellion, in which they misinterpreted their own history by declaring that all the evils that had fallen upon them had resulted from attacks made upon idolatry, and they deliberately declared their intention to continue their idolatrous practices. To this attitude Jeremiah replied by first answering their argument, declaring that their sorrows were the result of their idolatry, rather than, as they affirmed, the result of their turning from idols. Continuing, he declared that the judgment of God was determined against them, that they should be consumed, and only a small remnant should escape ultimately from Egypt. He ended by declaring that the sign of Jehovah to them should be the defeat of Pharaoh Hophra, and his handing over to those who sought his life.

The messages of Jeremiah to the chosen people end at this point, and there is inserted a special word to Baruch. It is evident that this faithful ally of the prophet had become depressed. He had manifestly hoped for great results, and was at once rebuked and comforted. He was charged not to seek great things for himself; and promised that his own life should be preserved.

The third and last section of the division containing the prophet's ministry is occupied with his messages concerning the nations. The first of these has to do with Egypt, and consists of two prophecies. The earlier one described the army of Egypt, in its preparation and advance, and declared that this was in reality the coming of the day of the vengeance of Jehovah. In general terms the prophet predicted the doom of Egypt. The second distinctly foretold the defeat of Egypt by Nebuchadrezzar, the king of Babylon. This visitation was that of Jehovah, and the agent was Nebuchadrezzar. The prophecy ends with the message of comfort to Jacob, who, while afflicted, is yet not to be utterly destroyed, but corrected by judgment.

The word concerning the Philistines was a foretelling of the coming against them of a scourge from the north, which would utterly break their power. In figurative language the prophet then described the sorrow which would overtake the proud, yet broken people.

B. The Prophet's Ministry

The word of the Lord concerning Moab was one of judgment, which nevertheless closed with a gleam of hope. The judgment was described first from the standpoint of the scourge. The widespread extent of it was foretold, and the affliction and helplessness graphically set forth. The judgment was then spoken of from the standpoint of Moab, that is to say, the long security of Moab, and his freedom from affliction was recognized, as was also his self-confidence. In contrast with this, the judgment was announced. All his past security was to end, and his strength to vanish. Finally, in a long passage, full of tremendous power, the judgment of Moab from the standpoint of the onlooker was described. Surrounding nations were called upon to observe and to lament, while yet they recognized the justice of the judgment, as it was a punishment for Moab for the sin of magnifying himself against the Lord. The prophet himself, observing the judgment, broke out into mourning and lamentation, with sobs describing the desolation, until at last, in one brief sentence, he announced the promise of Jehovah, that finally He would restore the captivity of Moab, and indicated that until that time of the Divine intervention the judgment of Moab must continue.

Against the children of Ammon, Jeremiah raised a protest because their king was in possession of Gad. He declared that by the fierce judgment of war they were to be dispossessed and driven forth. The message ends with a gleam of hope, in which the prophet foretold the bringing again of the captivity of the children of Ammon.

Concerning Edom, destruction was foretold, in spite of her wisdom. The reference to wisdom in Teman would seem to be a satirical literary allusion to the fact that it was the birthplace of Eliphaz, the counselor of Job. The destruction was described in figurative language, and the prophet declared, that notwithstanding the arrogancy and security of the people, Jehovah would bring them down into the dust. The destruction of Edom was intended to be a warning to the whole earth.

Damascus was described in her decay, and in the destruction determined against her by the Lord of Hosts. This reference to Damascus is brief, for it does not seem that in Jeremiah's time there was anything like intimate relationship of any sort between her and the chosen people. It is evident, however, that as his vision swept the horizon he saw that she also was within the circle of the Divine government, and that judgment was determined against her.

Kedar and Hazor represent the Arab peoples, the former such as were nomadic, the latter those who dwelt at settled centers, and yet not in walled cities. Against both of these Nebuchadrezzar, the king of Babylon, was to be the instrument of judgment.

The prophecy against Elam was one of judgment, ending once more with a gleam of hope. Of Elam nothing can be said with any certainty. It is evident, however, that in the far-reaching vision of Jeremiah she was seen as under the Divine displeasure, and consequently to be visited by the Divine judgment.

The last of the prophecies concerning the nations has to do with Babylon. Throughout the whole of Jeremiah's prophetic utterances, she has been seen as the instrument of God's judgment. Finally, on account of her own sin and corruption, that judgment must inevitably fall upon her. That is the great burden of this message. It is perfectly evident throughout that the prophet had in mind the nations of Judah and Israel, and what he said concerning Babylon had its direct bearing upon these as the people of God. The prophecy falls into two parts, the first foretelling Babylon's doom and Israel's delivery; the second indicating Israel's responsibility in view of this doom determined upon Babylon. In general terms the prophet announced the coming overthrow of Babylon, and described the repentant return of the children of Israel and Judah. He then more definitely described the destruction of the city of Babylon. A confederacy of nations would come against her, and destroy her, and that because she had rejoiced and been wanton in her dealing with the people of God. That people, though scattered and driven away, would be gathered and restored, while the iniquity of Israel and the sins of Judah would be pardoned. The prophecy increased in power as it proceeded, and Jeremiah foretold the completeness of the overthrow. There was to be the utter humbling of her pride, and the absolute destruction of her power. The instrument of the destruction would be a people from the north, but the judgment would be that of the invincible Jehovah. In the second movement the prophet again declared the determination of Jehovah to bring about the complete overthrow of Babylon, in order to ensure the deliverance of His people. To emphasize this, he described the invincible power of Jehovah, as Creator and Sustainer of the world, in the presence of Whom man is vanity. He thereupon described the judgment, first recognizing that Babylon had indeed been an instrument in the hand of Jehovah for the accomplishing of His judgments, but proceeding to declare that Jehovah was now against Babylon, and that therefore she must become a desolation without inhabitant, repeating finally the truth that the purpose of His judgment was the deliverance of His people. Upon the basis of these great declarations Jeremiah, in the name of Jehovah, made his appeal to the people of God, urging them to escape from the midst of Babylon, and declaring again the certainty of her doom. The prophecy concerning Babylon closes with an account of the charge which Jeremiah gave to Seraiah to write these words and read them in Babylon. Here the words of Jeremiah end.

The last chapter consists of an historical appendix, written, as the final words of the previous chapter show, by another hand. It first repeats in brief form the story of the capture of the city, and chronicles the oppression of the people which followed. A list is then given of Nebuchadrezzar's captives, and the story of Jehoiachin's position in Babylon is told.

LAMENTATIONS OF JEREMIAH

A THE SOLITARY CITY *i.*	B THE SOURCES OF HER SORROW *ii.*	C THE PROPHET'S IDENTIFI- CATION *iii.*	D THE DESOLA- TION *iv.*	E THE APPEAL OUT OF SORROW *v.*
I. The Desolation 1-11	I. The Act of the Lord 1-10	I. In Affliction 1-21	I. The Description 1-12	I. "Remember, O Lord" 1-18
II. The Confession 12-22	II. The Affliction of Iniquity 11-17	II. In Assurance 22-33	II. The Cause 13-16	II. "Turn Thou us unto Thee" 19-22
	III. The Appeal of Penitence 18-22	III. In Appeal 34-54	III. Vain Help 17-20	
		IV. In Assurance 55-66	IV. Hope 21-22	

LAMENTATIONS ✳ ✳ ✳ ✳

IN THE SEPTUAGINT the Lamentations are prefaced with these words: "And it came to pass, that after Israel had been carried away captive, and Jerusalem made desolate, Jeremiah sat weeping, and lamented this lament over Jerusalem, and said. . . ." This serves to show that, long before the coming of Christ, they were considered by Jewish scholars to be the work of Jeremiah.

In his prophecy Jeremiah is revealed as a man having a keen sense of the righteousness of judgment because of sin, and yet overwhelmed with sorrow for his people. Throughout the whole of his ministry he shrank from the difficulty of his work, and yet manifested heroic loyalty to the will of God. In this brief book of Lamentations the spirit of the man is strikingly revealed. There is no exultation over the fulfillment of his predictions; and there is a twofold loyalty manifest throughout, first to God in the confession of sin, and then to his people in the expression of their sorrow.

The chapter-division of the book is the natural one. It consists of five poems, the titles of which may thus be written: the Solitary City (i.); the Sources of her Sorrow (ii.); the Prophet's Identification (iii.); the Desolation (iv.); the Appeal out of Sorrow (v).

A. THE SOLITARY CITY

In this poem there are two movements. The first describes the desolation of the city as to her relationships with other nations, and as to her internal condition, declaring the cause to be that she "hath grievously sinned." In the second the city personified bewails her affliction, appealing to the passer-by, and describes her sorrow; she then confesses the justice of the desolation which has overtaken her, appealing to Jehovah for sympathy and deliverance.

B. THE SOURCES OF THE SORROW

In the second poem the prophet dealt with the sources of the sorrow. He first affirmed that it was the result of the direct action of Jehovah, and was manifest in material and spiritual judgments. He then broke out into a description of the affliction of iniquity, as to the actual sufferings endured, and the even more painful contempt of the nations. The poem ends with a double appeal: first that of the prophet to the people, in which he urged them to penitence; and secondly that of the people to Jehovah, in which they described their affliction.

C. THE PROPHET'S IDENTIFICATION

In this central and longest poem Jeremiah identified himself completely with the experiences of his people. In the first movement, in language which throbs with pain, he described his own sorrows, recognizing, through all, the action of Jehovah, as the almost monotonous repetition of the pronoun "He" reveals. This recognition of the fact that judgment is the work of Jehovah, compelled the ending of this dirge by the affirmation of hope. The next movement is one of assurance, in which the prophet, having in the previous section recognized Jehovah's activity in judgment, now recognized His activity in mercy. This section ends with

E. *The Appeal Out of Sorrow*

an expression of submission to judgment and a song of hope. The third movement is one of appeal, in which the prophet first recognized the justice of the Divine visitation, and then earnestly appealed to the people to turn to God in true penitence, ending with a declaration of his own sorrows. The final movement is one which first celebrates in song the deliverances already wrought for the prophet by Jehovah, and concludes with a declaration of his consequent assurance that God would yet act on behalf of His people.

D. THE DESOLATION

The fourth poem is for the most part a dirge of desolation, which nevertheless ends in a song of hope. The prophet described the disaster in Zion, and the consequent degradation of the people, and then proceeded to show that the sins of the prophets and the priests constituted the cause of the disasters, and declared that these prophets and priests were therefore hated of the people. In the next place he showed how vain had been their hope of help from men, and described the remorselessness of their enemies. The last movement is a satirical address to Edom, and a declaration to Zion of coming deliverance.

E. THE APPEAL OUT OF SORROW

The final poem is an appeal to Jehovah. It first calls upon Him to remember, describing the actual desolation, the affliction of all classes, and the consequently prevalent sorrow. Then, affirming confidence in the abiding throne of Jehovah, it appeals to Him to turn them unto Him. The last word of this poem and collection is a wail out of the then present distress.

EZEKIEL—*The Prophet of Hope*

A THE PROPHET'S PREPARATION *i.—iii.*	**B** REPROBATION *iv.—xxvi.*	**C** RESTORATION *xxv.—xlviii.*
Title Page.　　2. 3		
I. The Visions　i.	**I. Results of Reprobation** **iv.—xiv.**	**I. The Nations　xxv.—xxxii.**
i. Fire.　　1 and 4 ii. Living Ones. 　　　　5-14 iii. Wheels.　　15-21 iv. The Likeness. 　　　　22-28	i. The Four Signs.　　iv.—v. ii. The Denunciations.　vi.—vii. iii. The Judgment.　　viii.—xiv.	i. The Doom of Four—Ammon, 　Moab, Edom, Philistia.　xxv. ii. The Doom of Two—Tyre and 　Zidon.　　xxvi.—xxviii. 24 　(Parenthesis Restoration of 　Israel.　　　　25-26) iii. The Doom of One—Egypt. 　　　　xxix.—xxxii.
II. The Voice **ii.—iii.**	**II. Reason of Reprobation** **xv.—xix.**	**II. The Nation** **xxxiii.—xxxix.**
i. The Message. 　　　ii.—iii. 3 ii. The Equipment. 　　　iii. 4-15 iii. The Responsi- 　bility.　　16-21 iv. The Commission. 　　　　22-27	i. The Two General Figures. 　　　　xv.—xvi. ii. The Riddle.　　xvii. iii. The False Excuse.　xviii. iv. The Lament.　　xix.	i. The Watchman.　　xxxiii. ii. Shepherds, false and true. 　　　　xxxiv. iii. The New Order. 　　　xxxv.—xxxvi. iv. The Vision of the Bones. 　　　　xxxvii. v. The Last Enemy. 　　　xxxviii.—xxxix.
	III. Righteousness of Rep- **robation　xx.—xxiv.**	**III. The Restored Order** **xl.—xlviii.**
	i. Vindicated to Elders.　xx. 1-44 ii. The Song of the Sword. 　　　　xx. 45—xxi. iii. The Utter Evil of the City. 　　　　xxii. iv. Oholah. Oholibah.　xxiii. v. The Destruction of the City. 　　　　xxiv.	i. The Temple.　　xl.—xlii. ii. Jehovah.　　xliii. iii. The Service of the Temple. 　　　xliv.—xlvi. iv. The River.　　xlvii. 1-12 v. The Land.　　xlvii. 13-23 vi. The People.　　xlviii. 1-29 vii. The City.　　xlviii. 30-35

EZEKIEL * * * *

OF THE PROPHET Ezekiel personally we only know that
he was a priest, and the son of Buzi. If the expression "the
thirtieth year" in the opening verse of the book refers to his
age, which is probable, seeing that he was a priest, and that
thirty was the age at which they commenced their work, he
must have been twenty-five years of age when the captivity
commenced. During the whole of those years Jeremiah was
exercising his ministry. This would account for the evident
influence exercised upon Ezekiel by the teaching of
Jeremiah. His method was superlatively that of symbolism.
The book is full of visions, symbolic actions, similitudes,
parables, proverbs, allegories, and open prophecies. He was
the prophet who supremely looked through the then existing devastation to ultimate deliverance. Recognizing the
fact of the reprobation of the people by Jehovah, and the
righteousness thereof, he yet foretold a glorious restoration,
basing his conviction upon his conception of the character
of God. The main object of his prophesying would seem to
have been the comfort of the exiles, and their preservation
from the idolatry by which they were surrounded. The book
falls into three main parts, the first describing how the word
of the Lord came expressly to him, by visions and in a voice;
the second dealing with the reprobation of the people of
God; and the last foretelling their restoration, and indicating the methods by which it would be brought about. It may

be divided thus: the Prophet's Preparation (i.-iii.); Reprobation (iv.-xxiv.); Restoration (xxv.-xlviii.).

A. THE PROPHET'S PREPARATION

The division dealing with the prophet's preparation falls into two sections, the first describing the visions he saw, and the second the voices he heard. The second and third verses, which are really parenthetical, may be treated as a title page. This gives the date, states the fact that the word came expressly to him, and indicates the place in which he saw the visions and heard the voice.

The visions were inclusive visions of God. They proceeded in four manifestations. The first was that of a cloud swept into sight by a stormy wind, surrounded by brightness, and continually flashing forth in glory. The second was the appearance out of the midst of this fire, of four living ones, who moved in rhythmic unity. The third appearance was that of wheels which rotated in harmony with each other, and in co-operation with the movements of the living ones. The last appearance was that, first of a firmament overarching the ceaseless activity of the living ones; above the firmament a voice was heard, and then the likeness of a throne was seen, and finally a Person was manifested, of the nature of fire, surrounded by a glory like that of the rainbow. In the presence of the manifested glory Ezekiel fell upon his face, and then heard the voice. This voice called him to listen, and then commissioned him to deliver the message of God to the children of Israel, charging him that he was to speak it whether they would hear or forbear. The commission was ratified by the symbolism of a roll handed to him, which he was commanded to eat. He obeyed, and found the roll in

B. Reprobation

his mouth "as honey for sweetness." Continuing, the voice announced to him what his equipment for the fulfillment of his mission would be, warning him of the difficulties awaiting him, promising him that he should be strengthened for his work, and charging him to be loyal to the word of the Lord. In an interval he was borne up by the Spirit, and carried to the midst of the captives, where he sat "astonied" for seven days. The word of Jehovah then came to him again, laying upon him his responsibilities anew. He was first reminded of the source of the message, and told that his first responsibility was that of hearing, and his second that of speech. He was called into the plain, where once again he saw the glory of Jehovah as he had seen it by the river. A double charge was again laid upon him, the first part of which was that of silence, and the second that of speech.

B. REPROBATION

The second division of the book contains the messages of the prophet concerning the reprobation of the chosen nation. These fall into three parts. In the first, by symbol and speech, he described the results of reprobation; in the second he declared its reason; and in the last he proclaimed its righteousness.

The results of reprobation were first symbolically set forth in four signs. These were immediately followed by general denunciations. Finally the coming judgment was dealt with at length, as to its cause and its process.

Ezekiel's first sign was that of a tile, upon which he portrayed a city, around which were depicted all the forces of a siege. His second sign consisted of a posture. For three hundred and ninety days he lay upon his left side, and for forty days upon his right, prophesying during the whole period against Jerusalem. The third sign was that of the food of which he partook during the period of the three hundred and ninety days. The fourth was that of the shavings of his hair from head and face. This hair was divided into three parts, a third was burned, a third was smitten with the sword, and a third was scattered to the wind. This last sign was carefully explained. The hair symbolized Jerusalem, and the treatment of it indicated the method of the Divine judgment against it.

These signs were followed by denunciations. The first foretold the coming judgment of the sword against the whole land, and the consequent scattering of the people. In this process of judgment a remnant would be spared, in order that the lesson might be learned. The prophet was charged to deliver this message of the sword with vehemence, and to make clear the fact that vengeance moved toward the purpose of making the people who had forgotten, know Jehovah. The second dealt with the fact of the completeness of the judgment. Its keynote was expressed in the words "an end." The prophet declared that an end was determined upon the land, and upon the people; and that it should be accomplished by the act of God. He then proceeded to describe that end. Its first manifestation would be the paralysis of the people, so that although the trumpet was blown to the battle, and all was ready, yet none moved forward, being overcome by terror and grief. This paralysis would issue in poverty, not wholly in the absolute lack of silver and gold, but in the awful consciousness that these things were useless as means of deliverance from the wrath

B. Reprobation

of Jehovah. All this, finally, would produce the confession of overwhelming perplexity, and no interpreter would be found. The second denunciation ended, as did the first, by indicating the purpose of the vengeance: "They shall know that I am the Lord."

The long prophecy, descriptive of the cause and process of judgment, came to the prophet as he sat in his own house in the presence of the elders of Judah. In its first movement it described the idolatry in Jerusalem, which was the sin to be visited with punishment. The prophet first saw the image of jealousy at the entrance of the inner court of the house of God. He then saw, through a hole in the wall, all secret abominations before which the elders of Israel were burning incense. In the third place he was shown the depravity of the women of Israel, who were seen weeping for Tammuz. Finally, in the inner court men were seen with their backs toward the Temple, worshipping the sun. On account of this utter corruption of the people, Jehovah would proceed in judgment.

The next section of the message reveals the fact of the Divine discrimination in judgment. A man with an inkhorn passed through the midst, and set a mark upon the foreheads of such as mourned the abominations. These were to be spared, while all the rest were to be slain. The vision appalled the prophet, and he cried out in intercession, but he was told that the sin of Israel and Judah was great, and therefore the punishment was irrevocable.

The prophet then described the process of judgment. He was first granted a preliminary vision. The man with the inkhorn gathered coals of fire from between the cherubim, and scattered them over the city. Out of the midst of visions of the glory of God, similar to those which he had seen by the river Chebar, this fire was taken.

Again the prophet saw the princes of the people devising iniquity; and, instructed of the Spirit, he uttered a denunciation of them, and declared God's vengeance against them. One of the princes died, as he prophesied, and he appealed to Jehovah in terms of intercession. This appeal was answered by the declaration that Jehovah would protect those scattered among the nations, that eventually they should be restored, but that vengeance would inevitably fall upon such as were persistent in their sin. Again there was granted to him a vision of the glory of God, but he saw it departing from the city. Returning from the height of these visions, the prophet uttered in the hearing of the captives all the things that the Lord had showed him.

He was next commanded, in the sight of these people, to act as an exile going forth from his country. In answer to the inquiry of the people as to the meaning of what he did, he foretold the capture of the people and the princes in Jerusalem, and their carrying away to Babylon. By the sign of his own method of eating and drinking, he was charged to foretell the desolations which would fall upon the inhabitants of Jerusalem. The people of Israel declared in proverbs the failure of prophecy, or the distance of its fulfillment; and Ezekiel was charged to announce that the things foretold would immediately be fulfilled.

The next movement in the prophesying was that of a denunciation of false prophets and false prophetesses. The evil inspiration of the former was described, and its disastrous effect declared. Their destruction was foretold, and its reason

B. Reprobation

made clear. They had seduced the people by promising peace, when judgment was determined. The prophetesses had been guilty of the same iniquity for the sake of hire, and their judgment was equally sure.

Certain of the elders of Israel came to Ezekiel, and he was instructed by Jehovah to declare to them that, while idolatry remained in their heart, the only answer of Jehovah to them must be that of punishment.

This determined attitude of judgment was then explained to Ezekiel, first by a statement of principle. In days of willful and persistent corruption men as righteous as Noah, Daniel, and Job could not prevent the operation of vengeance, but only save their own souls by their righteousness. The application of this to the sore judgments against Jerusalem would prove to the prophet how that all that the Lord had done had been not without cause.

This final word as to the results of reprobation leads naturally to the part of the prophecy dealing with the reason thereof. This reason is first set forth under two general figures; secondly, in the form of a riddle; thirdly, as an answer to a false excuse; and finally, in a great lament.

The figures were familiar, because they had been used by former prophets. The first was that of the vine, and the second that of the adulteress. As to the vine, the prophet declared its uselessness as a tree, and its still more pronounced uselessness when burnt; the intention of which declarations was to show that the only value of a vine is in the fruit it bears. The application of the figure was made immediately to Jerusalem, whose inhabitants were to be given to the fire on account of their trespass.

The second figure the prophet wrought out at greater

length. It was that of Jerusalem, the faithless city, as
an adulteress. Maintaining his figure throughout, he traced
the history of the city. An abandoned child, born and forsaken, was found and nurtured by Jehovah. At maturity the
child was taken in marriage, and loaded with benefits. Then
as wife she trusted in her beauty, and turned to harlotry, in
which she prostituted her husband's wealth. This harlotry
had been worse than the common, in which the harlot
receives gifts, in that in this case she had bestowed gifts to
seduce others. The punishment of the adulteress was that of
stripping and shame. Yet this very process was intended to
produce in the heart of the sinning city the shame of repentance. The last movement is one in which the prophet foretold the restoration of the wife by the remembrance of the
covenant and its re-establishment by Jehovah.

The prophet then, commanded by Jehovah, put forth a
riddle. A great eagle came upon Lebanon, took off the top
of the cedar; carried away the seed of the land, and planted
it in a fruitful soil, where it became a spreading vine. Toward a second eagle it bent its roots, that he might water it.
The vine was denounced for this act of treachery, its judgment being that it should be plucked up by the roots, and
withered by the east wind. The riddle was then explained.
The first eagle was the king of Babylon, who carried away
the king of Jerusalem, and planted the seed royal in Babylon.
The second eagle was the king of Egypt, whose help Zedekiah
sought, and who was punished by Jehovah in consequence.
The riddle ended with the promise of Jehovah that He
would ultimately plant again a cedar in the mountain of the
height of Israel, and as a result there should be universal
recognition of the activity of Jehovah.

B. Reprobation

The people at this time were quoting a proverb, "The fathers have eaten sour grapes, and the children's teeth are set on edge," by which they intended to lay the blame of their present suffering upon their fathers. The truth of this the prophet denied, first by illustrations, declaring that the righteous man lives, that the wicked son of a righteous man dies, that the righteous son of a wicked father lives. He then stated the principle that God deals with individuals directly, and consequently that the sinner, turning to righteousness, should live; and the righteous man, turning to sin, must die. Then in the name of Jehovah he appealed to Israel to turn from transgression, and declared that God had "no pleasure in the death of him that dieth."

The final movement in this section is that of the lament of the prophet over Jehoahaz, in which he first described Judah, the lioness mother, and the captured whelp; then over Jehoiachin, the second whelp, and his capture; finally, over Zedekiah, whose mother, Judah, was like a vine plucked up, and destroyed by fire proceeding out of her rods, that is, from her children.

In the next section we have a series of prophecies, showing the righteousness of reprobation. This was first vindicated to the elders; secondly, celebrated in the song of the sword; thirdly, declared in a description of the utter evil of the city; fourthly, shown in a description of the sins of Samaria and Jerusalem; and finally, manifested in a description of the destruction of the city.

Certain of the elders of Israel came to inquire of the Lord, and Ezekiel was commissioned to answer them. This he did, first by reviewing their past history, and showing how God had dealt with them for His name's sake, in delivering them from Egypt; in delivering them in the wilderness; and in sparing them there. He then examined the relation of the present sin to the past. The fathers had sinned in the land; so also had the sons; and consequently they were punished. He then foretold the future. The Lord God, by a mighty hand, would gather His people to the wilderness and discipline them, and sanctify His name among them. As a result, Israel would be restored, and Jehovah's name sanctified among the nations; and all this for His name's sake.

The prophet was then commissioned to prophesy against the forest of the south, that a fire should be kindled in it. Not understanding the meaning of the message, he made his appeal to God, that men would say to him that he was a speaker of parables, and immediately the explanation was given. The sword of Jehovah was about to proceed against the land of Israel. The prophet's anguish in the presence of the judgment was to become a sign to the people. All this prepared the way for the song of the sword, in which in graphic language the process of its sharpening, and its readiness for use were described; and its commission was uttered. The song was immediately followed by an interpretation, announcing that the king of Babylon was coming against the city, and the prince of Israel was to be degraded by Jehovah, who would overturn until the coming of the rightful king. This interpretation was followed by a brief address to the children of Ammon, who had drawn the sword, commanding them to sheathe it, and declaring the judgment decreed against them.

The next movement described the utter evil of the city. Its fundamental sins of bloodshed and idolatry were named, and the resultant evils of oppressions by princes, irreligion,

B. Reprobation

lewdness, and greed were described. On account of these things, the judgment of Jehovah would be terrible, and would proceed to purpose which was illustrated under the figure of the furnace into which Israel was cast. Again the prophet described the corruption of the inhabitants, first in general statement, in which he described a land with no water, having no teaching; and the springs as polluted, having no prophets; and then proceeded to make particular charges against priests, princes, prophets, people. He concluded by describing the utter hopelessness of the case. There was no man to stand in the gap. Therefore the fire of wrath must proceed upon its way.

The next prophecy dealt with the sins of Samaria and Jerusalem under the figure of two women, Oholah and Oholibah. Samaria was charged with unfaithfulness in her confederacy with Assyria and Egypt, this being the cause of her judgment. Jerusalem was charged with unfaithfulness with Assyria, with Babylon, and with Egypt, this being the cause of her judgment. In other terms the prophet declared their sins. They were guilty of idolatry and bloodshed, profanation of the sanctuary, and unholy alliances. Returning to the figure, he declared them to be worthy of judgment by righteous men, of stoning by consent of the assembly, in order that the land might be purged.

Under this section the last prophecy described the destruction of the city. This was first done under the parable of the caldron set upon a fire, filled with water, and made to boil, which symbolized the coming destruction of Jerusalem and its people.

The prophet was then bereft of his wife, and commanded not to mourn, in order that he might be a sign to the people of coming judgment. Ezekiel was then told that the news would be conveyed to him of the fall of the city, and that in that day his mouth would be opened, and he would be able to speak with assurance the messages of Jehovah.

C. RESTORATION

The last division of the prophecy deals with the subject of the ultimate restoration of the chosen nation. It falls into three sections. The first has to do with the nations; the second with the Nation; and the last describes the restored order.

The prophecies concerning the nations fall into three groups. The first pronounced the doom of four, the second the doom of two, and the third the doom of one.

The doom of four dealt with Ammon, Moab, Edom, and Philistia. Ammon had mocked the people of God in the day of their desolation, therefore they were to be destroyed. Moab had rejoiced in the degradation of Judah, therefore judgment was determined against it. Edom had been brutal in her treatment of Judah, and therefore was to be made desolate. Philistia had taken vengeance with perpetual enmity, and therefore vengeance was determined against her. Each of these dooms ended with the same thought—that these people by judgment should know Jehovah.

The doom of two dealt with Tyre and Zidon, but principally with Tyre. Concerning her the prophet first made a general statement describing her sin and the judgment determined against her, declaring that the purpose was that she should know Jehovah. He then described in detail the destruction of the city by Nebuchadrezzar, and foretold the lamentation of the princes over her downfall.

–254

C. Restoration

At the command of Jehovah, Ezekiel then took up a lamentation for Tyre, which first described her commercial supremacy and enterprises, and then in language full of force foretold her commercial ruin. The prophecy concerning Tyre ended with a message to its prince, and a lamentation for its king. To the prince the prophet declared his sin to have been that of pride, which thought of himself as a god, and boasted accordingly. His judgment was to be, that by humiliation and destruction, even to the pit, he should learn that he was a man, and not God. The lamentation concerning the king of Tyre first described his glory, and his appointment by God to his original position. The prophet then described his sins, and their consequent judgment. Unrighteousness was found in him, and therefore he was cast out of the mountain of God. Pride filled him, therefore he was cast down in the presence of kings. For the multitude of his iniquities a fire devoured him, and he was burnt to ashes.

Judgment was to fall upon Zidon that she might know the Lord; and that there should be no more a pricking brier to the house of Israel. Immediately following this prophecy dealing with the doom of two is a brief parenthesis describing the restoration of Israel; the prophet declaring in the name of Jehovah that she should be gathered and settled, in order that her people should know that Jehovah was their God.

The doom of one had to do with Egypt. It consists of seven prophecies, which are placed here, not in the order of their delivery. Throughout these prophecies the purpose of judgment is constantly declared to be that of making Jehovah known. The first is against Pharaoh, and all Egypt. His sin the prophet declared to be the pride which claimed the river as his own creation, and the doom he poetically described as the taking of Pharaoh as a great fish out of his river, and casting him upon the land. That doom he then proceeded to foretell as the coming of a sword upon the land of Egypt, and the scattering of its people among the nations. After forty years he declared that Jehovah would gather them again, and in their own land make them a people degraded, no more to rule over the nations. The second prophecy foretold that the instrument of judgment should be Nebuchadrezzar, and the capture of Egypt would be his wage for the defeat of Tyre. The third prophecy described the process by which Nebuchadrezzar would accomplish this purpose of Jehovah. His stroke would fall on the multitudes, on the idols, on the cities. The fourth prophecy was directed against the power of Pharaoh, and declared that the Lord would break his arms, and strengthen those of the king of Babylon for the accomplishment of His purpose. The fifth prophecy was against the greatness of Pharaoh. That greatness was first described as that of a stately cedar in Lebanon, and then its destruction was foretold, first under the same figure, and then by a graphic and awful picture of the descent of Pharaoh into Sheol. The sixth prophecy was a lamentation for Pharaoh, in which his doom was first described, and then its widespread effect. Again the prophet declared that the destruction of Pharaoh and of Egypt would be brought about by the sword of the king of Babylon. The seventh prophecy was a wail for the multitudes of Egypt, in which the descent to death is portrayed, and all the companies of the dead from among the nations are represented as companions of Pharaoh and his hosts in the underworld.

–256

C. Restoration

Ezekiel next delivered a series of messages concerning the chosen nation. The first described the watchman; the second dealt with shepherds, false and true; the third set forth the new order; the fourth consisted of a vision of the valley of bones; and the fifth dealt with the last enemy.

The first message to Israel described the function and responsibilities of the prophet under the figure of a watchman. The duty of the watchman was to give warning of the approach of a foe. Ezekiel occupied that position. He was charged to declare to the people in the midst of their sins that Jehovah had no pleasure in the death of the wicked, and that they were to remember their responsibilities. Past acts of righteousness would not atone for present transgression. Past sin would be pardoned if the sinner turned to Jehovah. Upon the basis of this announcement the prophet defended Jehovah against the people who charged Him with being unequal in His ways. Immediately upon the delivery of this message fugitives who had escaped from the sack of Jerusalem came to the prophet. He was prepared and commissioned to deliver to them the message of Jehovah. The attention of the people was aroused, but they were disobedient to his voice.

The next prophecy dealt with the one Shepherd. Its first movement was an indictment of the false shepherds, through whom the evil things had happened to the chosen people. They had cared for themselves, and neglected the flock, with the result that the flock was scattered and devoured. Therefore Jehovah was against the shepherds, and required His sheep at their hands. This indictment was followed by a description, full of beauty, of Jehovah's method of deliverance. He Himself would come to search for His sheep. His government would proceed in strict discrimination and righteous administration. The message ended with the promise of the appointment of the one Shepherd under Whose rule order would be restored, blessing would be bestowed, and peace established.

The prophet then described the new order by contrasting Mount Seir with the mountains of Israel. The sin of Mount Seir had been that of perpetual enmity, and its judgment would be that of perpetual desolation. Its guilt had been that of the possession of Jehovah's land, and its punishment would be that of dispossession. The mountains of Israel were to be delivered from their enemies, and to be made abundantly fruitful. This prediction the prophet was charged to explain by affirming the fact that their own sin had been the reason of their sufferings, and by declaring that for the sake of His holy name they would be restored. A description of the method of restoration followed. The people were to be gathered from all countries, and cleansed from filthiness, and spiritually remade. The results of restoration would be that they should dwell in their own land, and in place of desolation there should be fruitfulness. The conditions of restoration were that Jehovah would be inquired of for these things, and its purpose that He should be known.

There was now granted to the prophet the great vision of the valley filled with bones. Over these bones he was commanded to prophesy. He obeyed, and beheld the bones coming together, and being clothed with sinews and flesh. Again he was commanded to prophesy to the wind. He obeyed, and saw the corpses in the valley stand upon their feet, a living army. This vision was the outcome of a proverb in which the people had declared, "Our bones are dried up, and our hope is lost, we are clean cut off." The application of the vision was made in the declaration that God would bring His people from their graves, and make them live. Having thus foretold the renewal of the people, the prophet was commanded to take two sticks and join them into one, and to declare to the people, by an explanation of his action, that God would gather the scattered ones from among the nations, and make them one under the dominion of a new king, and within the terms of a new covenant.

The final message concerning the nation dealt with matters far removed from the times of the prophet. He described the final antagonism of Gog, who with his allies would gather, under Divine compulsion, and in malice, against Israel. The prophet declared that this coming would be against Jehovah. He then proceeded to foretell the antagonism of God to the gathered hosts. The destruction of the enemy would be brought about by the act of Jehovah, completely and terribly; and the issue would be the restoration of the whole house of Israel.

The final movement in the prophecies of restoration described the restored order, and dealt with the Temple, Jehovah, the service of the Temple, the river, the land, the people, and the city.

Fourteen years after the sack of Jerusalem, Ezekiel was given visions of the ultimate restoration of the scattered and desolate people. His description of the new Temple commenced with the courts, of which he described the outer and the inner. Passing to the Temple proper, he portrayed it first from the outside, describing the actual Temple, with its holy place, and holy of holies; then the side chambers, finally the separate building; ending with general dimensions of the inner court, the house buildings, and the separate building. He then gave a description of the internal wood-work and ornamentation. Returning to the buildings, he described the chambers in the inner court, and their uses, ending with external measurements of the whole.

His next vision was that of the return of Jehovah to His house. The visions which he had seen by the river Chebar appeared again, and all the glory moved into possession of the new Temple. Again he heard the voice declaring that Jehovah had taken up His abode in the house, and that Israel should no more defile His holy name. Then follows a paren-thesis, which chronicles the charge delivered to the prophet to show this house of future glory to the house of Israel, that she might be ashamed of her iniquities. The prophet then described the ordinances of the altar, giving its measure-ments and the arrangements for its consecration.

The next section described the service of the new Temple. The gate by which the God of Israel entered would be kept shut. The place of the prince was appointed, and the prophet was charged to pay careful attention to the instruc-tions concerning the ordinances of the house. No aliens would be allowed to minister therein. The Levites would be restored to the service of the sanctuary, and the priests to their sacred offices. Careful instructions were given for the support of priest, Levite and prince. The duties of the prince would be to provide for the offerings. The actual services were next set forth. The feasts, the Sabbaths and months, the freewill offering, the daily burnt-offering, were all ar-ranged for. Instructions were given concerning the in-heritance of the sons of the prince, and the prophet was shown the boiling-houses.

C. Restoration

The prophet was brought back again to the door of the house, and there beheld the wonderful symbolic river proceeding under the threshold past the altar. He watched it in its course, and observed its marvelous growth and its life-giving effect.

The new boundaries and divisions of the land were next described, and careful instructions were given concerning the disposition of the people. At the center was the sacred land, occupied by priests and Levites, the city, and the prince. To the north places were appointed for Dan, Asher, Naphtali, Manasseh, Ephraim, Reuben, and Judah; and to the south places for Benjamin, Simeon, Issachar, Zebulun, and Gad.

The last vision granted to Ezekiel was of the city in the south of the sacred land. Its gates and dimensions were given; and the final words of this prophet of hope announced the name of the city, Jehovah-shammah, "The Lord is there."

DANIEL—*The Prophet of Interpretation*

<table>
<tr><td colspan="3">

A
THE HISTORIC NIGHT
i.—vi.

</td><td colspan="3">

B
THE PROPHETIC LIGHT
vii.—xii.

</td></tr>
</table>

<table>
<tr><td colspan="2">

I. The Reign of Nebuchadnezzar

</td><td>

i.—iv.

</td><td colspan="2">

I. Belshazzar's Reign

</td><td>

vii.—viii.

</td></tr>
</table>

i. Daniel's History.	i.		i. Daniel's first Vision in first year.		vii.
ii. Nebuchadnezzar's Dream.	ii.		*a.* The Vision.		1-14
iii. Nebuchadnezzar's Pride.	iii.		*b.* The Explanation.		15-28
iv. Nebuchadnezzar's Manifesto.	iv.		ii. Daniel's second Vision in third year.		viii.
			a. The Vision.		1-14
			b. The Explanation.		15-27

<table>
<tr><td colspan="2">

II. The Reign of Belshazzar

</td><td>

v.

</td><td colspan="2">

II. Darius' Reign

</td><td>

ix.

</td></tr>
</table>

i. The Carousal.	1-4		i. Daniel and the Prophecy of Jeremiah.	1-2
ii. The Writing.	5-12		ii. Daniel's Confession and Prayer.	3-19
iii. Daniel.	13-29		iii. The Coming of Gabriel.	20-23
iv. The Fulfillment.	30-31		iv. The Revelation.	24-27

<table>
<tr><td colspan="2">

III. The Reign of Darius

</td><td>

vi.

</td><td colspan="2">

III. Cyrus' Reign

</td><td>

x.—xii.

</td></tr>
</table>

i. The Appointment of Daniel.	1-3		i. The Introductory Apocalypse.	x.
ii. The Plot.	4-15		ii. Prophetic History.	xi.
iii. The Deliverance.	16-24		iii. The Last Things foretold.	xii. 1-3
iv. The Proclamation.	25-28		iv. The Closing of the Book.	xii. 4-13

DANIEL   *   *   *   *

DANIEL WAS CARRIED away into captivity before Ezekiel, having been among the number of those captured by Nebuchadnezzar in his first invasion, in the third year of Jehoiakim. His whole life from that time would seem to have been spent in Babylon. His personal history is a remarkable one, in that notwithstanding the fact that he was of the captive race, he rose to positions of power in three kingdoms, those namely of Babylon, Media, and Persia; and this, moreover, not as the result of any deflection from unswerving loyalty to the God of his fathers. His prophecies deal in detail far more fully with Gentile nations than with the history of the Hebrew people. In the midst of the densest darkness he was the medium through which the light of the Divine government shined. His ministry was exercised largely in the atmosphere of visions, and its nature was that of interpretation.

The first half of the book is occupied with historic matter, giving us pictures of the times and conditions in which he lived. The second half of the book deals with visions and their interpretations, and thus constitutes his prophetic message. The book thus falls into two divisions: the Historic Night (i.-vi.); the Prophetic Light (vii.-xii.).

A. THE HISTORIC NIGHT

During the reign of Nebuchadnezzar, Daniel came into favour and power. The king would seem to have been impressed by the people he had conquered, and desired that some of the choicest of their young men should be included among his own confidential servants. Among those selected were four specially named, and among the four, Daniel. These were set apart for training and preparation for the fulfilment of their official duties. This training lasted for three years, and included special physical attention, their food and drink being supplied from the king's table. Daniel at once manifested his strength of character in the purpose he formed to abstain from the king's meat and wine. His attitude was characterized by courtesy, and he asked for a ten days' test. The test vindicated his purpose, and Daniel and his friends were allowed to proceed with their training. At the end of that training they were presented to Nebuchadnezzar, approved by him, and appointed to positions in the kingdom.

In the second year of his reign Nebuchadnezzar, troubled by dreams, called together his magicians, and sought their interpretation. Their difficulty consisted in the fact that he could not tell them his dream, and demanded that they should discover it and interpret it. Being unable to do so, he was furious, and commanded their destruction. In this decree the Hebrew youths were involved. Daniel sought an interview of the king, and asked for time, promising to show the king the interpretation of his dream. This being granted, he at once gathered his friends together, and they betook themselves to prayer. In answer to that prayer the secret was revealed to him in a vision of the night. He then stood before the king, and first, in language full of confidence and dignity, ascribed to God the glory of the interpretation he was about to give; exonerating the wise men from any blame in their inability to interpret the dream. He then vividly described the image of the king's dream, and proceeded to an interpretation of its meaning. Tracing the progress of events through the successive kingdoms of Babylon, Media, and Persia, Greece, Rome, the ten kingdoms, and the final setting up of the kingdom of heaven, he showed that there would be a process of deterioration. This interpretation carried conviction to the mind of Nebuchadnezzar, who at once recognized the supremacy of God, and rewarded Daniel by setting him over the province and the wise men.

The next story is that of the pride of Nebuchadnezzar in setting up in the plain of Dura a great image of gold. There may have been a connection between this and the interpretation of the dream which Daniel had given. The head of gold in the image of Nebuchadnezzar's dream symbolized Babylon. Nebuchadnezzar's image was all of gold, and perhaps revealed his conception of the power of Babylon. To this he commanded all peoples to bow down in worship. This would also explain the attitude of the dauntless three who declined to bend their knee to the image. In the first place it was an act of idolatry; and moreover, such obeisance on their part might have been construed into a recognition of the continuity of the power of Babylon, of which the Divine revelation to Daniel had predicted the downfall. With splendid heroism they cast themselves upon God, and were supernaturally delivered from the fierce fire of the furnace. This deliverance more deeply impressed Nebuchadnezzar, and he made a decree that no word should be spoken against the God of Shadrach, Meshach, and Abednego, and promoted them in the province of Babylon.

The last story connected with the reign of Nebuchadnezzar

consists of the king's own manifesto, setting forth the dealings of the Most High God with him. It opens with an ascription of praise, then proceeds to tell the story of his own humbling before God, and ends with a description of his restoration, and a final ascription of praise. In the midst of his prosperity he had a dream which filled him with fear, and his magicians were unable to interpret it to him. Again he sent for Daniel, and minutely described his vision of the tree growing to great height, and then cut down, so that only roots and stump were left. Daniel "was astonied," evidently because he saw the application of the dream to the king. He nevertheless, in loyalty to truth, interpreted to him its meaning, declaring that he, by the decree of the Most High, would be driven out a madman from the ways of men for a long period, and appealing to him to turn from sin. A year later the dream was fulfilled. In the midst of a proud boast he was stricken with madness. Finally restored to reason, he recognized the God of Heaven, and was restored to his kingdom, and uttered the praise of the Most High.

The next scene is cast in the reign of Belshazzar. A man of profligate habits, he had succeeded to the throne of his father. In the midst of a great carousal there appeared to him a mystic hand, writing on the wall his doom and that of his kingdom. Again the wise men were unable to interpret the meaning; and Daniel, who evidently was not now in proximity to the king, who did not seem to know him, was sent for. The attitude of Daniel before him was full of dignity and heroic loyalty to God. With clear, incisive words he first declined all the king's gifts, and then charged upon him his guilt. Continuing, he proclaimed God as seated high over the thrones of earth and interpreted the writing as indicating God's knowledge of the kingdom and His determination to end it; His estimate of the king; and finally the future of Babylon, as divided among Medes and Persians. With dramatic and terrible force the story declares, "In that night Belshazzar the Chaldean King was slain. And Darius the Mede received the kingdom."

The last scene in the historic portion is in the reign of Darius. Having come into the kingdom, he appointed Daniel as one of three presidents, and proposed to set him over the whole realm. This naturally stirred up jealousy in the hearts of the other presidents and satraps, who with great cunning planned his downfall. Knowing that they would be unable to find occasion against him, save in the matter of his relation to God, they induced the king to sign a decree which would necessarily involve Daniel. His loyalty never swerved; he continued to observe those acts of worship which had been his custom. Against the desire of the king, he was cast into the den of lions, and was supernaturally delivered. This deliverance issued in a proclamation made by Darius, and Daniel prospered through his reign, and in the reign of Cyrus.

B. THE PROPHETIC LIGHT

During the reign of Belshazzar two visions were granted to Daniel, which constituted the prophetic light of that particular period. The first of these was of four beasts arising from the sea, the last of which had ten horns. In the midst of these there arose another, which destroyed them. The vision then became that of the setting of thrones, and the appearing of the glory of One Who overcame the beasts, and received dominion, and glory, and a Kingdom. These visions troubled Daniel, but an interpretation was given to him, first in general terms. The beast symbolized four kings, and the final vision indicated that the saints of the Most High should yet receive and possess the Kingdom for ever and for ever. A particular interpretation of the meaning of the fourth beast, and the horns, was vouchsafed to him; and the ultimate value was again declared to be the government of Jehovah, and the final establishment of His Kingdom over all others. The whole matter troubled the prophet, but he kept it in his heart.

Two years later another vision came to him. It was that of a ram with two horns pushing westward, northward, and southward. As he watched, a he-goat attacked the ram, and overcame him, and magnified himself. Four horns appeared, out of one of which there came another, which grew until it had broken down the sanctuary. A voice of a holy one inquired as to how long this should continue, and the answer was given to Daniel. Again he pondered the vision, and sought to understand it, and an interpretation was granted to him. The two-horned ram represented the united power of Media and Persia; the rough he-goat was the king of Greece. Against him a fierce one should arise, succeeding through policy, but ultimately being broken without hand. The effects of the vision upon Daniel was such that he fainted, and was sick. Being restored, he continued to fulfill his office in the kingdom, until the hour came in which, as we have already seen, he interpreted the writing to Belshazzar, and Darius succeeded to the throne.

In the first year of the reign of Darius, Daniel became conscious that the seventy years of judgment upon Jerusalem, foretold by Jeremiah, were drawing to a close. He set himself to personal prayer and penitence on behalf of his people, making confession of their sin, and pleading their cause. He besought the Lord that the reproaches which had fallen upon Jerusalem might be put away, and as the men of vision had so often done, he based his plea upon the honor of the name of the Lord. In the midst of this intercession Gabriel came to him, declaring to him first of all that he was "greatly beloved," urging him to consider the matter, and understand the vision. He then made a revelation to him concerning the Divine program. Seventy weeks were decreed upon the people and the city. These were divided into three periods, the first of seven weeks, the second of sixty-two weeks, and the third of one week.

The last things were revealed to Daniel in the reign of Cyrus. In the third year of his reign Daniel was mourning and fasting for three weeks. Following this mourning there appeared to him, as he was by the river Hiddekel, a Person glorious in appearance, in the presence of Whom he was reduced to weakness, and evidently filled with an overwhelming sense of awe. This glorious One touched him, and then addressed him in words full of tenderness, and subsequently gave him a prophetic history of what should befall his people in the latter days.

That history dealt first with Persia, showing how there should be three kings, and yet a fourth "richer than they all." It then foretold the coming of a mighty king whose kingdom would be divided after his death. Proceeding, it described the conflict between the kings of the north and they of the south in the centuries following, until there should arise one contemptible in person, but gaining the kingdom by flatteries. The reign of this one, undoubtedly Antiochus Epiphanes, is described at greatest length. The last things were then foretold; the coming of Michael, and the subsequent time of trouble; beyond that the resurrection, and the advent of a new age. Daniel was charged to shut the book and seal it to "the time of the end." In mystic language he heard the man clothed in linen swear "by him that liveth" that these things should be for "a time, times, and a half." Being filled with a sense of mystery, he asked what would "be the issue of these things"; and was answered that the words were "shut up and sealed till the time of the end," and assured that to such as waited there would be blessing, and that he would rest, and yet stand in his lot at the end of the days.

HOSEA—*Spiritual Adultery*

HOSEA   ✳ ✳ ✳ ✳

HOSEA DATED HIS prophesying by giving the names of four kings of Judah and one of Israel. This reveals a remarkable length of prophetic utterance. His voice was heard in reigns which covered no less a period than one hundred and twenty-eight years. The probability is that he exercised his ministry between sixty and seventy years. The period covered was undoubtedly the darkest in the whole history of the kingdom of Israel. Political life was characterized by anarchy and misrule. The throne was occupied by men who obtained possession by the murder of their predecessors, and the people were governed by military despotism. Foreign alliances involved the nation in inextricable confusion. These alliances, moreover, resulted in the introduction of the corrupting influences of Syrian and Phoenician idolatry. The conditions were terrible in the extreme; luxurious living, robbery, oppression, falsehood, adultery, murder, accompanied by the most violent intolerance of any form of rebuke.

In the first part of the book we have an account of the preparation of Hosea for the delivery of his messages, and in the second part a condensed epitome of his prophetic utterances. The prophecy falls into two divisions—the Training of the Prophet (i.-iii.); the Teaching of the Prophet (iv.-xiv.).

A. THE TRAINING OF THE PROPHET

In the account of the training of the prophet for his work there are three distinctly marked movements—his domestic life and national conscience; his home tragedy, a revelation; and his dealing with Gomer, a command and a revelation.

The statement, "When the Lord spake at the first," is a declaration made by Hosea long after the event. Looking back, he understood that the impulse which resulted in heart agony was also part of the Divine method of teaching him. There is no reason to believe that Gomer was outwardly impure in the days when Hosea married her. In the picture of the domestic life which follows, the supreme matter is its revelation of Hosea's national conscience. There were born to him three children, and in the naming of them he revealed his conviction concerning the condition of his people. While this was a dark outlook indeed, yet the section ends with words which show that the prophet's faith was unshaken in the final fulfillment of the first Divine purposes, in spi ˕ of all contradictory appearances.

No details of the unfaithfulness of Gomer are given; but in the second movement the prophet is seen nursing his own agony, and by that process learning the true nature of the sin of his people as God knew and felt it. All that Hosea said concerning Gomer was also the language of Jehovah concerning Israel. As she had violated her covenant with him, so had Israel with Jehovah. In the latter part of the section the prophet speaks for Jehovah only, the tragedy in his own life being the background of illustration. The Divine attitude was that of the severity of love, which determined upon stern measures in order ultimately to win again the sinning and wandering people.

Hosea was taught the truth of the tenderness of the Divine heart by the command of Jehovah to love, and find, and restore his sinful and wandering bride. Through his obedience he entered into fellowship with the amazing tenderness of God, and was thereby prepared for the delivery of the messages which followed.

The method of his training for work may thus be summarized. Out of his communion with God in the days of prosperity he was able to see the true condition of his people. He was conscious that on account of their sin, the judgment of Jehovah threatened them; that on account of their obstinacy, mercy was not obtained; and that the issue of all could only be that they should be a people cast out from their place, power, and privilege.

Out of his own heart agony he learned the true nature of the sin of his people. They were playing the harlot, spending God's gifts in lewd traffic with other lovers.

Out of that personal suffering he came to an understanding of how God suffered over the sin of His people, because of His undying love.

Out of God's love, Hosea's new care for Gomer was born; and in the method God ordained for him with her, he discovered God's method with Israel.

Out of these processes of pain there came a full confidence in the ultimate victory of love.

Thus equipped he delivered his messages, and through them all there sounded these deepest notes of sin, of love, of judgment.

B. THE TEACHINGS OF THE PROPHET

In any attempt to analyze and tabulate the teaching contained in this second division of the book, it must be remembered that the prophetic utterances cannot be treated as verbatim reports. As they here appear, they are rather the gathering up of the notes or leading ideas of a long period of preaching. In our analysis the method is that of indicating, not the periods at which the messages were delivered, but rather their subject matter.

They fall into three distinct cycles, dealing with pollution and its cause; pollution and its punishment; and the love of Jehovah.

In dealing with pollution and its cause the prophet first preferred a general charge against the nation. Israel was summoned to attend and hear the word of the Lord because He had a controversy with the inhabitants of the land. The charge made was that of the absence of truth and mercy and knowledge of God, and the consequent widespread existence of all kinds of evil. The result was to be seen in the mourning land, the languishing people, and the fact that man's dominion over nature was lost.

The prophet next declared the cause of the sin and more carefully described the results. The cause was that of the pollution of the priests. Priest and prophet stumbled, and the people were destroyed for lack of knowledge. As the priests multiplied they sinned, and their glory was changed to shame. The result was the pollution of the people. Following the example of the priests, they had ended in lack of understanding. The prophet declared that God would not punish for the smaller offense of physical harlotry, but for the more terrible outrage of spiritual adultery which lay behind it. In this connection he counseled Judah to take warning by the terrible example of Israel.

Having thus declared the cause of pollution, the prophet's next message was specially addressed to priest, people, and king. First to the priests and the king as leaders and responsible, though the people were included as having followed the false lead. The message affirmed the Divine knowledge of the condition of affairs, and announced the inevitable judgment which must follow. A threefold method of judgment was indicated. First that of the moth and rottenness, which is slow destruction; secondly, that of the young lion, which is strong devouring judgment; and finally, that of withdrawal, which is the most terrible of all. The section closes with the plaintive plea of the prophet which constituted his appeal in consequence of the judgment threatened. In its local application it was a call to return to Jehovah, based upon the certainty of the Divine pity, and a declaration of the equal certainty of prosperity if there were such a return to Him. The appeal is full of beauty, and has in it Messianic values, for all that the prophet declared finds its fulfillment only in the Christ, by way of His first and second advents.

Passing to pollution and its punishment, the prophetic word first stated the case as it existed between Jehovah and His people. The Divine attitude toward the people was affirmed to be that of perplexity. In the presence of the shallowness of their goodness, Jehovah had adopted different methods in His desire for their welfare. The human response had been that of persistent transgression and treachery, the proofs of which were to be found in Gilead and Shechem. The true state of affairs was that of the Divine desire to heal, frustrated by the discovery of pollution, and by their persistent ignoring of God. The pollution of the nation was manifest in the king, the princes, and the judges. The prophet described Ephraim as mixing among the people, with reference to the widespread influence of that tribe; as a cake not turned, indicating utter failure, being undeveloped on one side, and on the other destroyed by burning; as a silly dove, indicating fear and cowardice. The statement of the case was concluded by a declaration of the utter folly of the people whom God was scourging toward redemption. They responded by howling, assembling, and rebelling.

From this statement of the case the prophet turned to the pronouncement of judgment. This he did first by the figure of the trumpet lifted to the mouth, uttering five blasts, in each of which the sin of the people was set forth as revealing the reason of judgment. The first blast declared the coming of judgment under the figure of an eagle, because of transgression and trespass. The second emphasized Israel's sin of rebellion, in that they had set up kings and princes without the authority of Jehovah. The third dealt with Israel's idolatry, announcing that Jehovah had cast off the calf of Samaria. The fourth denounced Israel's alliances, and declared that her hire among the nations had issued in her diminishing. The fifth drew attention to the altars of sin, and announced the coming judgment.

The judgment is then described in detail. Its first note was that of the death of joy; Israel could not find her joy like other peoples; having known Jehovah, all to which she turned in turning from Him, failed to satisfy. The second note was that of the actual exile to which she must pass; back to the slavery of Egypt and Assyria, away from the offerings and feasts of the Lord. The third was that of the cessation of prophecy; the means of testing themselves would be corrupted. The fourth declared the nemesis of fornication; the prophet traced the growth of this pollution from its beginnings at Baal-peor, and clearly set forth the inevitable deterioration of the impure people. The fifth and last was that of the final casting out of the people by God, so that they should become wanderers among the nations. This section closes with the prophet's recapitulation and appeal. The whole case is stated under the figure of the vine. Israel was a vine of God's planting which had turned its fruitfulness to evil account, and was therefore doomed to His judgment. The result of this judgment would be the lament of the people that they had no king who was able to save them, and chastisement would inevitably follow. The last word was that of earnest and passionate appeal to return to loyalty.

The third cycle of the prophecy sets forth the love which Jehovah had for His people, notwithstanding their sin. This section contains a declaration of this attitude of Jehovah towards His sinning people, and is for the most part the speech of Jehovah Himself. He sums up, and in so doing declares His sense of the awfulness of the sin, pronouncing His righteous judgment thereupon. Yet throughout the movement the dominant notes are those of His love, and the ultimate victory of that love over sin, and consequently over judgment. Thrice in the course of this great message of Jehovah to the people, the prophet interpolates words of his own. In studying the section it is necessary to take the words of Jehovah in sequence, and then the interpolations of the prophet in sequence also. This division will easily be made by examination of the text.

The message of Jehovah falls into three clearly marked movements which deal respectively with the present in the light of past love; the present in the light of present love; the present in the light of future love.

In the first, Jehovah reminded the people of all His past love for them in words full of tenderness, setting their present condition in its light, and crying, "How shall I give thee up?" His own inquiry was answered by the determined declaration of the ultimate triumph of love, and the restoration of the people.

In the second, Jehovah set the present sin in the light of His present love. The sin of Ephraim and its pride and impertinence were distinctly stated, and yet over all, love would triumph. Jehovah declared Himself to be the God Who had delivered from Egypt, and Who would be true to the messages of prophets, to the visions of seers, to the similitudes of the ministry of the prophets.

Finally He set the present condition of Israel in the light of His future love. Sin abounded, and therefore judgment was absolutely unavoidable. Nevertheless, the almighty strength of love must overcome at last.

Turning from this main line of the Divine message, we must examine the prophet's interpolations. These set forth the history of Israel indicating their relation to Jehovah, and pronounce judgment. They form a remarkable obligato accompaniment in a minor key to the majestic love song of Jehovah, and constitute a contrasting introduction to the final message of the prophet.

The first of them reveals the prophet's sense of Jehovah's controversy with Judah, and His just dealings with Jacob. The second was reminiscent of Jacob's history, and made a deduction and an appeal. The third traced the progress of Israel to death, beginning with the flight to the field of Aram, through the exodus from Egypt and preservation to the present, in which Ephraim was exalted in Israel, offended in Baal, and died. The last declared the doom. It was indeed the last word of man, the pronouncement of awful judgment, and constituted the plea of "guilty," to which the answer of Jehovah, as revealed in His message, was that of the victory of love.

The cycle closes with a final call of the prophet, with the promise of Jehovah. The call was to the people to return, because they had fallen by iniquity. It suggested the method as being that of bringing the words of penitence, and forsaking all false gods. To this Jehovah answered in a message full of hope for the people, declaring that He would restore, renew, and ultimately reinstate.

JOEL—*The Day of the Lord*

<table>
<tr>
<td>

A
THINGS PRESENT
i.—ii. 27

</td>
<td>

B
THINGS TO COME
ii. 28—iii.

</td>
</tr>
<tr>
<td>

Title Page.   1

I. Locust Plague and First Meaning
i. 2-20

i. The Call to Contemplation.   2-12
ii. The Call to Humiliation.   13-20

II. Locust Plague and Deeper Teaching
ii. 1-27

i. The Trumpet of Alarm and Answer of God.
     1-14
ii. The Trumpet of Repentance and Answer
of God.   15-27

</td>
<td>

I. The Dispensation of the Spirit
ii. 28-32

i. Initiation and Characteristics.   28-29
ii. Signs of Ending and Coming of the Day
of the Lord.   30-31
iii. Deliverance from Terrors of that Day.   32

II. The Day of the Lord   iii.

i. God's Dealings with His Ancient People.
     1-8
ii. God's Judgment of the Nations.   9-16
iii. The Restoration of Israel.   17-21

</td>
</tr>
</table>

JOEL * * * *

JOEL WAS SPECIALLY a prophet to Judah. It is impossible to speak dogmatically concerning the date of his prophesying. Internal evidence makes it plain that he was one of the earliest, or one of the latest, of the prophets. The burden of his message was the Day of the Lord. It seems to be one remarkable utterance rather than notes of a ministry covering a long period, as in the case of Hosea. A terrible locust plague which had devastated the entire country was the occasion of its deliverance. He spoke of things which were evident to those whom he addressed, then predicted an immediate judgment, and finally looked far on to the ultimate Day of the Lord. Thus the book may be divided into two parts—Things present (i.-ii. 27); Things to come (ii. 28-iii.).

A. THINGS PRESENT

In the first division there are two sections. Joel interpreted the meaning of the actual locust plague, and then declared that it was a sign of yet severer judgment imminent. In dealing with the actual locust plague, he called the old men and all the inhabitants to contemplation. Singling out the drunkards, the worshippers, the husbandmen, and the vine-dressers, he reminded them of the completeness of the devastation, showing how it had affected all classes. He then proceeded to call the people to humiliation. Beginning with the priests, he included the whole nation, and at last voiced the cry of the people.

Having thus dealt with the actual visitation and its terrible devastation, and having called the people into the place of humiliation, the prophet rose to a higher level, and interpreted the visitation as indicating a deeper and more terrible judgment which threatened them. In doing this, he made use of the figure of the blowing of a trumpet.

The first blast sounded a note of alarm as it announced the approach of the Day of Jehovah. With the figure of the locusts still in mind, he described the swift, irresistible, and all-consuming character of the armies which were about to come as the scourge of God upon the people, being careful to declare that this whole movement would be under the command of Jehovah. The prophet, however, declared that God still waited. If the people would return to Him, He would spare them.

Then the second blast of the trumpet called for an assembly of the people in the attitude of repentance. The character of the assembly was to be that of a fast, and its constitution the actual gathering together of all the people, from the youngest to the oldest. Being assembled, they were to cry for mercy, the ultimate reason being that the nations should not say, "Where is their God?" To such attitude Jehovah would respond in grace. The prophet insisted that both the things of judgment and the things of mercy were in the government of God; the first, rendered necessary by the people's neglect of Him; the second, made possible by their return to Him. At this point ended the second chapter of the prophecy in the Bible of the Hebrews. The prophet, having indicated the judgment imminent, and called the people to

-284

repentance; and having, moreover, declared the merciful attitude of Jehovah toward such repentance, had come to the end of his message as it had to do with things then present.

B. THINGS TO COME

He now moved on to a yet higher level, and there was granted to him a vision of the final Day of the Lord, of which the things then present were but the shadow and forecast. In this second section he dealt wholly with things to come. The great word introducing it is *afterward*. Some of the things foretold have now been fulfilled, some are still in the future.

In looking toward the distant Day of Jehovah, Joel saw an intervening period of an entirely different character. This he first described, ending his message with a declaration concerning the Day of the Lord, which was the real burden on his spirit.

Of the intervening period, he declared that its initiation would result from the outpouring of the Spirit upon all flesh. It would be characterized by prophecy, dreams, and visions. The signs of the end of this period and of the approach of the Day of the Lord, would be "wonders in the heavens and in the earth." From the terrors of the Day such as called upon the name of the Lord were to be delivered.

This is a perfect description of the Pentecostal age in which we now live, with a statement of the signs which will precede its end, and a declaration of the way of deliverance from the terrors immediately to follow.

Finally, the prophet saw in the far distance the ultimate Day of Jehovah. In this He will first restore Judah and Jerusalem, and then find His scattered people Israel. Following this, His judgment of the nations is to proceed. The last vision of the prophet is that of the complete restoration of the ancient people, in which Jehovah will dwell in Zion—a city holy and full of prosperity.

AMOS—*National Accountability*

A DECLAMA-TIONS *i.—ii.*	B PROCLAMATIONS *iii.—vi.*	C REVELATIONS *vii.—ix. 10*	D RESTORA-TIONS *ix. 11-15*
Title Page. I. 2			
I. Damascus i. 3-5	**I. Jehovah's Verdict and Sentence** iii.	**I. The Locusts** vii. 1-3	**I. Restoration. Preliminary** 11-13
II. Gaza i. 6-8	i. Privileged People to be Punished. 1-2 ii. The Prophet's Vindication of himself. 3-8 iii. Reason of Punishment. 9-15	Judgment Threatened and Restrained. **II. The Fire** vii. 4-6	i. "I will." ii. "That they may."
III. Tyre i. 9-10	**II. Jehovah's Summons** iv.	Judgment Threatened and Restrained.	**II. Restoration. Progressive** 14
IV. Edom i. 11-12	i. Indictment of the Women. 1-3 ii. Final Summons to the People. 4-13	**III. The Plumb Line** vii. 7-9	i. "I will." ii. "They shall."
V. Children of Ammon i. 13-15	**III. Lamentation and its Causes** v.—vi.	Judgment Determined. (Historical Interpolation. vii. 10-17)	**III. Restoration. Permanent** 15
VI. Moab ii. 1-3	i. The Lamentation. v. 1-2 ii. The Sequence of Explanations. v. 3-17 iii. The Double Woe. v. 18—vi.	**IV. The Basket of Summer Fruit** viii.	i. "I will." ii. "They shall."
VII. Judah ii. 4-5		Judgment at Hand.	
VIII. Israel ii. 6-16		**V. Jehovah** ix. 1-10 Judgment Executed.	

AMOS ✳ ✳ ✳ ✳

AMOS WAS PRACTICALLY contemporary with Hosea. In the reign of Jeroboam he came out of Tekoa to Bethel. In all probability his messages were delivered during the short period when Jeroboam was king of Israel and Uzziah king of Judah. The latter years of the reign of Jeroboam were characterized by great material prosperity on the one hand, and on the other by the prevalence of injustice, oppression, and vice. The poor were ground down under the heel of the rich. This material prosperity was construed by the people as evidence of Divine protection, while yet they were forgetful of the requirements of the law.

The burden of his message is that of national accountability, which he delivered in a series of declamations against the nations as such; in set addresses to the chosen people; in a series of visions which deal with the coming judgment; and in a brief final word, prophetic of ultimate restoration.

The book falls naturally, therefore, into these divisions: Declamation (i., ii.); Proclamation (iii.-vi.); Revelation (vii.-ix. 10); Restoration (ix. 11-15).

A. DECLAMATION

The second verse of the first chapter gives us the key to the book. Jehovah declared Himself in judgment.

Beginning at the point furthest from Israel, the prophet delivered his messages to the nations as such. Each in turn is seen to pass before Jehovah and receive sentence.

The sin of Syria had been that of cruelty. Jehovah's patience had been manifested. At last sentence was uttered; the flame would devour; all defense would be useless, and the people would be driven into captivity.

The sin of Philistia had been that of the slave trade. Here, as before, and as in each subsequent case, the form of the declaration reveals the patience of God. Philistia would be visited with the devouring flame, her inhabitants be cut off, and even the remnant perish. Phœnicia's special guilt had been that, in spite of the covenant made, she had acted as a slave agent. Edom was doomed for determined and revengeful unforgiveness. The children of Ammon were specially denounced for cruelty based upon cupidity.

Moab's chief wickedness had been her shocking and vindictive hatred.

Having thus uttered the word of God concerning the surrounding nations, thereby revealing the fact of His government over all, the prophet turned to Judah, and declared that she also was to share the doom of the other nations, because she had despised the law of Jehovah, and had not kept His statutes.

Finally, he spoke to Israel. All the foregoing had been in preparation for this. He described the sins of Israel in detail and with almost startling directness. He charged the people with injustice, avarice, oppression, immorality, profanity, blasphemy, and sacrilege. Moreover, he declared that their sin had been greatly aggravated by the privileges which they had enjoyed. They had seen the Amorites destroyed before them for the very sins which they themselves had subsequently committed. They had been brought up out of

B. Proclamations

Egypt, and so knew the power of Jehovah. They had raised up sons for prophets, and young men for Nazarites. These sons they had corrupted, having given wine to the Nazarites, and silenced the prophets. The sentence against them was that of oppression and judgment; from which there should be no possibility of escape.

B. PROCLAMATIONS

Having thus uttered the declamations of Jehovah's judgment upon all the nations, the prophet proceeded to deliver his special message to Israel. This was done in a series of three discourses. In each the introductory word is "Hear this word."

The first discourse consists of a statement of Jehovah's verdict and sentence. It opens with a simple declaration that the privileged people were to be punished; their privileges were named, and their punishment announced.

In view of the probability that the people would object to this message, the prophet, in an interpolation, defended himself. By a series of seven questions he illustrated a principle which may thus be stated—an effect proves a cause. The illustrations may thus be summarized: communion proves agreement; the lion roaring proves the prey; the cry of the young lion proves the prey possessed; the fall of a bird proves the bait; the springing of the snare proves the bird to be taken; the trumpet proves alarm; calamity in the city proves Jehovah. From this principle the prophet deduced an application: Jehovah hath roared, therefore fear; Jehovah hath spoken, therefore prophesy.

Turning back to the main argument, Amos proclaimed

the punishment of the privileged, and declared its reason. The reason was stated to the heathen, who were invited to witness the justice of the doom.

The second discourse consists of Jehovah's summons to the people.

It commences with a severe and terrible indictment of the women. He addressed them as "Ye kine of Bashan," which description reveals the fact of the degradation of womanhood to mere animalism. The prophet described their doings, declaring that they oppressed the poor and crushed the needy, and said unto their lords, "Bring and let us drink." Their doom would be that they would be taken away with hooks, that is, in shame and helplessness, and in the presence of judgment would take refuge in wild flight.

He then uttered the final summons to the people. In this call there was a piece of stinging satire. They were to come to Bethel to transgress; to Gilgal to multiply transgression. Their sacrifices they were to offer every morning instead of once a year; their tithe every third day instead of every third year; their sacrifice was leavened; they made freewill offerings and published them.

He then described God's patience and their perversity. He had spoken to them by famine, by drought, by blasting and mildew, by pestilence and sword, by earthquake. After each description the prophet declared, "Yet have ye not returned to me." All this culminated in a great call, "Prepare to meet thy God."

The third discourse was a description of Jehovah's judgment. This opened with a lamentation for the virgin of Israel, "She shall no more rise, she is cast down upon her land; there is none to raise her up." Following this the prophet uttered a sequence of explanations, each commenc-

ing with the words, "Thus saith the Lord." Finally he pronounced the double woe. Two classes of the sinning people
were addressed. First those who desired "the day of the
Lord," that is most evidently, according to the description,
the hypocrites. They were religionists who kept feasts, observed solemn assemblies, brought burnt meal and peace
offerings, sang songs and made melody with viols; but who,
nevertheless, were living the life of sin. With tremendous
force the prophet described God's attitude toward such: "I
hate, I despise. . . . I will take no delight. . . . I will not
accept . . . neither will I regard. . . . I will not hear." Jehovah's call was for righteousness and judgment. The "day
of the Lord" for the hypocrites would be one of darkness
and destruction. The second class were the indifferent, those
"that are at ease in Zion." The prophet described them as
living in luxury and abandoned to animalism, declaring that
against them Jehovah would proceed in swift and terrible
judgment.

C. REVELATION

In this division the prophet gave a fivefold vision of judgment, introduced in the first four cases by the words, "The
Lord God shewed me." The last vision was that of Jehovah
Himself. The vision of the locusts declared judgment to be
threatened and restrained in answer to intercession. The
prophet saw the locusts eating up the grass, and made intercession on behalf of the people. In answer to this Jehovah
repented, and judgment was arrested. The vision of the fire
had the same significance. The prophet saw the devouring
fire, and interceded. His intercession was answered by Jehovah's repentance, and the judgment was restrained. The
vision of the plumb line is different. Jehovah was seen stand-

ing by a wall testing it with a plumbline. Having done so, He appealed to the prophet. No charge was made; but it is evident that as Amos beheld, he realized all the irregularities the plumb line revealed. There was no intercession. Doom was determined.

So long as prophecy was mingled with messages of mercy it was tolerated by the people. Directly that element was missing, hostility broke forth, and we have an interpolation upon the revelation, giving the story of the opposition of Amaziah and the answer of Amos. This Amaziah was an imposter, and yet held the position of priest of Bethel. He reported to Jeroboam what Amos was saying, advising his exile. He, moreover, attempted to appeal to the fear of Amos, and advised him to flee to Judah. The answer of Amos was full of dignity born of the consciousness of the Divine authority of his commission. He declared that he was no prophet, but that Jehovah had taken him and spoken to him, thus he had become a prophet in very deed. Then, answering Amaziah, he declared that God's judgment would overtake him.

The next vision, that of the basket of summer fruit, indicated the imminence of the judgment. Jehovah declared that the end was come, that He would not pass by them any more. This announcement was followed on the part of the prophet by an impassioned address to the money-makers, in which he first declared the effect of their lust for gain. They swallowed the needy, and caused the poor to fail. He described the intensity of that lust; the new moon and sabbath were irksome. Then there is a figurative description of judgment which declared Jehovah's perpetual consciousness of these things, and His consequent retribution. The final issue of judgment the prophet declared to be a famine of the words of the Lord, as a result of which there would come eager and fruitless search, followed by the fainting of the youth for lack.

The final vision was that of judgment executed. In this there was no symbol, no sign. We hear the manifesto of Jehovah Himself. It is one of the most awe-inspiring visions of the whole Bible.

The message proceeded in two phases. First an announcement of judgment, irrevocable and irresistible; secondly, a declaration of the procedure as reasonable and discriminative. Jehovah is seen standing by the altar, declaring the stroke of destruction to be inevitable, and all attempts at escape futile, because He has proceeded to action. While the judgment is to be reasonable and discriminative, the claims in which Israel had trusted were nothing. They became as children of Ethiopians. Philistines and Syrians had also been led by God. The eyes of Jehovah were on the sinful kingdom. The sifting process must go forward, but no grain of wheat should perish.

D. RESTORATION

The phrase "In that day" indicates the closing message of restoration and all that is to precede it. It is now declared that the reason of the Divine judgment is not revenge, but that it is the only way in which it is possible to usher in the restored order upon which the heart of God is set. The process of restoration is described as threefold. First, preliminary, "I will raise up . . . that they may possess." Then as to progress, "I will bring again the captivity . . . they shall build the waste cities . . . plant vineyards . . . make gardens." Finally, the permanent, "I will plant them . . . they shall no more be plucked up."

OBADIAH—*The Curse of Cowardice*

OBADIAH   ✳ ✳ ✳ ✳

THERE IS NO personal history of Obadiah, and it is impossible accurately to fix the date of his prophecy. The only ground on which it may be done is that of the capture of Jerusalem, to which reference is so clearly made. Certain passages in Jeremiah, apparently quoted from this book, make it probable that the capture referred to is that by Nebuchadnezzar. The corrected tense in verses 12-14 in the Revised Version, "Look not," instead of "Thou shouldest not have looked," would seem to indicate that the prophecy was uttered before the fall of Jerusalem, and not after it. The nation at this time was a hive of political disturbance. The people were divided into factions and parties. Fierce passions characterized these parties, and evil counsels prevailed. The whole nation was rushing headlong toward a great catastrophe. Obadiah had a vision of the attitude of Edom toward the chosen people in their calamity, and his message was delivered concerning them. It was not spoken to Edom, but to Israel, and was intended as a word of comfort for those who, loyal to Jehovah, were yet suffering with the whole nation. Its message falls into two parts: The Judgment of Edom (2-16); the Restoration of Israel (17-21).

A. THE JUDGMENT OF EDOM

The prophecy opens with a peculiarly dignified and authoritative introduction, which sets forth the method of communication, the value of the message, its subject, and a confirmatory coincidence.

The doom of Edom was announced in an address of Jehovah which asserted His act, declared the proud attitude of Edom, and announced the superior power of God. This was followed by the commentary of the prophet, consisting of his exclamations of astonishment, and his address to Edom, which declared that the events and men in which Edom had trusted were working Jehovah's will. This commentary was followed by a second address of Jehovah, foretelling the destruction of the wise men and the dismay of the mighty.

The reason for the doom was then stated. First broadly, Edom had done violence to his brother Jacob. In the day of Jacob's struggle Edom stood aloof, and subsequently joined the enemies. Then, in the form of a warning, the prophet indicated the attitude of Edom: in the day of disaster, "Look not"; in the day of destruction, "Rejoice not"; in the day of distress, "Speak not proudly"; in the day of calamity, "Enter not into the gate, . . . look not on affliction, . . . lay not hands on substance"; in the day of distress "Cut not off . . . deliver not up."

While these words were spoken as a warning, they declared exactly what Edom would do, and the final word of judgment announced the doom impending.

B. RESTORATION OF ISRAEL

While the prophet saw the coming judgment, and uttered his curse upon the cowardice of the people who rejoiced in the calamity, he yet saw the day of restoration, and spoke of it for the comfort of the afflicted people. He first declared

B. Restoration of Israel

that there should be a delivered remnant in Mount Zion which should be holy. He then foretold the fact that the people would be victorious, a conquering people, possessing their own land. The final word of the prophecy is the final word of all prophecy, "The kingdom shall be Jehovah's."

JONAH—*Condemnation of Exclusiveness*

A THE FIRST COMMISSION *i.—ii.*		B THE SECOND COMMISSION *iii.—iv.*	
I. The Prophet's Commission and Disobedience	**i. 1-3**	**I. The Prophet's Commission and Obedience**	**iii.**
		i. The Commission.	1-2
		ii. The Obedience.	3-4
		iii. The Result.	5-10
II. Jehovah's Interposition	**i. 4—ii.**	**II. The Prophet and Jehovah**	**iv.**
i. The Tempest.	i. 4-14	i. Jonah displeased.	1-3
ii. Jonah cast out.	i. 15-17	ii. Jehovah.	4-8
iii. The Experiences of the Deep.	ii. 1-9	iii. Jonah distressed.	8
iv. The Deliverance.	ii. 10	iv. Jehovah.	9-11

JONAH   ✳ ✳ ✳ ✳

JONAH WAS THE son of Amittai. There can be no reasonable possibility of doubt as to his identity with the prophet referred to in 2 Kings xiv. 25. These names, Jonah and Amittai, occur nowhere else in the Old Testament. It is evident therefore that Jonah exercised his ministry about the time of the accession of Jeroboam II. This would make him an early contemporary of Hosea and Amos.

The relation of the Hebrew people to foreign nations at this period was characterized by a strange contradiction. They were making political alliances with outside nations, while yet religiously they were bitterly exclusive. Both these attitudes were wrong in the measure in which they misinterpreted the Divine attitude and prostituted the Divine purpose. The book as we have it was undoubtedly written for Israel, and is a prophetic story.

In narrating his own experience in the matter of his commission to Nineveh, Jonah intended to teach his people the lesson of the inclusiveness of the Divine government, and thus to rebuke the exclusiveness of their attitude toward surrounding peoples.

The book naturally falls into two parts: the First Commission (i., ii.); the Second Commission (iii., iv.).

A. THE FIRST COMMISSION

In this first division we have the prophet's account of Jehovah's command, his own disobedience, and the Divine interposition.

There was evidently no doubt in his mind that the command was from Jehovah. In order to understand how strange a commission it must have seemed to Jonah, it is necessary to remember the national prejudice of the Hebrew against all other peoples in the matter of religion. Believing in Jehovah as a loving God, they yet thought of Him as their God exclusively. The charge to deliver a message to a city outside the covenant, and one moreover which was the center of a power which had been oppressive and cruel, must have been a startling one to Jonah. His attempt to escape was an act of willful disobedience. The statement that he went out from the presence of the Lord is equivalent to a declaration that he abandoned his prophetic office and work. Circumstances seemed to favor him, as he found a ship at Joppa going to Tarshish. Outside the path of duty he recognized that he was chargeable to himself, and with a touch of fine, if mistaken, independence he paid his fare.

His going out from the presence of the Lord did not, however, ensure his escape from His government. All the forces of nature are at the command of God, and are pressed into His service when need requires. The ship had started on her course, but Jehovah sent out a wind. The incidents of the storm are full of interest. In reading the account of it one cannot help feeling that Jonah when he ultimately wrote the book which tells the story of his failure had indeed learned the lesson which he intended to teach others, for the men outside the covenant are revealed in such a way as to suggest how much of good was in them. Terrified by the storm, and at their wits' end, they nevertheless made every possible effort to save the life of Jonah. The governing God however, Who had sent out the wind, presided over the casting of the lots, and at last Jonah was cast out into the deep. There he was received by the fish, *prepared*. In the midst of the strange and awful circumstances he poured out his soul in anguish before God. The prayer, as chronicled, consists of quotations from the book of Psalms. It is exactly the kind of cry which a man, familiar with the sacred penitential writings of his people, would utter in such circumstances. [Again Jehovah interfered, and the prophet was released.]

B. THE SECOND COMMISSION

Immediately he was charged to go to Nineveh. There is a fine revelation of the patient grace of God toward His servant in the declaration, "The word of the Lord came unto Jonah *the second time*." With a new sense of the authority of Jehovah, Jonah arose and obeyed.

It was a strange and startling thing for Nineveh, this coming into it of a man who had been cast out to the deep; and it is easy to understand how the monotony of his declaration, that within forty days Nineveh should be destroyed, would fill the hearts of the people with terror. They heard, they believed, they were filled with fear, and repented from the greatest to the least. This repentance on their part was answered by the repentance of God, so that the doom was averted, and the city was spared.

All this leads to the final picture of the controversy between Jonah and Jehovah, which revealed in the most vivid light, on the part of Jonah, the attitude of the ancient people which his story was intended to correct; and on the part of Jehovah, that attitude of care for, and patience with all sinning peoples, which they so little understood. The prophet was angry because mercy had been exercised toward those outside the covenant. Of course, behind this was a strict sense of justice. He could not comprehend why a people so cruel and oppressive should be spared. It seemed a violation of justice, and in his anger he asked that his own life might be taken. The wrong of this attitude lay in the fact of Jonah's knowledge of God. He declared that he knew Him to be "a gracious God, and full of compassion, slow to anger and plenteous in mercy." The answer of Jehovah is a wonderful revelation of His patience. It consists of a question: "Doest thou well to be angry?" Without reply the prophet went out of the city, and in distress and resentment sat in a booth of his own making to watch the course of events.

Again the overruling of Jehovah was manifest in the *prepared* gourd, the *prepared* worm, and the *prepared* sultry east wind. So great was the anger and anguish of the prophet that he fainted, and asked again that he might die. Jehovah repeated His question, but now with a new application, "Doest thou well to be angry for the gourd?" He who had been angry that the city was not destroyed, was angry that the gourd was destroyed, and he answered the inquiry by affirming, "I do well to be angry, even unto death."

Thus the last picture we have of Jonah is that of a man still out of harmony with the tender mercy of God, and the last vision of Jehovah is that of a God full of pity and compassion even for a city such as Nineveh, and willing to spare it as it returned to Him in penitence. Thus in the story, Jonah unveils an episode in his life which reflected upon him, as it revealed a side of the Divine nature of which the people had no appreciation. It was a revelation far in advance of the age in which Jonah exercised his ministry.

–304

B. *The Second Commission*

As a matter of fact, the people as a whole never came to understand it, and thus in his persistent displeasure Jonah represented the nation in its ultimate failure to understand the deepest truth concerning their God.

MICAH—*Authority False and True*

A TO THE NATIONS— CONCERNING THE CHOSEN *i.—ii.*	B TO THE RULERS— CONCERNING THE COMING ONE *iii.—v.*	C TO THE CHOSEN— CONCERNING THE CONTROVERSY *vi.—vii.*
Title Page. 1 **I. The Summons i. 2-4**	**I. Sin and consequent Judgment iii. 1-12**	**I. The Prophet vi. 1-2** The Summons.
II. The Proclamation of Jehovah i. 5-7	i. The Princes. 1-4 ii. The Prophets. 5-8 iii. All Ruling Classes. 9-12	**II. Jehovah vi. 3-5** A plaintive Appeal.
III. The Prophetic Message i. 8—ii. 5	**II. The Coming One and consequent Deliverance iv.—v.**	**III. The People vii. 6-7** Questions of Conviction. **IV. The Prophet vi. 8-9** The Answer.
i. Lamentation of the Prophet. i. 8-10 ii. A wailing Description of the Judgment. i. 11-16 iii. The Cause stated. ii. 1-5	i. The Vision of restored Order. iv.—v. 1 ii. The Deliverer and the Deliverance. v. 2-15	**V. Jehovah vi. 10-16** A terrible Charge.
IV. The False Prophets ii. 6-11		**VI. The People vii. 1-10** Confession and Hope.
V. The Promise of Deliverance ii. 12-13		**VII. The Prophet vii. 11-13** The Answer of Hope. **VIII. The People vii. 14** At Prayer. **IX. Jehovah vii. 15** The Answer of Peace. **X. The Prophet vii. 16-17** Faith expressing the Promise. **XI. The People vii. 18-20** The final Doxology.

MICAH   * * * *

MICAH PROPHESIED IN the early part of the reign of king Hezekiah. He was contemporary with Isaiah. He began his ministry after Uzziah's death, and it must have closed in the early part of Hezekiah's reign, for the idolatries which he rebuked were done away at Hezekiah's reformation. His message was peculiarly to the cities, as centers affecting the national thought and action. This he distinctly affirmed in his opening words. The prophecy is a declaration of a Divine program, and consists of three addresses, each beginning with a call to hear. Micah declared to those in authority in the cities, which were centers of authority, the messages of the One Whose authority is supreme.

The book may thus be divided: a Message to the Nations concerning the Chosen (i.-ii.); a Message to the Rulers concerning the Coming One (iii.-v.); a Message to the Chosen concerning the Controversy (vi.-vii.).

A. TO THE NATIONS CONCERNING THE CHOSEN

This first message consists of a summons, a proclamation of Jehovah, and a prophetic message based upon the proclamation. This division ends with an account of the interruption of the false prophets, and finally the promise of ultimate deliverance.

In the summons the prophet had clearly in mind the attitude of Jehovah toward the whole earth. All peoples were called upon to attend. Israel was Jehovah's medium of teaching, if not in blessing, then in judgment. He witnessed among the nations by His dealings with Israel. The description of His coming forth from His place is full of poetic beauty. Under the figure of a great upheaval of nature the prophet described the advent of God.

The proclamation of Jehovah first declared the cause of judgment. It was "for the transgression of Jacob . . . for the sins of the house of Israel." The reason of judgment was declared to be the apostasy of the whole nation as evidenced in the cities. He next described the course of judgment, commencing with the destruction of the city, and the destruction of false religion. The city wherein was gathered the wealth and wherein authority was exercised, was to be demolished, and the religion of apostasy swept out.

Upon the basis of this proclamation the prophet delivered his message. This opens with a personal lamentation expressive of his own grief concerning the incurable wounds of the people.

This is followed by a wailing description of the judgment. The passage is a strange mixture of grief and satire. At the calamity he was grieved. Because of the sin he was angry. This merging of agony and anger flashes into satire. The connection or contrast is not easy to discover. A translation of the proper names appearing in this section may enable the reader to discover the remarkable play upon words which runs through it.

Following this, the prophet stated the cause of the imminent judgment. The sin consisted in the devising of evil at night, the practicing of it in the morning, and the abuse of authority. Covetousness, expressing itself in oppression,

B. *To the Rulers Concerning the Coming One*

was the peculiar sin of the rulers. Against this Jehovah proceeds in just retribution: "I devise an evil." The prophet then described the mockery of observers who would imitate their sorrow, and finally declared that they would be utterly dispossessed.

Micah was interrupted by the false prophets, who protested against his message, basing their objection upon the goodness of God. To them Jehovah's answer was that the changed and rebellious attitude of His people accounted for the change in His attitude toward them. Against the people misled by false prophets Micah indulged in indignant satire. The first message, delivered in the hearing of the nations, closes with words spoken to Jacob. It is an indefinite promise of deliverance yet to come.

B. TO THE RULERS CONCERNING THE COMING ONE

Addressing himself directly to the rulers of the people, in this second message the prophet described their peculiar sin, and announced the coming judgment. He then foretold the coming of the one true Ruler, and the consequent deliverance.

In dealing with the sins of the rulers, he first addressed the heads or princes, charging them with being corrupt. As to character, they hated the good, and as to conduct, they spoiled the people.

Turning to the prophets he declared that their sin consisted in the fact that they made the people to err, exercising their sacred office for their own welfare. If they were fed they were prepared to cry peace; if they were not fed they made war. Judgment must overtake them in kind. Micah defended his own ministry by putting it into contrast with others.

He finally dealt with all the ruling classes, and his summary of their sin is forceful. The heads judge for reward; the priests teach for hire; the prophets divine for money. As a result of their sin, judgment must fall on Zion and Jerusalem.

From this scene of a corrupt people governed by corrupt rulers, the prophet lifted his eyes, and looking into the future, saw the day when, under true government, deliverance should be wrought and the Divine order established. In this look ahead he saw the mountain of Jehovah's house established, and the peoples flowing into it. Out of Zion the Lord would come forth, and the Word of the Lord from Jerusalem. The result of this establishment of Divine authority would be the cessation of war, and peaceful possession of the land with all its benefits.

In the light of this future deliverance the prophet addressed himself to the present. In the midst of affliction there was assurance. Even while the cry of pain and travail was heard there was hope. He declared that there was to be yet further pain and suffering, but that the day of deliverance was certain.

Having thus described the coming deliverance, Micah uttered the wonderful prophecy concerning the Deliverer and the deliverance under His administration. The Person of the Deliverer is first described. He is One Whose goings forth are from of old, and when He comes it will be to Bethlehem Ephratah. His program is next described. Its first movement will be that of abandoning the people, and the second that of gathering and feeding them. The central declaration of the whole prophecy is found in this connection: "This man shall be peace." The local application of the foretelling is seen in the fact that Micah described the victory as one over Assyria. Its far-reaching value has become perfectly evident by the literal and local fulfillment. Concerning this coming deliverance the prophet then uttered the word of Jehovah which declared that in that day there will be the destruction of all the false confidence which had ruined the people through the period of their sin and unbelief.

C. TO THE CHOSEN CONCERNING THE CONTROVERSY

This closing section is dramatic and magnificent. The prophet summoned Israel and the mountains to hear the controversy of Jehovah with His people. The key word is "Jehovah . . . will plead."

From there the address falls into dramatic form. It sets forth the controversy in which Jehovah, the prophet, and the people take part. Jehovah utters a plaintive appeal in which He asks His people what He has done to weary them. In answer to this the people inquire how they may appear before Him in view of the complaint made against them in His appeal. This inquiry of the people the prophet then answers, telling them what Jehovah requires of them. Immediately the voice of Jehovah is heard crying to the city and describing its sins, declaring them to be the reason of His visitation. This constitutes a terrible charge against them. Following it, the people break forth into a lamentation which is of the nature of a confession, submission to judgment, and hope.

The prophet then breaks out into an answer of hope, which yet ends with the consciousness of the necessity for judgment. Following this the people offer prayer for the guidance of Jehovah; and Jehovah answers with a promise that He will guide them as of old. Then the prophet in faith repeats the promise Jehovah has made.

The last movement is that of a great final doxology uttered by all the people, which celebrates the patience of God, and His certain restoration of His people.

NAHUM—*Vindication of Vengeance*

A VERDICT OF VENGEANCE *i.*	B VISION OF VENGEANCE *ii.*	C VINDICATION OF VENGEANCE *iii.*
I. Subject and Method 1	I. Preliminary Declaration 1-2	I. Vice declared and Vengeance 1-3
II. Jehovah 2-8	II. The Vision of Vengeance 3-10	II. Vice described and Vengeance 4-7
III. The Verdict 9-14	III. The Prophet's Exultation 11-13	III. Vice dissected and Vengeance 8-17
IV. The Cry to Judah 15		IV. Vice destroyed 18-19

NAHUM * * * *

NOTHING MORE IS known of the prophet Nahum than is declared in the title. He was a native of Elkosh, but this town cannot be located with any certainty. Some place it in Assyria, and defend this by the traditions, and by his evident acquaintance with local terms. Some place it in Palestine, and quote his reference to Lebanon, Carmel, and Bashan. The location is uncertain and unimportant.

The date of the prophecy must have been after the fall of Thebes, 663 B.C. (see iii. 8, where No-amon refers to Thebes), and before the fall of Nineveh, 606 B.C. This is sufficiently definite, and there is practical unanimity concerning the date.

There is suggestiveness in the meaning of the prophet's name, which signifies "the full of exceeding comfort."

At the time of the utterance of the prophecy, the northern kingdom had been destroyed, and the ten tribes dispersed. The prophet's message was to Judah, and it was delivered almost certainly during the days succeeding Hezekiah's reign, and probably in close connection with Manasseh's return from captivity. The Assyrian power was at its very height, and the descriptions given of it reveal its arrogance and habitual oppression of others. Nahum was not sent to Nineveh, as Jonah was. The time of such opportunity for her was forever passed. The message of Nahum was that of the full end determined. It was a declaration of the vengeance of God upon Nineveh, and may thus be divided: the Verdict

-*315*

of Vengeance (i.); the Vision of Vengeance (ii.); the Vindication of Vengeance (iii.).

A. THE VERDICT OF VENGEANCE

The prophet preceded the announcement of the verdict by a section dealing wholly with Jehovah Himself. In this we find, first, a declaration of His character, then a revelation of His majesty, and finally an affirmation of His method. As to His character, He is a God of vengeance and yet the central fact of His nature is that He is slow to anger.

Under the figure of a storm the prophet set forth the overwhelming majesty of Jehovah. The description of the storm moves in two sections—a hurricane on the sea, a simoom over the land. He finally described the method of God; as toward His friends He is "good, a stronghold"; toward His foes "he will make a full end."

Having thus set forth the majesty of Jehovah, the prophet proceeded to declare His verdict concerning Nineveh. Addressing himself to Nineveh, he inquired, "What do ye imagine against the Lord?" This hints at the deepest sin of Nineveh, namely, that she had set herself up wilfully against the power of God. In answer to his own question Nahum affirmed the irresistible nature of the judgment which must fall upon the city, and finally made his central charge against her; "There is one gone forth out of thee, that imagineth evil against the Lord, that counselleth wickedness." This charge in all probability referred to the blasphemous boasts of Sennacherib chronicled in Isaiah xxxvi. 18-20 and xxxvii. 10-13. As other prophets had summoned the nations to attend to God's controversy with Israel, Nahum addressed himself to the chosen people, declaring that the yoke of Assyria should be broken.

The last word in this first section is one which was addressed to Judah. The verdict of vengeance on Nineveh was an evangel to Judah.

B. THE VISION OF VENGEANCE

Having thus announced the verdict the prophet proceeded to describe the process of vengeance. He declared that the "hammer" had come up against Nineveh, and ironically advised her to prepare. He then gave in detail the process of Nineveh's destruction. The interpretations of this description greatly differ. I suggest that it falls into three clearly defined parts. First the conflict (3-5); secondly the conquest (6-9); finally the consummation (10). The picture of the conflict is a graphic one. We first see the attacking army outside the walls, then the defending host within the city. The battle itself is next described. The conquest of the city is secured by the act of God: "The gates of the rivers are opened. "It is interesting to remember that Diodorus Siculus mentions an old prophecy that the city would never be taken until the river became its enemy. He moreover declared that during an enemy's attack the river burst its banks, and washed away the wall for twenty stadia. Continuing, Nahum described the city under the figure of a woman and her attendants. They flee, and the enemy capture the spoil. Finally the consummation of judgment was announced. Nineveh "is empty, and void, and waste." The utter collapse of the people was set forth in figurative language. 'The heart melteth" indicates the failure of inward courage. "The knees smite together" indicates the failure of outward courage; the anguish in the loins the resulting agony; and the faces waxed pale the ultimate death.

The prophet then immediately broke forth into exultation. The den of the lions was gone, all the cruelty of Nineveh was at an end. He moreover recognized this as the righteous act of God. It was His act of vengeance. He was against Nineveh, therefore the overthrow was complete.

C. THE VINDICATION OF VENGEANCE

This last movement of the prophecy is devoted wholly to the vindication of Jehovah in His action with regard to Nineveh, and is a fitting defense of the introductory declarations concerning His character. Here in detail vice and vengeance are shown in their interrelation, the first being the reason of the second, and the second, therefore, the inevitable result of the first. There are four movements in this final message.

In the first vice is declared, and vengeance also. The prophet described Nineveh as a "bloody city," evil and cruel. A graphic description of vengeance, consisting of seven illustrations, followed.

In the second movement he more particularly described both the vice and the vengeance. The national method had been that of whoredom, that is, idolatrous practices; and witchcraft, that is, deceptive methods. The national influence had been that of selling nations and families. Jehovah's vengeance was then described, and its unquestioned righteousness in the inquiry, "Who will bemoan her? whence shall I seek comforters for thee?"

In the third movement vice and vengeance were dealt

C. The Vindication of Vengeance

with in yet greater detail. Addressing himself to Nineveh, Nahum inquired, "Art thou better than No-amon?" The argument being that if No-amon, or Thebes, which was not so corrupt as Nineveh, had been destroyed, and that notwithstanding her strength, how much more certain was the destruction of Nineveh, in view of her greater corruption! In the case of Thebes strength had been of no avail. In the case of Nineveh her corruption had canceled her strength. The vengeance of Jehovah was then set forth as proceeding from the outlying country to the very centers of the national life. First the outer fortresses are captured, then the gates of the land and the approaches to the capital, until finally the city itself is seen in a state of siege, and both the commercial and governing centers are destroyed.

The last section is a weird declaration of the destruction of Assyria. The shepherds, the nobles, and the people are dealt with in judgment. The universal verdict agrees as to the righteousness of the judgment. There is to be no healing, and because of the universal oppression exercised by Assyria, there will be great rejoicing over her downfall.

The message of Nahum was to Judah, and if delivered in the period of the reformation under Manasseh it was singularly appropriate as a message of encouragement and of solemn warning. Coming back from Babylon it was probable that the hearts of the people were fearful lest their old enemy Assyria should trouble them again. This message of Nahum would greatly strengthen and assure them, as it taught that Jehovah was still actively governing, and was on the side of those returning to loyalty.

Coming back from captivity in repentance for past sins, the people heard a solemn warning against repentance which was evanescent. Nineveh had repented under the preaching of Jonah and had been restored, but having returned to her sins the day of repentance was passed, and doom was determined. Jehovah is slow to anger, but He can by no means clear the guilty.

HABAKKUK—*The Problems of Faith*

HABAKKUK   * * * *

OF HABAKKUK NOTHING more is known than his name, and that he was in all probability a Levite. There is no serious discrepancy in the opinions concerning the date of his prophesying. Internal evidence brings it into relation with the Chaldean invasion, so that the range is from 635 to 586 B.C. This invasion was punishment for Manasseh's sin, and yet did not occur until after the death of Josiah, in the reign of Jehoiakim. When he delivered his message, the condition of things calling for reformation still existed. The probability, therefore, is that he prophesied during the closing years of Manasseh, or during the reign of Amon, which was earlier than Zephaniah, who prophesied in the days of Josiah. A description of the times of Manasseh, Amon, and the early days of Josiah, is contained in 2 Kings, xxi., xxii., and the prophet's description (i. 2-4) would exactly coincide. The book is a prophecy, and yet its methods differ from any other. The burden of the prophet is that of the problems of permitted evil, and the using of the Chaldeans as the instrument to scourge evildoers less wicked than themselves.

In this book we have a man of faith asking questions and receiving answers. A comparison of i. 2 with iii. 19 will give an indication of the true value of this book. Opening in mystery and questioning, it closes in certainty and affirmation. The contrast is startling. The first is almost a wail of despair, and the last is a shout of confidence. From the affirmation of faith's agnosticism we come to the confirmation of agnos-

ticism's faith. The book is a movement from one to the other.
The door of exit and entrance is ii. 4. The former part is a
pathway leading thereto, and the latter is the highway leading therefrom. The book falls naturally into two parts: the
Prophet's Problems (i.-ii. 4); the Prophet's Proclamations
(ii. 5-iii.).

A. THE PROPHET'S PROBLEMS

In this first division we have the prophet's statement of
the problems which vexed his soul.

The first was that of the apparent indifference of Jehovah
both to his prayer and to the condition of prevailing evil. It
is such a problem as could only occur to a man of faith. Take
away God, and there is no problem. He indicated the whole
condition of affairs by the one word "violence," and then
proceeded to describe it in greater detail. To this Jehovah
replied that He was at work, but that the prophet would not
believe if he were told. He then proceeded to declare explicitly that His method was that of raising up the Chaldeans
as a scourge against His people.

This answer of Jehovah, while strengthening the faith of
the prophet, immediately created a new problem. This he
stated by first affirming his faith, and then expressing his
astonishment that Jehovah should use such an instrument,
for notwithstanding all Israel's sin, she was more righteous
than the Chaldeans. Thus the method of God constituted
a new problem. The prophet declared his determination
to watch and wait. This was the attitude of faith and honesty.
He knew that God had an answer, and would give it; and
therefore he determined to wait. The answer came immediately. The prophet was first commanded to write, and to

B. *The Prophet's Proclamations*

make his writing plain for easy reading. The vision granted to him was stated in the words: "Behold, his soul is puffed up, it is not upright in him: but the just shall live by his faith." That is the central revelation of the prophecy. It is a contrast between the "puffed up" and the "just." The former is not upright, and therefore is condemned; the latter acts on faith, and therefore lives. The first is self-centered, and therefore doomed; the second is God-centered, and therefore permanent. This was the declaration of a great principle, which the prophet was left to work out in application to all the problems by which he was surrounded. From this point the prophecy becomes a proclamation of the contrast, and therefore an affirmation of faith in spite of appearances.

B. THE PROPHET'S PROCLAMATIONS

These fall into two parts. The first is concerning the "puffed up," the second concerning the righteous.

In the proclamation of the "puffed up," the viewpoint is that of the sin of such and its consequent judgment. He first described the "puffed up" as haughty, ambitious, conquering, against whom he then proceeded to pronounce woes. In considering these the progress is to be carefully noted. The first was against ambition, which was described. The judgment pronounced against it was that of the revolt of the oppressed, and retribution in kind. The second was against covetousness, that lust for possession which led to the destruction of the peoples for increase of personal strength. Its judgment was to be that of the breaking out against the oppressor of the subjugated people, the stones and beams of the house testifying. The third was against violence, the infliction of cruel sufferings upon the subjugated. Its judgment was that the very cities so built should be destroyed. The fourth was against insolence, the brutal act of making a man drunk and then making sport of him. Its judgment was to be retribution in kind. The fifth was against idolatry, the description of which was wholly satirical. Its judgment was declared to be that of the unanswering gods. The final statement of the prophet in this connection declared that he had found the solution: "The Lord is in his holy temple." The apparent strength of wickedness is false. Jehovah reigns.

In the proclamation concerning the righteous the viewpoint is that of the majesty of Jehovah, and the consequent triumph of His people. It consists of a psalm which is a prayer. In the first movement the prophet declared his recognition of the Divine interference, and his consequent fear. He then proceeded to celebrate the greatness of Jehovah as manifest in His dealings with His ancient people. The last section of the psalm expressed the fear and the faith of the just. The contemplation of the judgment of the "puffed up" had filled him with fear, yet he triumphed in God. Describing the circumstances of utter desolation, he declared his determination in the midst of them to rejoice, and announced his reason for this determination.

ZEPHANIAH—*The Severity and Goodness of God*

<table>
<tr><td colspan="2">A
THE DAY OF WRATH WITH AN APPEAL
i.—ii.</td><td colspan="2">B
THE DAY OF WRATH AND ITS ISSUE
iii.</td></tr>
<tr><td>Title Page.</td><td>1</td><td></td><td></td></tr>
<tr><td>I. The Day of Wrath</td><td>i. 2-18</td><td>I. The Day of Wrath</td><td>1-8</td></tr>
<tr><td>i. Announced in General Terms.
ii. Described Particularly.
iii. Described as to Character.</td><td>2-6
7-13
14-18</td><td>i. The Woe Declared.
ii. The Reasons Declared.
iii. The Final Word.</td><td>1
2-7
8</td></tr>
<tr><td>II. The Appeal</td><td>ii.</td><td>II. The Issue of the Day</td><td>9-20</td></tr>
<tr><td>i. The Cry of the Nations.
ii. The Call to the Remnant.
iii. The Argument.</td><td>1-2
3
4-15</td><td>i. The Gathering of a Remnant.
ii. The Remnant Addressed.</td><td>9-13
20-14</td></tr>
</table>

ZEPHANIAH ✳ ✳ ✳ ✳

THE PROPHECY IS clearly dated in the reign of Josiah. From the genealogy of Zephaniah it is evident that he was a prince of the royal house, and about the same age as Josiah. In all probability, therefore, he uttered his prophecy when the reformation of Josiah was in progress. It is remarkable that he makes no reference thereto, speaking only of the sin of the people, and the consequent swift judgment of God upon them; finally describing a restoration, the details of which had no counterpart in the work of Josiah. This omission is to be accounted for by a reference to the story of the finding of the book of the law by Hilkiah, and the word which Huldah the prophetess uttered in answer to the messengers sent by Josiah. She declared that because the king was sincere, God would spare him, and that he should not share in nor even see the judgment; but she emphatically declared that the curses written in the book of the law were certain to fall upon the sinning people. The people took part in the reforms initiated by Josiah simply because the king led, and not out of any real heart-repentance. Zephaniah, speaking under the inspiration of the Spirit, and perfectly understanding that the outward appearance of reform was not indicative of a true change of heart, ignored it. He therefore more definitely perhaps than any other prophet, declared the terrors of the Divine judgment against sin. Yet to him fell the lot of uttering the very sweetest love-song in the Old Testament.

ZEPHANIAH

The great burden of the prophecy is that of the Day of Wrath. It may be divided into two parts: the Day of Wrath, with an Appeal (i. 2-ii.); the Day of Wrath, and its Issue (iii.).

A. THE DAY OF WRATH, WITH AN APPEAL

The first movement of this section is that of the prophet's declaration of the coming judgment of Jehovah. This he first announced in general terms, then described more particularly as to procedure, and finally as to character. This description opened with a comprehensive announcement: "I will utterly consume all things from off the face of the ground, saith Jehovah." Zephaniah then showed that to be a description of the creation in so far as it had become evil; man and the sphere of his dominion, the stumbling blocks with the wicked and the race, were to be consumed. The local application was that judgment would descend upon Judah and Jerusalem, falling upon those who had practiced idolatry, those who had indulged in mixed worship, those who had backslidden from following the Lord, and those who had never sought or inquired after Him. Proceeding to describe more particularly the judgment, the prophet announced the presence of Jehovah for the purpose of judgment. The stroke of that judgment would fall first upon the princes, then upon the extortioners, also upon the merchantmen, and finally upon those who were "settled on their lees," that is, those who were living on their wealth in idleness and indifference. He finally gave a graphic description of the day in which men should walk as blind, none being able to deliver them because Jehovah would make "an end, . . . a terrible end, of all them that dwell in the land."

—330

B. *The Day of Wrath and Its Issue*

After this declaration he uttered his great appeal, first to the nation as a whole, calling upon it to pull itself together before the opportunity for repentance should pass, before the hour of judgment should arrive. As though conscious that that larger appeal would be unavailing, he turned to the remnant, to such as were the "meek of the earth," and urged them to renew devotion. This appeal he enforced by argument, in which he again set forth the fact of the coming judgment upon the nations, interspersing his declaration with words of hope concerning the remnant. He first addressed the nations on the west, declaring that they should be utterly destroyed, and in their place the remnant of the house of Judah should feed their flocks. He next turned to the nations on the east, declaring that they should become a perpetual desolation, and that the remnant should inhabit their lands. He then turned to those on the south, declaring that they should be slain by the sword. Finally he declared that those on the north should be destroyed, and their cities made a desolation.

B. THE DAY OF WRATH AND ITS ISSUE

In this section the prophet yet more clearly set forth the sin of the people, and uttered the hopelessness of the case from the human standpoint. This gave him his opportunity to announce the victory of God, Who, notwithstanding the utter failure of His people, would ultimately accomplish the purpose of His love concerning them. The address opened with a declaration of woe against Jerusalem, which the prophet described as rebellious, polluted, and oppressing. The reason of the woe he then set forth with great care, first describing the city as a whole as one which "obeyed not

. . . received not correction, . . . trusted not in Jehovah, . . . drew not near to her God." The reason of the sin of the city was that of the corruption of the rulers, who are all referred to. Princes, judges, prophets, and priests alike had failed, each in their distinctive office. In the midst of the city, Jehovah the Righteous One had brought forth His judgment, but His presence had been insulted. He had, moreover delivered the people, but their answer to His deliverance had been that of increased and persistent corruption. In the presence of this utter hopelessness the prophet cried, "Therefore wait ye for me, saith Jehovah." This was the first gleam of hope. The very hopelessness and sin of the people made Divine action necessary, and that action would be that of judgment. The judgment, however, would be but the prelude, for immediately the prophet had declared it to be inevitable, he proceeded to describe the ultimate restoration.

From this point the prophecy is clearly Messianic. Zephaniah gave no picture of the suffering Servant, nor any hint of His method. He only dealt with the ultimate result to Israel. This he first described as the turning "to the peoples a pure language" by Jehovah gathering again all His dispersed ones. In that gathering the "proudly exulting ones," that is, the false rulers, would be deposed, while in the midst of the city the afflicted people who trust in the name of Jehovah would be established. Zephaniah then addressed himself to the remnant, charging them to sing and rejoice because their enemy should be cast out, and their true King, Jehovah, be established in the midst of them. He next called them to true courage and to service. The prophecy reached

B. *The Day of Wrath and Its Issue*

its highest level as Zephaniah described the attitude of God in poetic language under the figure of motherhood. Jehovah in the midst of His people will rejoice, and from the silence of love will proceed to the song of His own satisfaction.

HAGGAI—*The Duty of Courage*

A FIRST PROPHECY *i. 1-11*	B SECOND PROPHECY *ii. 1-9*	C THIRD PROPHECY *ii. 10-19*	D FOURTH PROPHECY *i. 20-23*
Introductory. 1	Introductory. 1-2	Introductory. 10	Introductory. 20-21a
I. The Reason **2**	**I. The Reason** **3**	**I. The Message** **11-19**	**I. The Reason**
Neglect of the Lord's House. The Time not come.	The Old Men. Disappointment.	i. Appeal to Priests and Principles Deduced. 11-13 ii. Application of Principles. 14-19	Ratification of Promise. "I will bless."
II. The Message **3-11**	**II. The Message** **4-9**	**II. The Reason** **19a**	**II. The Message** **21b-23**

i. Their own Houses.
   3-4
ii. Consider your
   Ways.   5-7
iii. The Reason of
   Failure.   8-11
	i. The Call. 4a
	ii. The Immediate
	   Promise. 4b. 5
	iii. The Larger
	   Promise. 6-9
	See Zechariah. i. 1-6
		The Delay of Blessing.
		Disappointment.
			i. The Shaking of
			   False Authority.
			   21b-22
			ii. The Establishment
			   of True Authority.
			   23

III. Historic Inter- **lude** **12-15**		**III. The Promise** **19b**	

i. Obedience.   12
ii. Encouragement.
   13
iii. Enthusiasm.
   14-15			

HAGGAI ✳ ✳ ✳ ✳

OF HAGGAI'S PERSONAL history nothing is known, but
the dating of his prophecy is very exact. It is noticeable that
for the first time a Gentile date is given. Darius reigned during the years B.C. 521-486, so that Haggai's four messages fell
within four months in the years B.C. 520-519. For the understanding of the conditions in which he exercised his
prophetic ministry the book of Ezra must be studied; a tab-
ulation of the leading events in connection with the return
from Babylon will help us thus to place his prophecy:

B.C. 536. Return from Babylon under Zerubbabel (Ezra
iii. 1-4). Altar built. Sacrifices offered. Feast of Tabernacles.

B.C. 535. Foundations of the Temple laid. Opposition of
Samaritans and cessation of building.

B.C. 520-519. Prophesying of Haggai and Zechariah. The
people recommenced building.

B.C. 515. The Temple completed.

Thus it will be seen that the work of rebuilding the Temple had ceased, and in order to stir up the leaders and people to their duty in this matter these messages were uttered.

The book is naturally divided by the four messages the
prophet delivered: the First Prophecy (i. 1-11); the Second
Prophecy (ii. 1-9); the Third Prophecy (ii. 10-19); the
Fourth Prophecy (ii. 20-23).

A. THE FIRST PROPHECY

The prophet Haggai delivered his first message on the first day of the sixth month of the second year in the reign of Darius, and it was especially addressed to those in authority. The people were excusing themselves from building by declaring that the time had not come. To this the prophet replied by reminding them that they were dwelling in their own cieled houses, while the house of God was lying waste. He called them to consider their ways, reminding them of the long-continued material failure in the midst of which they had lived. He then urged them to build the house of God, declaring that all the failure to which he had already referred was of the nature of Divine punishment for their neglect of His house. There was an immediate response to the appeal of Haggai, first on the part of the governor and priest, and then by the people. This response was followed, first, by a word of encouragement, in which the prophet declared that Jehovah was with them; and secondly, by new enthusiasm on the part of the people.

B. SECOND PROPHECY

About seven weeks later, on the twenty-first day of the seventh month of the same year of the reign of Darius, Haggai delivered his second message. This was addressed to Zerubbabel the governor, Joshua the priest, and all the people. A comparison of Ezra iii. 13 with this message will show how certain of the old men who remembered the former house lamented the comparative inferiority of this. Such memory tended to dishearten the people, and the prophet appealed to them to be strong and to work, promising in the name of Jehovah His immediate presence and help. Upon the basis of this promise he then rose to the height of a more gracious one. The central phrase of this large promise is difficult of interpretation, "The desire [singular] . . . shall come [plural]." Perhaps the simplest explanation is to be found in the use made of the connected words in the letter to the Hebrews (xii. 25-29). It is evident that in this promise there is a revelation of an order of Divine procedure which is manifested in the method of both the first and second advents of the Messiah. That order may thus be briefly summarized: "I will shake;" "the desire shall come;" "peace." Thus the disheartened on account of lesser material glory were called to look for the spiritual glory which would be the crowning splendor of the new. After this prophecy Zechariah delivered a message (Zech. i. 1-6).

C. THIRD PROPHECY

About two months later, on the twenty-fourth day of the ninth month of the same year in the reign of Darius, Haggai delivered his third message. In this the people are addressed through a colloquy with the priests. The content of this prophecy shows that after three months of hard building there were still no signs of material rewards, and the people were again disheartened in consequence thereof. As a result of his questioning of the priests and their answers Haggai taught the people that their present obedience could not immediately result in material prosperity because of their past sin. Yet the final word of this third message is a promise of blessing: "From this day will I bless you."

D. FOURTH PROPHECY

The last message of Haggai was delivered on the same day as the third, and was an enforcement and explanation of the final promise, "I will bless you." It consisted first of a repetition of the declaration of Jehovah's determination to shake, carried out in greater detail, in order to reveal the fact that He would destroy all false authority and power; and finally in the promise of the establishment of true authority.

ZECHARIAH—*The Apocalypse of the Old Testament*

ZECHARIAH * * * *

THE ASSOCIATION OF Zechariah with Haggai has already been seen. Of the prophet himself we are only sure that he was the son of Iddo (Ezra v. 1, vi. 14). In the book of Nehemiah reference is made to a priest named Iddo (xii. 4) and to his son Zechariah (xii. 16). If these references are to the same persons, Zechariah was also a priest.

The first part of the book is carefully dated, and contains prophecies closely related to those of Haggai, having practical bearing upon the work of the Temple building. The latter part of the book is undated, and deals with three distinct events in the history of the people. The time was all-important. The Messiah had been promised through the chosen nation. Prior to the Edict of Cyrus that nation was practically dead, and, indeed, was being buried in its captivity. This is clearly evidenced by the smallness of the remnant who had interest and enthusiasm enough to return (Ezra ii.). Yet through this remnant the coming of Messiah was made possible, as to a human channel. This fact gives us the clue to the difference between the first and the second parts of the prophecy of Zechariah. In the first he urged the people to build the Temple by prophecies which showed the far-reaching effect of such work in the coming and Kingdom of Messiah. In the latter part he dealt more in detail with certain events leading toward that great future.

The book, therefore, naturally falls into two parts: Messages during the Building of the Temple (i.-viii.); Messages after the Building of the Temple (ix.-xiv.).

A. MESSAGES DURING THE BUILDING OF THE TEMPLE

In this first division there are three messages. The first was local and immediate. The second consisted of a series of visions setting forth God's ultimate purpose for His people Israel. This was followed by a brief historic interlude; and the third message consisted of a threefold answer of Jehovah to an inquiry on the part of the people concerning the observance of certain fasts.

About a month after Haggai's second prophecy, in which he had encouraged the people who were in danger of being disheartened by the memory of the past, Zechariah uttered his first prophetic word. He gave them another view of the past, intended to warn them. He reminded them that Jehovah was sore displeased with their fathers, and warned them not to walk in the same sins. Thus the value of his first message was that from another standpoint he urged the people to be obedient to the message of Haggai. While they were lamenting the departed greatness, they were also to remember how it had been lost, and not repeat the folly. Haggai encouraged them by looking on to the new spiritual glory, while Zechariah exhorted them by looking back to the past of disobedience.

Two months after Haggai had delivered his last message, which was one of hope for the future, as it declared that Jehovah would destroy false authority and establish the true, Zechariah delivered his great message consisting of eight symbolic visions. There are three methods of interpreting

–342

these visions. First, that which confines their significance to the times of Zechariah. Secondly, that which spiritualizes very much by application to the Church. Thirdly, that which makes them refer to events still in the future. I adopt the third. The first is untenable because the things declared have not yet been fulfilled. Any attempt to explain the glorious announcements of the defeat of the foes of Israel and her victories, by the poor conditions then existing, and continuing until Messiah, is to suppose the prophet guilty of the wildest and most foolish exaggeration. The second involves exposition in inextricable and endless confusion, for there are things which will not admit of spiritualization. Moreover, to apply to the Church the order and service herein revealed is to contradict New Testament teaching as to her order and service. This series of visions constitutes the Old Testament Apocalypse, or unveiling of God's final dealings with Israel.

Under the figure of the myrtle trees Israel is described as "in the bottom," or, far better, as the margin reads, "in the shady place." It is the day of her overshadowing, but she is yet watched. The whole earth is sitting still and at rest. The angel watcher makes appeal to Jehovah on behalf of Jerusalem and the cities of Judah, and is answered with "comfortable words." These words declare Jehovah's determination to deliver and re-establish His people. This vision therefore is a picture of Israel as she has long been, and still is, outcast from privilege and position, yet never forgotten by Jehovah, Who declares His determination ultimately to return to her with mercies, and to restore her to favor.

The second vision of horns and smiths, while indefinite as to detail, yet carries its own explanation. The horn is a symbol of power, and the four stand for the powers which have scattered the chosen people. The smiths are the symbol of that which destroys power, and stand for those who are to break the power of the horns. The vision therefore foretells the ultimate overthrow of Israel's enemies.

The vision of the measuring line reveals the condition of Jerusalem which will result from the overthrow of her enemies. The young man with a measuring line goes forth to measure the restored city, and is prevented from doing so by an angel messenger, who in figurative language declares to him that Jerusalem will be such that it is impossible to measure. The nature of that prosperity is indicated in the statement that the presence of Jehovah will make walls unnecessary, and its extent is declared to be so vast as to make walls impossible. In view of this remarkable vision of ultimate prosperity the prophet uttered his call to the scattered people to return, making the declaration of Jehovah's determination, and calling them to rejoice thereat.

As the first three visions have dealt principally with the material side of Israel's tribulation and restoration, the remaining five deal with her moral and spiritual influence.

The vision of Joshua, first clothed in filthy garments, and then cleansed and charged by the angel of Jehovah, shows how the nation, having failed through sin, is restored by way of moral cleansing to the priestly position and function of access to God and mediation.

The vision of the candlestick immediately following sets forth Israel as fulfilling the Divine intention. The candlestick was the symbol of Israel as the light-bearer amid the darkness. The two olive trees refer in the first place to Zerubbabel and Joshua, the governor and the priest, and thus finally to the offices of priest and king as they would be realized and fulfilled in the Person of the Messiah. Through these the Spirit would be communicated to Israel, and so the light would shine.

The vision of the flying roll represents the principle of law as it will be administered by Israel when she fulfills the true ideal. It is the curse upon evil in action and in speech, and that not merely pronounced, but active. Thus while Israel stands as priest mediating, and as light bearer illuminating, she will also affirm and apply the principle of law in the midst of the earth.

The vision of the ephah shows what will be the result of this application of law. The ephah is the symbol of commerce, and the woman, according to the distinct declaration of the prophecy, is the personification of wickedness. Thus the principle of wickedness is to find its final vantage ground in commerce. This, however, is to be centralized in the land of Shinar, where the tower of Babel was erected, and Babylon was built. The vision teaches that even in the administration of restored Israel the spirit of lawlessness will still exist, but that it will be restricted in its operations.

The last vision, of the chariots driven from between the mountains of brass, is symbolical of the four winds or spirits of heaven going forth from the presence of the Lord to walk to and fro in the earth, and suggests finally that in the day of restoration the administrative forces of righteousness will be spiritual.

After the delivery of this second message there followed a great symbolic act. Skilled workmen prepared crowns of silver and of gold which were set upon the head of Joshua.

To him, thus crowned, the prophet foretold the coming of One Who should fulfill the predictions made in the message of the visions. His office was to be dual—that of priest and king. The crowns which Joshua wore during this ceremony were retained for a memorial in the Temple of the Lord. The final words of the prophet reveal the purpose he had in his heart in all that he had said. It was that the work of Temple building should be continued.

The third message of Zechariah was uttered nearly two years later, on the fourth day of the ninth month of the fourth year of Darius. It was a fourfold answer to an inquiry made by the people concerning the necessity for observing certain fasts. The history of these fasts is contained in 2 Kings xxv. One was established in the tenth month, in connection with the besieging of the city. The next occurred in the fourth month, and commemorated the taking of the city. The third was held in the fifth month in memory of the burning of the city, and the last in the seventh month, in which Gedaliah was murdered. The inquiry was confined to the fast of the fifth month, as to whether it was necessary to continue its observance. The answer of the prophet was delivered in four statements of what Jehovah had said to him.

The first of these answers declared that the fasts had been instituted not by Divine command, but entirely upon the initiative of the people themselves. It declared also that they should consider the messages which had been delivered to them before the occasion which gave rise to the fasts of which they now complained.

The second answer reminded them that God sought the execution of justice and the manifestation of mercy, rather than the observance of self-appointed fasts. It also reminded them that they had refused to hear the call of justice, and therefore all the evil things which had befallen the city had resulted. The inference of the answer was that had they been obedient, the occasion of the fasts would never have arisen.

The third answer was full of grace. It declared that God was jealous for Zion, that He was returned to it, and that therefore its prosperity was assured, notwithstanding the fact that these people saw only the devastation which caused their lamentation. Because of the certainty of this restoration, the prophet appealed to the remnant to be strong and build, promising them in the name of Jehovah that, instead of being a curse, they should become a blessing. Reaffirming this Divine intention to restore, the prophet called the people back to the attitudes which the second answer had declared God sought, those, namely, of the execution of justice and the manifestation of mercy.

The final answer to their question was a declaration that Jehovah would turn all their self-appointed fasts into feasts, and that the city, the destruction of which had caused the appointment of these fasts, should become the center to which many peoples and the inhabitants of many cities should come to seek Jehovah.

B. MESSAGES AFTER THE BUILDING
OF THE TEMPLE

In this second division there are two messages. The first the prophet described as "The burden of the word of the Lord upon the land of Hadrach"; and the second as "The burden of the word of the Lord concerning Israel." The first deals with the rejection of the anointed King, and the second with the enthronement of the rejected King.

The first message is characterized by the prophet's vision of three outstanding events in the future of his people. These are set in the light of the Kingship of Messiah. Each foretelling is merged into, or connected with, the glorious hope of the people of God. The three events referred to are the coming of Alexander and the protection of the city; the victory of Judah under the Maccabees; the final Roman overthrow of the city and the scattering of the people. These are all related to the Messianic hope. The first merges into a great triumph song concerning the King; part of the prophecy contained therein has now been fulfilled, and part is still unfulfilled. The second passes to a description of Jehovah's triumph through His people, and of all the blessings of His Kingdom; this is wholly unfulfilled. The third is accounted for by the rejection of the true Shepherd when He appeared.

In the first movement the prophet announced the coming of the King. He foretold the preservation of the city of Jerusalem in days when Syria, Phœnicia, and Philistia would be overcome by the enemy, who, acting under Jehovah, would thus execute His judgments upon them. This prophecy was in large measure fulfilled by the coming of Alexander the Great. He captured Damascus and Sidon, and after a siege of seven months, Tyre itself. He then marched against Gaza and razed it to the ground. In the course of this campaign he passed Jerusalem more than once, but never attacked it. Thus, according to the prophecy of Zechariah, the city was preserved for the coming of the King. That coming he then foretold, calling upon Zion and Jerusalem to rejoice, declaring the character of the King, and announcing His complete victory.

The prophet proceeded to describe the King's program. He foretold a coming triumph for Zion against Greece, under the direct guidance and in the might of Jehovah. This prophecy was fulfilled in the victory gained by Judas Maccabæus over Antiochus Epiphanes. This victory led him to describe the yet greater and final victory of the people of God. He introduced this description by appealing to Zion to ask help of Jehovah, and immediately declaring His intention to accomplish their deliverance. Consequent upon this determination on the part of Jehovah, the people would be strengthened. The prophet finally, speaking in the name of Jehovah, described His regathering of the people. "I will hiss for them . . . I will sow them . . . I will bring them out . . . I will bring them into . . . I will strengthen them."

The last movement of the message is one in which the prophet described the rejection of the King. He first foretold the coming of judgment under the figure of the Roman fire, devouring the people and spoiling the glory of the false shepherds. The reasons of this judgment he then declared to be the rejection of the anointed King. This King is portrayed as having two staves, one called Beauty, which signified grace, and the other Bands, which signified union. This true Shepherd rejected the false, and then was Himself rejected of the people. It is noticeable that the prophet spoke of that rejection from the standpoint of Divine interference. Beauty was cut asunder, the price being thirty pieces of silver, and the result was the breaking asunder of Bands. The result of this rejection of the true Shepherd would be the restoration of the false, and the consequent affliction of the people. The last note of this message pronounced woe upon the worthless shepherds.

Thus the prophet foresaw the Roman victory over the chosen people following their abandonment of their true King.

The second message has to do with things wholly future. The King spoken of in the previous burden, Whose rejection was there foretold, is now seen as coming into His Kingdom. This the prophet described in two movements, which are complementary. In the first he looked at the opposing nations as they will be dealt with in judgment, and at Israel as she will be restored through the acknowledgment of her true though rejected King, and by her own spiritual cleansing. In the second movement he viewed the same events from the standpoint of the King, beginning with His rejection and then describing His coming, day, process, and administration.

The final victories of the King are described as to the nations and as to Israel. By the strength of Jehovah operating through His people, the strength of the nations is discomfited, and perfect victory is assured. This victory over the nations will issue in the restoration of Israel to supremacy under the government of One Whom they had pierced. This, however, will be brought about when, recognizing their sin, the chosen people repent with mourning. In that day, by way of a fountain opened to them, Israel will be cleansed from all the things which have defiled and degraded her.

The prophet finally described the ultimate victories as to the King, commencing with a description of the smiting of the Shepherd and the scattering of the sheep. In this proc-

B. Messages After the Building of the Temple

ess of scattering a remnant would be loyal, and they would become the people of Jehovah. The prophet then proceeded to describe the ultimate day of the Lord, which would be ushered in by the coming of Jehovah in the Person of His King to the Mount of Olives. This advent would initiate the new processes of the settlement of the land, and the cleansing of Jerusalem by judgment, to be followed by the establishment of the Kingdom in which all nations would gather to Jerusalem as a center of worship, those refusing being punished, while all life would be consecrated.

MALACHI—*Unconscious Corruption*

A FUNDAMENTAL AFFIRMATION *i. 1-5*	B FORMAL ACCUSATIONS *i. 6—ii.*	C FINAL ANNUNCIATIONS *iii.—iv.*
Title Page. 1		

I. The Sensitive Word
   of Jehovah   2a
	I. Against the Priests
	   i. 6—ii. 9
		I. The Coming One iii.

	i. Their Corruption declared.
	   i. 6-14
	ii. The Punishment
	   threatened. ii. 1-9
		i. Announcement of Advent.
		   1-6
		ii. Appeal to the Nation.
		   7-15
		iii. Attitude of the Remnant.
		   16-18

II. The Skeptical
   Question   2b
	II. Against the People
	   ii. 10-16
		II. The Coming Day
		   iv. 1-3

III. The Answer in Proof
   2c-5
	III. Against All ii. 17	III. The Closing Words
		   iv. 4-6

MALACHI ✳ ✳ ✳ ✳

NOTHING MORE IS known of Malachi than the book which bears his name reveals. The word Malachi means messenger, and this has given rise to the supposition that it is a title rather than a name. While it is probable that Malachi was indeed the actual name of the prophet, its significance is most suggestive, for throughout the prophecy the burden of the message of Jehovah is supreme, and the personality of the messenger is absolutely hidden.

The connection of this prophecy with the work under Ezra and Nehemiah is evident. The abuses against which Malachi made his protest, namely a polluted priesthood, mixed marriages, and failure to pay tithes, were those which existed during the time of Nehemiah. Malachi is mentioned neither by Ezra nor Nehemiah; probably, therefore, he prophesied after their time. It would seem as though the special evils, which they set themselves to correct, still existed side by side with correct outward observances. The attitude of the people is revealed in the sevenfold "Wherein" (i. 2, 6, 7, ii. 17, iii. 7, 8, 13).

The prophecy falls into three parts: Fundamental Affirmation (i. 2-5); Formal Accusations (i. 6-11); Final Annunciations (iii.-iv.).

A. FUNDAMENTAL AFFIRMATION

After the introductory word, which really constitutes the Title Page, the message begins almost abruptly with the tender and sensitive word of Jehovah to His people: "I have loved you." This is the real burden of the prophecy; everything is to be viewed in the light thereof.

The prophet then, in an equally brief sentence, indicated the attitude of the people toward Jehovah: "Wherein hast thou loved us?" The only explanation of such a question possible is that the people, conscious of the difference between their national position and their past greatness, and of the apparent failure of fulfillment of the prophetic promises, called in question the love of Jehovah.

This skeptical question the prophet answered by reminding them of Jehovah's love for Jacob, and His hatred of Esau; of His destruction of Edom, and His deliverance of Israel.

B. FORMAL ACCUSATIONS

Having thus made his fundamental statement, the prophet proceeded to utter his formal accusations. These fall into three groups, those against the priests, those against the people, and those against the nation in general.

In dealing with the priests, he declared their corruption, and indicated the line of their punishment. He charged them with profanity, in that they had despised the name of Jehovah; with sacrilege, in that they had offered polluted bread upon His altar; with greed, in that none of them was found willing to open the doors of His house for nought; with weariness, in that they had "snuffed at" the whole system of worship as "a weariness." In the study of these accusations against the priests, it is most evident that they resented the charges made against them, as the recurrence of the questions—"Wherein?"—shows. This makes it evident that the prophet was protesting against a formalism which was devoid of reality. Against them he therefore uttered the threatenings of Jehovah. Their blessing were to be cursed, and the punishment of corruption would be that they should be held in contempt by the people. In the midst of this declaration occurs a passage full of beauty describing the true ideal of the priesthood.

The prophet specifically charged the people with two sins, and in each case pronounced judgment upon them. He introduced this charge by the enunciation of a principle— that of the common relationship of all to God as Father, and the declaration of the consequent sin of dealing treacherously with each other. The first specific sin was that of the mixed marriages of the people, while the second was that of the prevalence of divorce.

The final accusation was against the whole nation, and consisted of a charge of accommodating doctrine to the deterioration of conduct. In the presence of ethical failure, the people were declaring that, notwithstanding the doing of evil, Jehovah delighted in the people, and were inquiring skeptically, "Where is the God of judgment?"

C. FINAL ANNUNCIATIONS

The last division of the book contains the prophet's announcement of the coming of Messiah. It falls into three sections dealing with the coming One, the coming Day, and uttering the closing words.

The prophet announced the advent of Jehovah's Messenger, describing His Person, the process of His administration, and finally declaring the principle of the unchangeableness of Jehovah.

He then appealed to the nation, generally calling them

to return, and then making a twofold charge against them of robbery and of blasphemy. To each of these they responded with the same inquiry, "Wherein?" thus showing that the people, like the priests, were observing formalities of religion while deficient in true spiritual life.

In the midst of this widespread apostasy there was a remnant yet loyal to Jehovah, which the prophet first described, and then addressed, declaring to them Jehovah's knowledge of them, and determination concerning them.

All this leads to his great declaration concerning the coming Day. This Day he described in its twofold effect. Toward the wicked it would be a day of burning and of destruction. Toward the righteous it would be a day of healing and of salvation.

The closing words of the prophet called upon the people to remember the law of Moses, promised the coming of a herald before that of the day of the Lord, and ended with a solemn suggestion of judgment.

Part II:

THE NEW TESTAMENT

MATTHEW—*Jesus Christ the King*

A HIS PERSON *i.—iv. 16*	B HIS PROPAGANDA *iv. 17—xvi. 20*	C HIS PASSION *xvi. 12—xxviii.*
I. His Relation to Earth **i.—iii. 12**	**I. His Enunciation of Laws** **iv. 17—vii.**	**I. His Cross and His Subjects** **xvi. 21—xx.**

	i. A Nucleus Gathered.
	         iv. 17-25
		i. The Cross and the Glory.
		         xvi. 21-28

i. Genealogy.   i. 1-17
ii. Birth.   i. 18—ii.
iii. Herald.   iii. 1-12
	ii. The Manifesto. v.—vii.
	   a. The Nature. Character.
	                 v. 3-12
	   b. The Purpose. Influence.
	                v. 13-16
	   c. The Laws. v. 17—vi.
	   d. The Dynamic. vii. 1-12
	   e. The Final Words.
	               vii. 13-29
		ii. The Glory and the Cross.
		         xvii. 1-21
		iii. The Cross and the Resurrection. xvii. 22-23
		iv. Instructions to His Disciples.
		         xvii. 24—xviii.
		(The Multitudes. xix. 1-22)
		v. Instructions to His Disciples.
		         xix. 23—xx. 28

II. His Relation to Heaven **iii. 13-17**	**II. His Exhibition of Benefits** **viii.—ix. 34**	**II. His Rejection of the Hebrew Nation** **xxi.—xxiii.**

i. Attestation.
ii. Anointing.
	i. First Manifestation and
	   Result. viii. 1-22
	ii. Second Manifestation and
	   Result. viii. 23—ix. 17
	iii. Third Manifestation and
	    Result. ix. 18-34
		i. The Entry. xxi. 1-17
		ii. Opposition and Parabolic
		   Denunciation. xxi. 18—xxii.
		iii. The Final Woes. xxiii. 1-36
		iv. Withdrawal. xxiii. 37-39

III. His Relation to Hell **iv. 1-11**	**III. His Enforcement of Claims ix. 35—xvi. 20**	**III. His Predictions to His Subjects** **xxiv.—xxv.**

i. Testing.
ii. Triumph.
	i. The Twelve. ix. 35—xi.
	ii. Conflict with Rulers. xii.
	iii. Parables of the Kingdom.
	               xiii. 1-52
		i. The Disciples' Questions.
		         xxiv. 3
		ii. The Detailed Answers.

(IV. 12-16. Connecting
iii. 17 with xi. 2)
	iv. Increasing Opposition.
	        xiii. 53—xvi. 12
	v. The Confession of Peter.
	         xvi. 13-20
		IV. His Passion
		xxvi.—xxviii.
		
		i. Preliminary. xxvi. 1-30
		ii. The Suffering.
		         xxvi. 31—xxvii.
		iii. The Triumph. xxviii.

MATTHEW   * * * *

MATTHEW WAS A Hebrew, whose calling in life was that of a taxgatherer under the Roman government. His writing evidences his acquaintance with the Hebrew Scriptures, and especially with those which foretold the coming of the Messiah King. Thus, both in his religious thinking and the prosecution of his daily calling he was familiar with the idea of government.

His story of the life and work of Jesus is naturally therefore a setting forth of the King and His Kingdom. The book falls into three parts. In the first Matthew introduces the Person (i.-iv. 16); in the second he tells the story of the Propaganda (iv. 17-xvi. 20); and in the last chronicles the events of the Passion (xvi. 21-xxviii.).

A. THE PERSON OF THE KING

The King is presented to us in a threefold relation: to earth, to heaven, and to hell.

As to the first, after the manner of His nation, the genealogy which sets Him in purely Jewish legal relationship is given. Then follows the account of His birth, and it is the only account of the origin of the unique Personality of Jesus which is at all able to satisfy the reason. In a mystery passing our comprehension, the King is Son of God, and Son of Mary. Chronologically there is a great gap between the birth and the baptism, which is filled by the years of human growth and development at Nazareth. As the days approached for the commencement of His propaganda, His herald, the last of the long line of Hebrew prophets, appeared to the nation; and with a baptism of water, and words of authoritative rebuke and hope, he announced the advent of the King.

Crowning the ministry of the herald, the King appeared, and was baptized in Jordan. In connection with that baptism His relation to heaven was manifest. There was first the coming upon Him of the Spirit. This was the sacred ceremony by which He was set apart to the exercise of the Kingly office. Simultaneously with the anointing, the silence of the heaven was broken, and the words of the Father attested Him King. The second psalm should carefully be read in this connection. The declaration, "I am well pleased," attested the perfection of the life which had been lived in seclusion, especially in the light of the fact that by baptism the King's submission to the Divine will for all the purposes of redemption was symbolized.

Immediately from the lofty experiences of anointing and attestation the King passed to the lonely conflict of the wilderness. Here He came into grips with the archenemy of the race, the conspirator against heaven's order. The devil attacked Him in the threefold fact of His human personality, the material basis, the spiritual essence, and the vocational purpose. In every case victory was on the side of the King, and that by simple submission to the law of God. Thus His royalty was created and demonstrated by His loyalty.

Behold, this is our King! Sharer of our nature, and yet bringing into it the Divine nature. Appointed to rule by God Himself, and equipped for administration by the plenitude of the Spirit. Meeting every onslaught of the foe, and triumphing! Surely we may trust Him. The only adequate expression of trust is obedience.

B. THE PROPAGANDA OF THE KING

The next division contains the account of the propaganda of the King, in which there are three movements: the enunciation of laws, the exhibition of benefits, and the enforcement of claims.

He first gathered around Him a nucleus of disciples. Some of these had been called in the earlier Judæan ministry, which Matthew does not record. They were now called to abandon their fishing in order to be with Him.

After a period of teaching in the synagogues of Galilee, He gathered these disciples, and gave to them His manifesto, in which He first insisted upon the supreme importance of character in His Kingdom; and declared its purpose to be that of producing influence, which He illustrated under the figures of salt and light. He then enunciated His laws, prefacing them with a prelude on the importance of law. His laws fall into three groups: first, those of human interrelationship, which He illustrated by two quotations from the Decalogue, dealing with murder and adultery; and two from the wider law of Moses, dealing with truth and justice, adding a new law of love, even toward enemies. Next came the laws of Divine relation, which declared the principle that life was to be lived before God rather than before men, and then was illustrated by application to alms, to prayer, to fasting. Finally He revealed the necessity for a superearthly consciousness, as He warned them against covetousness and against care. Passing to the great subject of the dynamic, in the power of which it would be possible for His subjects to obey His ethic, He first warned them against censoriousness, and enjoined discrimination; then declared to them that in answer to their asking, seeking, knocking, they would receive, find, and the door would be opened, because they had to do with a Father. The last words of the manifesto were of the nature of invitation, warning, and the uttering of the Kingly claim. The effect produced upon the multitude who had listened to the manifesto uttered to the disciples was that of astonishment at His authority.

While the King had described His Kingdom to the faithful few in the hearing of the multitude, His will was that it should include all men within its embrace. His mission was not to compel by force of arms, but to constrain to willing submission to Himself. In order to do this He went forth, working to illustrate the benefits which must come to such as lived within His Kingdom. This working of wonders was no merely spectacular display on the part of Christ. It was a setting forth of the fact that He was King in all the realms by which their lives were affected. There are three distinct movements noticeable, each culminating in an effect produced upon the crowds.

In the first He demonstrated His power in the purely physical realm by healing leprosy, palsy, and fever, and with an astonishing ease, all that were sick. Thus the King of righteousness in ethical ideals, proved Himself able to correct all disability in the physical realm resulting from sin. The result of this first manifestation of His power was a spontaneous and apparently enthusiastic determination to follow Him on the part of some. Following, however, is not easy. He immediately presented the difficulties of the way, and yet insisted on the absolute importance of coming after

Him by calling men to break with every other tie rather than fail in this matter.

In the second movement the King's power was seen operating in other spheres. He was Master of the elements, He exercised imperial sway in the mystic spirit world, He claimed authority in the moral realm. The result produced upon the multitude by these manifestations was that they were afraid, and glorified God.

The third manifestation included the first two in its exercise of power, in both physical and spiritual realms. He recalled the spirit of the child of Jairus to its clay tenement, and by the healing of a woman revealed His method of answering faith by the communication of virtue. The result produced upon the multitudes now was that they were filled with wonder, and the Pharisees suggested an explanation, to which they gave more definite voice later.

The section dealing with His enforcement of claims opens with a brief paragraph, full of suggestiveness, revealing the King's heart, as in the presence of all the needs of men He is ever moved with compassion. He now called twelve of His disciples, and commissioned them as apostles. His charge to them included instructions which affected their immediate work, and indicated the lines of the work of their successors to the end of the age. This commissioning of the apostles was immediately followed by four illustrations of the kind of obstacles which confronted the King in His work. The perplexity of the loyal was manifest in the question of John; the unreasonableness of the age in His description of its children; the impenitence of the cities in His denunciation of them; and finally, the blindness of the simple.

The King is then seen in conflict. Opposition to Him became active. Twice the rulers attacked Him concerning His attitude to the Sabbath. They attempted to account for His power by attributing it to complicity with the devil. With supercilious unbelief, they asked a sign. Moreover, He had to contend with opposition which must have been more painful to Him than that of His avowed enemies. His own mother, unable to understand Him, sought to persuade Him to abandon His work.

In the presence of this increasing opposition the King uttered His great parables of the Kingdom. These may be divided into two groups: first, those spoken to the multitudes; secondly, those spoken to the disciples only. In the first there are four parables, revealing the method of the King, the method of the enemy, the worldly growth of the Kingdom, and the introduction of the corrupting influence of leaven. In the second there are four parables, the first three viewing the Kingdom from the Divine standpoint, the last teaching the responsibility of those to whom the revelation was committed.

Proceeding with His work the King encountered increasing opposition from His own, from the false king Herod, from Pharisees and scribes, and from Pharisees and Sadducees. In the intervals of this clearly marked growth of antagonism there were remarkable manifestations of Kingly power, revealing to such as had eyes to see, how beneficent was His rule.

At last a crisis was reached. At Cæsarea Philippi He gathered His disciples about Him, and asked them in effect what was the result of the work He had been doing. Their answers were remarkable, but none of them, reporting the opinions of the multitude, satisfied His heart, and He challenged them as to their opinion. Peter's confession opened the way for the King's entry upon His final work. He had fulfilled the first movement of His ministry, that of revealing to at least a handful of souls the truth concerning His Person, and His relation to the Divine economy. Henceforth there would be a new note in His teaching, a further revelation in His attitudes.

C. THE PASSION OF THE KING

The King practically broke with the multitudes at Cæsarea Phillippi. Henceforward His principal work was directed to leading the little group of His own into deeper appreciation of the meaning of His mission. The multitudes, however, perpetually broke in upon His teaching, and He always answered them in blessing. With regard to His own, His teaching now centered around the Cross. At once they became afraid, and a distance between Him and them is observable. To three of their number He granted a marvelous revelation of His glory. Yet even there the central thought was that of the Cross. During the days that followed all the disciples' preconceived notions of royalty, of greatness, of the value of material things, were rudely shaken as He declared to them the way to the crown must be that of the Cross. Yet let it be carefully observed that He never mentioned the Cross without also announcing the fact of resurrection.

As the end approached, the King went to Jerusalem. All Old Testament history, from Abraham, culminated in that hour. For long years the greatness of the Hebrew people as a nation had passed away. The Roman eagles were spread above the standards of their own national life. To them the long-expected King had come, enunciating the laws of the Kingdom, exhibiting its benefits, enforcing its claims. They had rejected the laws, despised the benefits, refused to yield to the claims. At last the King quietly, majestically, authoritatively rejected them. With quiet precision He prepared to enter the city, and, having arrived, occupied the throne of judgment, uttering words of righteous discrimination, dealing with all objections until they were silenced. Thereupon He pronounced the final woes, and uttered the inevitable sentence.

Having officially rejected the nation, He again devoted special time to His disciples. His action in Jerusalem had strangely puzzled them. He had offended the rulers past the possibility of reconciliation, and with a dignity which must have appalled His own, had flung the whole ruling class away. They came to Him with an incoherent outbreak of questioning: "When shall these things be? and what shall be the sign of thy coming, and of the end of the age?" Whatever they meant by these questions, the King treated their inquiry as threefold: first, concerning "these things"; secondly, concerning His coming; finally, concerning the "end of the age." The King Who had been rejected by His own, and Who in turn had rejected them in their national capacity, manifested nothing of doubt, nothing of disappointment, nothing of discouragement. From the midst of apparent failure and disaster He quietly and calmly surveyed the ages, claiming for Himself the position of continual supremacy.

For us the Via Dolorosa is always bathed in the sunlight of the resurrection. It is a little difficult to observe those dark and awful days in which the earthly ministry of the King ended. The ultimate victory is always sounding its triumphant music in our ears. And yet we must walk this way with Him meditatively, and in some senses experimentally, if we would share the travail that makes His Kingdom come. Therefore, as we read and ponder the tragic story, let us pray for such illumination of His sorrows by the Spirit as shall give us to have some fuller consciousness of the cost at which our royal Master won the glorious victory. In proportion as we are able to do this, our songs of triumph will be richer, fuller, when striking death to death, He comes forth, never again to know defeat, but to move with sure and unerring progress to the ultimate victories.

A solemn awe takes possession of the spirit as the final movements in the progress of the King are considered. No more radiant light ever fell from human love upon the sorrowing Christ than that of Mary's appreciation of His sorrow as expressed in her act of worship, and no more terrible darkness ever came to Him from human selfishness than that of Judas' treachery. A sad and solemn gathering, yet thrilling with hope, and merging in music, was the passover feast. There the types and shadows of the past had their fitting ending in the presence of the Antitype and the Substance.

And now the King passed into the darkness. We cannot accompany Him. We may reverently stand upon its outer margin, and listen with bowed heads to the sob of the unutterable deep, as in a death-grapple in the darkness, He took hold upon the spoiler of His people. In the garden the last shadows of temptation fell, and the final triumph of devotion was won. Terrible beyond all human comprehension was that to which the King passed. Glorious beyond all finite explanation was the stern triumph of the will which yielded itself at cost to the accomplishment of the One and only Will. That vast sea of sorrow broke in angry and hissing waves upon the shore, and from that surf we gain some faint and far-off notion of the sea. Then solemnly we follow Him by reading again and again the awful story of the mind of love, stronger than death.

All sorts and conditions of men were gathered about the Cross, and though at the moment they did not realize it, it was in their midst, the King's great throne, at once a throne of judgment and a throne of grace. From it they parted, some to the right, others to the left, according as they crowned or crucified.

Man's last and worst was done. The King was dead. From the moment of His dying none but tender hands touched Him, and from the moment of His burial none but loving eyes saw Him.

The night has passed, the day has dawned. A new glory is on the whole creation. It will be long years, as men count time, ere the groaning ceases, and the sob is hushed, but the deepest pain is passed in His pain, and the wound of humanity is staunched at its center. Strange new glories break in the dawning of the first day of the week.

The King's followers, discouraged and scattered, were gathered together, while a new heroism possessed them. For one brief while He tarried, and at last, with a majesty of authority such as man had never known, He uttered His commission, and declared His abiding presence.

Reverently, and with meaning such as mortals never knew, there pass our lips in His presence words often uttered, but

C. The Passion of the King

never before with such confidence or courage, "Long live the King," and in answer we hear His words spoken, a little later, to a lonely man in an island of the sea, "I am alive for evermore."

MARK—*Jesus Christ the Servant*

A SANCTIFICATION *i. 1-13.*	B SERVICE *i. 14—viii. 30.*	C SACRIFICE *viii. 31—xvi.*
I. "John Came" **1-8**	**I. First Disciples and First Work i. 14—iii. 12**	**I. Anticipated viii. 31—x.**
i. According to prophecy. 1-3 ii. Prophesying. 4-8	Galilee. i. Works. i. 14—ii. 12 ii. Words. ii. 13-28 iii. Works and Words. iii. 1-12	i. New Terms. viii. 31—ix. 1 ii. New Manifestations. ix. 2-27 iii. Teaching. ix. 28—x. 45 iv. The Healing of Bartim æus. x. 46-52
II. "Jesus Came" **9-13**	**II. Appointment of Twelve and Advance in Toil iii. 13—vi. 6**	**II. Approached** **xi.—xiv. 42**
To i. Obedience. 9 ii. Anointing. 10-11 iii. Testing. 12-13	Galilee. Gerasene's Country. Judæa. i. Twelve Appointed. iii. 13-19a ii. Continued Toil and Teaching. iii. 19b—vi. 6	i. Jesus and the City. xi. 1-26 ii. Jesus and the Rulers. xi. 27—xii. 34 iii. Jesus and the Multitudes. xii. 35-40 iv. Jesus and the Disciples. xii. 41—xiv. 42
	III. Commission of Twelve and Co-operation in Service vi. 7—viii. 30	**III. Accomplished** **xiv. 43—xv.**
	i. The Apostles' Departure. vi. 7-13 ii. Herod and Jesus. vi. 14-16 (Account of Murder of John. vi. 17-29) iii. The Apostles' Return. vi. 30-32 iv. The Feeding of the Multitudes. vi. 33-44 v. The Disciples and the Storm. vi. 45-52 vi. Healing the Multitudes. vi. 53-56 vii. The Scribes and Pharisees. vii. 1-23 viii. Journeying. vii. 24—viii. 30	i. Disciples. xiv. 43-72 Betray. Forsake. Deny. ii. The People. xv. 1-15 Yield to Priests. Clamor for Blood. iii. The Rulers. xv. 16-47 Slay. Bury. **Conclusion xvi.** The Risen One. The Commission. The Ascension. "The Lord working with them."

MARK   ✳ ✳ ✳ ✳

MARK WAS THE personal friend of Peter, and throughout his gospel the influence of this friendship is manifest. The outlook therefore is that of a man himself familiar with toil, as were all the fishers of the Galilean lake. In this gospel we find Jesus presented as the Servant. He goes forward in unremitting submission to the calls of service, but it is impossible in His presence to indulge the familiarity which breeds contempt, or to feel the pity which proceeds from a sense of superiority. The only contempt we feel as we watch Him at His work is for ourselves, who so miserably fail in our devotion; the only pity possible is for our own patent and infinite inferiority; and this is as it should be. The kingly and submissive are two sides of one quality in the nature of God. Even He is most royal when He stoops to service. In setting forth the wonders of Jesus as the servant of God Mark deals with His Sanctification (i. 1-13); Service (i. 14-viii. 30); Sacrifice (viii. 31-xvi.).

A. SANCTIFICATION

In this division there are brought before us the remarkable movements through which Jesus was set apart to service. The keynote of the first section, which describes the work of the herald, is contained in the words *"John came."* His coming was in fulfillment of prophecy, and his mission was prophetic. The keynote of the section introducing Jesus is contained in the words *"Jesus came."* At the Jordan He entered upon a new phase of toil. Through all the years, in the commonplaces of life, He had been serving. Now, by baptism, He deliberately identified Himself with sinners, and so set His face toward the specific service which He had come to render. In connection with His baptism He was anointed, and His fitness was attested by the voice of the Father. He then immediately passed into the wilderness, where, as Servant, in perfect submission, He met in conflict the one who had rebelled against submission, and overcame him. He then stood upon the threshold of His work, wholly surrendered, perfectly equipped, and already victorious.

B. SERVICE

The division setting forth the perfect service of Jesus falls into three sections, the first dealing with His first disciples, and first work; the second with the appointment of the twelve, and an advance in toil; the third with the commissioning of the twelve, and co-operation in service.

Coming into Galilee, He first called four men into association with Himself, choosing those already trained to some form of work to be associated with Him in His. At Capernaum He entered the synagogue on the Sabbath day, and amid its rest, He continued His toil. Under the influence of His teaching, a demon-possessed man interrupted, and became the mouthpiece of the evil spirit within him. The testimony was remarkable. He spoke of Jesus as "the Holy One of God," and in the uttering of the words confessed his own defeat. From the synagogue God's Servant passed to the home, and healed a woman, who immediately became herself a servant, ministering to Him and others. Multitudes gathered to Him, and He healed them with perfect ease.

B. Service

From the press of the crowds He escaped to the mountain for a period of communion with His Father. There the clamor of eager disciples broke in upon Him, and He passed on, continuing His toil in other cities. Leprosy, palsy, and sin in quick succession presented themselves before Him, and He dealt with each powerfully and finally. Following this series of works is a series of words in which He first vindicated His method with sinners: His presence at the feast of the publican was that of the Physician; He was there to heal. He then vindicated His disciples' joy; how could they be sad while He was with them? Again He indicated His attitude toward the Sabbath by declaring that the Son of Man was Lord thereof. His anger in the synagogue with the lack of tenderness in the hearts of His accusers revealed the keen sensitiveness of His own heart. Deep and pure emotion is always costly. The last paragraph in this section reveals His ceaseless activity; multitudes pressed upon Him with their woes and wounds and weaknesses; there was no limit to His power; He touched, and they were healed.

The time had now arrived for calling others into fellowship with Himself. This He did, deliberately making His own choice upon the basis of unerring wisdom. Those chosen were appointed first to be with Him, and secondly to be sent forth. It was now that the opposition of His relatives was manifest. It was the opposition of affection so far as His mother was concerned. She felt that His toil without cessation was a sympton of madness. It must have caused Him acute suffering that neither His mother nor His relatives understood Him. Without break His toil proceeded. The rulers suggested that He was in league with the powers of evil. In denying the charge the Lord made use of some of the most solemn and awful words that ever fell from His lips. He did not say that these men had committed the unpardonable sin, but that they had approached the confines thereof in attributing to Satan the works of God. To carry that suggestion out, and finally reject Him Who did the works is the unpardonable sin. After His warning to the rulers He revealed the positive facts concerning the Kingdom in the present age in a series of parables. Once we have a picture of Him resting, and it is pre-eminently suggestive that His rest was in the midst of a storm. Even here He was disturbed by His disciples, and readily responded in glad service on their behalf. Arrived upon the other shore, He was at once at work again. He healed the demoniac, and then, besought by the men of the city, passed back over the sea, and there, in answer to the sob of a father's heart, accompanied him to the home into which death had come. On the way disease approached Him in the person of a woman, weak and trembling, yet confident; and she was answered with the virtue of His healing. He came to Nazareth, and there the blighting influence of self-centered prejudice was forcefully illustrated. The wonder of His words and works was patent to them, but because He was one of them, they were offended.

Through all this section it must be remembered that the disciples were fulfilling the first part of their appointment. They were with Him. They had not yet been sent forth. Following Him they beheld His method, and became imbued with some measure of His Spirit. By the way of this comradeship He was preparing them for immediate service, and commencing their preparation for the larger work which would devolve upon them in the days when He, as to bodily presence, was removed from them.

–374

B. Service

The apostles having thus been with Him for a period were commissioned and sent forth. They were to be the servants of the Servant, and consequently it was necessary that in every way they should represent Him. The attitude of service was emphasized by the poverty of their going: no bread, no wallet, no money. There were three essential matters in their equipment. They were to go shod with sandals, they were to go two by two, they were to go in His name. Thus tenderly the Master provided for all necessities, and swept aside all superfluities. His instructions concerning the method of their work were simple yet drastic. In any city or village they were to accept the hospitality of one dwelling, and refuse to go to others. They were not to conform to conventionalities which would consume their time, and hinder their work. They would not be everywhere received. This was no part of their responsibility. The story of the murder of John is told at this point in the narrative of Mark, in explanation of a fear which possessed the heart of Herod as he heard of the work of Jesus. The disciples returned to Jesus and reported everything. He invited them to a desert place for rest, which they never reached. Yet the short voyage over the sea with Christ must have been rest for them. His presence is home, His voice is music, His look is sunshine, His touch is life. Arrived on the other shore the multitude were waiting, and with perfect readiness the great Servant of God sacrificed His own rest and quietness that He might minister to their needs. Back again across the sea to escape the crowd, and for Jesus a short respite on the mountain, while His disciples returned yet once more over the sea at His bidding. Their sorrow brought Him to them miraculously, and mightily; and the storm was stilled. Again He gave Himself in unstinted outpouring to the multitudes as He healed their sick. Then followed a discussion with the scribes and Pharisees in which He revealed the difference between tradition and commandment, the former being the law of custom, and the latter the law of God. The final movements in the section reveal Him still at work, casting out demons, healing the deaf, feeding the multitude, and healing the blind. These works were interspersed with instructions given to His disciples. The Pharisees asked a sign, and with a sigh He declared that none should be given. Finally He gathered His own about Him at Cæsarea Philippi and the issue was that of Peter's confession. Thus through all this section Jesus is seen ceaselessly occupied in service, and calling into fellowship with Himself men who, while lovingly loyal, yet so imperfectly understood Him as to be unable to enter in full measure into the sacred comradeship.

C. SACRIFICE

In the final division the ministry of service merges into its highest sphere, that of sacrifice. Again there are three sections, which deal with sacrifice anticipated, approached, and accomplished.

Immediately after the confession at Cæsarea the Master began to speak to His own disciples concerning His Cross, and they were filled with fear. The people were thronging Him still, and in their hearing He uttered words the infinite meaning of which neither they nor the disciples knew at the time, insisting upon the absolute necessity that men following Him should do so by the way of self-denial and the Cross. From the number of His disciples He selected three to be "eyewitnesses of his glory." Passing down from the "holy mount" they were surrounded by the multitudes, and His power was manifested in His healing of the boy possessed of an evil spirit. With the departure of the crowds the disciples inquired as to the reason of their failure in dealing with this case. Answering them directly He led them forth quietly, and as far as possible privately, through Galilee in order that He might teach them still further concerning the Cross. At Capernaum He rebuked their disputation concerning greatness, and uttered some of the most solemn words that ever fell from His lips as to the necessity for the renunciation of everything which would be likely to prevent the highest realization of life. Coming into the borders of Judæa He answered the Pharisee's question concerning divorce, and immediately afterwards received the children and blessed them; and then dealt with the young ruler, and answered the question of the disciples concerning the mystery of His dealing with him. Thus He passed on, His face set toward Jerusalem, walking alone, while His disciples followed behind. Yet He waited for them, and instructed them further concerning His Cross, and two of their number asked for positions of power. The last picture in this section in which the Cross is so evidently anticipated is that of Jesus responding to a cry of need as He healed Bartimæus, and thus added another to the company of disciples who followed in His train.

In the next section the Lord is seen with definite determination approaching the final sacrifice of Calvary. The happenings are all in the neighborhood of Jerusalem. In his story of the entry Mark gives none of the effects produced upon Jerusalem and the Pharisees, save those which reveal the recognition of His Kingship. That is remarkable in the light of the fact that this is the gospel of the Servant. Yet it is in perfect harmony with Christ's own teaching that the Chief of men is so by virtue of being the Servant of all. The cursing of the fig tree, and His explanation of the act are separated by the story of the cleansing of the Temple. The pretext for selling and money-changing was that of rendering service to worshippers. This was carried on in the Court of the Gentiles, who were thus robbed of the right to their place of worship. This explains Christ's words, "a house of prayer for all nations." There was no home for Him in His city, and no rest for Him in His house. Therefore "every evening he went forth out of the city." He came into final conflict with the rulers as they challenged Him as to His authority for cleansing the Temple. That challenge He answered by uttering the parable of the vineyard. Calmly He told them of His own casting out at their hands, and announced in fulfillment of prophecy His final victory as Chief of the corner. With magnificent ease He dealt in turn with the attacks of Pharisees and Herodians, of Sadducees and the lawyer. Having silenced these rulers He solemnly warned the people against the scribes, and the contrast between the popular view of them and His estimate is most remarkable.

Mark then chronicles His instructions to His disciples concerning giving, and concerning things to come. As the hour approached for the final movements of sacrifice two opposing forces were working in different ways toward the same end. Judas plotted with the chief members of the Sanhedrin for the destruction of Jesus; Jesus prepared for the seclusion necessary to the delivery of His last discourses and the eating of the passover. At last He and His own approached Gethsemane. No apostle witnessed its agony. Heaven and hell watched the conflict. None can fathom its mystery, and darkness, and suffering; the sense of death, the weight of sin, the awful fear. We are bowed to the dust in its presence as we remember that our sin is its explanation.

The last section of this division and indeed of the whole gospel tells the story of the accomplishment of sacrifice. The solemn and awful solitude of Gethsemane was disturbed by the coming of the traitor. All the worlds touched by man are represented in the Garden. Hell let loose in the priest-inspired rabble, led by Judas, himself "a devil," on whose face is depicted the feverish fierceness of fear. Earth trembling, cowardly, and impetuous, in the disciples in folly and flight, led by Peter. Heaven quiet, calm, regal, in the Person of the Son of Man, the Servant of God. Again in solemn silence we ponder the story of His death. Its reaches go far out beyond our dreams. It is well to be silent. Joseph of Arimathæa, according to Hebrew law, contracted defilement by coming into the presence of Pilate, and so made it impossible for him to take part in the approaching feast. That defilement was made deeper by his contact with the Dead. Yet what keeping of the feast he had, in that he cared with tender hands for the Holy One of God, Who was never to see corruption!

Mark's story closes as it began. One brief chapter in our Bible contains the story of resurrection, of the days in which He tarried on the earth, of His glorious ascension. There is a calm dignity about the brief account of the ascension, which is a most appropriate end to the gospel of the Servant. He sat down at the right hand of God, His service ended, and so rendered that the most fitting place for Him is the place of highest honor, the Servant of God took the place of Chief of all. Yet His triumph did not issue in cessation of activity, for as His servants, in obedience to His parting instructions, went forward to preach the Word everywhere, He worked with them, and gave the signs which confirmed the truth of their message. The last manifestation of the grace which had been so conspicuous in personal service was that He sent His disciples forth to carry on His work, while He accompanied them.

LUKE—*Jesus Christ the Man*

A PERFECT *i.—iii.*	B PERFECTED *iv.—ix. 36*	C PERFECTING *ix. 37—xxiv.*
Prologue i. 1-4		**Prelude** ix. 37-50
I. Being and Birth i. 5—ii. 39	**I. Temptation. First Process and Issue.** iv. 1-14 **The Devil**	i. Symbolic Miracle. 37-45 ii. The Disciples. 46-50
i. Angelic Annunciations. i. 5-38 ii. The Two Mothers. - - - i. 39-56 iii. The Births. i. 57—ii. 39	i. The Challenge. 1-2 ii. The Process. 3-12 iii. The Issue. 13-14	**I. Purpose and Preparation** ix. 51—xviii. 30 i. Purpose. ix. 51 The Key to all that follows. ii. Preparation. ix. 52—xviii. 30 The Journey. The Prophet Priest Correcting and Instructing all Classes. Disciples as such. Multitudes. Rulers as responsible. Individuals according to need.
II. Childhood and Confirmation ii. 40-52	**II. Teaching. Second Process and Issue.** iv. 15—ix. 27 **Man**	
i. Growth. 40 ii. Confirmation. 41-51 iii. Advancement. 52	i. Induction and things following. iv. 15—vi. 11 ii. The Twelve. vi. 12—viii. iii. The Issue. ix. 1-27	**II. Approach and Accomplishment** xviii. 31—xxiv. 12 i. Approach. xviii. 31-34 The Key to all that follows. ii. Accomplishment. xviii. 35—xxiv. 12 The Priest making atonement alone. *a.* "Up to Jerusalem." xviii. 35—xix. 44 *b.* "Delivered to Gentiles." xix. 45—xxiii. *c.* "The Third Day." xxiv. 1-12
III. Development and Anointing iii.	**III. Transfiguration. Third Process and Issue.** ix. 28-36 **God**	
i. The Ministry of John. 1-20 ii. Anointing and Attestation. 21-22	i. The Process is in the perfecting already considered. ii. The Issue.	**III. Administration** xxiv. 13-53 i. The New Interpretation creating Passion. 13-35 ii. The New Comradeship creating Confidence. 36-43 iii. The New Commission creating Responsibility. 44-49 iv. The New Benediction creating Worship. 50-53
(Genealogy iii. 23-38)		

LUKE * * * *

LUKE WAS A Greek and a physician. He wrote moreover to a Greek, his friend Theophilus. These facts enable us to appreciate his standpoint, and thus to approach the study of this gospel intelligently. The Greek ideal was that of the perfection of the individual, and Luke sets Jesus before us in all the perfection of His human nature, showing how it transcends, by virtue of the work He accomplished, anything which the highest conceptions of Greek culture had ever conceived. His presentation of Jesus falls into three distinct parts, in which he shows Him as Perfect (i.-iii.); Perfected (iv.-ix. 36); Perfecting (ix. 37-xxiv.).

A. PERFECT

The opening paragraph constitutes a prologue, in which Luke carefully stated the method of his writing, giving the sources of his information, and declaring that he had "traced the course of all things accurately." That is pre-eminently the method of the artist who from a mass of material produces an orderly statement.

Following that method, he first presented the Person of Jesus in three movements; His being and birth; His childhood and confirmation; His development and anointing.

As to the first, he gave the account of the angelic annunciations, which account was immediately followed by that of the songs of the Mothers, and of the birth of Jesus. Thus he dealt first with the physical side, showing that this Child came into human nature, but not as the result of human will or act.

The next picture presents the Child at about twelve years of age, when according to Hebrew custom, He was presented for confirmation, and became a son of the law. The outstanding impression is that of the mental, as with perfect naturalness, in questions and answers, He revealed an intellectual capacity which astonished the rulers of His people.

The final movement in this division tells the story of the baptism and anointing of Jesus. Here the special revelation is that of the spiritual perfection of the Man as He set His face toward His life work. Thus the threefold perfection of Jesus is set forth.

In connection with the last of these three movements, Luke gave an account of the ministry of John, which is followed by the genealogy which traced the descent of Jesus, even on the human side, through all mediating men to God Himself.

B. PERFECTED

Having thus shown what may be termed the natural perfection of Jesus, Luke proceeded to tell the story of how He was perfected by processes of testing. Of these there were three; that of temptation, in which He dealt with the underworld of evil in the person of its prince, the devil; that of teaching, in which He dealt with the world of men about Him; and that of transfiguration, in which the supreme value is the revelation of His relation to God.

The first of these was a process in which, led by the Spirit, He challenged evil, and sustained by the Spirit, met all its onslaughts, and gained full and final victory. The whole

B. Perfected

temptation was in the realm of the manhood of Jesus. The words with which He rebutted the attacks of Satan were quotations from the Divine law for the government of human life. He deliberately abode in the will of God as revealed in that law, and so overcame the enemy at every point. The issue Luke declared in the words, "When the devil had completed every temptation, he departed from him for a season," and "Jesus returned in the power of the Spirit into Galilee . . . and taught." This statement reveals the exhaustive nature of hell's onslaught; but the thoroughness of the temptation is the completeness of the victory.

The second process and issue reveals the perfecting of Jesus in relation to men. In the synagogue at Nazareth with which He was perfectly familiar from youthful association, He claimed the fulfillment of prophecy in His own Person, and was immediately rejected as the men of Nazareth attempted to do Him violence. Luke next gave a series of pictures revealing different aspects of His work in Capernaum; teaching, mastery over demons and disease, and healing of all who came to Him.

He then told how Jesus called the twelve into a mountain, and appointed them to apostolic office and service; and passing from the mountain came with them into the midst of the multitudes, and repeated portions of the great manifesto which Matthew records as having been given at an earlier point in His ministry. Jesus then passed over the national barrier and brought blessing to the house of a Roman centurion. The next picture is that of the meeting, in the gateway at Nain, between death and the Lord of life, with the transformation of the procession of death and sorrow into the triumphant march of life and joy. Following is the ac-

count of John's inquiry, with Christ's answer and consequent
address to the multitudes; then the story of the scene in the
house of Simon, and the account of His journeying with the
twelve through cities and villages, teaching by both parables
and miracles.

Finally, the twelve were sent forth alone on a mission
from which they returned flushed with victory. He led them
apart, ultimately to Cæsarea Philippi. There the confession
of Peter illustrated His perfection as a Teacher, as it declared
the essential truth concerning Him. Jesus immediately commenced the second stage in the training of His own disciples,
as turning toward the supreme work of the Cross, He prepared them by announcing it to them.

The third and last process and issue, that of transfiguration, would perhaps be more accurately described as an issue resulting from the process of all so far considered. The
story of the transfiguration is that of the coming to final
perfection of the human nature of Jesus. Up to this point the
life had been probationary. A perfect instrument had nevertheless been subjected to the testing of temptation, and of
responsibility. In both He had been victorious, mastering
all attacks made upon Him by the underworld of evil, and
living so absolutely at the disposal of God as to have been
the Instrument through which light had shined upon others.
Thus through innocence and holiness He came to that
transfiguration, or metamorphosis, by which without death
He, in His humanity, was prepared to pass from the earthly
scene into all the larger spaces of the life that lay beyond. In
the glory of this mountain we see Him revealing the ultimate intention of God, and the consequent consummation
of human nature. The contrast between this Man and all

other men who must pass to death because of sin, became most vivid in this hour. At this point in the narrative of Luke the utmost reach of the Greek ideal was realized. This is the absolutely perfect human Being. All the rest of the story has to do with sacrificial work on behalf of others.

C. PERFECTING

The Greek teachers had recognized the necessity for sacrifice in order to the realization of personal perfection, but that a perfect One should suffer for the imperfect was new, and this is the story of the last division of the gospel.

Fittingly Luke placed the story of the healing of the demon-possessed boy immediately following the account of the transfiguration. The only begotten Son of God met an only begotten son of man. Having turned His back upon His right of entry to the larger life, descending into the valley, He came into contact with one, devil-possessed, and so prevented from the possibility of entering into the life that now is. Immediately He cast the devil forth, and gave the boy back to his father. It was a symbolic miracle, suggesting that work to which He was now passing, as His face was toward the Cross; and became the occasion of a conversation with His disciples in which He corrected their false views of greatness and of dignity.

This last division is centered in the Cross, and falls into three parts. The first deals with the purpose and preparation; the second with the approach and accomplishment; and the last with the administration.

The purpose is declared in the words, "When the days were well nigh come that he should be received up, he steadfastly set his face to go to Jerusalem." That is the key to all that follows in this section. Anything in the nature of detailed analysis is almost impossible. The Prophet Priest is seen pressing resolutely and yet quietly on toward the city and the Cross. On the way He was perpetually occupied in correcting all kinds of mistakes made by all kinds of people; and instructing as He went. In turn He dealt with His disciples concerning varied matters; addressed the multitudes, and manifested His power on their behalf; rebuked the rulers as responsible; answered the criticism of His enemies; and scattered helpful words and beneficent deeds among the people, according to their individual requirements. It was wholly a ministry of prophecy, revealing superlatively the darkness in which the people were living, flinging up into startling distinctness the sins of the time, and thus supremely and overwhelmingly revealing the necessity for that very work, the accomplishment of which was the reason of His first coming; and moreover, of His recent descent from the mount of transfiguration. The perfect One, perfected to demonstration in the process of His own life, is now seen doing the preparatory work in order to the perfecting of those who need His help.

The next section commences with the words, "He took unto him the twelve, and said unto them, Behold, we go up to Jerusalem," and with the declarations He made in connection therewith. It may be analyzed around this affirmation of Jesus. Thus we have first the account of the immediate approach, as He and His disciples took their way through Jericho to Jerusalem. On the journey He healed Bartimæus, and entering into the house of Zacchæus excited

C. *Perfecting*

the astonishment and opposition of those who observed Him. Because He was nigh the city, He uttered the parable which predicted His own rejection, and indicated the responsibility which would rest upon His representatives after He had gone. At last He entered the city itself, in the midst of acclamations; and His own attitude is revealed in a wonderful merging of tenderness and terror, as He swept over the city, and uttered the prediction of its coming doom.

Then follows the account of how He was "delivered to the Gentiles." His first act was to cleanse the Temple. This was followed by the criticism and questioning of the authorities, to which He replied directly, accompanying His answers by parables of denunciation. Then came the beginning of the end. The priests and the devil are seen in coalition. Their one central work was to get rid of Jesus. They were afraid of the people, but at last they gained their vote and crucified Him. He gathered His apostles about Him, and the shadow of the ancient ceremonial ritual was merged in the substance of the new Feast. He gave them fresh instructions, which indicated the necessity henceforth for forethought and arrangement in all their service for Him.

Luke now brings us into the land of shadows. In Gethsemane we see Jesus keenly alive to the terrible nature of the passion baptism, but resolutely abandoned still to His Father's will. Immediately all the storm of the malice of devils and the sin of man broke upon His head. Judas the betrayer kissed Him to death. Peter the boaster blundered with a sword, followed afar, and finally polluted the night air with blasphemy. The servants that held Him mocked and beat Him. The council formally and definitely rejected

Him. Nevertheless the figure of the Christ is still commanding and arresting. He passed through this hour with the firm
step of a Conqueror. To Judas He spoke strong and awful
words, which opened perdition before him. Peter He looked
back to penitence and tears. In the hands of brutality He
opened not His mouth. To the council He formally declared
His high office, and coming dignity. Out of the hour and
power of darkness He brought light and victory for all the
enslaved; and proved that in the toils of His foes, and in the
extremity of His weakness, He was yet mightier than all the
power of the adversary; and by victory won through defeat
He turned the hour of darkness into the daybreak of the
race. Two men saw Jesus for the first time, Pilate and Herod.
The one sold his conscience to save his position. The other,
having no conscience left, endeavored to satisfy his morbid
sensual curiosity with a new thrill, and the only thrill he
gained was the tragic silence of the Son of God.

The story of the Cross itself is told by Luke with sublime
simplicity. We stand again on the margin of the sea of unutterable anguish, and remember that His submerging was
for our rescue. What it meant to Him of suffering, and to us
of deliverance, is only understood as we remember that He
exhausted all the force of its sweeping waters; and we now
stand on the far side with Him, singing the triumph song
of those whose judgment is passed, and whose heaven is won.
What mingled feelings of disappointment and love must
have filled the heart of Joseph as he laid the body of Jesus in
his garden grave. Thank God forever, for the love of this
heart that found resting place for the sacred body which was
never to see corruption.

And thus we reach "the third day." No human eye saw

the resurrection. The failure of the disciples to believe Him concerning His return out of death prevented their watching for it, and the keepers were not permitted to behold; for emerging from the graveclothes, without discomposing them, He left the tomb before the stone was rolled away. Yet while no human eye saw the daybreak, men everywhere were soon to walk in the full light of the glorious day.

The last page of Luke's gospel gives us some suggestive glimpses of the personal administration of the priestly work of Jesus. All the appearances were to His own, and all He did was on their behalf. The story of the walk to Emmaus is full of fascination. Two men in unbelief, and yet in love declared, "We hoped that it was he which should redeem Israel." To them He gave new interpretation of the Scriptures with which they were familiar, which created a burning of heart, which consisted in the kindling of a new passion for Him, and for the enterprises of His heart.

Then with startling abruptness He revealed to them the new comradeship existing between them, which created their confidence for all the coming days. Coming into their midst through closed doors, He invited them to see His hands and His feet, and know that it was He Himself, and moreover, He ate a piece of broiled fish.

He then gave them a commission which indicated the relation of all the past and the future in the economy of God to Himself; the ancient writings, the law of Moses, and the prophets, and the psalms concerned Him. Their ultimate message was of His suffering and resurrection. In order to the preaching of repentance and remission to all the nations, His disciples were first to enter into the experience, and so to become witnesses.

The last vision of Him is that of hands outstretched in priestly benediction as He left them, in consequence of which they returned to the Temple and to worship; thus, through His priesthood, fulfilling their own.

JOHN—*Jesus Christ the Word of God*

A FROM EVERLASTING *i. 1-18*	B GOD MANIFEST *i. 19—xix.*	C TO EVERLASTING *xx.—xxi.*
I. The Word Essentially 1-14	**I. In the World** **i. 19— xii.**	**I. Abiding Life** **xx. 1-18**

i. The two Relations.
   1 and 14
ii. The two Creations.   2-13
	i. Prologue. i. 19-51
	ii. The Manifestation.
	             ii.—xi. 46
	iii. Epilogue. xi. 47—xii.
		i. The Tomb Empty. 1-10
		ii. The Lord Alive. 11-18

II. The Witnesses 15-17	**II. To His Own** **xiii.—xvii.**	**II. Abiding Light** **xx. 19-31**

i. The Old. John, Prophet.
                15
ii. The New. John, Apostle.
              16-17
	i. Love. xiii.—xiv. 15
	ii. Light. xiv. 16-31
	iii. Life. xv.—xvi.
	iv. The Prayer of the Word.
	               xvii.
		i. The Disciples. 19-23
		ii. Thomas. 24-29
		iii. Unrecorded Signs. 30-31

III. The Word Evangeli- **cally 18**	**III. By the Cross** **xviii.—xix.**	**III. Abiding Love xxi.**

	i. Love: deserted and
	   faithful. xviii.—xix. 16
	ii. Light: eclipsed and
	   dawning. xix. 17-30
	iii. Life: laid down and given.
	             xix. 31-42
		i. Breakfast. 1-14
		ii. Love Triumphant. 15-23
		iii. Unrecorded Deeds. 24-25

JOHN * * * *

JOHN WAS A mystic in all the highest senses of the word. Conscious at once of the things patent, and of that vast realm of the spiritual, of which the material is but a partial and transitory manifestation, he came into fellowship with the profoundest things in the Person of his Lord. Turning to the gospel according to John, we find ourselves immediately compelled to worship. The same personality is presented to us as that with which we have grown familiar in the earlier stories. From the beginning, however, we are conscious of a new assertion on the part of the writer, and a new quality about the Person. As we proceed, we find that the change is not that of difference, but an unveiling and explanation. The revelation of this gospel is that of God manifest in flesh. The central division dealing with this is introduced by a brief but pregnant one, showing how the Word came from the everlasting conditions into those of time and human sense; and is followed by one presenting Him in the new everlasting conditions arising out of His incarnate presence in human history. These divisions therefore may thus be stated: From Everlasting (i. 1-18); God Manifest (i. 19-xix.); To Everlasting (xx., xxi.).

A. FROM EVERLASTING

In the study of this division it is necessary that the first and fourteenth verses should be read in connection. The first declares the everlasting relation of the Word; the fourteenth the fact of His temporal manifestation. In each statement there are three parts, those of the first being immediately related to those of the second.

Lying between the two verses referred to, the glories of the Word are dealt with in the varied processes of God's relation to humanity. All creation has proceeded through Him. All life has been derived from Him, and the inner light of humanity has ever been His shining within the consciousness of the race.

Following this preliminary paragraph the evangelist recorded the double witness of John the prophet, and John the apostle, the messages of hope and realization, respectively.

The final verse announces the evangel, and constitutes a key to all that is to follow. The evident need of man is the vision of God. This he lacks. It is granted to him through the Son Who speaks from the bosom of the Father.

B. GOD MANIFEST

The main division of the gospel deals with the Word as the manifestation of God in time. It has three sections—manifestation in the world, manifestation to His own, manifestation by the Cross.

The manifestation in the world is introduced by a prologue, giving the account of the ministry of John the Baptist, and of the gathering of the first disciples of Jesus. In response to the inquiry of the rulers, the herald directed their attention to Another than himself, identifying Him as the Lamb of God, which description, to be appreciated at its true value, must be heard with the ear of the Eastern. The Lamb was suggestive of sacrifice, and this is em-

B. God Manifest

phatically declared in the statement, "who taketh away the sin of the world."

There immediately follows the account of the gathering to the Lord of His first disciples. Men are seen finding the One for Whom men everywhere are waiting. They came seeking Messiah, and found that He had already found them.

We now approach the actual manifestation in the world. Yet here again John grouped some initial signs and wonders in order to introduce the more formal showing. This grouping is full of artistic and spiritual beauty. The matters dealt with have to do with life and light, and move in an interesting circle. The first sign was that of life in its creative power, exercised at Cana, in turning water into wine. This was followed by the wonder of light manifested in Jerusalem upon the great subject of worship, first in the cleansing of the Temple as the House of God, and in the interests of Gentile worshippers who had been excluded by the traffic established in the courts; and then in the instruction of a man, honest, sincere, and inquiring, as to the deeper meanings of the Kingdom of God, and the possibility of human entrance thereto. After this first sign and wonder at Jerusalem, the evangelist introduced the double witness of John the prophet, and of himself, John the apostle. The former was the last voice of the old dispensation, and constitutes a dignified recessional, culminating in the declaration, "He must increase; but I must decrease." The latter was the experimental declaration of the new, and constitutes a triumphal processional, ending with the declaration, "He that believeth on the Son hath eternal life; but he that obeyeth not the Son shall not see life, but the wrath of God abideth on him." Then sweeping on in his circle, and so returning toward the point from which he started, he recorded the wonder of light in the spiritual illumination of a woman in Samaria, and her instruction as to the deepest meaning of worship; and returning to Cana described the second sign which revealed life operating in restoration. Whereas in the first division of the gospel the cosmic relations of Christ are set forth in their widest reaches, in this introduction to the formal showing, His relation to human life and history is set forth.

The formal showing consists of the grouping of such works and words as show the Word manifesting God in life, and light, and love.

The manifestation of life is threefold. It is first shown as having its source in God, and mediatorially in His Son, Who is the Word. This is first set forth by the account of the healing of the man at the pool. On the Sabbath day Jesus arrested and healed a man who for thirty and eight years had been in the grip of infirmity. This action was immediately followed by controversy, in the course of which Christ claimed that what He had done had been of the nature of co-operation with His Father, Whose Sabbath had been broken by man's sin. This claim stirred up their opposition, because in it He made Himself equal with God. In a discourse resulting from their criticism Jesus lifted the controversy into the highest realm as He declared His right to work this miracle on the Sabbath to be that of His fellowship with His Father, as Source of life. The key verses of the discourse are the twenty-first and the twenty-sixth.

John recorded His fourth and fifth signs, the first that of the feeding of the multitude, and the second that of the stilling of the storm as the disciples crossed the sea to the other side. The outcome of the sign of the feeding of the multitude was the great discourse on the bread of life, in which rebuking them for their eagerness concerning material sustenance, He declared Himself to be that Bread of life, out of heaven, which was necessary for the sustenance of life eternal. The sign of the stilling of the storm was for the disciples only, and was granted to them in an hour when in all probability they were both perplexed and disappointed that He had not consented to be made King by popular acclaim on the basis of His power to feed the multitudes with material bread. They were shown thereby His power over Nature. The claim of Christ to be the Bread of life gave rise to perplexity in the minds both of the Jews, and of His own disciples, each of which stated their difficulties, and Christ dealt with them in turn. The teaching was on so high a level as to sift the ranks even of the disciples, many going back to walk no more with Him.

In the next section the Word is revealed as the Satisfaction of life. The central declaration is that of Christ's invitation on the last day of the Feast of Tabernacles, in which He challenged all human need under the figure of thirst, and claimed to be able perfectly to satisfy it. The effect of the manifestation is seen in the disputes and divisions occurring as the result of His teaching. Through all this the positive theme is developed as Jesus answered questions and corrected misapprehensions.

The record now deals with the Word as light. This section is introduced by a paragraph universally conceded to have been added by a later hand than that of John. In set discourse Jesus definitely claimed to be Light, maintaining His claim in the controversy which followed. This claim was then illustrated by the introduction of the account of the miracle wrought on the blind man. Jesus is recorded to have repeated His claim before bestowing on him his sight. The gift of sight was in itself symbolic of the mission of the Word in the midst of the darkness of human unbelief. The whole of the subsequent controversy gathered round the same idea, and the development in the testimony of the man to Christ is a remarkable illustration of the illumination of spiritual life by the Word of light.

Finally, in the formal showing, we have the revelation of love. There is the closest connection between the subject of this section and that of the preceding one. In the former a man was excommunicated by the rulers of the Jews because of his truthful testimony to what Christ had done for him. Being so excommunicated Christ received him, and accepted his worship. In the scheme of revelation His discourse concerning the new community of believing souls is recorded, and in this He is seen in the ultimate revelation of His love, under the tender and beautiful figure of the Shepherd Who lays down His life for the sheep, first in the death by which He delivers them from the marauding wolf; and secondly in that infinite mystery by which through such death He takes the life again, and communicates it to them. The highest and final expression of love is found in this teaching, and the supreme declaration concerning the nature of God is made by Christ when He declared that His Father loved Him because He laid down His life, that He might take it again. This teaching was naturally followed by further controversy, in the course of which Jesus declared that the final argument for those who did not know Him personally was that of His works.

B. God Manifest

John now recorded the seventh and final sign in the manifestation in the world. It contains all the elements of love, of light, and of life; and makes a profound appeal, in that these essential things of God are seen in relation to individuals and family life. The love is declared in the midst of circumstances which seem to contradict it. The home at Bethany had ever been open to Jesus; and one of the family circle, the much beloved brother, lay sick unto death. When appealed to, Jesus did not seem to respond with any earnestness, and yet in this connection the affirmation of love was made. Then as He went with His disciples toward the scene of sorrow, those who went with Him are seen walking in the light, and thus triumphing over appearances. Finally, at the grave of Lazarus the life had its most remarkable revelation in the world in His words, "I am the resurrection," and in His work as He raised Lazarus.

The section dealing with the manifestation in the world ends with an epilogue, which gathers up in a series of movements the results following the ministry of Jesus. The effects upon His foes were seen in the plotting of the priests, and His inability to walk openly among the Jews. The effects upon His friends were seen as they gathered about Him at the social board, and were superlatively set forth in the anointing spikenard of Mary. The general issues among His own people, the Jews, were revealed in the curiosity which made them crowd to see Lazarus, and the fact that many of them believed on Him; and, finally, in the popular acclaim of the Galilæans as He rode into the midst of the hostile city of Jerusalem. Moreover, the interest of the Gentiles was seen beginning, as the Greeks came to Him, and He revealed the fact that it was necessary for them also to find Him by the way of the Cross. These illustrations and results are followed by a summary. In that summary John first recorded the broad issues of the manifestation in the world. On the one hand, blind unbelief in fulfillment of the word spoken by Isaiah; and on the other, fearful belief on the part of many who loved the glory of men more than the glory of God. Thus the epilogue is linked to the prologue. John then chronicled what perhaps were the last words uttered in the way of public teaching and appeal by Jesus.

The second movement in the manifestation of God by the Word now commences. In it are recorded the works and words in which Jesus dealt exclusively with His own. The essential revelations are the same, but they are now made to that inner circle of believing souls who are able to understand more perfectly the Divine manifestation, and consequently they touch a profounder depth.

The first section is pre-eminently an unveiling of His love. This took the form of a supreme act of lowly service. Jesus laid aside His garments, and girded Himself with a towel —that is to say, He adopted the very badge of slavery. It was the most marvellous revelation of the love of God expressing itself in terms of service. Following this action He gave His disciples instruction concerning the perfected union between Himself and them, based upon love, and expressed in mutual service. In this connection occurred the solemn act of the exclusion of Judas. Love then proceeded to speak to them in terms calculated to help them in view of the fact that He was about to leave them. This discourse was thrice interrupted by the inquiries of certain of His disciples.

The next section has pre-eminently to do with light, as it would be granted to His own by the coming of the Paraclete, consequent upon the completion of the work of the Word. The gift of the Spirit would be bestowed by the Father in answer to the intercession of Christ, and His office would be that of interpreting the things of the Christ. Thus, through the going of Jesus, the disciples would pass into new light as well as into new realization of love.

The last movement in the farewell discourses has to do with life. As in dealing with love He spoke of Himself; and with light, of the Spirit; so now in dealing with life He speaks of Himself perfected in His own by the Spirit. The new union is illustrated by the figure of the vine, and He emphasized the conditions upon which the disciples would become fruitful. The truth thus symbolized of the relation of the disciples to Himself in the bond of life He then spoke of in greater detail as to its purpose, its law, its relation, and its appointment; and finally communicated the value of this relationship for the world. Under the law of love His own would have fellowship with Him in suffering, and fellowship with the Spirit in witness. This led on to a declaration of the work of the Spirit in the world; and consequently of the work of the Spirit in equipping the disciples for the fulfillment of their work in the world. These final discourses to His own ended with His gracious declaration that the sorrow of His going would soon be turned into new joy; a summary of the meaning of His mission; and a last word of warning.

Following the discourses we have the great prayer of the Word. This again follows the threefold line of life, of light, and of love. The essential fact of life is unfolded as He spoke of His relation to His Father, and uttered His own petition. The fact of light is revealed as He spoke of His relation to the men by whom He was surrounded, and uttered His petitions for them. The fact of love is supremely evident in His prayer for the Church, which also thrills with His care for the world. He prayed for the unity of His own, that the world might believe, and that the world might know; and for their ultimate perfecting by being with Him and beholding His glory in the ages to come.

The final movement in the manifestation of God by the Word describes that manifestation by the Cross. It is first an unveiling of love, deserted and yet faithful. Love is now seen at its mightiest as it proceeds in strength through weakness. Voluntarily, and yet with the movement of a Conqueror, He bends to suffering. All this is revealed in the story of the betrayal, and of the two trial scenes. While the foes of the Word opposed, the friends failed; and Pilate, neither friend nor foe, sacrificed justice in the interests of self-preservation.

At the center of the manifestation by the Cross light is eclipsed, and yet flashes forth in new radiance. The darkness gathers as men crucify, while yet the attitude of the Word, and the two sayings from the Cross chronicled by John, suggest dawning rather than eclipse, victory rather than defeat.

The final fact in the manifestation by the Cross is that of life laid down and yet thus given. The pent-up suffering of the long hours found vent in one brief and fearful cry, "I thirst"; and the victory in the mightiest of all cries, "It is finished." In sublimity and simplicity John chronicled the most stupendous fact in human history in the words, "They crucified him." There is no detailed description, and again the only fitting attitude is that of the subdued spirit, which,

C. To Everlasting

in consciousness of the terribleness of the scene, shuts it out from all curious contemplation. Sorrow is crowned as to its measure, for never was such before or since; as to its value, for the cup there drained to the dregs will for evermore overflow with the elixir of a new life for a death-doomed race. Exquisitely beautiful is the story of His burial. After the accomplishment of the redemptive work, God suffered no rude hand to touch even the dead body of the Man of manifestation. Two secret disciples paid the last tender offices of respect to their Lord. Joseph found Him a grave in a garden, and Nicodemus brought wealth of spices for His entombment.

C. TO EVERLASTING

The last division of the gospel is brief but full of suggestion and value. As the first division declared the way by which the Word came from ages past into time, this reveals the abiding conditions of the Word toward His own in all the ages to come. Abiding life is manifest in the empty tomb and the living Lord. Abiding light is seen in His appearances to His disciples, and His patience with Thomas. Abiding love has manifestation which touches the simplest and sublimest things of human life. Its interest in material necessity is seen in the breakfast provided for toil-tired fishermen. Its provision for all spiritual need is seen in its dealing with Peter.

John closed as he began. His first statement concerned the eternal Word. His last declares that words can never express all the facts, even of His tabernacling in the flesh. Thus as at the beginning we stood in wonder in the presence of the bewildering eternities, at the close we stand in amazement in view of the infinitudes which have yet been condensed into manifestation in a Person upon Whom we may look, to Whom we may listen, Whom indeed we may handle, and yet Who forever defies any to say all that is to be said concerning Him.

ACTS—*The Church Formed and Witnessing*

A THE CHURCH FORMED *i.—ii. 4*	B THE CHURCH WITNESSING *ii. 5—xxviii.*
I. The Key Note **i. 1**	**I. In Jerusalem** **ii. 5—vii.**

The Continuity of Christ.
  i. King. Proceeding to Empire.
  ii. Servant. Serving and Suffering.
  iii. Man. Realizing and Revealing.
  iv. God. Manifest.
	i. The First Impression. ii. 5-13
	  ii. The First Message. ii. 14-47
	  iii. The First Opposition. iii.—iv. 31
	  iv. The First Communism. iv. 32-37
	  v. The First Discipline. v. 1-16
	  vi. The First Persecution. v. 17-42
	  vii. The First Organization. vi. 1-7
	  viii. The First Martyr. vi. 8—vii.

II. The Last Glimpse of the Old Conditions **i. 2-26**	**II. In Judæa and Samaria** **viii. 1-25**

i. Christ Alone.
  ii. Disciples Alone.
	i. The Scattered Witnesses. 1-4
	  ii. Samaria. 5-25

III. The Creation of the New
                    ii. 1-4
	III. To the Uttermost Part of the Earth
	                    viii. 26—xxviii.

i. The Units.
  ii. The Unity.
	i. Toward Africa. viii. 26-40
	  ii. Toward Asia. ix.—xvi. 5
	    a. Saul. The Instrument Found. ix. 1-31
	    b. Peter. ix. 32—xi. 18
	    c. Barnabas and Saul. xi. 19-30
	    d. Herod. xii. 1-24
	    e. Paul. The Instrument Commissioned.
	                    xli. 25—xiii. 4
	    f. Paul. The Instrument Used. xiii. 5—xiv.
	    g. The Council at Jerusalem. xv. 1-35
	    h. Separation between Barnabas and Paul.
	                    xv. 36—xvi. 5
	  iii. Toward Europe. xvi. 6—xviii. 18
	  iv. In Asia. xviii. 19—xxvi.
	    a. Ephesus. xviii. 19-21
	    b. Visitation. xviii. 22-23
	    c. Ephesus. xviii. 24—xix.
	    d. Three Months in Europe. xx. 1-6
	    e. Troas. xx. 7-12
	    f. Journey to Jerusalem. xx. 13—xxi. 16
	    g. Jerusalem. xxi. 17—xxiii. 30
	    h. Cæsarea. xxiii. 31—xxvi.
	  v. In Europe. xxvii.—xxviii.
	    a. The Long Journey. xxvii.—xxviii. 15
	    b. Rome. xxviii. 16-31

ACTS ✳ ✳ ✳ ✳

LUKE IS THE author of this book, and, as the opening
words indicate, he intended that it should be a companion
to his "former treatise," and, indeed, a continuation of the
story told therein. The Gospels have been principally occupied with the Person of Christ, while they have also declared so much of His doing and teaching as was necessary
for the understanding of His work. The book called the
Acts of the Apostles is principally occupied with the beginnings of that more perfect unfolding of His teaching, and
that mightier operation of His power, consequent upon the
accomplishment of the work of the Cross. In the Gospels we
have seen the perfection of His Person, but both as to doing
and teaching He has been limited, as He Himself said, "But
I have a baptism to be baptized with; and how am I
straitened till it be accomplished!" (Luke xii. 50). "I have
yet many things to say unto you, but ye cannot bear them
now. Howbeit when he, the Spirit of truth, is come, he
will guide you into all truth" (John xvi. 12, 13).

In this book we see Him in the unstraitened power, resulting from the accomplishment of His exodus, working by the
Spirit through the Church; and we hear His voice speaking through the Spirit to the Church; and through the Spirit
and the Church to the world. Perhaps the title more correctly
indicating the true scope of the book would be, the Beginning of the Doing and Teaching of Christ, by the Spirit,
through the Church. It falls into two unequal parts as to

quantity, the first being absolutely necessary to an understanding of the second, the second revealing the issues of the events chronicled in the first; the Church formed (i-ii. 4); the Church witnessing (ii. 5-xxviii.).

A. THE CHURCH FORMED

After referring to his former treatise, and in a few brief sentences epitomizing its contents, Luke first presents us with a last glimpse of the old conditions. Christ was still alone, in that His disciples did not yet understand the real meaning of His mission, or of their own. They inquired as to whether He would now restore the kingdom to Israel, and He corrected the false thinking by declaring Himself to be a new Center, and that they would be witnesses to Him, not to Israel only, but to the uttermost part of the earth. After His ascension, the disciples waited in obedience to His command, because they were unequal to the carrying on of His work, or the delivery of His message, until the Spirit had been poured out upon them.

The account of the formation of the Church needs little exposition. It is brief and sublime, and yet perfectly simple. In the upper room was a company of units, all together as to bodily association, yet separated from the Lord and from each other. By the mighty fire-baptism of the Holy Spirit the separated units were fused into one unity. Every individual member was joined to Christ, and so all shared the common life, thus becoming an organism through which Christ was able to carry on His work. In that hour began the new and unlimited ministry of Christ, by the Spirit, in and through His own, for the sake of the world.

B. THE CHURCH WITNESSING

The second division stands in close relation to the commission of Jesus as recorded in the first. He declared that they should be His witnesses "in Jerusalem, and in all Judæa and Samaria, and unto the uttermost part of the earth." The story of the witnessing of the early Church is told in that order.

The first section gives an account of the witness of the Church in Jerusalem, and is of perpetual interest as it reveals the first things. The first impression produced upon the city was that of amazement, perplexity, and criticism. This was immediately followed by the first message delivered in the power of the outpoured Spirit. In it there are two main facts noticeable. First, Peter's use of Old Testament Scriptures; and secondly, his clear declarations concerning Jesus of Nazareth. He connected the strange happenings of that wonderful day with the foretelling of their own Scriptures, and so made evident the fact that the new was the continuation and consummation of the old. He then proceeded to show that the result had been achieved through the Man of Nazareth, Whom they had rejected. The result of the message was glorious and immediate. It produced conviction, which under instruction, resulted in conversion.

The next section tells the story of the first opposition showing its cause, its instigators, and its effect. The healing of a man at the Temple gate Peter distinctly attributed to the immediate power of the risen Christ. Opposition at once followed, caused by this clear testimony of the apostles to the resurrection, and instigated by the priests. For the first time the apostles are seen on their trial. There was no definite charge preferred against them. It was rather a court of inquiry before which they stood, instituted evidently with a desire to find a charge. Peter's answer was remarkable for its splendid daring and absolute definiteness. Being released, the apostles rejoined their own company, and all betook themselves to prayer, asking for boldness. The answer was sudden and startling, the place being shaken, and themselves filled with the Spirit. This was not a second Pentecost; but rather the gracious manifestation of the continued presence of the Spirit in the hour of a grave danger. Their fear was abandoned, and their courage renewed.

If the Name was persecuted from without, within there was the realization of a most delightful fellowship. Under the Lordship of Christ, and having His mind, these early disciples emptied themselves, and served each other. The basis of the first communism was that of the essential spiritual unity of the disciples. They were of one heart and one soul. Its method was that of apostolic distribution, according to the need of individual members. One notable instance is given, that of Barnabas, who in a magnificent venture of faith sold his land, and laid the proceeds at the feet of the apostles.

The story of the judgment of Ananias and Sapphira is that of the first discipline, and utters its solemn warning to all who may be tempted to make an outward profession which is not in keeping with the inward fact and experience. It constitutes an almost overwhelming revelation of the awful atmosphere of purity, which made impossible the presence of hypocrisy and deceit within the borders of the early Church.

B. The Church Witnessing

At last the opposition flamed into actual persecution. Its inspiration was Sadducean. The new movement was essentially spiritual. The Sadducees were wholly rationalistic. The scene presented at the trial is remarkably vivid. On the one side the most august and representative assembly that Judaism could bring together; on the other a handful of men, not one of their number a man of mark or note, judged by the standard of the time; yet men whose names were to live, and whose work was to abide, while the others have only found a place in human history because of their connection with these despised followers of Jesus. As a piece of human wisdom Gamaliel's advice was excellent, but it was impossible that it should be followed. The claims of Christ are such that they cannot be let alone.

The first organization grew out of murmuring within the fellowship. The appointment of deacons issued in the increase of the Word of God, and the multiplication of the number of the disciples.

From the ranks of the diaconate a Christian martyr first sealed his testimony with his blood. The attack upon him was popular rather than priestly, and this was the first manifestation of such an outbreak. The charge against him was that of having spoken against the Temple, and his defense was an answer thereto. It consisted of a masterly review of the history of the nation, from the call of Abraham to the rejection of Jesus; and was intended to emphasize the fact that God had never been limited or localized, that the Temple was merely a part of His method, which did not exist at the beginning of their history, and may now as surely be dispensed with. Such argument and directness could produce but one result. Convinced that his argument was unanswerable, their rage was stirred against him. The dying Stephen was granted a glorious vision of his Lord. He saw Him standing, and thus fulfilling one aspect of His great priesthood.

The popular outburst against Christianity was felt by the whole Church, and as a result its members were scattered throughout Judæa and Samaria. Of this organized persecution, Saul of Tarsus was the appointed leader. Among the scattered witnesses, Philip, one of the recently chosen deacons, passed to the city of Samaria. The work under his ministry was one of arrest and conviction. A great company believed, among the number Simon the sorcerer, whose history stands as a warning against any attempts to procure the filling of the Spirit for merely selfish purposes. The apostolic visitation of the Samaritans was followed by a tour through the villages.

Then follows the last and largest section, which deals with the witness of the Church toward the uttermost part of the earth. One brief story tells how the evangel came into Africa. Philip acting under direct guidance took a journey of at least thirty miles to declare the Word to an Ethiopian eunuch. The issues are not chronicled, but the fact abides that that eunuch was one of the dark-skinned sons of Africa.

The movement toward Asia commenced with the finding of the instrument. Saul, the appointed prosecutor of the Nazarene sect, while traveling in the interest of that appointment, was, to use his own word, "apprehended"; and henceforth became the Master's "chosen vessel unto the Gentiles." Instructed more perfectly in the Way by Ananias, he received the fullness of the Holy Spirit. The change of attitude in Saul immediately issued in a change of attitude toward him. The persecutor was persecuted. At once the

B. *The Church Witnessing*

disciples who had feared him became his guardians, and made provision for his escape from the determined attempts that were being made on his life.

At this point the history returns to Peter. He is seen busily occupied in his Master's service. "He went throughout all parts," and stories are told of his visits to Lydda and Joppa. Then commenced the larger movement of the witness to Jesus in connection with the conversion of Cornelius. God by special revelation attracted the first of the "all nations" toward the evangel; and by the same method prepared the first messenger to declare that evangel. In the house of Cornelius, Peter declared that there had come to him a new perception, breaking down his prejudices, and broadening his outlook. As he spoke, the light that had broken out upon the ancient people on the day of Pentecost flashed forth upon these, and the new converts were baptized by the Holy Ghost; and then as a sign of the essential baptism they were baptized in water. The prejudices of the Hebrew Christians gave way slowly, and Peter in Jerusalem spoke in defense of his action, setting the fact of the Divine visitation against the theories of the critics. It is interesting to notice how amenable they were to the evidences as declared.

Antioch now became the new base of operations for missionary enterprise. The news of an apparently irregular proceeding there reached the brethren in Jerusalem, and they sent down Barnabas for purposes of investigation. Recognizing the movement as of God, he went to Tarsus to seek Saul, almost assuredly knowing that his special mission was to the Gentiles; and a year's work in Antioch followed under the direction of these two men.

While this movement was in process of initiation, the

church in Jerusalem was passing through a new period of persecution under Herod. Peter was imprisoned, and supernaturally delivered. There is a graphic contrast incidentally revealed between the opposing forces; Herod, sensual and sinning, at last descended even to receiving worship, and was smitten by the Divine judgment; the Word of God grew and multiplied.

The new departure at Antioch, the beginning of which was chronicled in the previous section, now became operative. Paul, the new instrument, was commissioned by the action of the church at Antioch in co-operation with the Spirit of God; and there follows an account of his first labors. Sent out from Antioch, he visited Cyprus, and then from Paphos passed through Perga to Antioch in Pisidia; and on through Iconium and Lystra, to Derbe. Turning back through Lystra, Iconium, Antioch in Pisidia, and Perga, he called at Attalia, and reached Antioch. It is the story of a prevailing ministry accompanied by persecution.

The account of the first Christian council follows. It opened with much desultory discussion, after which two serious contributions resulted in final decision. In connection with this council Peter makes his last appearance in the record, in a weighty utterance in defense of Gentile inclusion. James pronounced judgment, and, with remarkable unanimity, action was taken in the interest of this larger work. The separation between Barnabas and Paul is an interesting revelation of the imperfection of the best men. Paul found a new companion in Timothy, and they journeyed together visiting the churches.

The beginning of the second missionary journey was noted for an almost startling experience. The Spirit hurried Paul onward against his inclination. Arrived at the coast, the vision of the man of Macedonia explained that strange constraint of the Spirit, and in answer to that vision the apostle's European ministry commenced. At Philippi, which was a Roman colony, he found himself nearer than ever to the center of earthly government. The story of the progress through Philippi, Thessalonica, Berea, Athens, to Corinth, is one of continued triumph, notwithstanding difficulty. In each case testimony was borne, and results followed, and all the while the sense of responsibility and of resource was the inspiration of continuity in service and patience in suffering.

Turning back into Asia, we have in brief compass the chronicle of what in those days must have been long journeys. Proceeding from Corinth to Ephesus, on to Cæsarea, to Jerusalem, where he stayed long enough to salute the church, Paul returned to Antioch, and the second missionary journey ended. From here we see him starting upon his third journey, passing first over the old ground, revisiting the newly formed churches, strengthening believers in their faith.

During Paul's absence, Apollos, a Jew by birth, yet trained in all Greek thought, exercised a ministry which was at first limited by the fact that his knowledge of Jesus was only that obtained through the ministry of John. More accurately instructed by Priscilla and Aquila, he passed into Achaia, and making Corinth his center of operations, did much to strengthen the believers.

The story of the return of Paul to Ephesus is full of interest. He first led into the fuller light the band of men who had been influenced by the ministry of Apollos, and for three months he preached in the synagogue. Then, because of the opposition raised against him, he secured the school of Tyrannus, where he exercised his ministry for two years with wonderful effect. A new opposition manifested itself at length, stirred up by those whose craft was in danger, and resulting in actual riot.

This was followed by a return to Europe, and a three-months' stay in Greece, of which there is practically no account given. Paul then set out upon his last long journey through Jerusalem toward Rome. At Troas the account of his converse with the saints is a wonderful revelation of his enthusiasm for Christ. There is a great restlessness manifest in his attitude, which undoubtedly is to be explained by the declaration made in the previous section, "I must also see Rome." As we follow Paul from Troas to Miletus, from Miletus to Tyre, from Tyre to Jerusalem, we find him calm and confident, his face set toward Jerusalem, while yet his spirit was evidently urging him toward Rome.

Arrived at Jerusalem the apostle was received by the elders, and at once rehearsed the story of the wonderful triumphs of the Word among the Gentiles. A strong spirit of opposition to his work manifested itself among the Jewish section of the Christians. In order to pacify this section Paul consented for a moment to a policy of compromise in the matter of the men with a vow. Disturbance followed which led to his ill treatment, and subsequent arrest by the Roman captain. In his great defense before the multitudes the last word he was permitted to utter was the word "Gentiles." Immediately the whole fury of the crowds broke out, and they clamored for his blood. Thus in a moment of crisis, in loyalty to the call of Christ which came so long ago in the Temple vision, he broke forever with all the trammels of that system; and from thenceforth to the end, through suffering and through bonds, he fulfilled his high calling as the apostle of freedom, as messenger of that Christ in Whom there is neither Jew nor Greek.

The resourcefulness of Paul is evidenced in his attitude in the midst of these trying circumstances. His appeal as a Roman citizen was the climax of a remarkable threefold method. He spoke in the Greek tongue, and so obtained the opportunity of speech; he addressed the Jews in the Hebrew tongue, and so gained their attention; and now claimed the privileges of Roman citizenship. Yet the strain upon him was great, and in this connection is manifest the graciousness of the midnight vision, when the Lord stood by him, and in words which must have been as sweetest music to the heart of His troubled servant said to him, "Be of good cheer"; and by a new commission "so must thou bear witness also at Rome," sealed his own wish, "I must also see Rome." A conspiracy was hatched to encompass his death, but he was rescued. Before Felix, Paul uttered a defense which affords a splendid illustration of the strength and dignity of one who was conscious that he had nothing to hide and nothing to gain by concealment and distortion of truth. His address was courageous, courteous, and clear. His defense before Agrippa, while eloquent in defense of his own cause, was yet directed toward an attempt to capture the king's conscience and constrain it toward Christ.

The account of the last recorded voyage of the apostle is full of interest. It would seem as though all the forces were combined in an effort to prevent his coming to the city on the seven hills. At last he arrived, and a great day dawned for the Gentile world. In loyalty to his brethren after the flesh, notwithstanding all the opposition they had offered to him in Asia, and the bitterness of the persecution that followed him to Jerusalem, in Rome also he delivered his first message to them. Here also, however, he was compelled to turn from them to the Gentiles, and the last picture we have of him is that of his dwelling in his own hired house, receiving all who came to him, preaching the Kingdom of God, and teaching the things concerning the Lord Jesus Christ.

Thus ends the story of the first things in the history of the Church. The book is evidently a fragment. From the center, Christ, the lines are seen proceeding in every direction, but the uttermost part of the earth is not reached.

ROMANS—*Christ the Salvation of God*

INTRO-DUCTION *i. 1-15*	A THE GOSPEL—UNTO SALVATION *i. 16—xi.*	B THE TRANSFOR-MATION—BY SALVATION *xii.—xv. 13*	CON-CLUSION *xv. 14—xvi.*
	Fundamental Affir-mation i. 16-17	**Final Appeal** **xii. 1-2**	
I. The Address **1-7**	**I. Condemnation.** **The Gospel needed** **i. 18—iii. 20** i. The Gentile Con- demned. i. 18-32 ii. The Jew Condemned. ii.—iii. 8 iii. The Whole World Guilty. iii. 9-20	**I. Simplicity.** **Personal Life** **xii. 3-21** i. The Character of Humility. 3 ii. The Consciousness of Communion. 4-8 iii. The Conduct of Simplicity. 9-21	**I. Personal** **Matters** **xv. 14—xvi. 23**
II. Personal **Interest** **8-13**	**II. Salvation. The** **Gospel Message** **iii. 21—viii.** i. Justification. iii. 21—v. ii. Sanctification. vi.—viii. 17 iii. Glorification. viii. 18-39	**II. Submission.** **Relative Life** **xiii.** i. Definition. 1-10 ii. Inspiration. 11-14	**II. Closing** **Doxology** **xvi. 25-27**
III. The Reason **of the** **Letter** **14-15**	**III. Objections Dis-** **cussed ix.—xi.** i. Election. ix. ii. Rejection. x. iii. Restoration. xi.	**III. Sympathy.** **Relative Life** **xiv.—xv. 13** i. Sympathy as Tolera- tion. xiv. 1-12 ii. Sympathy as Edifica- tion. xiv. 13-23 iii. Sympathy as Hospi- tality. xv. 1-13	

ROMANS ✳ ✳ ✳ ✳

OF THE FOUNDING of the church at Rome we have no authentic details. The hypotheses are, that it was one of the earliest churches; that it was founded by "sojourners from Rome" who were present on the day of Pentecost and carried the evangel to the imperial city; that Paul wrote this letter in Corinth during his three months' stay there after the uproar in Ephesus; and that Phœbe's approaching visit to Rome (xvi. 1, 2) offered him the opportunity of sending it to the church there.

This letter is the foundation document of the Pauline system of teaching. It is intended to set forth clearly God's way of salvation for ruined man. The argument falls into two main parts, the first dealing with the Gospel Unto Salvation (i. 16-xi.); the second dealing with the Transformation by Salvation (xii.-xv. 13). These are preceded by an Introduction (i. 1-15), and followed by a Conclusion (xv. 14-xvi.).

INTRODUCTION

The writer introduced himself as an apostle of Jesus, and greeted his readers as "beloved of God, called saints." He then declared his personal interest in them, telling them how he thanked God for them, made mention of them in his prayers, and longed to see them. Pre-eminently conscious of how strategic a point for the Kingdom of God Rome was, he earnestly desired to see them that he might impart "some spiritual gift." As that was impossible, he wrote this letter. In this connection he wrote those ever memorable and illuminative words which declared him to be a debtor, and ready to discharge his debt.

A. THE GOSPEL—UNTO SALVATION

This first division of the letter opens with a fundamental affirmation, and then proceeds to discuss the condemnation which made the Gospel necessary; the salvation, of which the Gospel was the message; and finally, certain objections likely to be raised in the minds of the Hebrew readers.

The fundamental affirmation declares the gospel to be one of power, that is, equal to accomplishment, and therefore infinitely more than the presentation of an ideal, or the enunciation of an ethic. The one condition upon which this power becomes operative is indicated in the phrase, "to every one that believeth." The nature of the provision which the Gospel announces is that of righteousness at the disposal of unrighteous men.

In dealing with the condemnation which made the Gospel necessary the apostle commenced with the Gentiles. After announcing the general principle that "the wrath of God is revealed . . . against ungodliness and unrighteousness," he proceeded to declare the measure of Gentile knowledge to be that of the revelation of the power and Divinity of God through created things. Their sin consisted in the fact of "holding down the truth in unrighteousness," in that they deified that which revealed, instead of worshiping the One revealed. Their judgment consisted in their being abandoned to their own sin of refusing to act upon the measure of light received.

A. *The Gospel—Unto Salvation*

The Jew is next described as one who condemned
Gentile sins under the impression that the possession of the
law ensured some kind of benefit to him. All such confidence
is swept aside as the Jew is charged with practising the evils
which he condemns. The failure of the Jews is then stated
in greater detail. They did actually possess in the law the
form of knowledge and truth. By a series of questions the
apostle inferentially charged them with actual failure in
conduct, and so with the sin of blaspheming the name of
God among the Gentiles; finally declaring that a Jew who
is merely one outwardly, is not a Jew. He then turned to a
brief discussion of certain objections which would almost
inevitably be raised. First, "What advantage then hath the
Jew?" to which he replied, "Much every way," and then
spoke of one—that they were entrusted with the oracles of
God. To the inquiry, if faith failed on the part of man would
God be unfaithful, he replied that it is impossible for God
to be unfaithful, but showed that His faithfulness is to His
own character; and that if a man sin, He judges him; if he
repent, He forgives him.

He then includes both Jew and Gentile, and utters an appalling verdict concerning the whole race in the quotation of
a series of passages from the Old Testament. The whole
world is guilty.

In dealing with the Gospel message the first subject is that
of justification. The scheme is first summarized. To the condemned race "a righteousness of God hath been manifested,"
which is at their disposal. It is witnessed by the law and the
prophets. It is appropriated by the faith of any, "for there is
no distinction." In the development of the theme the apostle
dealt more explicitly with the consequent facts, namely that

the righteousness of God is at the disposal of those who believe. The charge against the race is repeated, "All have sinned." Immediately the provision of grace is announced. That provision operates through the medium of redemption, accomplished by Christ Jesus, through propitiation in His blood. Thus the work of the Cross is set at the heart of this evangel of salvation, and is seen to be a fulfillment of God's purpose, by God's Son, for the vindication of God's righteousness, in the action of God's forbearance. The condition of human appropriation is that of faith in Jesus. This evangel is founded upon eternal justice. Justification is the act of God, through Christ, in response to faith. The apostle declared that this method of imputed righteousness in response to faith was in harmony with the whole history of Israel. This he illustrated at length from the history of Abraham.

The values or privileges of justification are dealt with under two heads, those experienced by the individual believer, and those at the disposal of the race. The privileges of the individual believer are intimately connected with the essential things of God, grace and glory, which Christ came to reveal. They carry a twofold responsibility; that of a peace with God, which means the end of controversy, and that of rejoicing, which is based upon the certainty of His ultimate victory. The effect of this new relationship to God is that all life is changed, and even tribulation becomes the minister of progress. The values of justification, as at the disposal of the race, are set forth by a contrast between the first and last Adam. As far as the evil results of the first Adam's sin have spread, so far do the benefits of the last Adam's work extend. By faith in the last Adam, man can be set free from the effects of the disobedience of the first Adam. By continuity in the disobedience of the sins of the first Adam, man is excluded from the values of the work of the last Adam.

Sanctification is the experimental appropriation of the virtue, as well as the value, of the work of Christ. In the last section the opposing principles of action were seen to be faith in Jesus, and continuity in sin. The question is now asked, Can both these govern life? This is answered by insistence upon the fact of the believer's identification with Christ in death, and in life, and the responsibilities of such identification. The negative responsibility is declared first, "Even so reckon." Sin is not to reign in the mortal body. The mastery of the life by the desires of the flesh is no longer necessary, by reason of the new life possessed in Christ. The positive responsibility is that of presenting ourselves as "alive from the dead." This new obligation resting upon the believer is then illustrated by the figures of the bond-slave and marriage. The servant of sin is the slave of sin. The servant of righteousness is the bond-servant of righteousness. The believer is freed from the covenant of law by death, and brought into new covenant with Christ by life. The death which frees him is the death of Christ; the life which enables him is the life of Christ. A change of masters will produce a change of service, and a change of covenant changes the center of responsibility.

This argument is then illustrated by one of the great personal and experimental passages of the Pauline writings. The pronouns change from the plural to the singular. The apostle gives a picture of his religious experience up to the time of his meeting with Christ; his condition before law, his experience at the coming of law, and his subsequent experience under law; all of which prepares the way for the description of the new experience of such as are not under law but under grace. From the fearful sense of condemnation they pass into the consciousness of no condemnation. From the slavery of the law of sin and death they emerge into the law of the spirit of freedom and life. Then follows a detailed contrast between life in the flesh and life in the spirit.

Glorification is dealt with by an onward look from the midst of that suffering to which Paul had already referred. The apostle first suggested, and then declined, a comparison between the sufferings and the glory. In the light of the accomplished redemption, the apostle sees all things working together, even through processes of pain which express themselves in groaning, toward the ultimate good. That pain of Nature is the consciousness of the saint, but finally and supremely that of God Himself. This assurance issues in the triumphant challenge of the believing soul to all the forces which can possibly be against it; and the unfolding of God's plan of salvation ends with the cry of an assured triumph.

The certainty of no separation creates the sorrow of fellowship with Christ in the presence of the need of man. Its first expression, in the case of the apostle, was toward his brethren after the flesh. After an enunciation of glorious facts concerning Israel, facing their present condition, he was conscious that it appeared as though the Word of God had come to nought. This was not so, because the promises made were not to a people after the flesh. The purpose of election was character, and its principle was the mercy and compassion of God. God exercises that mercy toward those who believe. The apostle then selected an illustration from the opposite condition, that namely of the willful hardening of the heart against God, and shows how God finally hardened the man who had persistently hardened himself. The sovereignty of election was then insisted upon by the use of the ancient figure of the potter; and finally the declaration was made that the Gentiles are chosen to become a people of God because they attain righteousness by faith, while Israel failed as a nation through seeking to establish righteousness apart from faith. Thus the choice of God is of such as believe. The test is the Son of His love.

Again declaring his affection for his own people, and his desire for their salvation, the apostle proceeded to discuss the way of return. Israel had been rejected because of her rebellion, in spite of the fact that the hands of God had been spread out continuously toward her. The original purpose of God, however, is retained. A temporary casting off of the nation after the flesh, and the bringing in of the Gentiles is in itself a movement toward the ultimate fulfillment of the original Divine intention. He then solemnly warned the Gentile Christians that if God spared not natural branches, neither will He spare those grafted in, save upon the one condition of belief. Unbelieving Israel had been rejected as a nation, in order that the outside world which they failed to bless might receive salvation. Through the accomplishment of that larger purpose, blessing would return to Israel. The doxology which follows forms the conclusion of the whole doctrinal statement of the epistle.

B. TRANSFORMATION—BY SALVATION

The second division of the letter opens with an inclusive final appeal, which the apostle proceeds to apply in a description of the transformed life, in its simplicity, submission, and sympathy.

The word "therefore" links all that is now to be said with everything that has already been said. Because of the grace of God the believer is called to certain attitudes and actions. The first of these is that of personal abandonment to God. Man, essentially a spirit, is to make his own body the sacrificial symbol of his worship. The spirit is evidently God's; the body is therefore presented to God; the mind is thus renewed according to the will of God.

One of the first and positive proofs of abandonment to the will of God is the character of humility. The test of humility is the consciousness of communion. To illustrate this the apostle uses the figure of the body, wherein the importance of each member is measured by its contribution to the whole. A list of gifts, bestowed as within the one body of Christ, is then given. The character of humility finally expresses itself in the conduct of simplicity. Love is to be without hypocrisy; that is, without acting; that is, simple.

Submission to authority was specially necessary for Christians living in Rome at the time of the writing of this letter. Yet the apostle so stated it as to leave clearly in view the abiding principles rather than the local coloring. The first law in the life of the Christian is his abandonment to the will of God. When earthly authority is exercised in harmony therewith, obedience is enjoined. Necessarily, therefore, when authority comes into conflict with Divine laws the

Conclusion

Christian must refuse to obey, even at the cost of suffering. Abandonment to the will of God is evidenced, moreover, before the world at large by the discharge of all just debts. The incentive to realization of the surrendered life is that the children of the Lord are to walk as in the day, even though the night is round about them.

The final expression of the surrendered life is that of sympathy, which is first dealt with as toleration. This is illustrated by a discussion of the matter of diet, and the matter of days; and he insists upon the fact that there is but one throne of judgment, and that therefore we have no right to usurp the function in relation to our brethren. Sympathy, however, is more than toleration, it is edification. Therefore the highest principle of freedom is abandonment of a right, if need be, for the good of a weak brother. The one final test, and perhaps the severest test of conduct possible, is enunciated in the words, "whatsoever is not of faith is sin." Yet once more, sympathy is also hospitality. This is inculcated in the injunction, "Receive ye one another." The most powerful line of argument for this conduct is that of the example of Christ.

CONCLUSION

The epistle being ended as to its statement of doctrine, and the application thereof to life, the apostle turned to personal matters. In the course of this conclusion incidental revelations of his methods and ideals of Christian service occur which are very valuable. Touching and beautiful is his request for the prayers of those to whom he wrote. The section of salutation is full of interest. Twenty-six different persons are named. Two-thirds of the names are Greek, and in all probability are names of persons Paul had actually known in his work in Asia. Throughout these salutations there is manifest the apostle's consciousness of the inter-relationship of the saints as being dependent upon their common relationship to Christ. It is this very consciousness of unity that caused the solemn note of warning as he referred to certain false teachers. Once more he turned to salutations, but this time from those associated with him at Corinth.

The epistle closes with a doxology, in which the apostle refers to that perpetual purpose of love, which, having been kept in silence through ages, had now been manifested in this evangel, in order that through all the coming ages there might rise the song of glory to God; and he reverently ascribed the glory to Whom it was thus evidently due.

I CORINTHIANS—*Christ and His Church.*
The Medium of Work

INTRO-DUCTION *i. 1-8*	A CORRECTIVE— THE CARNALITIES *i. 9—xi.*	B CONSTRUCTIVE— THE SPIRITUALITIES *xii.—xv.*	ILLUSTRATIVE CONCLUSION *xvi.*
	Fundamental Proposition i. 9		

I. The Writers i. 1
 	
i. Paul.
ii. Sosthenes.
	I. Divisions
	    i. 10—iv.
	
	i. The Wisdom of Words, and the Word of the Cross.
	    i. 10—ii.
	ii. Causative Carnality corrected. iii.—iv.
		I. The Unifying Spirit xii.
		
		i. The Creation of Unification 1-3
		ii. The Administration of Unification. 4-7
		iii. The Realization of Unification. 8-31
			I. Concerning the Collection 1-4
			
			II. Paul the Worker 5-9

II. The Church 2-8
 	
i. Nature   2
ii. Character.   4
iii. Equipment,   5-8
	II. Derelictions
	    v.—vi.
	
	i. Discipline. v.
	ii. Disputes. vi. 1-11
	iii. Desecration.
	    vi. 12-20
	
	III. Difficulties
	    vii.—xi.
	
	i. Concerning Marriage. vii.
	ii. Concerning Things sacrificed to Idols. viii.—xi. 1
	iii. Concerning Women. xi. 2-16
	iv. Concerning the Lord's Supper. xi. 17-34a
	v. Conclusion. xi. 34b
		II. The Unfailing Law xiii.—xiv.
		
		i. The Law. xiii.
		ii. The Law at Work. xiv.
		
		III. The Ultimate Triumph
		    xv. 1-57
		
		i. The Gospel of Christ's Resurrection. 1-11
		ii. The Importance of Christ's Resurrection. 12-34
		iii. Intellectual Difficulties. 35-50
		iv. The Assurance and Challenge. 51-57
		
		Final Injunction
		    xv. 58
			III. Timothy the Worker 10-11
			
			IV. Apollos the Worker 12
			
			V. Injunctions to Workers 13-14
			
			VI. Interrelation of Workers 15-18
			
			VII. Salutations 19-24

I CORINTHIANS ✳ ✳ ✳ ✳

THE HISTORY OF the founding of the Corinthian church is found in Acts xviii. In the days of the apostle Corinth had become the virtual capital of Greece. It was famous for its wealth, magnificence, and culture. "To live as they do at Corinth" was an expression of the time which suggested conditions of luxury and licentiousness, for the city was a veritable hotbed of all kinds of impurity.

The church existing in the midst of this most appalling corruption was influenced by it in more ways than one, and this letter was immediately addressed to the correcting of the disorder arising from this influence. It has been called the epistle of New Testament Church order. While that is perfectly true, it describes rather that which is incidental than that which is fundamental. It is a treatise dealing with Church order, but always in view of the fact that the Church is an instrument for the accomplishment of a certain purpose; and pre-eminently, therefore, it is the epistle which deals with the fitness of the Church for fellowship with Jesus Christ in His work.

After a general Introduction (i. 1-8) the epistle falls into two main parts. The first is Corrective, and deals with the Carnalities (i. 9-xi.); the second is Constructive, and deals with the Spiritualities (xii.-xv.). It ends with an illustrative Conclusion (xvi.).

I CORINTHIANS

INTRODUCTION

In his introduction, after referring to himself as "an apostle . . . through the will of God," and associating Sosthenes with what he was about to write, Paul prepared the way by addressing the Church, describing it as to its character, "sanctified in Christ Jesus, called saints"; and as to its equipment, "enriched in him."

A. CORRECTIVE. THE CARNALITIES

In this division the first thing is the statement of a fundamental proposition, in which the apostle declared that the Church was called into the fellowship of Jesus Christ the Lord, and affirmed the faithfulness of God to such fellowship.

From that point he proceeded to deal with the manifestations of the dominance of the carnal nature in the Corinthian church, which proved that they were not living as saints, and therefore were not fulfilling the responsibilities of fellowship.

The first subject dealt with is that of the divisions which had arisen among them. The key to the understanding of these divisions is found in the phrase, "the wisdom of words." Each teacher, whether Paul, or Apollos, or Cephas, had laid emphasis on some distinctive phase of truth. The Corinthians had grouped themselves into parties around these emphases. A corrective for such schism would be found in an understanding of "the word of the cross." Then followed a contrast at length of the wisdom of the age, as manifested in "the wisdom of words," with the wisdom of God, as revealed in "the word of the cross." Reminding them of his own method when he first came to them, he was careful to declare that "the word of the cross" was indeed one of surpassing wisdom, dealing with the deep things of God, and the natural man could not receive it.

He then proceeded to show the real meaning of these divisions. They arose out of the carnality of the Corinthian Christians. This carnality had expressed itself in their partiality for certain teachers, and therefore the apostle was careful to teach the subservience and sublimity of the work of the ministry. The subservience is manifest in the fact that all contribute to the final result upon which the heart of God is set. The sublimity is evidenced in the fact that all co-operate with God. Elaborating the figure of the Church as the building of God, he declared that all exercising the ministry of the Word were building upon the foundation of Jesus Christ, and that the value of their work would ultimately be tested by Him. The point of the argument is that the supreme matter is the building, and the builders are subservient. Continuing, he rose on to a yet higher level as he declared the purpose of the building—"ye are a sanctuary of God." "The Spirit of God dwelleth in you." In the light of this almost overwhelming statement the apostle wrote the most searching and solemn warning against the destruction of the Temple. Summarizing his argument that the wisdom of the age is foolishness with God, he proceeded to show that all things belong to such as receive the revelation; both the teachers, and all the facts and forces which touch personality and affect it. Returning to the subject of the Christian teachers, the apostle defined their responsibility as being "ministers of Christ," and their work as that of "stewards of the mysteries of God." Such a conviction produced independence of the judgment of men, and remitted everything to the

final test of the Lord Himself. Then followed a passage laden
with scorn for the folly of the Corinthian Christians, and
characterized by keen satire. It would seem, however, as
though this faithful steward of the mysteries of God feared
lest the impetuous sweep of his anger should be misunderstood, and he hastened to close the section in words full of
tenderness.

The apostle now passed to other evidences of the carnality
of the church. The first was that of a lack of discipline. A
case of immorality utterly bad, judged even by the low
standards of morality current in Corinth among the Gentiles, had brought no sense of shame to the church, and consequently no action had been taken in the matter. The
church was called to immediate and drastic dealing therewith, in order first to the ultimate salvation of the excommunicated man; and secondly, to the purification of the
church, which would suffer in its corporate capacity through
the toleration within its borders of the leaven of evil. From
the particular illustration he deduced the general principles
upon which the church must ever act in the presence of evil
within her borders. The wicked man must be put away from
the company of the saints.

The next dereliction dealt with was that of the submission of disputes to heathen tribunals by members of the
church. The teaching is clear and remarkable, and has an
application for all time. Disputes among saints should be
settled between saints, and wholly within the confines of the
church. This decision he based, first, upon the fitness of the
saints for judging such things; and secondly, upon the unfit-
ness of unbelievers for the same work.

The last dereliction may be described as desecration of

the temple of God by impurity of personal life. The apostle laid down principles revealing the limitations of Christian liberty, and declaring that the believer joined to the Lord "is one Spirit"; and affirmed therefore that all the functions and powers of the life must be dominated by that Spirit. Such a statement revealed, as in a flash, the awful heinousness of all such sin.

The last section of the corrective division arose out of difficulties which had arisen in the church concerning which they had sent inquiries to the apostle. Very much of this is necessarily local. His answers, however, contained principles of permanent application. Concerning marriage the principles enunciated were that marriage is in itself honorable and right, that when the marriage union exists between converted and unconverted men and women the believer is not to take the initiative in bringing about a dissolution. If, on the other hand, the unbeliever is the acting person, no blame attaches to the Christian. The all-governing fact in the life of the Christian is that he is the Lord's bond-servant, and must so act as in loyalty to, and fellowship with, Him. The daughters of the King are to settle the question of marriage always and only within this sphere, consenting or refusing according as such action will help or hinder their highest realization of the fulfillment of His purposes.

The next difficulty had to do with things sacrificed to idols, and from the discussion of the local circumstances we may deduce a principle of permanent application. Love demands the consideration of the weakness of others. In the course of the argument he contrasted knowledge and love: "Knowledge puffeth up," "love edifieth"; and showed that the Christian desire must be to edify, and therefore that love rather than knowledge is to be the true principle of action. The apostle illustrated the principle by his own action in another matter. He claimed the right to cease working for his own living, and to look to them for material support. He declared that, while he had that right, he did not exercise it. This illustration carries out the true value of the first principle laid down. His knowledge of right would have puffed *him* up. Love resulted in *their* building up. The same principles he then enforced by illustrations from the religious and athletic feasts. The one master principle obtaining in the mind of those who ran in the races he expressed in these words: "So run that ye may obtain." The goal of the Christian is not merely his own crowning, but the ultimate realization by all of the purposes of the Lord; so that the question whether things sacrificed to idols must be eaten, must be decided in the light of the necessity for bringing all present matters into subservience to that final issue of the goal.

Continuing to deal with the same subject, he persistently set it in the light of such principles as cover the whole field of life, and illustrated the fact that privilege is not in itself assurance against ultimate failure by reference to the example of Israel. They were guilty of four sins; idolatry, fornication, tempting Jehovah, and murmuring. Because of these, notwithstanding their baptism to Moses, their eating of spiritual food, and drinking spiritual drink, they were overthrown. The warning based upon the illustration is contained in the words, "Wherefore let him that thinketh he standeth take heed lest he fall." To this warning he added the gracious declaration, "God . . . will . . . make also a way of escape. . . . Wherefore, my beloved, flee from idolatry." Then, in sudden and startling fashion, he gave the greatest argu-

A. Corrective. The Carnalities

ment for the Christian position by putting the Christian feasts into contrast with idol feasts. The position is summarized in the teaching that the test of Christian action is expediency, and the test of expediency is edification. This summary is followed by local instructions, and finally the whole teaching is condensed into the form of two governing principles, first, "Do all to the glory of God"; and second, "Give no occasion of stumbling."

Dealing with the question of the position of women in the Corinthian assembly, he taught that woman bears the relation to man that man bears to Christ. Man bears the same relation to Christ as that which Christ bears to God. If we commence this argument from the highest fact, the relation of Christ to God, three great facts are borne in upon the mind. God is equal with Christ, God co-operates with Christ, God is the Head of Christ. Carrying this out, we see that Christ has made Himself equal with man for co-operation with man, while yet He is the Head of man. Again following the argument, man is equal with the woman in Christ, for co-operation with her in Christ, while he is yet her head in Christ. The application of the principle is that woman has a right to the exercise of ministry, but that in such exercise she must ever recognize the headship of man. Knowing that this might be misconstrued into an argument for the inferiority of woman, which would lead to their being despised in Corinth, he declared that in the Lord neither is without the other. Both are needed for the fulfillment of His purposes.

The last matter discussed at length in this section was that of the Lord's Supper. In their observance of this sacred ordinance, which was intended to be the symbol of communion, they had manifested differences and divisions. The condition of affairs existing is a startling revelation of the carnality of the church. In order to correct these abuses he first told them the simple story of the institution of the sacred feast, and then declared its value to the world, and in solemn words warned them against the condemnation consequent upon unworthy eating and drinking. Thus closed the distinctively corrective section of the letter. There were other matters needing attention, but these the apostle dismissed in the words, "The rest will I set in order when I come."

B. CONSTRUCTIVE. THE SPIRITUALITIES

Turning from the corrective section of his letter, to the constructive, the apostle devoted himself to dealing with the spiritualities, which conditioned the order of the church, and equipped her for her service, under three heads; the unifying Spirit, the unfailing Law, the ultimate Triumph.

In setting forth the great truth of the unification of the Church by the Spirit of God the apostle first showed how the union was created. The master principle is that of the Lordship of Jesus, and the power both for confession and obedience is that of the Holy Spirit. In the administration of the unification, the unifying force is God in the three Persons of His Trinity. Within the unity there is variety of gifts, ministries, workings. The whole truth may be summarized thus; the Spirit bestows the gifts or capacities; the Lord directs the service; God bestows the power. This three-fold fact the apostle then dealt with in greater detail. The diversities of gifts by the Spirit is set forth in the enumeration of nine separate and distinct gifts, all of which are bestowed by and under the control of the one Spirit. The ministrations of the Lord are illustrated under the figure of the body, wherein diversity is recognized as the consent of all members to the government of the Head, that government creating the principle of power and unification. The subject of the workings of God is introduced by a fundamental statement, "God hath set," and then an illustrative list of eight manifestations of ability follow.

The teaching concerning the unifying Spirit ended with the injunction to desire earnestly the best gifts, and the promise that the apostle would show the most excellent way to obtain them. That he now proceeded to do by dealing with the unfailing law. That law briefly is love, and in the chapter which is so full of beauty we have his analysis of love. He set forth first its values, showing it to be the strength of service, the energy of equipment, the dynamic of devotion; and then named its virtues in a double seven; finally declaring its absolute victory in the all-inclusive declaration "Love never faileth," which declaration he demonstrated by comparison between the things that pass and the things that abide, of which latter he declared love to be the greatest.

Having thus dealt with the law, he proceeded to show how it operates, returning to the subject of gifts. The whole teaching here may thus be stated; the desire for the best gift is to be tested by the profitableness of the gift in the edification of another, and thus finally the inspiration of true desire is love.

Finally the apostle turned to the discussion of the ultimate triumph, setting in its light all the difficulties and disorders of the little while. Dealing first with Christ's resurrection, he claimed that it was established by three lines of proof:

his preaching, and the results following in their own experience; that the resurrection was in harmony with the declarations of Scripture; that it was attested by a company of those who actually saw Him after resurrection. He then set forth the importance of the doctrine of resurrection in regard to the salvation and the resurrection of the saints, in regard to the program of God, and in its bearing on present conduct. Turning to the discussion of intellectual difficulties, he practically summarized them in two questions: "How are the dead raised up?" and "With what body do they come?" Dealing with mistaken ideas concerning the doctrine of resurrection, he claimed that death was in itself a process of resurrection, and that there might be continuity of personality without identity of the material body, but insisting that the new body would come in some sense out of the old. All through he used the illustration of the single grain of seed. In answer to the second question, "With what body do they come?" he described, in a wonderful passage, the new body as being soul-governed. Finally he uttered anew his assurance of the fact of resurrection, and ended the whole argument with a magnificent challenge to death which breathes the spirit of triumph over it.

He then made his ultimate appeal, which must be read in close connection with the fundamental proposition. Having shown the perils of the carnalities, and corrected them by a declaration concerning the spiritualities, he laid upon the saints to whom he wrote the solemn charge that they should be "stedfast, unmovable, always abounding" in that fellowship into which they had been placed in the "work of the Lord."

ILLUSTRATIVE CONCLUSION

The conclusion is local and personal, yet nevertheless is an interesting commentary upon the theme of the whole letter. The idea of fellowship in service obtains from first to last, as to the collection for the troubled saints at Jerusalem, as to the apostle's own manifold activities, as to Timothy, and Apollos, and other loved ones who help in the work and labor; until at last the Lord in Whose work all are engaged is declared; and those who love Him not are pronounced Anathema. The final word is that of the grace of the Lord as a message of blessing to Corinth, and in that the apostle has fellowship also, in that he sends to them his love in Christ Jesus.

II CORINTHIANS—*A Sequel*

INTRO-DUCTION *i. 1-11*	A THE MINISTRY *i. 12—vii.*	B THE COLLECTION FOR THE SAINTS *viii.—ix.*	C PAUL'S COMING TO CORINTH *x.—xiii. 10*	CON-CLUSION *xiii. 11-14*
I. Salutation **1-2** i. The authoritative Note. 1a ii. The inclusive Note. 1b. ii. The Salutation. 2	**I. Personal Vindication** **i. 12—ii. 11** i. A Defense of Principle. i. 12-22 ii. An Explanation of Action. i. 23—ii. 4 iii. Parenthesis. ii. 5-11	**I. The Example of the Macedonians** **viii. 1-5**	**I. His Authority** **x.** i. His Appeal to them to be obedient. 1-6 ii. His Answer to the criticism of the Christ party. 7-11 iii. The Claim to Divine Authority. 12-18	Words of Cheer
II. Thanksgiving **3-11** i. The Values of an Experience of Suffering. 3-7 ii. The Experience from which the Values came. 8-11	**II. Concerning the Ministry** **ii. 12—v.** i. Its Power. ii. 14—iv. 6 ii. Its Tribulation. iv. 7-12 iii. Its Hope. iv. 13—v. 10 iv. Its Impulse. v. 11-19 v. Its Aim. v. 20-21	**II. The Deputation** **viii. 6—ix. 5**	**II. His Apostleship** **xi.—xii. 18** i. His Apology for Boasting. xi. 1-4 ii. His Boasting. xi. 5—xii. 10 iii. His Apology for Boasting. xii. 11-18	
	III. The Consequent Appeal **vi.—vii.** i. For Consistency. vi. 1-10 ii. For Consecration. vi. 11—vii. 1 iii. For Continued Fellowship. vii. 2-16	**III. The Results to follow** **ix. 6-15**	**III. His Program** **xii. 19—xiii. 10** i. The real purpose of his Writing. xii. 19-21 ii. His Procedure on Arrival. xiii. 1-10	

II CORINTHIANS ✳ ✳ ✳ ✳

THE SECOND LETTER to the Corinthians was evidently the outcome of the first. Titus, and perhaps Timothy also, had communicated to the apostle certain facts concerning the reception of his first letter. There were in Corinth those who imputed wrong motives to him, denied the sufficiency of his apostolic credentials, and practically refused to believe in him. In this letter the apostle answered these people, vindicating his claim and his conduct. In doing this he remarkably revealed his heart, and declared how high and holy was his conception of the office of the ministry.

If the first epistle was that of the Church prepared for work by corrective and constructive statements, this may be said to be a picture of the apostle himself as a worker, in suffering, in love, and in the consciousness of the authority conferred upon him by God.

The letter does not easily lend itself to analysis, but may be divided by the principal subjects dealt with. Introduction (i. 1-11), the Principles of the Ministry, an Answer to Criticism (i. 12—vii.); the Collection for the Saints, an Exhortation (viii., ix.); the Visit to Corinth, a Vindication of Authority (x.-xiii. 10); Conclusion (xiii. 11-14).

INTRODUCTION

After the salutation, the apostle, before dealing with the matters calling forth the letter, wrote of a great trouble through which he had passed, and expressed his joy in the comfort that had come to him, principally on account of the ability to comfort others arising therefrom. He had passed through some affliction in Asia, in all probability a sickness in which he had come nigh unto death. He recognized the aid afforded him by their prayers, speaking of his deliverance as a gift bestowed upon him by them. Thus appealing to their love and sympathy, he prepared them for much he was about to write in defense of himself against the misinterpretation of some in Corinth.

A. THE MINISTRY

The attitude of those in Corinth who were hostile to him arose out of their misconception of the true vocation of the Christian minister; and in this first division of the letter he wrote first in personal vindication, then in instruction concerning the ministry, and finally in appeal to them.

He began by reminding them inferentially that he did not purpose according to the flesh, but rather under Divine guidance realized through the Lordship of Jesus, and interpreted by the Spirit.

He then explained the action which they had criticized, that namely of his not having come to Corinth, according to his declared purpose. He had remained away, out of love for them, that he might spare them, and to this assertion he called God to witness. His sorrow over their sin was such that his coming would have been in sorrow, and thus would have brought sorrow to them. He had therefore written, that the cause of the sorrow might be removed. Having thus referred to his first letter, the apostle returned to the subject of the incestuous person with which he had dealt therein. Evidently they had followed out his instruction, and dealt in discipline with the wrongdoer; and the effect had been salutary in his case. He now urged them to the duty of manifesting their love by restoring this one to their fellowship. He urged this action, "that no advantage may be gained over us by Satan; for we are not ignorant of his devices."

Perhaps nowhere in the New Testament is the subject of the ministry set forth in its sublimity as in the section following. Paul first dealt with its power. Describing the work of the ministry as a long triumphant march, he cited the Corinthian church as an evidence of the fact. That triumph was due to the fact that the ministry was no longer of the letter, but of the Spirit. This told the secret of victories won, and revealed the nature of the power of the ministry. Passing more deeply into the statement of the reason of the power and triumph of the ministry, he declared the greater glory of the ministration of righteousness by the life-giving Spirit. It was the declaration of a message of transforming life which was demonstrated by the transformation wrought in those who declared the message. The culminating statement in the discussion of the subject of power declared that the God of original creation has shined in the heart giving the "light of the knowledge of the glory of God in the face of Jesus Christ." The earlier part of the paragraph declares the results of which this statement reveals the cause. They are, as to the ministry, "we faint not," "we have renounced the hidden things of shame," "we preach . . . Christ Jesus as Lord"; as to the hearers the negative result only is referred to, that namely of the veiling of the Gospel, the apostle affirming that it is only a veiled Gospel to those who perish. To summarize, the apostle first declared that the ministry is a triumphant march, and that the church at Corinth was the credential of the fact. The reason for this is that it is a ministry exercised in the power of the Spirit, and consequently transforming life. Finally it is a ministry through which God Who said, "Let there be light" at the beginning, says it again in the human heart, so that the darkness is dissipated, and the life is transformed.

This ministry, so full of triumph, is yet exercised through great tribulation. The treasure is in earthen vessels, and these are subject to affliction. This is a revelation of a great principle in all successful work. It is through the breaking of the earthen vessel that light flashes out upon the pathway of others. Yet throughout this statement also the other truth is recognized. The power is such that all the pressure upon the earthen vessel is not sufficient to destroy it.

Yet once more, tribulations are endured because of the hope which burns brightly in the midst of travail. The ultimate triumph will be that of resurrection; and by comparison with the weight of glory, the burdens and afflictions of the ministry are light. Moreover, tribulation is seen to be a process which issues in victory. Through the travail comes the birth, through the suffering comes the triumph, through the dying comes the living. Beyond the present tabernacle in which there is groaning, is the house of God.

These visions produce no carelessness, but consecration. At the portal of the ultimate stands the judgment seat of Christ, where He will test our work, destroying that which is unworthy, and purifying even the best of its dross.

He next declared the twofold impulse of the ministry to be the fear of the Lord and the love of Christ. The second is the exposition of the first. Much is gained by the change in the Revision from the word "terror" to the word "fear."

Finally the aim of the ministry is that men may be reconciled to God.

Upon the basis of this teaching concerning the ministry the apostle made his first appeal. Beseeching the Corinthians to be reconciled to God, he urged his argument by a description of the methods of his own ministry. This was an appeal not to outsiders, but to his children in the faith, and was for consistency, as though he would say to them, You are reconciled to God, be reconciled to God; you have received the grace of God, receive it not in vain.

He immediately followed with an appeal for consecration. In words full of tenderness, he pleaded with them, by declaring his love for them, and that they were not straitened in him, but in their own affections. He called them to separation, citing the great promises of God. These promises create the profoundest argument, not only because they appeal to the highest sentiment, but also, and especially, because in their fulfillment will be found power sufficient for the perfecting of holiness. The call is to separation, and to the putting away of filthiness of both flesh and spirit. Where this call is obeyed, the promises will be fulfilled, and at once the process of perfecting in holiness will go forward.

The section culminates in an appeal full of local coloring and suggestion. The apostle, evidently conscious that in the case of some, at least, he had been excluded from their affection, in a great cry gave expression to the hunger of his heart when he wrote, "Make room for us." He then referred to the period of his sorrow in Macedonia, of his joy when

Titus told him that they had received and been obedient to his letter, and his final word was one of magnificent hopefulness, "I rejoice that in everything I am of good courage concerning you." Perhaps there is hardly a chapter in the writings of Paul in which the heart of the man is more perfectly revealed; and the charm of it is to be found in the natural humanness which is manifested, and yet which all the while is under the constraint of that love of Christ which makes the fear of the Lord the supreme motive in all life and service.

B. THE COLLECTION FOR THE SAINTS

The apostle now turned to the subject of the collection for the saints at Jerusalem, concerning which he had written in his previous letter. First he reported the action of the churches in Macedonia. They had given according to, and even beyond, their power. Their method was that they gave themselves. If self is given, nothing is withheld.

Then with extreme delicacy the apostle urged the Corinthians to emulate so excellent an example, citing the example of Christ. Turning to the business side of things, he told them that Titus and another were sent to encourage them in the carrying out of their liberality, and was careful to show the necessity for avoiding any chance of misinterpretation in matters financial, as he wrote, "We take thought for things honorable, not only in the sight of the Lord, but also in the sight of men." He then declared the credentials of Titus and the other, and appealed to them to act in such a way as to prove their love, and vindicate his glorying on their behalf.

In concluding the subject of the collection for the saints

the apostle declared that he was not urging them to give. That they would do, but he was desirious that their giving should be glad and spontaneous, and that they should be well in advance in the matter of bounty, and not, as he says, in the matter of extortion. In order to stimulate them, he declared that such giving was of the nature of seed-sowing, and that ever means harvest. In order that the harvest may be bountiful let the sowing be bountiful. He excluded two methods of giving, first, "grudgingly," that is, very literally, sorrowfully; "or of necessity," that is, the giving of such as simply give from a sense of duty, and have not found the higher impulse of delight. For the correction of these false methods he declared "God loveth a cheerful giver." He then proceeded to declare the advantages of giving, or, if we may apply his own figure here also, to describe the harvest resulting from such sowing as he urged. The first of these was the fact that they would fill up the measure of the wants of the saints. That in itself was good, but the outcome was even better. Through such ministry they would create the cause of glory to God. And yet again, they would reap the intercession of those they helped—a harvest of precious value. The final word concerning this whole subject was an expression of thanks to God for His unspeakable gift, for the apostle knew that the remembrance of that would do more than all his argument to stimulate the generosity of those who had received the inestimable blessing.

C. THE APOSTLE'S COMING TO CORINTH

In the third division of the letter Paul vindicated his authority in an argument that centered around his proposed visit to them, and the criticisms which had been passed on him. In this division he seems to have had in mind more especially the minority who had been opposed to him. He first pleaded with them that there might be no necessity for him to change the methods that characterized his actions when amongst them. Evidently some had criticized him as courageous in his absence, while they declared him to be lowly when present. He declared his readiness if need be to be courageous in their presence. In answer to the criticism of those who evidently had declared themselves to be Christ's as the reason for their opposition to him, he in turn declared that he also was Christ's, and announced his ability to use his authority if necessary, finally claiming that he had such authority directly from the Lord, and did not depend upon self-commendation.

Having thus referred to authority, he proceeded to claim the authority of apostleship. After apologizing for boasting and stating the reason why he was compelled to do so, he proceeded to boast of his apostleship, commencing with the remarkable statement that he was "not a whit behind the very chiefest apostles," as his exercise of the apostolic office proved in its manner, its method, and its motive. He then plunged into a comparison between himself and some whom the Corinthians had received, giving the credentials of his ministry in a passage which gathers up into its sweep facts concerning himself, which at once place him in the very front rank of the servants of Christ. Yet if he himself must needs glory, he determined that it should be in the things that concerned his weakness, and called God to witness as to the truth of what he wrote. His boasting now took on a new and startling characteristic. In the history of his apostleship there had been something supernatural, and not to be finally ex-

C. The Apostle's Coming to Corinth

plained. Of this he would glory. He had received direct and remarkable revelations which it was not possible for him to speak of in detail. The purpose of these revelations had evidently been that of giving him courage and confidence in his work, for their peril lay in the direction of his becoming "exalted overmuch." With reference to the thorn in the flesh, which followed the revelations, he declared, "Now will I rather glory in my weaknesses, that the power of Christ may rest upon me." As the section concerning his apostleship commenced with an apology for boasting it closes in the same way. Yet he declared, "Ye compelled me." As his actual glorying began with a statement of his apostolic authority by comparison with others, so now he ended in the same way. "In nothing was I behind the very chiefest apostles, though I am nothing."

As the letter drew to conclusion the apostle was careful to make perfectly clear what his attitude in writing had been. All his dealing with them had been conditioned within three facts; first, it had been in the sight of God; second, it had been in Christ; and third, it had been for their edifying. He cared little for their approval of his conduct, but much for their being approved before God. Out of such desire he delivered his message under the sense of responsibility to God, and with a consciousness of its authority, because he spoke in Christ.

Finally he announced the method of his third coming to them to be that of a severe investigation, and declared that when he came they would have a proof of Christ's speaking in him. He then urged them to personal examination. They were to test themselves, and to prove whether they were in the faith.

CONCLUSION

The last words are words of cheer. A series of brief exhortations indicate what their true attitude should be. Then follows the declaration that "the God of love and peace shall be with you," and all concludes with the benediction, and it is to be carefully noted that this letter, which is perhaps the severest that the apostle wrote, yet ends with the benediction in its fullest and most gracious terms.

GALATIANS—*Christ the Emancipator*

INTRO-DUCTION *i. 1-10*	A AN APOLOGY. DEFENSE OF THE GOSPEL *i. 11—ii.*	B AN ARGUMENT. DECLARA-TION OF THE GOSPEL *iii.—v. 1*	C AN APPEAL. DEMANDS OF THE GOSPEL *v.—vi. 10*	CON-CLUSION *vi. 11-18*
I. Personal Introduction 1-5 i. Direct. 1a-2 ii. Parenthetical. 1b iii. Salutation. 3-5	**I. The Authority of Paul's Gospel i. 11-24** i. Received directly. 11-12 ii. Obeyed without consultation. 13-17 iii. Rejoiced in by the Church of Judæa. 18-24	**I. Justification is by Faith iii. 1-14** i. An Appeal to Galatian Experience. 1-5 ii. Faith the Reason of Abraham's Blessing. 6-9 iii. Law cannot justify. 10-12 iv. The Cross of Christ the Basis of Faith. 13-14	**I. Freedom must be Maintained v. 1-12** i. The Law of Liberty. 1 ii. The Alternatives. 2-6 iii. The Appeal. 7-12	**I. The Conclusion in "large letters" 11**
II. The Occasion of the Epistle 6-10 i. Another Gospel. 6-7 ii. The Anathema. 8-9 iii. The Apostolic Passion. 10	**II. Authority confirmed by Conference ii. 1-10** i. The Reason of the Going to Jerusalem. 1-5 ii. The Happenings at Jerusalem. 6-10 **III. Authority maintained in Conflict with Peter ii. 11-21** i. The Dissimulation of Cephas. 11-13 ii. The Resistance of Paul. 14-21	**II. The Relation of the Law iii. 15-29** i. The Promise. 15-18 ii. The Law. 19-24 iii. The Faith. 25-29 **III. Illustrative Enforcements of the Truth iv.—v. 1** i. Childhood and Sonship. iv. 1-10 ii. A Personal Appeal. iv. 11-20 iii. Ishmael and Isaac. iv. 21—v. 1	**II. Freedom is to Realization v. 13-26** i. Not fleshly License. 13-15 ii. Life in the Spirit is Victory over the Flesh. 16-26 **III. Freedom is Mutual vi. 1-10** i. One another's Burdens. 1-2 ii. His own Burden. 3-5 iii. Liberality. 6-10	**II. A Summary Contrasting Teachers 12-16** i. "They." 12-13 ii. "We." 14-16 **III. The Apostle's Credential 17** **IV. The Benediction 18**

GALATIANS * * * *

GALATIA WAS A district of Asia Minor, and is first mentioned in connection with Paul's second journey. No details are given of his work in this region, but in all probability in connection with that first visit the churches addressed in this epistle were formed. He visited them again, establishing them.

In these brief references, however, no particulars are given concerning them. The letter shows that Judaizing teachers had found their way into the region, and as a result much harm had been wrought among the new converts. These teachers had questioned the apostle's authority, contradicted his doctrine, and so produced conduct contrary to the Christian standard.

The epistle was written with a view to the correction of these errors. After an Introduction (i. 1-10) it falls into three divisions; an Apology, the Defense of the Gospel (i. 11-ii.); an Argument, the Declaration of the Gospel (iii.-v. 1); an Appeal, the Demands of the Gospel (v.-vi. 10), Conclusion (vi. 11-18).

INTRODUCTION

In the beginning of most of his epistles Paul definitely declared his apostleship. In this instance he defended that declaration more emphatically than in any other introduction. With extreme care both on the negative and positive sides he made his claim. There are no personal salutations, but he does not omit the general salutation of the gospel.

As there are no words of personal salutation, so also there are no expressions of thankfulness for their condition. Instead of the usual "I thank my God," he wrote, "I marvel." The false teachers were perverting the Gospel of Christ. So terrible a thing was this to the mind of the writer that twice in the introduction a curse is pronounced upon those causing the trouble. The line of teaching followed by these men is not definitely stated, but may be gathered by an examination of the epistle. The one thing certain is that it was subversive of the evangel of the Cross, and there is a note of passion in this introduction which runs throughout the whole letter.

A. AN APOLOGY. DEFENSE OF THE GOSPEL

In defense of the Gospel the apostle wrote an apology which falls into three parts, the first being a statement of its authority, the second a declaration that such authority was confirmed by conference; and the third, an account of how that authority was maintained in conflict with Peter.

The apostle first enforced the Divine origin and consequent authority of his Gospel by three arguments deduced from his own experience. He had not learned it from others, but had received it by direct revelation from Jesus Christ. He had obeyed its call without consultation. Holding no conference with flesh and blood, not even going up to Jerusalem, he had departed into Arabia. When at last he had come to Jerusalem, it was not for official recognition, but to make the acquaintance of Peter; and his only relation to the church of Judæa was that he gave it occasion of rejoicing in the success attending his work. The Divine element vindicating the authority of his Gospel is clearly marked. There was first the revelation to him of Jesus Christ, by which he received his Gospel; then the revelation in him of the Son of God, which constituted the inspiration and power of his obedience; and finally such revelation through him that the churches of Judæa glorified God in him. The argument of all this is that the authority of his Gospel is demonstrated, by the fact that he received it directly, by the effect it produced on him, and by what it had accomplished through him.

Having thus dealt with the Divine authority of his Gospel, the apostle proceeded to claim that that authority was confirmed by a conference which he had with the elders in Jerusalem fourteen years after his conversion. He declared that he went up by revelation in the interests of his work, and because of false brethren. He declared that at that conference the elders of the church imparted nothing to him; nay, rather, having heard him, they acknowledge the rectitude of his conduct, and the soundness of his positions, and gave to him and his colleague, Barnabas, the right hand of fellowship. Thus the authority of his Gospel was confirmed by conference.

His third argument was that of the maintenance of the authority of his Gospel even in conflict with Peter. The dissimulation of Peter was of so grave a nature that Paul rebuked him before the whole company of believers, urging upon him the necessity for consistency, declaring that it was because the law could not justify that they had put their faith in Christ; thus showing the absolute futility of returning to legal observances and distinctions, from all of which they had already turned. He ended his apology by the great word of personal testimony in which he outlined the Christian life as to both its negative and positive aspects. "Crucified with Christ," "No longer I that live," these declare how the believer has died to law; "Christ liveth in me," "I live in faith," these reveal how, through identification with death, the believer henceforth lives unto God.

B. AN ARGUMENT. DECLARATION OF THE GOSPEL

Having thus defended the Gospel, the apostle now proceeded to declare its essential message. This he did by first affirming that justification is by faith; then by showing the relation of the law to this; and finally by illustrative enforcement of the truth.

In affirming that justification is by faith, he appealed first to Galatian experience, describing the course of their spiritual life; Jesus Christ "set forth"; the Spirit received by faith; suffering resulting, and the Spirit supplied, and wonders wrought by faith. Showing that faith was the reason of Abraham's blessing, he declared that the true sons of Abraham are they that are of faith. This affirmation of faith as the condition of blessing led him to a statement of the alternative, and it is almost startling in its definite clearness. "As many as are under the works of the law are under the curse," for the law curses imperfection, cannot justify, and demands perfection. From this curse of the law Christ, by His Cross, delivers. Thus His Cross becomes the basis of the faith which justifies.

He then proceeded to show the relation of the law to this

Gospel. The covenant of faith, based upon a promise, was four hundred and thirty years older than the law; and therefore the law could not make it void, or add to it. The law, then, was a temporary arrangement only until the coming of the Seed, to which it led on, because through faith in that Seed the promise originally made to faith would be realized. Therefore the law exercised discipline, and watched over conduct, and so was a custodian; until Christ, by settling the question of sin, created the foundation for faith, and vindicated its confidence. Christ not only opened the prison-house by dealing with sin; He also communicated to those believing, a new life. That new life cancels all old differences. Thus the newborn are Abraham's seed, not according to, or by the way of law, but according to promise. This is the Christian doctrine of liberty from the law.

In illustrative enforcement of the truth, the apostle first instituted a comparison between the old and the new under the figure of the difference between childhood and sonship. Under the old economy men were children, that is, minors. Under the new, God sent forth His Son to provide redemption, and His Spirit to provide regeneration, whereby those trusting become sons, that is majors. On the basis of that contrast he revealed the peril threatening those who turned back to the old, under which God was unknown. In Christ He is known, and to turn back is to return to weak and beggarly elements, that is, to things unable to lift, and poverty-stricken.

At this point the apostle wrote a tender and beautiful personal appeal. Reminding them of the way in which they had received him, he asked if he became their enemy by telling them the truth; and immediately put into contrast with himself those who had been troubling them, ending his appeal with an outcry like that of a mother.

Then, asking them if they really desired to be under the law, he put the law and the Gospel into contrast by a comparison between Ishmael and Isaac; the first being the son of the bondwoman, and the second the son of the free woman. Those in Christ are the children of promise, who must therefore cast out the bondwoman.

C. AN APPEAL. DEMANDS OF THE GOSPEL

The last division of his letter is a great appeal setting forth the demands of the Gospel. In this the writer first declared that freedom must be maintained; then showed that freedom is in order to the realization of purpose; and finally taught that freedom is mutual.

The law of liberty is stated in the opening sentence. Its privilege is described in the words, "For freedom did Christ set us free"; and its responsibility in the positive "Stand fast," and the negative "Be not entangled." The alternatives of entanglement and freedom he then dealt with more fully. The former meant severance from Christ; the latter separation from all the things that spoil. This teaching that freedom must be maintained he concluded with an appeal in which he challenged them as to who had hindered them, and declared his confidence toward them in the Lord.

Continuing, he insisted upon the necessity for remembering that freedom is in order to realization. Their liberty was not intended to be fleshly license, but rather the law of life in the Spirit; and he put into contrast the works of the flesh, and the fruit of the Spirit.

Conclusion

Having thus broadly dealt with the principle, the apostle made some application thereof. The attitude of the free toward failure in others is to be that of gentleness and service toward restoration. The attitude of the free toward those who are burdened, that is, oppressed, weighed down with sorrow or suffering, is to be that of helping to bear such burdens. The attitude of the free toward personal responsibility is to be that of bearing the burden, realizing that none can assist.

CONCLUSION

After a personal reference, somewhat obscure, but which suggests a physical affliction, making it necessary for the apostle to write in large characters, he summarized the whole subject of the false teachers. The principle upon which they had acted is that of desiring to make a fair show in the flesh in order to escape persecution. As against this, his attitude had been that of glorying in the Cross. He finally pronounced peace and mercy upon such as walked by that rule of glorying, and upon the "Israel of God." The use of this phrase at the close of the letter is suggestive in the light of his argument that the true seed of Abraham consists of the sons of faith, and that the Jerusalem which is from above is the mother of those who are justified by faith.

With a touch of fine independence he wrote, "Henceforth let no man trouble me; for I bear branded on my body the marks of Jesus." The very shame and suffering and persecution which the false teachers would escape, the apostle declared had stamped him with the true insignia of his office. The scars upon his body left by the stripes and the stones spoke of his loyalty to, and fellowship with, his Master; and rendered him splendidly independent of all human opinion, and declining to be troubled by any man. The letter closes with a benediction.

EPHESIANS—*Christ and His Church.*
The Eternal Vocation

INTRO-DUCTION *i. 1-2*	A THE CHURCH—THE HEAVENLY CALLING *i. 3—iii.*	B THE CHURCH—THE EARTHLY CONDUCT *iv.—vi. 18*	CON-CLUSION *vi. 19-24*
	Inclusive Preliminary Benediction i. 3		
I. The Message 1	**I. Predestination** **I. 4-23** "Before the Foundation of the World." i. The Predestined Purpose. 4-6 ii. The Predestined Method. 7-14 iii. The Parenthetical Prayer. 15-23	**I. Concerning the Church iv. 1-16** i. Basic Unity. 1-6 ii. Growth. 7-16 iii. Ultimate Unity. 13	**I. Personal Conclusion** **19-22**
II. The Salutation 2	**II. Edification ii.** "Now . . . made nigh." i. The Materials. 1-10 Individuals the Workmanship of God. ii. The Building. 11-22 The Union of such Individuals in the one Church.	**II. Concerning Conduct iv. 17—vi. 9** i. Individual. iv. 17—v. 21 ii. Family. v. 22—vi. 4 iii. Household. vi. 5-9	**II. Resultant Final Benediction** **23-24**
	III. Vocation iii. "Unto all generations for ever and ever." i. The Personal Parenthesis. 2-13 ii. The Great Prayer. 1 and 14-19 iii. The Great Doxology. 20-21	**III. Concerning Conflict vi. 10-18** i. "Put on the Armor." ii. "Take up the Armor." iii. "Stand."	

EPHESIANS   ✳ ✳ ✳ ✳

IT IS OPEN to question whether this letter was originally sent to the church at Ephesus alone, or to a group of churches in Asia, of which Ephesus was one. The words "at Ephesus" are considered to be doubtful. The fact that there is no salutation, or directly personal matter in the letter, would seem to lend force to the idea that it was intended for a group of churches. Unlike many of the other letters of Paul, this one does not seem to have been called out by any local circumstance, but is rather a document concerning the whole Church.

The absence of local coloring makes it unnecessary to dwell upon the history of the church at Ephesus. All of it, so far as recorded, is to be found in the Acts, and in the Apocalypse.

The letter may be spoken of as the Manifesto of the Church's ultimate vocation. In it the apostle is no longer dealing in detail with the fundamental doctrine of salvation as he did in the letter to the Romans, nor with the Church's equipment for present service, as in those to the Corinthians; but with the still more glorious matter of the Church's eternal vocation. This, however, is not a doctrine revealed merely for the sake of the instruction of the intelligence of the believer. It has its bearing upon the present life, and while the first half of the epistle deals with the heavenly calling, the second half shows the effect that will be produced by an understanding of this upon the present life.

The contents may thus simply be analyzed; Introduction (i. 1-2); the Church, the Heavenly Calling (i. 3-iii.); the Church, the Earthly Conduct (iv.-vi. 18); Conclusion (vi. 19-24).

INTRODUCTION

The apostle introduced himself by claiming apostleship through the will of God, and then carefully defined those to whom the letter is addressed. He wrote to the saints, that is, to such as live by faith in Christ Jesus. He saluted his readers with the benediction of grace and peace.

A. THE CHURCH. THE HEAVENLY CALLING

The main object of the letter is suggested by the benediction which affirms the blessedness of God, and declares that He has conferred blessing upon the saints in Christ.

Following closely upon this introductory benediction, the subject of the Church's heavenly calling is commenced. It falls into three sections: Predestination, or the Church's origin; Edification, or the Church's construction; Vocation, or the Church's function.

Before the foundation of the world God chose One, even Christ, and all who put their faith in Him. God's predestination of the saints was to such relationship with Christ as should issue in their being holy, in order to the manifestation of His grace. Predestination was not only to this purpose, but included the method of redemption by blood, the revelation and consequent realization of grace in the character of such as believed. This doctrine of grace created desires in the heart of the apostle for the saints, which he expressed in prayer. This prayer asked that they might have a full knowledge of the purpose, and of the power at their disposal for its realization.

Passing to the subject of the edification, or building of the Church according to the predestined purpose and method, he first described the materials of the building. These are individuals living in the midst of conditions absolutely opposed to the will and purpose of God. These are made alive, raised up, made to sit in the heavenlies in Christ Jesus. The words "in Christ Jesus" refer to the whole process. Thus out of the deep and awful darkness God brings, through Christ, the materials with which He will build His Church. These are His workmanship as to preparation. The apostle then passed to the subject of the unification of these materials into one building. Writing to Gentiles, he declared that Jew and Gentile were to be united in Christ. Those united become "a holy temple in the Lord," the purpose of which is that it should be "a habitation of God in the Spirit." The creation of the temple is accomplished through the work of Christ. The incoming of the Spirit appropriates the temple according to the intended purpose. Thus the edification or building of the Church goes forward according to predestination.

Dealing with the vocation of the Church the apostle showed that God's dwelling therein is not finality, but rather equipment. By the Church, God Himself is equipped for the display of His blessedness. By the indwelling Spirit the Church is equipped for the fulfillment of her Divine purpose. That purpose is, that to the high intelligences, "the principalities and powers in the heavenlies," the Church is to be the medium for the manifestation of "the manifold wisdom of God." The stupendous magnitude of the subject is clearly set forth in the second prayer of the apostle, which proceeded through causes to an effect. The final petition was "that ye may be filled unto all the fullness of God." In order to this he prayed that they might be rooted and grounded in love, and so, strong to apprehend. In order to this he prayed that Christ might dwell in their hearts. In order to this he prayed that they might be strengthened with power through the Spirit. The division ends with the great doxology. So stupendous is the idea developed that in the presence of it faith staggers, save as it recognizes that God bestows power equal to the accomplishment of the purpose. That power is already at work in those who are saints by faith in Christ.

B. THE CHURCH. THE EARTHLY CONDUCT

The apostle at once moved to the application of this great doctrine to the present life of the Church, and dealt with it as it concerns the Church as such, as it affects conduct, and as it creates conflict.

The first responsibility of the Church is that it maintain the unity of the Spirit. Having described the unity as to the process of its creation, and its glorious inclusiveness, he dealt with its growth. In doing so he maintained the figure of his previous section, that of building; and yet it is the building of a living organism. To every individual, grace is given in order that all may grow up toward the ultimate fullness of the entire Church, which he described as a "full grown man, the measure of the stature of the fulness of Christ." There is an individual bestowment of grace from the Head in order that there may be mutual growth into right relationship, and simultaneous action, with the Head.

Turning to the subject of conduct, he dealt first with individual responsibility. In a series of eight remarkable contrasts, illustrating the difference between the old life and the new, he urged the believer to put off the former, and to put on the latter. These contrasts are between lying and truth, malice and mercy, stealing and giving, corrupting and edifying speech, hatred and love, purity and impurity, folly and wisdom, excitement and enthusiasm. This whole section of contrasts and injunctions must be considered and obeyed in the light of the opening words, which describe inclusively the earthly conduct of the people of the heavenly calling. "Walk worthily of the calling." Two commands may be spoken of as the dynamic centers. First, "Grieve not the Holy Spirit of God, in whom ye were sealed unto the day of redemption," and "Be filled with the Spirit."

Passing from the question of individual conduct the apostle approached that of the Christian family, dealing first with the heads thereof, husbands and wives. The wife is to be subject to the love of the husband, finding the fulfillment of the natural capacities of the love of woman in trusting so perfectly the loved one as to rejoice in his guidance and direction, knowing that it is the expression of his love. The apostle's teaching concerning the husband was the exact correlative of that concerning the wife. He spoke only of man's love, which is to be self-emptying, and is to have as its purpose the perfecting of the wife. The radiant vision of the perfect love of Christ to His Church, and the true ideal of the Church's love to Christ, is the pattern of the relationship which ought to exist between husband and wife. The heads of the household are to bear such relation to each other as is worthy of that high calling of the Church, which is made possible in the glorious union existing between her and her

Lord. Concerning children the apostle had two commands, which should be carefully distinguished. The first is that they are to obey, and the second that they are to honor their parents. Obedience is the attitude of the child under age, during the process of training, and ends with the coming of manhood and womanhood. The duty of honoring parents never ends. The responsibility of parents is stated only with reference to fathers. The exercise of authority is to be on the principle of reasonableness; and its method that of nurture, which suggests the thought of development; chastening, which includes restraint in all its forms; and admonition, which is that of warning.

The wider circle of the Christian household is dealt with as to the relationship between servants and masters. Servants are to obey, always remembering that their final reward comes from the hand of Christ. The master is ever to have in mind, as the revelation of his true relation to his servant, his own Master in heaven, and is to remember that with the Lord there is not respect of persons.

The last section of the second division of the letter deals with conflict. It is significant that at the close of so great an argument concerning the heavenly calling and the earthly conduct, the apostle should recognize the fact that life on earth after the pattern of the heavens necessarily brings conflict with all the forces that are opposed to God. He recognized that behind all the opposition of man is the more terrific opposition of spiritual forces. While the teaching realizes that the conflict is indeed a terrible one, there is not a single note that indicates the necessity for cowardly fear. Perfect provision is made for the saint in the "whole armour of God." If advantage is taken of this provision, conflict always issues in victory. The armor must not only be put on, it must be taken up; and the soldier must fight. His true attitude in conflict is that of dependence upon God in prayer.

CONCLUSION

The final injunction in the previous section concerning prayer, merges into the personal element with which the apostle concluded. They were to remember him as "an ambassador in chains." The letter closes with a benediction, consisting of words of peace and of grace, in which the Source of blessing, "God the Father and the Lord Jesus Christ," and the recipients thereof, "all them that love our Lord Jesus Christ in incorruptness," are brought together in suggestive sentences.

PHILIPPIANS—*Christ the Secret of Joy*

INTRO-DUCTION *i. 1-2*	A EXPERIENCE *i. 3-26*	B EXPOSITION *i. 27—iv. 1*	C EXHOR-TATION *iv. 2-20*	CON-CLUSION *iv. 21-23*
I. The Writers 1a	I. The Joy of Memory 3-11 i. Its Conscious-ness. 3-7 ii. Its Activity. 8-11	I. Manner of Life Worthy of Gospel i. 27-30 i. Stand fast in One. 27 ii. Nothing affrighted. 28 ii. To suffer with Christ. 29-30	I. An Illustra-tion Euodia and Syntyche 2-3 i. A Difference. 2 To be healed. ii. Neglect. 3 To cease.	I. The Saluta-tion of Saints 21-22
II. The Readers 1b	II. The Joy of Experience 12-18 i. The Value of Bonds. 12-14 ii. The Preaching of Christ. 15-18	II. The Mind of Christ ii. 1-18 i. Its Activity. 1-4 ii. Its Nature. 5-11 iii. Its Value. 12-18 (Parenthesis. Timo-thy and Epaph-roditus. 19-30)	II. The Treat-ment 4-9 i. For Differences. 4-7 ii. For Neglect. 8-9	II. The Bene-diction 23
III. The Saluta-tion 2	III. The Joy of Expectation 19-26 i. Christ shall be magnified. 19-24 ii. I shall abide. 25-26	III. Joy in the Lord iii. 1—iv. 1 i. The Peril. 2-3 ii. The Illustra-tion. 4-14 iii. The Responsi-bility. iii. 15—iv. 1	III. The Confi-dence 10-20 i. The Revival. 10-14 ii. The Beginning. 15-18 iii. The Future. 19-20	

PHILIPPIANS ✳ ✳ ✳ ✳

PHILIPPI WAS THE first city in Europe in which Paul preached. His letter to the Philippians differs from other of his writings in that it seems to have no definite scheme of teaching. It is, however, of the utmost value as a revelation of Christian experience. The word sin is not mentioned. The flesh is only referred to that it may be ignored. There are no direct reproofs, the nearest approach to one being the exhortation to Euodia and Syntyche. It is largely personal, a letter of the heart, written by one who loves to those whom he loves, and who love him. Its atmosphere is that of joy, and this is the more remarkable seeing that it was written from prison.

Some of the sublimest things concerning Christ and the Christian life are written here. Recognizing the difficulty of analysis, and remembering that the ultimate value of the letter is its revelation of the triumph of Christian experience in joy over all adverse circumstances, it may be divided thus: Introduction (i. 1, 2); Experience (i. 3-26); Exposition (i. 27-iv. 1); Exhortation (iv. 2-20); Conclusion (iv. 21-23).

INTRODUCTION

Paul's association of Timothy with himself in these introductions is an act of gracious identification with his beloved son in the faith. In this letter, for the first time, officers of the church are named in the introduction—"bishops and deacons." These, according to the New Testament ideal, are the two orders of the servants of the Church; first, the bishops, or overseers, who are entrusted with the spiritual responsibility; secondly, the deacons, who are to serve tables, or attend to the business details. It is worthy of notice that these are not named first, seeing that they are only of importance in the measure in which they serve the interests of all the saints.

A. EXPERIENCE

In writing to his children at Philippi the apostle first poured forth his own experience of joy, and in doing so revealed the joy of experience, and the joy of expectation.

His memory of them filled his heart with thankfulness, and the activity of such joy was that of prayer on their behalf. His ultimate desire for them was that they might approve the things that are excellent, in order that they might be sincere, and void of offense unto the day of Christ.

The apostle then turned to the subject of his experience in prison, using the phrase "my bonds" three times in quick succession. Thus we see the circumstances under which he wrote. He declared that these things "have fallen out rather unto the progress of the Gospel." It had become known that he was a prisoner because of his relation to Christ, and this had been his opportunity to testify for his Lord; and his brethren had become confident of the result. He rejoiced moreover in the fact that Christ was preached, even though some were doing it because of faction. All this is a radiant revelation of the triumph of Christian experience over all circumstances.

Out of the midst of such circumstances he looked on, and

B. *Exposition*

expressed his confidence that "Christ shall be magnified in my body, whether by life or by death." From the purely personal aspect, death would be very far better. On the other hand, to abide would be to have new opportunity of service. The triumph is on the side of that service rather than on that of selfish interest, even of the highest kind. He was confident that he would abide.

Thus his whole experience was that of joyful triumph over the most trying and difficult circumstances, because of his relation to Christ.

B. EXPOSITION

His interest in, and care for his children at Philippi now expressed itself in an exposition of that very experience which he had described, and he taught them what is the manner of the life worthy of the Gospel, what is the mind of Christ which will produce such manner of life, and finally described the attitudes which would enable them to rejoice in the Lord.

The manner of life worthy of the Gospel is that of maintaining unity, manifesting courage, and sharing in suffering. As in his own case the apostle measured all the circumstances of the hour by the effect they produced on the great work of the progress of the Gospel, so he tested the manner of life of these children of his love by the measure in which it ministered to the same great result.

In order to such manner of life the great necessity is the mind of Christ. This he first urged upon them, and then in a stupendous and stately passage unfolded the nature of that mind. Its master principle is that of love, first as the motive of self-emptying; and secondly, as the reason of Divine exalting. The examination of this passage should be undertaken in lonely and reverent contemplation. Turning back to Paul's first word in this section, "If there is therefore any comfort in Christ," and considering it in the light of this unveiling, its value is discovered. The statement introduced by the word "if" is seen to be of that superlative nature which admits of no contradiction. The manner of life which is worthy of the Gospel must be impulsed by the mind that was in Christ. The apostle therefore passed immediately to his next injunction, an examination of which reveals the value of the mind of Christ. There is to be the working out into visibility of that salvation which God wills and works within. The result of this will be that in the midst of a crooked and perverse generation they will be seen as lights in the world. Thus the whole section on the mind of Christ is seen to be intimately connected with the one that deals with the manner of life worthy of the Gospel. The life, love-impulsed in obedience to the indwelling of Christ, and love-controlled in submission to the Divine inworking by the Spirit, is in itself a light dissipating darkness. He declared in conclusion that if these ideals be fulfilled, there will be cause for glorying in the day of Christ, and therefore such as minister the Word may joy and rejoice, even though poured out as a drink-offering.

Immediately following is a passage in which he spoke of his hope of sending Timothy, and his determination to send Epaphroditus, in which the point of value is that of the principle of the apostle's selection of these messengers. Timothy is not among the number of those who seek their own.

B. Exposition

Epaphroditus he spoke of as "your messenger, and a minister to my need." He was to be sent back to help them, the apostle having noticed how he longed after them, and was troubled concerning them, because they had heard that he was sick.

Having appealed to the Philippian Christians to fulfill his joy, the apostle now urged them to rejoice. The ultimate attitude of life worthy of the gospel in the impulse of the mind of Christ is that of rejoicing. Having definitely stated the duty, the apostle proceeded first to warn them of the peril that threatens joy, that of conformity to the material ceremonies from which they had escaped, and ultimately laid upon them their responsibility.

Between this warning against the peril, and declaration of responsibility, we have his great autobiographical paragraph. This paragraph shows how he had lived in the midst of the things against which he warned them; and how, when apprehended of Christ, he turned from them to the attitude which he laid upon them as responsibilities. Thus the old story of his own experience becomes an illustration of how they might fulfill his injunction to rejoice. His past life was a remarkable one, in that it realized the possibilities of the old economy at their highest and best; but the vision of Christ was such that not by gradual elimination, or slow and tedious process, but immediately, he had counted all the things in which he had trusted as valueless. Turning to the positive side, he described the determination and devotion of his whole life to the one supreme object of apprehending that for which Christ had apprehended him.

Then follows his statement of the responsibility of those who are to fulfill the injunction to rejoice in the Lord. They are to walk by the same rule, that is, make progress, according to the principles already learned. He described the true attitude of the Christian, and in the midst of his description in a parenthesis for the sake of contrast, referred to those who were walking in such a way as to cause him sorrow. The true walk has as its motive the consciousness of heavenly citizenship, and its direction is toward the goal of life, which is the completion of salvation at the advent of the Lord. Therefore they were to stand fast in the Lord.

C. EXHORTATION

The last division of the letter is occupied with exhortation, and is in harmony with all that has preceded it. The apostle first gave an illustration of the necessity for exhortation, and then showed the treatment of all such cases, finally revealing his perfect confidence in his children at Philippi.

The illustration is that afforded by the case of Euodia and Syntyche. Evidently there had been some difference between them, which was to be healed; and moreover, in all probability on account of this difference, they had been somewhat neglected by others in the fellowship. This neglect was to cease.

Whereas that which follows has a far wider application than the case of Euodia and Syntyche, that wider application is most clearly seen if we consider the teaching first, as it would touch this particular case. Differences are to be dealt with by rejoicing, forbearing, praying, the result being that the peace of God will guard the heart and the thought. The peace of God is His quietness, His certainty based upon His

C. Exhortation

infinite knowledge and unlimited power. All possibility of neglecting certain of the saints because of their failure is for evermore corrected, as the things of glory and of beauty, which the apostle lists, are thought upon. These things, moreover, they were to do, and the result would be that the God of peace would be with them.

Drawing to the conclusion of his letter, the apostle expressed thankfulness for the loving thought manifest in the saints of Philippi in their having ministered to his need. This expression called forth words which afford a revelation of the deepest experience of his life. He is able to be content in any circumstances through Christ. And yet again he expressed his gratification at their care of him, in order that he might tell them the deepest reason of his thankfulness. It was not that he had been enriched, but that their giving meant "fruit that increaseth to your account." His confidence for them was finally based upon the Divine provision for them, which he expressed in the great and gracious words "My God shall fulfil every need of yours according to his riches in glory in Christ Jesus." The doxology is a fitting expression of the experience of the Christian as it has been revealed throughout the epistle. This prisoner of the Lord Jesus, recognizing his relationship to God, ascribed to Him the glory, and is thus seen to be superior to all the limitation of life which characterized his position. That ascription of glory, moreover, is "unto the ages of the ages," and thus the man who, as this letter reveals in its commencement, was living so much a day at a time that he did not know whether life or death awaited him on the morrow, was superior to all care on that account, because in Christ he stood in confident relation to the vast and unmeasured ages.

CONCLUSION

The final words are those of personal and tender salutation, followed by pronouncement of the single and inclusive benediction of the grace of the Lord Jesus Christ.

COLOSSIANS—*Christ and His Church. Mutual Fullness*

INTRO-DUCTION *i. 1-8*	A THE GLORIOUS CHRIST AND HIS CHURCH PROVISION *i. 9—ii. 5*	B THE CHURCH AND HER GLORIOUS CHRIST POSSESSION *ii. 6—iv. 6*	CON-CLUSION *iv. 7-18*
	Introductory i. 9-14 Prayer. i. The Need indicated. 9-12a ii. The Provision. 12b-14	**Introductory ii. 6-10** i. The Central Injunction. 6-7 ii. The Central Warning. 8 iii. The Central Truth. 9-10	
I. The Salu-tation **1-2**	**I. The Glorious Christ** **i. 15-23** i. The Person. 15-19 ii. The Purpose. 20-23	**I. The Church Identified with Christ** **ii. 11—iii. 4** i. The Argument. ii. 11-15 (Interpolated Application to Colossian Perils. ii. 16-19) ii. The Appeal ii. 20—iii. 4	**I. Recom-mendations** **7-9**
II. Thanks-giving **3-8** i. Faith. ii. Love. iii. Hope.	**II. The Glorious Church** **i. 24—ii. 3** i. The Mystery OF THE CHURCH. 24-26 ii. The Mystery OF THE CHRISTIAN. 27-29 iii. The Mystery OF THE CHRIST. ii. 1-3	**II. Christ Identified with the Church** **iii. 5—iv. 1** i. The General Responsi-bility. iii. 5-17 ii. The Particular Applica-tions. iii. 18—iv. 1	**II. Messages** **10-14** **III. Instruc-tions** **15-17**
	Conclusion The Reason for the State-ment. ii. 4-5	**Conclusion** Conditions. iv. 2-6	**IV. The Last Words** **18**

COLOSSIANS * * * *

WE HAVE NO information concerning the founding of the church at Colossæ, and it is probable that when this letter was written Paul had not visited it. The occasion of the writing of the letter seems to have been that information had reached the apostle that false teachers were troubling the church, attempting to supplement the Christian system by ascetic practices, and a doctrine concerning the intermediation of angels. The apostle combats these errors by declaring the absolute sufficiency of Christ. The epistle may therefore be described as a statement concerning the glory of Christ Who is the Head of the Church; and the consequent perfection of provision for the Church in Him.

This letter is, as to doctrine, correlative to that to the Ephesians. The Ephesian epistle deals with the glorious vocation of the Church in its union with the Head; the Colossian letter deals with the glory of the Head, as at the disposal of the Church. In this, the subject is that of the fullness of God in Christ, and the Church's participation in that fullness; in that the subject is that of the Church as the medium for the display of the glory of God in union with Christ. In dealing with his great theme the apostle first wrote of the glorious Christ and His Church; then of the Church and her glorious Christ, the first division being devoted to the subject of the Church's provision in Christ, and the second the Church's possession of Christ. The scheme of the epistle may thus be stated; Introduction (i. 1-8); The Glorious Christ

and His Church; Provision (i. 9-ii. 5); the Church and Her
Glorious Christ; Possession (ii. 6-iv. 6); Conclusion (iv.
7-18).

INTRODUCTION

After the usual introduction of himself as "an apostle
. . . through the will of God," Paul declared to the Colossian Christians the gladness of his heart at the news which
Epaphroditus had brought to him concerning them. The
reasons of his thankfulness are, first their "faith in Christ
Jesus"; second their "love . . . toward all the saints"; and
third their "hope . . . laid up . . . in the heavens." The
apostle indicated the connection between these essential
graces of Christian character. Faith in Christ issues in love to
the saints, and this sequence is consequent upon the hope.
In proportion as the heart is set upon the apprehension of
all that for which Christ has apprehended the believer, faith
is constant, and love profound.

A great carefulness of statement is evident in this letter.
In both divisions the same method is followed. The
systematic statement is preceded by an introductory word,
and followed by a suitable application.

A. THE GLORIOUS CHRIST AND HIS CHURCH.
PROVISION

The apostle introduced his subject by declaring the con-
stancy of his prayer, then presented the glorious Christ, and
the glorious Church, concluding with a statement of the
reason of his writing.

The apostle was conscious that the supreme need of those

to whom he wrote was that they might "be filled with the knowledge of his will," and that they might "walk worthily of the Lord." He was conscious of the absolutely perfect provision made for the saints in Christ, and his prayer merged into a declaration concerning it. Two words indicate the values of that provision—"delivered," "translated," that is, salvation out of and into. The old forces which dominated the life, and made impossible the achievement of good even when it was seen and admired, are no longer operative. From this slavery of darkness the saints have been delivered. They are brought into the "kingdom of the Son of his love." Instead of the power of darkness there is now the authority of light. Instead of the thraldom of the forces that spoil there is now the dominance of the One Who saves and perfects.

All this leads to his declarations concerning the glorious Christ. He first dealt with the glories of His Person. These he set forth in three relationships, by an inclusive statement. His relation to God is that of "the image of the invisible God." His relation to creation is that He is the originating Cause and the upholding Power thereof. His relation to the Church is that He is the Head. The whole truth is summarized in the sublime and awe-inspiring declaration that "it was the good pleasure of the Father that in him should all the fulness dwell."

He then passed to a statement of the glorious purpose of His earthly mission. The extent of that purpose is the reconciliation of all things to God. In the fall of man, discord was introduced into the cosmos. The purpose of God is to restore the lost harmony by reconciling all things to Himself. The immediate Agent of the restoration is Christ, and the method is that of the Cross. At the center of the order to be reconciled is man, and the issue of his reconciliation is his presentation "holy . . . without blemish . . . unreprovable."

The company of those redeemed constitutes the glorious Church, which is the Body of Christ. In dealing with this subject the apostle declared his joy in the fact that he had fellowship with Christ in the accomplishment of His purpose, and claimed the stewardship of the truth concerning the Church, and then dealt with it by referring to a threefold mystery. The first phase of the mystery is that of the Church itself, which is composed of Christian souls. The second phase of the mystery is that of the Christian in whom is Christ as the Hope of glory, and who is perfected in Christ. The final and deepest mystery is that of the Christ Himself. It is the mystery of the Incarnation, transcending all human apprehension, and yet demonstrated in the changed lives of those in whom Christ dwells, and to be manifested finally in the whole company of such as constitute the Church, which is the Body of Christ.

Taking this threefold mystery in the other order of statement, which is the order of the Divine procedure, we have first the mystery of God, even Christ; second, the mystery of Christ in man, the Hope of glory; and finally, the mystery of the perfected Church, Christ fulfilled in His Body.

This division he concluded by declaring that his reason for having so carefully stated this doctrine of Christ and the Church is that the Colossian Christians may not be deluded by persuasiveness of speech. Though he was absent from them, he declared that he was with them in spirit, finding his joy in the steadfastness of their faith in Christ.

—490

B. THE CHURCH AND HER GLORIOUS CHRIST. POSSESSION

The apostle introduced his subject by injunction and warning, and a general statement of truth; he then particularly declared the truth concerning the identification of the Church with Christ, and Christ's identification with the Church; concluding with a statement of the conditions upon which the saints are to possess their inheritance.

He first enjoined them that as they had received Christ the Lord they were to walk in Him, and solemnly warned them against any that would spoil them, ending his introduction by making the great central declarations of the epistle, that all the fullness of the Godhead bodily dwells in Christ, and that the saints are made full in Him.

In relation to Christ the believer stands in identification with His death, and with His resurrection. These facts are intimately connected with the glories of Christ dealt with in the earlier division of the letter. Union with the death of Christ means union with His purpose, that is, with His great work of reconciliation. Union with the resurrection of Christ means union with His Person, that is, with all the glories described. Thus, indeed, in Him the saints are made full, for they are reconciled through His death to the eternal order, and are equipped in His life for continued harmony therewith.

Immediately following this statement is a brief section dealing with the perils specially threatening the Church at Colossæ. It is evident that there were those who were attempting to bring believers into bondage to external observances, and the apostle urged them that they should allow no man to judge them in these matters. The other peril was that of false intermediation, and the consequent worship of angels, and he warned them against any such subservience, which is in itself false.

Returning to his teaching concerning the identification of the believer with Christ, he showed the necessity for living in response to the twofold fact of union already dealt with. In view of identification with Christ in death, they were not to submit themselves to ordinances, because the whole fact of their relation to evil was conditioned within the fact of their death in Christ.

Being through death set free from bondage to the commandments of men, believers are in life brought into captivity to the authority of Christ and the things of Christ. They are therefore to seek the things above, that is to say, the aspiration, the desire, the passion of the life is to harmonize with that of Christ. They are moreover to set their mind on these things. Thus the life of the Christian in union with Christ has to do with the things above. They create the activity, "seek the things"; they condition the aspiration, "set your mind on the things"; they constitute the anticipation, "Christ . . . shall be manifested . . . ye also."

The apostle then proceeded to show how Christ is identified with His Church in all the relationships of its present life. This discussion he introduced by a general statement as to responsibility. There must be answer to the fact of union in the putting to death of the things of the earth. Of these there are two lists given, one dealing with sensuality, and the other with bitterness of spirit. The injunction to put these things to death is based upon the affirmation that they have put off the old man, and have put on the new.

That which is a fact by faith, is to be made a fact in experience.

The responsibility is not merely the negative one, which consists in consent to identification in death; but also the positive one, which consists of consent to identification in life. They are charged to put on all the things of the Christ life. They are moreover to let the peace of Christ rule, and the Word of Christ dwell in them. The final and inclusive word is "whatsoever ye do, in word or in deed, do all in the name of the Lord Jesus, giving thanks to God the Father through him."

This general statement of responsibility is followed by practical injunctions, all of which show how Christ is identified with His people for the activities of the present life. These deal with the relationships between wives and husbands, children and fathers, servants and masters, all of them being set in the light of the supreme relationship to Christ.

This division of the letter closes with a statement of three matters of supreme importance in the life of the saint. The first has to do with prayer, which conditions the life in its relationship with God; the second has to do with the walk or behavior of the believer; the last deals with speech, these conditioning life toward those that are without.

CONCLUSION

The conclusion is local and personal. To the church at Colossæ he recommended Tychicus and Onesimus, and sent messages from those who evidently were with him. It is interesting to notice three of these were Hebrews, and three were Gentiles. He then gave instructions concerning his letters. The final words have in them a touch of pathos. Taking the pen from the one to whom he had been dictating, he wrote words which indicate at once his sense of limitation and his desire for sympathy, "Remember my bonds"; and ended with the simple benediction.

I THESSALONIANS—*Christ and His Advent*

INTRO-DUCTION *i.*	A THE WORK OF FAITH, "YE TURNED" *ii.*	B THE LABOR OF LOVE, "TO SERVE" *iii.—iv. 12*	C THE PATIENCE OF HOPE, "TO WAIT" *iv. 13—v. 22*	CON-CLUSION *v. 23-28*
I. Salutation 1	I. The Work of Faith 1-12 "Ye turned." i. "Not vain." 1 ii. The Ministry producing. 2-12	I. The Labor of Love iii. 1-10 "To Serve." i. The Sending of Timothy. 1-5 ii. The comforting Report. 6-8 iii. Thanksgiving and Prayer. 9-10	I. The Patience of Hope iv. 13-18 "To Wait." i. The "fallen asleep" at His Coming. 13-15 ii. The glorious Program. 16-17 ii. The Injunction to comfort. 18	I. The Final Desire of Assurance 23-24
II. General Thanksgiving 2-10 i. The Reason of Thanksgiving. 2-3 *a.* "Work of Faith." *b.* "Labor of Love." *c.* "Patience of Hope." ii. The Demonstration of the Reason. 4-9a iii. The Reason of the Demonstration. 9b-10 *a.* "Ye turned." *b.* "To serve." *c.* "To wait."	II. The Labor of Love 13-16 "To serve." i. Reception of the Word." 13 ii. Service and Suffering. 14-16 III. The Patience of Hope 17-20 "To wait." i. The Separation. 17-18 ii. The Advent. 19-20	II. The Patience of Hope iii. 11-13 "To wait." i. Separation. 11-12 ii. The Advent. 13 III. The Work of Faith iv. 1-12 "Ye turned." i. The Consequent Walk. Personal. 1-8 ii. Love of the Brethren. 9-10 iii. Toward them without. 11-12	II. The Work of Faith v. 1-11 "Ye turned." i. The Day of the Lord. 1-3 ii. "Ye Brethren." 4-11 III. The Labor of Love v. 12-22 "To Serve." i. Submission to Teachers. 12-13a ii. Mutual Relationships. 13b-15 iii. General Injunctions. 16-22	II. Personal Words 25-28

I THESSALONIANS ✳ ✳ ✳ ✳

THE CHURCH AT Thessalonica was founded amidst great and active opposition. The apostle being "sent away" by the brethren on account of the state of tumult existing in the city, went to Beræa and Athens, and on to Corinth, from whence this first letter was written. It is evident that the time elapsing between his departure from Thessalonica and the writing of this epistle was very short, for he refers to "being bereaved of you for a season of an hour."

Paul's anxiety concerning the church in the midst of persecution had been so great that he had sent Timothy from Athens to find out their state. His return and report called forth this letter. These facts will help us to understand the nature of the epistle. It is intended to be a message of comfort and instruction to those who are in the midst of persecution. The method is that of stating what the attitudes of Christian life really are, and thereby revealing the secrets of strength under such circumstances. The epistle may thus be analyzed: Introduction (i.); the Work of Faith, "Ye turned" (ii.); the Labor of Love, "To serve" (iii.-iv. 12); the Patience of Hope, "To wait" (iv. 13-v. 22); Conclusion (v. 23-28).

INTRODUCTION

In the salutation the apostle associated with himself Silvanus and Timothy, the former having been with him at Thessalonica at the time of the founding of the church; and the latter having been a special messenger to them, upon whose report the letter was based.

He then declared his thankfulness to God concerning them. The reason of this was his remembrance of three facts. These are the foundation-facts of Christian experience. The "work of faith" refers to belief of the Gospel; the "labour of love" refers to the activity of life after belief; the "patience of hope" refers to the attitude of waiting for the return of the Lord. The demonstration of the power of these facts he found in the memory of the way in which the Word came to them; in the fact that as the result of their reception of the Word they became imitators, and an ensample; and that consequently from them the Gospel sounded forth. Having thus declared his thanksgiving, and stated its reason, and given demonstration of the reason, he declared that these results in demonstration followed upon the fact that they "turned . . . to serve . . . and to wait." The connection between this threefold final statement and the threefold reason of thanksgiving is intimate. The "work of faith" consisted in turning "unto God from idols"; the "labour of love" consists in serving "the living and the true God"; and the "patience of hope" is constituted by waiting "for His Son from heaven." Around this threefold fact of their Christian experience the whole epistle circles. In each division all the facts are recognized, while only one has special treatment.

A. THE WORK OF FAITH

In this first division the apostle laid special emphasis on the "work of faith" which demonstrated his own spiritual authority, referring to their "labour of love" and their "patience of hope."

It is evident that some of the Jews in Thessalonica had been discounting the apostle in his absence. In answer to such detraction he first went back to the days when under great stress he preached to them and they believed, thus claiming that their work of faith, their turning from idols, was the supreme proof of the authority and power of his ministry. Their work of faith was not "in vain." The ministry producing it was characterized by boldness, by faithfulness, by tenderness, and by earnestness.

The demonstration of the apostle's authority was further emphasized by their "labour of love," the fact that they served the living and true God. Having received the Word, and worked the work of faith by the turning, they had treated it as the Word of God, and served even in suffering. Thus they had entered into fellowship with Him, and their fellow-believers in suffering. To serve the living and true God is a labor of love, that is to say, it is obedience to the law of love in the impulse of love, but it ever means more or less of suffering in the midst of those who are antagonistic to the revelation which God has made of His will through the Lord Jesus.

He finally referred to the great subject of the Lord's return, thus encouraging them in that "patience of hope" which consists in waiting for His Son from heaven. Loving them with a great love, earnestly desiring to see them, he was yet hindered by Satan, and for his own comfort and for theirs he reminded them of that glorious hope of the Church, the coming of the Lord Jesus, to which he looked forward for the one reward of all his toil, and pain, and suffering. That reward would consist in the presentation of these children of his ministry to Christ in the glory of His advent.

B. THE LABOR OF LOVE

In this second division the apostle laid special emphasis upon the "labour of love," illuminating the dark day by reference to the "patience of hope," and exhorting them to continue steadfastly in the "work of faith."

Conscious of the strain under which the saints at Thessalonica were living, the apostle had sent Timothy to see how they fared, and he had brought a comforting report of their "faith" and "love." These words indicate two root principles of the foundation-facts. Their work of turning from idols was the result of their faith. Their labor of serving the living God was the outcome of love. He thus rejoiced in that labor of love, which demonstrated the continuity of their work of faith.

In view of their loyalty to service in the power of love, the apostle again referred to that great light of hope, the coming Lord. He breathed out an earnest prayer that his way might be directed to them, and that they might abound in love. The purpose of both petitions was that their hearts might be "unblamable in holiness . . . at the coming of our Lord Jesus with all his saints." Thus in the midst of their suffering he flashed upon them the light of that glorious moment when character will be perfected, and the strain and stress of the process pass into the perfect satisfaction of the glorious results.

He then turned to exhortation, urging his beloved chil-

dren to be true to the attitudes of life assumed when they
received the Word, and by the work of faith turned to God
from idols. The first responsibility is that of personal purity.
He charged them that the will of God for them was their
sanctification, and that they should be in possession of their
own lives in obedience to God, under the dominion of the
Holy Spirit. He next indicated the true attitude of the
brethren towards each other, as being that of love, charging
them to abound more and more therein. Finally, he wrote
of their attitude toward those that are without, urging them
to live the life of quiet and honest toil, thus creating a testimony to the power of the Gospel to those outside.

C. THE PATIENCE OF HOPE

In the third division the apostle dealt specifically with the
"patience of hope," showing that their relationship to the
coming of the Lord was created by the "work of faith," and
again urging them to continuance in the "labour of love."

It is evident that some of the Thessalonian Christians had
fallen on sleep, and those remaining were afraid that in some
sense the departed ones had missed the realization of the
glorious hope of the personal advent of Jesus. In order to
correct that false impression the apostle dealt with the subject of the second advent in its relation to such as had fallen
asleep. He first declared that these will take precedence of
such as are alive at the advent, then in stately language he
gave the program of the advent, finally enjoining the sorrowing saints to comfort one another with these words.

It is important to notice that the next section opens with
the word "But." When we come to the second epistle we shall
see that this message of the apostle was misunderstood and

misinterpreted, because a clear distinction was not drawn between things which the apostle treated as separate. Having written to them of the coming of the Lord, he declared that he had no need to write to them of times and seasons, or of the day of the Lord; their work of faith had brought them into the position of "sons of light," and therefore they were to live in watchfulness and sobriety. The day of the Lord is to be a day of wrath. To it the saints are not appointed, but rather to salvation through our Lord Jesus Christ. Thus it is seen that the "work of faith," by which they turned from idols, is closely related to the "patience of hope," in which they waited for the Son.

In view of this glorious certainty of hope, he finally urged them to continue in the "labour of love," which consists in serving the living and true God. This they were to do by submission to the spiritual teachers who admonished them in the light of the glorious consummation, also by carefulness concerning mutual relationships through the admonishing of the disorderly, the encouraging of the fainthearted, the supporting of the weak, and long-suffering toward all. A series of general injunctions ends this section.

CONCLUSION

In conclusion the apostle made a final declaration of desire and assurance concerning these Thessalonian Christians. His desire was that they might be sanctified wholly by the "God of peace Himself." He evidently had no fear or doubt in his heart as to the issue, for he made the glorious declaration, "Faithful is he that calleth you, who will also do it."

Words wholly personal follow. Conscious of the difficulties of his position at Corinth, he sought an interest in their

Conclusion

prayers. The last words are those of most significant benediction, their faith and love and hope all centered upon the Person of the Lord Jesus Christ. Through Him grace had been manifested for their salvation. In Him they stood in the grace which conditioned their service and their growth. At His coming the grace of the first epiphany would merge into the glory of the second. Thus the apostle in a benediction including faith and love and hope, committed them to the Lord Jesus Christ.

II THESSALONIANS—*Christ and His Advent*

INTRO-DUCTION *i. 1-5*	A CONSOLA-TION *i. 6-12*	B INSTRUCTION *ii. 1-12*	C EXHORTA-TION *ii. 13—iii. 15*	CON-CLUSION *iii. 16-18*
	The Second Advent and their Tribulation	The Second Advent as to its Order	The Second Advent and their present Duty	
I. Salutation 1-2	I. The Revelation of the Lord Jesus i. 6-10 i. The Central Fact. Twofold Aspect. Rest to the Saints. Vengeance to the Evil. ii. The Union of the Saints with Him. The medium of Manifestation.	I. The Coming and the Day ii. 1-5 i. The Distinction. ii. The Signs of the coming of the Day. A falling away. Manifestation of man of Sin.	I. Chosen—Stand ii. 13-17 i. Chosen to Salvation. ii. Stand fast in the Truth.	I. Benediction 16 The need. The Lord.
II. Thanksgiving 3-5	II. The Prayer i. 11-12 i. Its immediate Desires. ii. Its ultimate Desire.	II. Lawlessness and the Lord Jesus ii. 6-12 i. The two Forces. Mystery of Lawlessness. One that restraineth. ii. The two revealings. The lawless one. The Lord Jesus.	II. Pray—Do iii. 1-5 i. "Pray for us." ii. Declaration of his confidence in them. III. Work iii. 6-15 i. The Apostolic example. Some neglecting their calling. ii. No work, no food! The mistaken one to be admonished as a brother.	II. Salutation 17 III. The Benediction 18

II THESSALONIANS * * * *

THIS LETTER WAS evidently intended primarily to correct certain mistakes which the Thessalonians were making concerning the second advent; and thereby to strengthen them in the midst of their suffering, and recall some of them to devotion to present duty. Whether these mistakes arose from misinterpretation of his first letter, or from the influence of false teachers, is matter of small moment. In all probability both these elements had contributed to the result. It would almost seem as if some spurious letters, purporting to have come from the apostle, had been used in order to teach views of the second advent which were untrue.

The idea that the great day of the Lord, in which He would take vengeance on evil men, was approaching, was calculated to weaken their patience; and it had already rendered certain of them careless and unsettled in the matter of their daily calling. The letter, therefore, sets their tribulation in the light of the advent, by showing its true relation thereto; corrects mistakes concerning the order of the advent; and urges them to devotion to duty. It may be divided thus: Introduction (i. 1-5); Consolation (i. 6-12); Instruction (ii. 1-12); Exhortation (ii. 13-iii. 15); Conclusion (iii. 16-18).

INTRODUCTION

Again the apostle associated Silvanus and Timothy with himself in the salutation. From this it would appear probable that the second letter followed the first quickly. The greeting is almost identical with that of the first. There is, however, the addition of the words "from God the Father and the Lord Jesus Christ" which he almost invariably used in subsequent letters.

He announced his thankfulness concerning them, giving a threefold reason—that of their present condition, the fact that they had been an argument for him, and the evidence of their patience. In dealing with their condition he did not refer to their hope. The two foundation facts dealt with in the earlier epistle are recognized, but the third is not mentioned. There is the most intimate interrelationship between faith, love, and hope. Whenever one of these, from any reason, is weakened, sooner or later the others languish.

A. CONSOLATION

In order to the consolation of those who were troubled through misinterpretation of the truth of the second advent, the apostle first dealt with the subject of the revelation of the Lord Jesus, and then told them of his perpetual prayer for them.

In dealing with the subject of the revelation he declared that it is to be for a definite purpose, that of vengeance. The connection of the saints with that apocalypse is, first, rest at the appearing; and finally, that they are to constitute the medium through which all His glory will be manifested and marvelled at in the succeeding ages.

"To that end," that is with such a consummation in view, the apostle prayed that God might count them worthy of such calling, fulfilling every desire and good work; the deepest desire of his heart being that at last in the fullness of inter-relation Christ may be glorified in them, and they in Christ.

B. INSTRUCTION

The apostle now made a clear statement of the order of events connected with the second advent of Jesus, in order to explain what he had already written, and to deliver them from the confusion of ideas which was threatening to diminish their steadfastness by dimming their hope. He did this in two sections; in the first of which he showed the distinction between the coming and the day; and in the second the relation between lawlessness and the Lord Jesus.

For "the coming of our Lord Jesus Christ" they were to wait, for it is to be the occasion of the gathering of the saints to Himself. The day of the Lord is not "just at hand," nor can it come until certain other matters have been accomplished. He warned them against confusing the hope of the parousia of Jesus with the fact of His manifestation to men, whereby shall be ushered in the day of the Lord.

Having thus referred to the day of the Lord, and to that revealing of the man of sin which is to precede it, the apostle described the present condition of affairs, and traced them toward the great crisis. Two forces are in conflict, "the mystery of lawlessness," and the "one that restraineth." The former is at work like leaven, fermenting, corrupting, and the manifestations of its presence are everywhere. The latter, as salt and light, prevents the spread of corruption, and utter darkness. This conflict is for a season. At the coming of Jesus the "one that restraineth" will be taken away, and "the mystery of lawlessness" will reveal itself in a person. In the day of the Lord, by the revelation of Jesus, the lawless one will be destroyed.

C. EXHORTATION

The last division is one pre-eminently of exhortation, in which he first described their position, and urged them to stand, then asked their prayer, and finally insisted upon the importance of work.

They were chosen to salvation, that is, ultimately, "to the obtaining of the glory of our Lord Jesus Christ." He charged them therefore to stand fast, and hold the traditions. Thus he warned them against allowing any part of the foundation truths at first declared to be forgotten, or to cease to have the proper influence upon their lives.

The appeal to them to pray for him and his work reveals how his heart was burdened and exercised about the work at Corinth and in other cities. Again he affirmed his confidence in them, and expressed hope for their continued patience.

The last section of this division is emphatic to the verge of severity. The apostle was dealing with a material evidence of weakness, and his words ring with authority, and admit of no possible manner of misconstruction. There were some in Thessalonica who were neglecting their lawful earthly callings, and had become chargeable to others, largely through misunderstanding of the doctrine of the second advent. This was wholly wrong, and contrary to the true meaning and intention of the hope of the advent. This the apostle urged upon their attention by the significant fact that, when he ministered the Word to them, he did not withdraw himself from the ordinary avocation of his daily life.

Conclusion

The matter was so serious that he charged those who were loyal to withdraw themselves from those who walked disorderly. In further enforcement the apostle laid down a great principle of life. "If any man will not work, neither let him eat." This is drastic and final. Any view of the advent, or, indeed, any view of life, which makes work distasteful, and causes its neglect, ought to, and must stay all food supplies. Again he charged them that, if any man disregarded these injunctions, they were to have no company with him.

CONCLUSION

The letter closes with words of tender desire on their behalf. He did not forget their troublous circumstances, and supremely desired peace for them. Peace, however, for him, was only associated with the Lordship of Jesus, Whom he here spoke of as "the Lord of peace," and Whose presence will assure them that blessing.

A personal salutation, and the apostle's declaration that his signature is guarantee of the genuineness of his writing, was for their safeguarding against spurious communications, such as had caused them trouble in the matter of the advent.

There is the addition of one little word to the final benediction as compared with its form in the first epistle. It is the word "all." Does not the apostle here take in the disorderly as well, and so reveal the greatness of his heart and love for them?

I TIMOTHY—*Christ and His Minister*

INTRO-DUCTION *i. 1-2*	A TIMOTHY'S CHARGE— THE CHURCH *i. 3—iii.*	B CHARGE TO TIMOTHY— THE MINISTRY *iv.—vi. 16*	CON-CLUSION *vi. 17-21*
I. Paul's Introduction of himself 1 · A Declaration of Authority.	**I. The Church and Man. Her Gospel i. 3-20** i. The Gospel. 3-11 ii. Experimental Illustration. 12-17 iii. Timothy Charged and Warned. 18-20	**I. His Duty toward the Truth iv.** i. The Perils of Spurious Pietism. 1-3 ii. The Breadth of true Godliness to be declared by Timothy as Corrective. 4-9 iii. The Strength in which he is to do this. 10-16	**I. Postscript 17-19**
II. Paul's Greeting to Timothy 2 A Revelation of Tenderness.	**II. The Church and God. Her Intercession. ii.** i. Common Prayer. 1-7 ii. The Worshippers. 8-15	**III. His Duty toward his Flock v.—vi. 2** i. Men. v. 1 ii. Women. 2 iii. Widows. 3-16 iv. Bishops. 17-22 (Personal Parenthesis v. 23-25) v. Servants. vi. 1-2	**II. Summing up 20-21a**

	III. The Church Herself. Her Officers and Office iii.
	
	i. Her Officers. 1-13
	  a. The Bishop. 1-7
	  b. Deacons. 8-13
	ii. Her Office. 14-16
	  a. The Depository of Truth. 14-15
	  b. The Truth Deposited. 16
		III. His Duty toward Himself vi. 3-16
		
		i. The Manner and the Method of the False Teachers. 3-10
		ii. Timothy's Duty by Contrast. 11-16
			III. Benediction 21b

I TIMOTHY ＊ ＊ ＊ ＊

THE SUBJECT OF Paul's association with Timothy is very full of interest, and of beauty. It is the story of a sacred and beautiful comradeship in Christ between an old and a young man. The apostle's references to Eunice and Lois would suggest a long acquaintance with them; and from the fact that Lystra is not far from Tarsus it has been conjectured that these women had been influenced by the apostle during the early days of his Christian life in which he lived there, before Barnabas sought him and brought him to Antioch. The first recorded visit to Lystra ended in the terrible stoning of the apostle, when he seemed to be dead. Almost immediately he returned to confirm the disciples. In all probability the boy Timothy was led to Christ then, for Paul speaks of him as his son in the faith, and on the occasion of his next visit Timothy is a disciple, "well reported of by the brethren."

It was at this time that the apostle officially set him apart to the work of the ministry, and from that time onward he shared his journeyings and helped him in his work. Near the end of the life of Paul, certain conditions obtaining in the church at Ephesus made it necessary that someone should be stationed there, having apostolic authority to set things in order. To this work Timothy was assigned. Paul's supreme passion was ever that of the well-being of the Church as "the pillar and ground of the truth," and he parted from Timothy, sacrificing his own personal comfort, as many tender touches reveal, in order that the church at Ephesus might be cared for.

This epistle was sent to Timothy at Ephesus, and contains such instructions as are necessary to fit him for the work he has to do. It may broadly be divided thus; Introduction (i. 1, 2); Timothy's Charge, the Church (i. 3-III. 16); Charge to Timothy, the Ministry (iv.-vi. 16); Conclusion (vi. 17-21).

INTRODUCTION

In the apostolic salutation two elements are revealed which characterize the whole epistle, those namely of authority and tenderness. Paul's introduction of himself is a declaration of authority. In order to the proper government of the church there must be duly constituted authority, and this is traced and set in its true relation. Paul's greeting to Timothy is a revelation of tenderness in his form of address, "My true child in faith"; and in the words of actual salutation, "Grace, mercy, peace."

A. TIMOTHY'S CHARGE. THE CHURCH

Through all the personal and local values of this section there may be discovered the apostolic conceptions of the Church itself, and these constitute the bases of interpretation. The apostle first had in mind the Church and man, her Gospel; then the Church and God, her intercession; finally the Church herself, her office and officers.

The Church's Gospel is the Gospel of "the blessed God," and therefore Timothy is to safeguard it against any different doctrine. The law is good, but it is for the lawless. All the things of evil, against which it protests, are absent in the lives of those obedient to sound doctrine. The power of the

Gospel is illustrated by an experimental passage in which he confessed the sin of the past, triumphed in the grace which overcame it, and claimed the service resulting. All ended in a great song of praise. Timothy is charged to "war the good warfare," which means a great deal more than fighting the good fight of faith in personal life. The words convey the thought of a campaign, and include all the responsibilities of the officer in command. He is to engage in the warfare, remembering the prophecies uttered concerning him, and holding faith in a good conscience. The apostle emphasized the urgency of his charge by words of warning, in which he cited instances of those who had failed.

The Church is not only called to proclaim to men the evangel of God, but to plead with God the cause of men. The apostle exhorted to the exercise of this function, which he described by the use of words covering the whole ground, "supplications, prayers, intercessions, thanksgivings." He then named the subjects of prayer, declared its warrant, and insisted that those who prayed should be clean in conduct and strong in character. The subject of the public assemblies of the church in Ephesus was evidently in the mind of the apostle as he described the demeanor and position of women.

In order to the proclamation of the evangel, and the exercise of intercession, the Church itself must be properly governed, and recognize the true meaning of her existence. Turning to the subject of government, the apostle dealt with two orders, bishops and deacons. The bishop is an overseer —that is, one whose duty it is to watch over the flock, and know them, to become acquainted with their condition and their needs. After declaring the excellence of the office, he proceeded to describe the qualifications necessary for its fulfillment. The picture is that of a perfectly balanced life, neither given to excess in any direction, nor ascetic. The office of the deacon was not inferior, but different. It was complementary and co-operative. In a description of the qualifications therefore for this work the apostle was as careful as when dealing with the calling of the bishop. He also recognized the possible necessity of appointing women to the office, under certain circumstances; and in a few words defined their qualifications, showing them to be practically the same as those for men.

All this leads to the final declaration of this first division, which is a remarkable and singularly beautiful description of the Church and her purpose. She is the house of God, and moreover, the pillar and ground of the truth—that is, the institution which upholds and manifests truth in the sight of all. This led the apostle further, and he declared what that truth was which the Church supports and reveals.

B. CHARGE TO TIMOTHY. THE MINISTRY

Having thus dealt with the Church as the charge committed to Timothy, the apostle charged Timothy as to how he was to fulfill his responsibility; and dealt with his duty toward the truth, his duty toward his flock, and his duty toward himself.

With regard to the first, Paul first definitely and solemnly warned him of an approaching danger. There would be a decline in faith consequent upon ascetic practices. The corrective consists in a declaration of the breadth of true godliness, which takes in life as a whole; both in its present and future realizations. Godliness does not starve any life, does not produce any crippling of the powers, has nothing to do with limitation. The secrets of strength for those who are called upon to defend the truth against error are next set forth. Hope is to be set on God. The teacher must be such a man as to carry conviction and command respect. In order to this, he must give himself to reading, exhortation, teaching, which words here undoubtedly all refer to the public work, and their combination suggests the true type of preaching. Again, in order to such public ministry there must be the cultivation of the gift, and then earnest devotion to the things to be declared. This is expressed in the charge, "give thyself wholly to them." No man gifted for the ministry can afford to devote himself, giving part of his strength of body or of mind, to other things. So sacred and so spacious is the glorious work that it demands the whole man. The general attitude therefore is expressed in the language, "Take heed to thyself, and to thy teaching." That is the duty of the preacher to truth, first the answer of his own life to its claims, and then the teaching of it to others.

The next section deals with the duty of the minister to his flock. His demeanor toward men and women is described. The large section devoted to widows indicates the local conditions and dangers. Elders in the church are to be held in honor and provided for. If an elder is found guilty of sin his public position demands public reproof for the sake of the maintenance of a general discipline. The responsibility in this connection is so great that the apostle solemnly charged Timothy as to how he is to act in the light of God, of Jesus Christ, and the elect angels. At this point in the letter there occurs a personal parenthesis; in all probability on a subject occurring to his mind at the moment, and dealt with immediately lest it should be forgotten. The last injunction of the apostle concerning Timothy's duty toward his flock indicated the line of his teaching of those Christian slaves who were members thereof. Those who serve unbelieving masters are to let their service be a testimony to the profession they make. Those who serve Christian masters are not to presume upon their spiritual relation to such as a reason for the neglect of duty. They are rather to serve all the more zealously, out of love and respect.

The apostle now reverted to the prime occasion of Timothy's appointment to Ephesus, that namely of the false teachers. His reference to this consisted of a scathing description of them, and a startling revelation of the real reason of their action. This prepared the way for his dealing with Timothy's duty toward himself. The apostolic form of address here recognized the character of Timothy, "O man of God." His charge to him was threefold: he was to flee, to follow, to fight. The young ambassador of the Cross is placed between the sad and sorrowful Jesus testifying to truth in the court of the Roman governor, and the glorious Person of the manifested King at the day of His advent.

CONCLUSION

The conclusion seems to be of the nature of a postscript. The final charge to Timothy had brought to the mind of the apostle the perils which threatened all those who were rich in this world, and for their sakes he described the true attitude of a Christian man. The letter closes in an outburst of personal appeal which seems to gather within itself all the varied tones of what had already been written—personal tenderness, apostolic authority, a great sense of wrong being done to truth, and consequent anger, with tremendous urgency in the special charge. Positive responsibility is that he guard the deposit; and negative that he turn away from the things which oppose. The brief final benediction is full of comfort. For such responsibilities as rested upon this man, how much was needed of the full grace of God; and there need be no anxiety, no panic, for that grace is ever the portion of such as are appointed to responsibility.

II TIMOTHY—*Christ and His Minister*

INTRO-DUCTION *i. 1-5*	A PERSONAL RESPON-SIBILITY *i. 6—ii. 13*	B CHURCH RESPON-SIBILITY *ii. 14—iii. 13*	C TRUTH RESPON-SIBILITY *iii. 14—iv. 5*	CON-CLUSION *iv. 6-22*
I. Personal Introduction 1 II. Greeting to Timothy 2	I. Gifts i. 6-18 i. The Injunction. 6-8 ii. The Incentives. 9-18	I. Present Perils and Duties ii. 14-26 i. The Workman and the Destroyers. 14-19 ii. The Lord's Servant. 20-26	I. The Scriptures and their Value iii. 14-17 i. "Abide." 14 ii. The Value of the Writings. 15-16 iii. The Purpose of Abiding. 17	I. Paul's final Attitudes iv. 6-18 i. As to his Ministry. 6-8 ii. As to his Associates. 9-13 iii. As to his Enemies. 14-18
III. Thanksgiving 3-5	II. Grace ii. 1-13 i. The Injunctions. 1-6 ii. The Incentives. 7-13	II. The Coming Troubles iii. 1-13 i. Description. 1-9 ii. Paul's Experience. 10-13	II. The Final Charge iv. 1-5 i. His Work. 1-4 ii. His Character. 5	II. The Last Salutation 19-22

II TIMOTHY * * * *

THIS SECOND LETTER to Timothy was also written from prison, and in all likelihood followed the first within a very few months. It is evidently a sequel to it. The troubles in the church were the same as those referred to before, and the charge to Timothy was of the same kind. The note of apostolic urgency seems to be accentuated. It is evident that Paul wrote again under a threefold consciousness. He was conscious of his own approaching departure. He recognized the evil existing in the church at Ephesus, and forecast the terrible days that are coming. He was, moreover, most acutely conscious of the grave responsibility resting on Timothy. In the light of the first two facts—his departure and the evil days at hand—he addressed himself to Timothy concerning his responsibility.

The epistle is consequently almost exclusively personal. His heart was set on this child of his own labor with solicitous anxiety, that he in turn might be faithful to his opportunity, both for his own sake, and for the sake of the truth.

The letter is intensely interesting as the last of Paul's writings, and as revealing the true attitude of the minister in days of declension and peril. The letter may be divided thus; Introduction (i. 1-5), Personal Responsibility (i. 6-ii. 13); Church Responsibility (ii. 14-iii. 13); Truth Responsibility (iii. 14-iv. 5); Conclusion (iv. 6-22).

INTRODUCTION

In this introduction there are two phrases differing from those used in the first letter. He described his apostleship as being "according to the promise of the life which is in Christ Jesus." This is particularly suited to this letter, which was intended to strengthen Timothy in view of his difficult work. He called Timothy his beloved child, and thus expressed a growing tenderness for him. The passage of thanksgiving breathes the very spirit of this affection.

A. PERSONAL RESPONSIBILITY

The subject of Timothy's personal responsibility the apostle dealt with first as to gifts, and secondly as to grace.

He first laid two injunctions upon him, to "stir up the gift," and not to be ashamed of the testimony. The gift bestowed upon him was that of capacity for oversight, and was characterized by power, love, and discipline. This two-fold injunction is emphasized by a twofold incentive, that namely of the greatness of the Gospel committed as a deposit, and of Paul's experience and convictions in relation to the responsibility of the ministry. The discussion of these is followed by an injunction, including a question of government and courage, and the paragraph ends with examples of those who failed, and of one who has been true.

Continuing, the apostle came to the subject of grace, and again there are two injunctions, "Be strengthened in the grace," "suffer hardship," the latter being illustrated by the soldier who is loyal to a king, the athlete who observes the conditions, and the husbandman who labors and waits. Here again the apostle passed from injunctions to incentives,

-520

and the first is expressed in the comprehensive words, "Remember Jesus Christ." This command recognized the limitations of human life, and called to definite acts and seasons of meditation. The apostle then passed to a lower level of incentive, that of his own experience, yet this would have special weight with Timothy, the child of his love. Paul's suffering is declared in the words, "I suffer hardship unto bonds, as a malefactor." His confidence flames out in the declaration, "The word of God is not bound." Turning finally from the supreme example of Jesus, and his own corroborative evidence of the possibility of triumph in service over suffering, the apostle quoted one "faithful saying," which at once set the principles of responsibility clearly before the mind. The foundation principle is that of identification with Jesus in death and resurrection, and the whole experience of Christian service is described in the words, "If we endure, we shall also reign with him." To understand these things is to feel the force of the warnings, "If we shall deny him, he also will deny us."

B. CHURCH RESPONSIBILITY

In charging Timothy as to his responsibility concerning the church, the apostle dealt with the perils and duties then present, and with the coming troubles.

His first duty to the church was that of the exercise of his gift, and the apostle's instruction gathered round the three-fold thought contained in the description of the spirit of the gift already stated. Placing the workman into contrast with the destroyers, he was to exercise power. This exercise was made necessary by the presence of those who were disputing about words, and indulging in "profane babblings." He was, moreover, to exercise his gift in the spirit of love, but in the definite administration of discipline. In order to all this he must himself flee aspirations and desires which are self-centered, follow the truth, and refuse questions likely to engender strife.

The apostle then turned aside to give Timothy a distinct foretelling of coming trouble. Even more trying times would come than those in the midst of which Timothy was then exercising his ministry, days characterized by "holding a form of godliness, but having denied the power thereof." In view of these coming troubles the apostle wrote of his own manner of life in order to prepare Timothy. He had passed through all manner of suffering, but always, through the strength and faithfulness of his Lord, unto victory.

C. TRUTH RESPONSIBILITY

Paul now turned to the question of Timothy's responsibility concerning the truth, dealing first with the Scriptures themselves, and then uttering his final charge. One word indicates the personal responsibility, and that is "abide." The words which indicate the values of the Scriptures are evidently carefully chosen: "teaching, reproof, correction, instruction." Their purpose is the making complete of the man of God in order that he may be prepared for his work.

His final charge had to do first with Timothy's work. The incentives are those of the final testing, and the very perils in the midst of which he labored. His work is stated in four words, "preach, reprove, rebuke, exhort," which exactly correspond to the values of the Scriptures already declared. Moreover, the measure in which he will be able to use the Word influentially for the edification of others, is the measure

Conclusion

in which he himself is established in character and conduct thereby.

CONCLUSION

In this conclusion we have in all probability the last written words of Paul preserved to us, and they declare his own final attitude as to his own ministry, as to his associates, as to his enemies. The final salutations are followed by the words "grace be with you." The one great theme of all Paul's preaching and teaching had been that of grace, and therefore this brief sentence forms a most fitting conclusion to the things he has written.

TITUS—*Christ and His Minister*

INTRO-DUCTION *i. 1-4*	A CHURCH GOVERN-MENT *i. 5-16*	B CHURCH BEHAVIOR *ii.*	C CHURCH AND STATE *iii. 1-11*	CON-CLUSION *iii. 12-15*
I. Personal Introduction 1-3 Divine authority.	I. The Office i. Elders. ii. Bishops (Comp. 5 and 7)	I. The Precepts ii. 1-10 i. Aged Men. 1-2 ii. Aged Women. 3 iii. Young Women. 4-5 iv. Young Men. 6-8 v. Servants. 9-10	I. The Church's Duty iii. 1-2	I. Personal 12
II. Address to Titus 4	II. The Functions i. God's Steward. 7 ii. The Teacher. 9	II. The Power ii. 11-15 i. The two Epiphanies. 11-13 ii. The Gift and its Purpose. 14-15	II. The Church's Impulse iii. 3-7	II. Zenas and Apollos 13
	III. The Character i. Blameless in family. 6 ii. Blameless personally. 7-8 iii. Blameless in doctrine. 9		III. The Method of Realization iii. 8-11	III. Post-script 14
	(Parenthesis Local Reason for the Instruction 10-16)			IV. Valuation and Benediction 15

TITUS   *   *   *   *

IT IS A remarkable fact that Titus is not mentioned in the Acts of the Apostles. All we know of him we gather from the writings of Paul. From the present letter we learn that he was a convert of the apostle. From the letter to the Galatians we learn that he was a Greek. In the second letter to the Corinthians there are sundry references to him. He met Paul in Macedonia, and gave him an account of the effect produced by his first letter to Corinth. He voluntarily undertook the completing of the collections for the saints at Jerusalem. Paul speaks of him as a partner and fellow-worker. He was sent to Corinth to make collections for the poor saints at Jerusalem. Finally, Paul declares his confidence in him.

The present epistle finds him in Crete for a temporary sojourn having a definite purpose. His stay there was to be short. There is uncertainty as to the foundation of the churches in Crete. Most probably they were the direct results of the day of Pentecost. Christian doctrine had been corrupted by Judaizing teachers. This, taken together with the natural characteristics of the Cretans, had brought about a state of disorder. Titus was sent to set things in order, and this letter contains his instructions. The epistle may be divided in the following way; Introduction (i. 1-4); Church Government (i. 5-16); Church Behavior (ii.); Church and State (iii. 1-11); Conclusion (iii. 12-15).

INTRODUCTION

Paul described himself first by the fundamental and inclusive truth, as the "bond-servant of God." His definition of apostleship follows, and is full and remarkable. He was an apostle "according to the faith of God's elect," that is to say, all his ministry was exercised within the limits of that faith. Its strength is indicated in the words, "in hope of eternal life." His salutation of Titus as "my true child after a common faith" suggests relationship in that which conditioned the relationship and apostleship of Paul.

A. CHURCH GOVERNMENT

The chief business of Titus in Crete was that of setting the church in order, and the apostle first discussed the true form of government as to its office, its functions, its character.

The office is that of the elder, which is coincident with that of the bishop. The function of the elder is declared to be that of a steward, which suggests general oversight, and management of the affairs of the household. The fulfillment of this will be realized by a recognition of the fact that he is a teacher. The function of the bishop, therefore, is not that of making laws and regulations, but that of interpreting the will of God as revealed in the sound doctrine, and insisting upon obedience. Only men of character are to be appointed to such office, and the apostle described the character as that of a threefold blamelessness. The bishop must be blameless in family life, blameless personally, blameless in doctrine.

The immediate reason for the work of Titus in Crete was that of the presence there of Judaizing teachers, who for filthy lucre's sake were perverting the truth and working havoc in whole houses. His method, therefore, would necessarily be that of severity. He was to reprove them sharply. The reason of the severity, however, is here, as always, that the highest purposes of love may be realized.

B. CHURCH BEHAVIOR

In showing what the behavior of the Church of God should be, the apostle first laid down particular precepts, and then declared the power in which it would be possible to obey. The behavior is to be such as befits sound doctrine, and he made application of this to the aged men and aged women, to the young women and young men, and finally to servants. It was of these last that he declared, "that they may adorn the doctrine of God our Saviour in all things," thus revealing the fact that the more difficult the circumstances in which Christian life is to be lived, the greater is the opportunity for revealing to the world the graciousness and glory of the government.

If these are the commandments laid upon the members of the Church, he proceeded to show that it is possible to obey them because of the resources at the disposal of every Christian. In a passage of singular beauty and power he declared the fourfold value of the grace of God. That grace had its epiphany at the first advent of Jesus. It first brings salvation; then teaches; next, through the result produced by teaching, denies ungodliness and wordly lusts; and throughout all these it directs the eyes of the saint toward the advent of glory. Thus the two advents are referred to. The first was the occasion of the epiphany of grace. The second will be the occasion of the epiphany of glory. In order to obey the precepts it is necessary to live in the light of the

-527

twofold relation to the advent of grace and the advent of glory. This description of the power of grace merges into a statement concerning the work of Christ through which the grace of God has become operative in the need of man.

C. CHURCH AND STATE

The final division, called forth by local circumstances, nevertheless clearly reveals the apostle's conception of the relation between Church and State. This he dealt with by declaring the Church's duty, the Church's impulse, and showing the method of realization.

The duty of the Church is first that of subjection to the authorities, secondly readiness to every good work, thirdly freedom from all evil speech, and finally the maintenance toward all men of the attitude of gentleness and meekness. The presence of such persons in any State is a positive benefit conferred. The multiplication of such lives serves to strengthen and establish the life and order of any nation.

There are certain facts which, being remembered, will contribute to the fulfillment of these ideals of life and conduct, in relation to the State. The first is that they should remember their own past; the second is that they should remember the Divine grace whereby the change has been wrought in them; and finally, they should recognize what is the value of their present position of life. This threefold memory of what we were, of how the change has been wrought, and of what we are, will serve ever to create the spirit of subjection to authority, when that authority does not conflict with submission to the will of God, will equip us for all honesty of toil, will silence all evil speech, and will generate an unceasing passion toward those that are without.

Conclusion

For the realization of these ideals of life by the local church Titus, as appointed to oversight, is held responsible. He is to fulfill his office as steward of God by the declaration of that which is profitable, by the shunning of all that is unprofitable, and by the persistent maintenance of discipline.

CONCLUSION

The conclusion of this epistle shows that it was written at an earlier date than that to Timothy, for the apostle was evidently at liberty, and choosing his own place of winter residence. He then dealt with matters of local significance, and closed with a benediction which harmonizes with his opening salutation. For the fulfillment of his work as steward of the house of God, and for the Church's submission to his direction, grace is needed and supplied.

PHILEMON—*Christ and Social Relationships*

INTRO-DUCTION 1-3	A THE APPROACH 4-7	B THE ARGUMENT 8-16	C THE APPEAL 17-21	CON-CLUSION 22-25
I. To Philemon	I. Thanks-giving for Philemon's Love	I. Paul Intro-duces his Subject by Introducing himself 8-9	I. Direct "Receive him as myself."	I. "Prepare me a Lodging"
II. Also the Church	II. Thanks-giving for Philemon's Faith	II. Paul strengthens his Argument by Refer-ences to Onesimus 10-16	II. I. O. U. III. U. O. Me IV. Confidence	II. Saluta-tion III. Bene-diction

PHILEMON   ✻ ✻ ✻ ✻

THIS LETTER IS of a purely personal nature. Its right to a place in the canon was called in question in the fourth century on the ground that its manner and content were beneath the dignity of the apostle. This opinion was surely the result of superficial examination, as, while it is perfectly true that the matter dealt with is of a personal and private nature, yet the whole method of dealing with it is a radiant revelation of the application of Christian principle to matters of individual life and social relationship.

After the introduction (vers. 1-3) the letter falls into three divisions; the Approach (vers. 4-7); the Argument (vers. 8-16); the Appeal (vers. 17-21); with a Conclusion (vers. 22-25).

INTRODUCTION

While the letter is addressed to Philemon, the apostle includes the members of his household, and the whole Church. The reason for this is, evidently, that upon the new social relationships existing among the members of the Christian Church, Paul is about to base his appeal on behalf of Onesimus.

A. THE APPROACH

After the usual salutation of grace and peace the apostle proceeded to declare his thankfulness for all he heard of the love and faith of Philemon. It is to be carefully noted that this love and faith was described as being "toward the Lord Jesus, and toward all the saints." He prayed for him that the fellowship of his faith might be effectual, and declared how much joy and comfort he had in the knowledge of the fact that the saints had been refreshed by Philemon. All this constituted a method of approach to the argument upon which he based the specific appeal which was the principal purpose of the writing of the letter.

B. THE ARGUMENT

The first movement in the apostle's argument was that of the introduction of himself. He declared that although he had full authority to command Philemon as to what befitted his profession of Christianity, he did not choose to do so. He chose rather to appeal to him upon the basis of his love. Setting aside his official authority, he set up the authority of their mutual love. Very tender, and full of the most sacred art, was his reference to himself as "the aged," and "a prisoner of Jesus Christ." It would have been very difficult for Philemon to have refused compliance with anything requested by one who was so highly esteemed and tenderly loved in the faith, especially in view of the fact that he was bowed beneath the weight of years, approaching the end of his life and ministry, and withal a prisoner bound in chains for the sake of the Gospel. Thus the apostle would capture him by this introduction of himself.

He then adopted a new method of argument by the way in which he referred to Onesimus. This man, a slave of Philemon, had run away from his master, and the most probable attitude of Philemon toward him would be that of a perfectly just anger. Of course, in reading this story the men must be measured by the standards of their own age. The more perfect light in which we are now living, and which makes the holding of slaves impossible, was then only beginning to break through the darkness, and its meaning was not perfectly apprehended. Therefore it was that Paul introduced the name of the runaway in the way in which he did, referring to him as "my child, whom I have begotten in my bonds." From these words it is evident that in some way Onesimus had come under the influence of Paul, and had been brought to Christ thereby. Reference to his relationship to Philemon immediately followed, but was introduced with a touch of playful humor; for the word Onesimus means profitable, and when the apostle wrote, "who once was unprofitable to thee, but now is profitable to thee and me," he was indulging in a play upon words.

C. THE APPEAL

At last the apostle reached the appeal. He asked Philemon to receive Onesimus as though he were receiving Paul himself. Seeing that there might be some difficulty in the way, the apostle made himself responsible for any debt which Onesimus owed Philemon, gently reminding the latter that he owed himself to Paul. He finally declared his confidence that Philemon would do as he asked, and even beyond.

CONCLUSION

Finally, the apostle expressed his hope that he would be able to visit Philemon; requested that a lodging should be prepared for him; sent salutations; and pronounced the benediction.

HEBREWS—*Christ the Final Speech of God*

INTRO-DUCTION *i. 1-2a*	A THE ARGUMENT FOUNDATIONS OF FAITH *i. 2b—x. 37*	B THE APPEAL FRUITFULNESS OF FAITH *x. 38—xii.*	CON-CLUSION *xiii.*
I. Unargued Truth i. God. ii. God speaks.	**I. Superiority of the Speech of the Son** **i. 2b—vii.** i. Superior to Angels. 　　　i. 2b—ii. (The Book of Genesis.) Exhortation and Warning. 　　　1-4 ii. Superior to Leaders. 　　　iii.—iv. 13 (The Books of Exodus and Joshua.) *a.* Moses.　iii. 1-6 Exhortation and Warning. 　　iii. 7—iv. 7 *b.* Joshua.　iv. 8-10 Exhortation and Warning. 　　　iv. 11-13 iii. Superior to Priesthood. 　　　iv. 14—vii. (The Book of Leviticus.) *a.* Aaronic. iv. 14—v. 10 Exhortation and Warning. 　　v. 11—vi. 12 *b.* Levitic. vi. 13—vii. 28	**I. The Witnesses** **x. 38—xii. 3** i. The Old Economy. A Cloud of Witnesses. 　　　x. 38—xi. ii. The New Economy. The One Witness. 　　　xii. 1-3	**I. Closing Injunctions** **1-17** i. Conduct of Faith. 1-6 ii. Anchorage of Faith. 　　　7-9 iii. Worship of Faith. 　　　10-15 iv. Fellowship of Faith. 　　　16-17
II. The Two Economies i. "Of old time." ii. "At the end of these days."	**II. Superiority of Consequent Relationships** **viii.—x. 37** i. The Better Covenant. 　　　viii. ii. The Better Worship. 　　　ix.—x. 18 iii. The Better Fellowship. 　　　x. 19-25 Exhortation and Warning. 　　　x. 26-37	**II. The Great Appeal** **xii. 4-29** i. The Perils.　　4-17 *a.* Failure to respond to Chastening.　4-13 *b.* Falling short of the Grace of God. 14-17 ii. The Encouragement. 　　　18-24 *a.* The Old. Terror and Majesty.　18-21 *b.* The New. Tenderness and Mercy. 22-24 iii. The Appeal.　25-29 *a.* "See that ye refuse not . . . for." 25-27 *b.* "Let us have grace . . . for."　28-29	**II. Personal Conclusion** **18-25**

HEBREWS ✳ ✳ ✳ ✳

THERE IS GREAT uncertainty as to the authorship of this treatise. Into the discussion we do not propose to enter. Its main subject is that of the superiority of the revelation of God in Christ to all that had preceded it. This is dealt with in order that the faith of Hebrew Christians may be established. For the strengthening of that faith the writer laid bare the foundations, and described the fruitfulness. Its purpose is to show the hopelessness of those guilty of apostasy from Christ, by revealing the perfection and finality of His message and work. The broad divisions are; Introduction (i. 1-2a); the Argument, Foundations of Faith (i. 2b-x. 37); the Appeal, Fruitfulness of Faith (x. 38-xii.); Conclusion (xiii.).

INTRODUCTION

The introduction takes us at once to the heart of the subject, and declares in compact form the truth upon which all the subsequent arguments and appeals depend. Two truths are taken for granted—the existence of God, and the fact that He reveals Himself to men. Two periods of revelation are referred to in the phrases, "of old time," and "at the end of these days."

A. THE ARGUMENT. FOUNDATIONS OF FAITH

The first division of the book is devoted to the argument which sets forth the superiority of the speech of the Son "at the end of these days" to all that had been spoken "of old time"; and claims the superiority of consequent relationships.

After the declaration that God now speaks in the Son there follows a sevenfold description of the glories of the Son, which perfectly includes all the economies of the past. In Him all voices merge into the one Voice, all signs are fulfilled in the one Manifestation, all visions shine through the essential Light. Thus emphasis is laid upon the authority and finality of the Christian revelation, and the absolute safety of the same as the groundwork of faith.

Then follows the detailed argument for the superiority of the Son to all the methods of the past. The Hebrews believed that their system was ministered by angels, and so was supernatural. The subject of the superiority of the Son to the angels is introduced by seven quotations from Old Testament Scriptures. The first two show the superiority of the Son in the matter of relationship to God. The Third claims the worship of the angels for the Son. The fourth, fifth, and sixth contrast the service of the angels with the supremacy of the Son. The seventh shows the superiority of the Son Who shares the Throne over those who are its ministers.

The epistle is characterized by occasional applications and solemn warnings. While the writer specially devotes himself to such statements concerning the foundations of faith as shall strengthen faith, he is careful to make such deductions as will reveal the peril of apostasy. The first of these warnings argues that if the ministration of angels had been of so steadfast a character, how much more the speech of the Son.

Continuing the argument concerning the superiority of the Son to the angels, the writer introduces a new statement.

A. *The Argument. Foundations of Faith*

He Who in essential nature was superior to them, yet for a period was made lower. Through His humiliation and the victory wrought therein, He passed back to the place of superiority, carrying with Him a new right of supremacy over man, to whose level He passed in humiliation.

The argument now passes to the second claim of superiority, that over human leaders. It includes in its process the superiority of the Son to Moses and Joshua, the man who led the people out, and the man who led the people in. It first institutes a comparison between Moses and Christ. Christ is the Son over the spiritual house, of which the Tabernacle was but the shadow, in which Moses was a servant. The contrast is striking, and the argument intended is, that if faith centered on the pattern and the men who built it, how much more may it confidently take hold upon the One Who in His own Person fulfills all that was shadowed forth by the servant of old, and by the pattern house in which he served.

Then follows the second exhortation and warning. Readers are reminded of what happened in the wilderness. The heart was hardened by unbelief, God was displeased, and they were shut out from rest. The whole force of the illustration is that of reminding those to whom the letter is addressed that if in the case of unbelief in the servant, men were shut out from rest, much more will that be true in the case of those who are disobedient to the Son. The reason why a generation perished in the wilderness is declared to be that "the word of hearing did not profit them, because it was not united by faith with them that heard." Notwithstanding the fact of this past failure the offer is repeated, this time, however, by the superior speech of the Son. All this gives urgency to the appeal with which the section opened, "Let us

–537

fear, therefore, lest haply a promise being left of entering into his rest, any one of you should seem to have come short of it."

In close connection, because the subject is virtually the same, the writer deals with the superiority of the Son over Joshua. Joshua completed that in human leadership, in which Moses failed. He led the people in. Yet while it is true that he led them into the land, he did not lead them into rest. What he failed to do, the Son accomplished; and this is referred to by the writer in the words, "He that is entered into his rest hath himself also rested from his works as God did from his."

The section showing the superiority of the Son to the leaders closes with an inclusive exhortation and warning, descriptive of the power of the Word of God.

The writer now passes to discuss the superiority of Christ as Priest. He first makes a statement of the fact of His priesthood, which he accompanies by appeals. Because Jesus, the Son of God, is a great High Priest, the appeal is made, "Let us hold fast our confession." Because of the nature of His priesthood, the appeal is made, "Let us therefore draw near." Then commences the argument by contrast. The two essential qualifications for a priest are a capacity for sympathy, and a vocation of God. These are fulfilled in Christ, as they never were in Aaron.

Having thus introduced the subject, the writer declares his sense of difficulty in dealing with it, because of the incapacity of the readers; and he appeals to them to leave the first principles, and press on to perfection; again in solemn and awful words warning them against apostasy.

Turning to the subject of the superiority of the priesthood

of the Son to the Levitic, the writer commences by taking his readers back in thought to Abraham, whose anchorage was the oath of God, which oath is ratified in the Person of our High Priest, Whose priesthood was after the order of Melchisedec. He then shows the superiority of the Melchisedec priesthood to the Levitic. The whole Levitic priesthood paid tithes to Melchisedec in the person of Abraham, from whose loins they sprang. Thus the living Priest received tithes from the dying, even while they were yet unborn, and He blessed them in the person of Abraham. Therefore it is evident that the Levitic priesthood is inferior to that of Melchisedec; and the priesthood of the Son is after the pattern of that of Melchisedec. In the next place he shows the inferiority of the Levitic priesthood in that it was unequal to the realization of perfection; and the superiority of the priesthood of Jesus is revealed in the fact that through Him a better hope has been given to men through which they draw nigh unto God, and perfection is realized.

The contrast is finally made vivid in two particulars, first, as to the oath of appointment; and second, as to the perpetuity of the office. These contrasts are marked by two phrases, each occurring twice, "they indeed," "but he." The High Priest is described finally as to character, "holy, guileless, undefiled, separated from sinners"; as to position, "made higher than the heavens"; as to mediatorial rights, the sacrifice of Himself once for all.

Having established the fact of the superiority of Christ, the argument now proceeds to deal with the superiority of the relationships consequent thereupon. The superiority of the Priest demonstrates the superiority of the place of the exercise of the priesthood, and thus finally demonstrates the superiority of the covenant. That superiority is threefold. It is internal rather than external; it is universal rather than local; and finally it is based upon the forgiveness of sins.

Upon the basis of the better priesthood and the better covenant there issues a better worship. The sanctuary is first described. The imperfection of its service is shown in the limitation and restriction of priestly service, because the ordinances were unavailing in the realm of conscience. In contrast to this, Christ entered a greater tabernacle through a greater sacrifice. Therefore His entry was once for all, because in the shedding of His own blood He dealt with sin finally. The superiority of the sacrifice is next emphasized. In this matter Christ is at once Priest and Sacrifice. He offered Himself through the eternal Spirit. The prominent thought in this section is that in the priesthood of Christ there is a place of worship unlocalized and unlimited. Into the better sanctuary through the better sacrifice, the worshipper may enter, in any place, and at any time, if he come through the better Priest.

Still dealing with worship, the subject of the superiority of the service is finally dealt with. In this connection, for special reason, the writer restates the fact of the superiority of the priesthood of Jesus, in the matters of sacrifices and offerings. The sacrifices of the old economy could never perfect men. By the One Sacrifice of Christ, He perfects for ever the sanctified. Moreover, through this offering and sacrifice of Christ the worshippers are brought into relationship with God, in which instead of consciousness of sin, there is delight in the doing of His will.

The better covenant and the better worship issue necessarily in the better fellowship. The privilege of the worshipper is that in union with the Priest he may approach with boldness. The responsibility of the fellowship is that the worshippers should "draw near," "hold fast," and "consider one another." The preparation for such approach is then clearly stated. All this is to be the more carefully observed because of the assurance that the High Priest Who ministers will appear again, and that the day is drawing nigh.

Then follows the fifth solemn warning of the epistle, which deals again with the sin of apostasy. The nature of that sin is described in terrible words: "trodden under foot the Son of God, . . . accounted the blood of the covenant . . . an unholy thing, . . . done despite unto the Spirit of grace." To those guilty of such sin there can remain nothing but judgment, and the fierceness of fire. The warning ends with words full of hope. They had "endured"; and are urged therefore not to cast away their boldness; and their faith is encouraged by a further reminder of the certainty of the second advent of Jesus.

B. THE APPEAL. FRUITFULNESS OF FAITH

The letter now passes to its second division, which consists of an appeal made by the writer, describing the fruitfulness of faith; and falls into two sections, in the first of which he masses the evidence by calling the witnesses; while in the second he makes his appeal.

Quoting from the prophecy of Habakkuk he shows that the principle of life is faith, and makes it clear that apostasy issues in death. This he then illustrates on the positive side. His first illustration is all-inclusive in its teaching concerning the spiritual origin of all things. He then passes in rapid review the outstanding names in the history of the Hebrew people, in each case showing that at the center of all their victories lay the principle of faith. He then gives a list of names, each one of which stands for some triumph through faith; and immediately following a list of deeds, all accomplished in the selfsame power. And yet again, he describes the suffering endured in the strength of faith. The matter of supreme interest in this massing of the witnesses is the variety of types of character, of circumstances, in all of which the principle of victory is the same. The fruitfulness of faith in all these is yet more clearly revealed in the closing declaration that none of them received the promise. Faith was strong enough to enable them to endure, postponing their final realization until the great promises of God should be perfectly wrought out in the history of men.

Having thus shown that faith was the abiding condition of victorious life under the old economy, the writer declares it to be the abiding condition of victorious life under the new. The one supreme Witness is presented to the mind as the Author and Perfecter of faith. Seeing the witnesses, and looking at the Witness, the readers are urged to lay aside weights, and the sin of unbelief, in order that they may run.

Then follows the great appeal. It opens by a careful and yet tender setting forth of the perils which threaten the life of faith. The first is that of failure to respond to chastening, and in order to safeguard them against such failure he explains the real meaning of their suffering and chastening.

The second peril is that of falling short of the grace of God, which falling short manifests itself in disputes, and differences, caused by moral failure; and he urges them to look carefully lest they so fail.

Then in order to their encouragement, the writer brings

graphically before the mind the contrast between the old economy and the new. The former was characterized by terror and majesty, of which he gives seven illustrations. The new is characterized by tenderness and mercy, of which he gives eight illustrations. The old revealed distance, and filled the heart with fear. The new reveals the way of approach, and should inspire with faith.

At last he utters the appeal itself. The first words, "See that ye refuse not him that speaketh," should be read in connection with the affirmation in the introduction of the letter, "God . . . hath spoken . . . in his Son." Between that first affirmation and this final appeal lie all the arguments concerning the superiority of the speech of the Son. The writer shows that greater privilege means greater responsibility, and consequently creates graver peril. Therefore they are charged not to refuse, and in order that they may not, they are further charged to have grace. The last word "Our God is a consuming fire" will affect the conscience according to its condition. The men of faith will rejoice in the fire which purifies; the men of apostasy will tremble in the fire which destroys.

CONCLUSION

The conclusion of the letter consists of a series of injunctions which illustrate the value of faith, in the superior relationships created by the revelation made through the Son. The conduct of faith will be that of love in all practical application. The encouragement of faith is, "Jesus Christ, the same yesterday, and today, and for ever." The worship of faith consists of leaving the old economy, by going without the camp, and entering into the new by worshipping within the veil. The fellowship of faith is to express itself in doing good and communicating.

The last paragraph is a personal conclusion, first urging the readers to pray for those in the ministry, and finally recording the prayer of the writer for those to whom his letter is addressed.

JAMES—*Christ and His Ethic*

INTRO-DUCTION	A FAITH AS A PRINCIPLE OF VICTORY IN TEMPTATION	B FAITH AS A PRINCIPLE OF ACTION TOWARD MEN	C FAITH AS A PRINCIPLE OF WISDOM IN SPEECH	D FAITH AS A PRINCIPLE OF PURITY IN CHARACTER	CON-CLUSION
i. 1	*i. 2-27*	*ii.*	*iii.*	*iv.*	*v.*
No Details of human Relation-ship, only that to Christ and God	**I. Temptation 2-15** i. As Adversity of Circumstances. 2-12 ii. As Allurement to Sin. 13-15 **II. The Principle of Victory. Faith's hold on the Word 16-25**	**I. The Failure 1-11** i. Judge not. 1-4 ii. "Ye Despise the Poor." 5-7 "Theirs is the Kingdom." iii. The positive Statement. 8-11 "If ye fulfil."	**I. A Warning to Public Teachers 1**	**I. The Failure 1-5** i. Wars and Fightings. ii. Arising from Lust. iii. Issuing in Envy. iv. Daring to lay Tribute on Prayer.	**I. Address to the Oppressors 1-6**
Letter addressed to Jewish Christians scattered abroad	i. The Admission. 16-17 Every good gift and perfect boon from God. ii. The Test. 18 Those born of the Word must realize the ideal. iii. The Responsibilities. 19-25 *a.* The Word received. 19-21 *b.* The Word obeyed. 22-25 **III. The Contrast 26-27** i. "Seemeth to be Religious." ii. "Pure Religion."	**II. The Correction 12-25** i. Injunction to act as those to be judged by the law of Liberty. 12-13 ii. The Profitlessness of Creed without Conduct. 14-20 iii. Two Illustrations. 21-25 **III. The Principle 26** The Central vein of the Epistle.	**II. The Tongue 2-12** i. Its Power for Evil. 3-6 ii. Its Untameable Nature. 7-8 iii. Its Inconsistency. 9-12 **III. The Effect of Faith 13-18** i. The Power of Silence. 13-16 ii. Wisdom from above the true Source of Speech. 17-18	**II. The Correction 6-10** i. The Gift. 6 ii. The Responsibility. 7-10 **III. The Principle 11-17** i. Toward Man. 11-12 ii. Toward God. 13-16 iii. Summary. 17	**II. Address to the Oppressed 7-12** **III. Final Words 13-20**

JAMES * * * *

THIS EPISTLE IS pre-eminently practical. The ethics of Christianity are perhaps more forcefully taught here than in any of the apostolic writings. The letter has often, therefore, been spoken of as being devoted to the subject of works; and Luther, imagining that it contradicted the doctrine of justification by faith as set forth by Paul, decided against its inspiration, denying its right to a place in the canon. It is easy to understand Luther's position when his times are remembered, and the necessity there was for insistence upon faith as the root principle of Christian relationship. As a matter of fact, however, there is no epistle which reveals more clearly the necessity for faith than that of James. While Romans deals with faith as the principle from which works issue, James insists upon works as necessary for the demonstration of faith. It is around the thought of faith that the epistle may best be analyzed. Introduction (i. 1); Faith as a Principle of Victory in Temptation (i. 2-27); Faith as a Principle of Action Toward Man (ii.); Faith as a Principle of Wisdom in Speech (iii.); Faith as a Principle of Purity in Character (iv.); Conclusion (v.).

INTRODUCTION

James introduced himself briefly and comprehensively as a servant of God and of the Lord Jesus Christ. His letter was written to the "twelve tribes which are of the dispersion"— that is, to Christian Israelites not resident in Jerusalem.

–547

A. FAITH AS A PRINCIPLE OF VICTORY IN TEMPTATION

The condition of these Christians was that of persons in the midst of temptation and trial; and in this first division James recognized the place of temptation, then dealt with faith as a principle of victory; finally drawing a sharp contrast between false and true religion.

First dealing with temptation as adversity of circumstances he declared that its issue is that they might be perfect and entire, lacking in nothing. He then cited three illustrations of this kind of temptation—lack of wisdom, lack of position, and lack of need, closing with a beatitude on such as endure. He then passed to speak of temptation as allurement to sin, declaring that God is never the Author of such, and showing that it consists in an appeal made to a proper desire to meet its demand in an improper way or time.

He next proceeded to show that the Word of God is the stronghold for faith as it meets temptation. Recognizing the fact that every good gift and perfect boon is from God, and therefore not evil in itself, James insisted that such as were born again must set forth the Divine intention in human life. The first responsibility in order to obedience is that the implanted Word should be received with meekness. The second responsibility is that of actual and active obedience to the Word thus received. In order to this the attitude must be that of looking into, and so continuing; that is, of determined attention to the Word, and abandonment to its claim.

This division closes with a remarkable contrast between false and true religion, between the man who thinks himself to be religious, and pure religion. Faith therefore fastening upon the Word is the principle of victory in temptation.

B. FAITH AS A PRINCIPLE OF ACTION TOWARD MEN

In dealing with faith as a principle of action toward men, James first described the failure of conduct which he condemned; and then gave the teaching which corrects such wrong conduct; finally crystallizing the argument in a brief statement of principle.

The failure he condemned was that of respect of persons which expresses itself in the worship of wealth. Those who are guilty of this conduct do not hold the faith of the Lord Jesus Christ. They despise the poor, whereas, according to the teaching of their Master, the poor are heirs of the Kingdom. While it is a good thing to fulfill the royal law of love to neighbors, it is an evil thing to have respect of persons.

To correct the failure James charged them first of all to speak and act as men to be judged by the law of liberty; and then, in one of the strongest passages in the whole letter, showed the profitlessness of faith which does not express itself in works, illustrating by reference to Abraham, the father of the faithful, and to Rahab, a woman outside the covenant. In each case faith was the vital principle, but it was demonstrated by works.

The closing declaration summarizes the division, and is indeed the central truth of the whole epistle. A faith which does not express itself in conduct is as dead as a body from which the spirit has departed.

C. FAITH AS A PRINCIPLE OF WISDOM IN SPEECH

After uttering a warning as to public teaching, James described the peril of the tongue, and finally showed the effect of faith upon its use.

When referring to false religion, the one illustration he gave was that of an unbridled tongue. He then showed the disastrous effects which may be produced thereby. Perhaps more burning and scorching words are hardly to be found in the whole of the New Testament. There would seem to be a contrast suggested between the tongue set on fire by hell, and the tongue of fire. Speech always waits for inspiration, and such inspiration comes out of the awful depths of evil, or from the Spirit of the living God.

He then declared that true wisdom and understanding will manifest itself in life; that is to say, he practically affirmed that the silence which is the outcome of faith is the most eloquent testimony to consistent life. In immediate contrast to the effects of unbridled speech, he described the true wisdom as to character and result; and the contrast is extremely vivid. In the description of the former there is the thought of tempest and conflict, strife and malice; in that of the latter there is the manifestation of calm and serenity, of quietness and love. Thus the effect of faith upon that natural character from which speech springs is shown; and thus the effect of faith upon speech itself.

D. FAITH AS A PRINCIPLE OF PURITY IN CHARACTER

Here again the writer described failure, corrected it, and finally declared the true principle of victory.

-550

Conclusion

The failure is that of wars and fightings arising from lust, issuing in envy, and daring even to lay tribute on prayer. He asked, "Doth the Spirit which he made to dwell in you long unto envying?" evidently intending to indicate that the only answer to such a question must be a negative one. The Spirit which God makes to dwell in us does not create desire which issues in envy. The character which is self-seeking and unclean results from lack of faith in God, manifested in failure to submit to the indwelling Spirit.

The Divine corrective to these terrible conditions is then dealt with, first as to the all-inclusive gift of God, and secondly as to human responsibility. The government is that of grace. The responsibility is marked in a series of injunctions.

Finally he revealed the true principle of purity. Faith in God will produce love, rather than censoriousness toward men. Secondly, faith in God means dependence upon Him which is actual and active.

CONCLUSION

In conclusion the writer addressed himself first in solemn indictment and terrible warning to the rich. The cry of the oppressed comes into the ears of God as a plea which is never heard in vain. In the balances and proportion of the Divine government, nemesis inevitably follows upon any gain which is the result of injury done to others.

Turning to those who suffer, he addressed to them words as full of tender comfort as those directed to the oppressors were full of fiery indignation. He called them to patience in the midst of testing, first with God in the understanding of the meaning of His perfect waiting for their perfecting, and then with each other. To patience and simplicity of speech he urged them by two examples—that of the prophets, and that of Job.

The last paragraph of the letter contains advice and instructions for differing experiences and things. "Is any . . . suffering?" "Is any cheerful?" "Is any . . . sick?" Those who suffer should pray. Those who are cheerful should praise. As to the sick, the whole paragraph, from verse fourteen to the end, must be read for correct understanding of any portion thereof. The raising of the sick is united with the forgiveness of sin, and immediately upon this statement there follows the injunction to confess sins. The particular cases of sickness in mind were those resulting from wrongdoing. The calling in of the elders of the Church indicated the relation between the sickness and matters of spiritual import. The use of oil was in itself an indication of the necessity for the employment of means. The instruction to pray shows that the Christian man will never depend upon natural means alone. The most important teaching of this final paragraph is that where sickness is related to wrongdoing, by confession and by recognition of church responsibility sin may be removed, and the sickness consequent upon it healed. The value of this exercise of confession and forgiveness is emphasized by the words with which the letter closes.

I PETER—*Christ the Strength of His People*

INTRO-DUCTION *i. 1-2*	A ESTABLISHED FOR TESTING IN CONFIDENCE *i. 3—ii. 1*	B ESTABLISHED FOR TESTING IN CONDUCT *ii. 4—iii. 9*	C ESTABLISHED FOR TESTING IN CHARACTER *iii. 10—v. 7*	D ESTABLISHED FOR TESTING IN CONFLICT *v. 8-11*	CON-CLU-SION *v. 12-14*
I. The Apostle and his Elect Readers 1	I. The Life of Faith i. 3-5 i. The Beginning. 3 "Begat us again." ii. The Issue. 4 "An Inheritance." iii. The Assurance. 5 ". . . . are guarded."	I. The Life of Holiness ii. 4-10 i. Composition. 4-6 Living Stone and living stones. ii. Quality. 7-8 The Preciousness of the Living Stone. iii. Vocation. 9-10 Exhibiting the excellencies.	I. The Life of Victory iii. 10-22 i. Principle. "If ye should suffer." 10-17 ii. Pattern. "Christ also suffered." 18-22	I. The Life of Conflict 8-9a i. The Adversary. 8 ii. The Attitude. 8-9a	
II. Explanation of "elect" 2	II. The Proving of Faith i. 6-12 i. The Value of Proof. 6-7 ii. The Principle of Believing. 8-9 iii. The Testimony of the Past. 10-12 III. The Practice of Faith i. 13—ii. 3 i. Personal. 13-21 ii. Relative. i. 22—ii. 3	II. The Practice of Holiness ii. 11—iii. 9 i. General Instructions Personal. ii. 11-12 ii. National Relationships. ii. 13-17 iii. Household Relationships. ii. 18-25 iv. Home Relationships. iii. 1-7 v. General Instructions Corporate. 8-9	II. The Process of Victory iv.—v. 7 i. The Equipment. "Arm yourselves with the same mind." iv. 1-11 ii. The Principle. "Partakers of Christ's Sufferings." iv. 12-19 iii. Responsibilities. v. 1-7	II. The Fellowship of Conflict 9b "The God of all grace." III. The Strength of Conflict 10-11	

I PETER * * * *

THIS LETTER WAS directed to the same persons as that of James. Its main purpose is the establishing of such as are passing through a period of suffering and testing. In the solemn days in which the Lord had foretold Peter's fall and restoration, He had said to him, "When once thou hast turned again, establish thy brethren." In both his epistles the apostle carried out that commission.

The letter abounds with references to his own experiences. Its twofold method is indicated in the closing words, "exhorting, and testifying" (v. 12). The word "exhorting" is derived from the same root as Paraclete, and thus reveals the nature of the exhortation. The word "testifying" means witnessing, in the sense in which the Lord had said to His disciples that they should be witnesses to Him. Thus in the power of the Paraclete, Peter exhorted, and emphasized his exhortation by testifying to Him of Whom the Holy Spirit is Representative and Administrator. These two aspects of the epistle are intermixed, the apostle perpetually passing from exhortation to testimony. The epistle may thus be divided; Introduction (i, 1, 2); Established for Testing in Confidence (i. 3-ii. 3); Established for Testing in Conduct (ii. 4-iii. 9); Established for Testing in Character (iii. 10-v. 7); Established for Testing in Conflict (v. 8-11); Conclusion (v. 12-14).

INTRODUCTION

The apostle introduced himself by the name which Jesus gave him, "Peter," and announced his apostleship. He described those to whom he wrote as "the elect," and explained the meaning of his own term. Election is "according to the foreknowledge of God." Its process of realization is "in sanctification of the Spirit." Its purpose is "unto obedience and sprinkling of the blood of Jesus Christ." He saluted his readers with the words of the new covenant; "grace" indicating all the favor of God operative through the work of Jesus; and "peace," the resulting condition and consciousness of the life.

A. ESTABLISHED FOR TESTING IN CONFIDENCE

In order to establish them for testing in confidence, he first described the life of faith; then showed the place of the proving of faith; and finally gave them practical exhortation as to the practice of faith.

As to the origin of the life of faith, he reminded them that the beginning of their life was by the act of God, in which He "begat us again" through the liberation of the life of Christ in resurrection. The final issue of this is that of an inheritance, all the characteristics of which are in direct contrast to the inheritances of earth. It is "incorruptible," while everything here is corruptible; it is "undefiled," while everything here is tainted with defilement; it "fadeth not away," while everything here is passing, even while it is possessed; it is "reserved in heaven," while everything here is overshadowed by the coming of death. The assurance of

A. *Established for Testing in Confidence*

the ultimate realization lies in the fact that the saints are guarded by the power of God.

The value of the present proving is the consequent vindication at the revelation of Jesus Christ. The principle of strength in the process of proving, is that of love which springs out of perfect confidence in the Lord Himself. The salvation which is to be revealed is even now received by faith, and so the joy of the present is of the nature of that which is to come; and out of this grows the victory of courage and gladness over all the grief of the manifold trials of today. He finally reminded them that this wonderful salvation had been the subject of the inquiries and the search of the prophets of old; and angels themselves had desired to look into them.

Having set the testing of their confidence in relation to its purpose, the apostle proceeded to practical exhortations, dealing first with individual, and then with relative responsibility. In personal life the attitude to be maintained is that of strenuous readiness for all present emergencies, in the absolute certainty of the ultimate issue. The ruling principle of obedience is to be that of relationship to God as children. He concluded the personal injunctions with the strongest argument it was possible for him to use. They had been redeemed at infinite cost. In dealing with the relative practice, the individual obedience is taken for granted. The only injunction laid upon the saints, conditioning their relation to each other, is that of love. The character of the love enjoined is described as being "from the heart fervently." The energy sufficient to enable obedience in this matter is that of the new birth, wherein life, containing forces equal to every demand, is received. The method of obedience is that of putting away all things contrary to the spirit of love, and the sustenance of life by the Word.

B. ESTABLISHED FOR TESTING IN CONDUCT

Passing from the subject of the testing of confidence to that which is closely allied, the testing of conduct, the apostle first dealt with the life of holiness, and the practice of holiness.

In dealing with the life of holiness he described the Church as a building, of which the chief corner Stone is the living Christ, and in which all members are living stones, deriving from Him a preciousness. The fellowship of this preciousness issues in fellowship in the suffering resulting from rejection by the men of the world. In a passage of remarkable force and beauty, the vocation of the Church is declared to be that of the manifestation of the excellencies of God.

The application of this master principle immediately follows. Generally, it means that the members of the Church are to behave as those not of the world, conducting themselves among outsiders in a seemly manner in order to silence slander, and vindicate God.

This general principle is then illustrated in its national bearing. Submission to God does not express itself in disobedience to earthly government, but rather in subjection to such.

The application to household relationships illustrates how things generally considered menial are transfigured in the light of Christian experience. Servants are to be subject, not only to masters who are reasonable, but also to the forward. For the encouragement of such the apostle quoted

C. *Established for Testing in Character*

the great example of Christ, to Whom they have returned, and in relation to Whom it is possible for them to obey.

The application to home relationships begins with the marriage relation. The attitude of the wife is to be that of subjection, the true adornment of woman being that of womanly character. The injunction to husbands is that they dwell with their wives according to knowledge. Thus the woman is to be subject to a love which acts in knowledge, and not in selfishness and ignorance. The final reason for the fulfillment of the true ideal of the marriage relationship is that "prayers be not hindered," a forceful suggestion that the whole married life is consecrated by mutual intercession.

The section closes with general exhortations to the cultivation of such disposition as shall fulfill the ideals in conduct.

C. ESTABLISHED FOR TESTING IN CHARACTER

The apostle now passed to the establishing of those tested as a result of their realization of the true Christian character, and he first described the life of victory, and then indicated the process of victory.

He commenced with a quotation from the Psalms, which calls to a life of holiness and declares a truth concerning the attitude of God towards men. In the light of this truth, those who suffer for character are urged to be zealous of that which is good. The one supreme responsibility is expressed in the words, "Sanctify in your hearts Christ as Lord." The perfect Pattern for the believer in order to victory is Christ Himself, and the apostle stated comprehensively the facts of the suffering and victory of Christ. These are, His death and resurrection; His descent into Hades and proclamation of the evangel; His ascension to the right hand of God and assumption of authority. The force of the argument in its bearing on suffering saints is that of showing how through suffering Christ reached a triumph. Through His suffering He was able to make proclamation of His evangel in Hades, and then to ascend to the place of final authority, even above all angels and authorities and powers. Through their baptism of suffering they also find their way into victory.

The process of this victory is, therefore, first that of being armed with the same mind. This mind belongs to the saints, and is a good conscience through the finished work of Christ. Let them act in the power of it by ceasing from sin and all those gratifications of the flesh-life which have characterized their past. The result of that will be their suffering, but the issue will be their triumph in the Gospel, as through them it is preached to others. The apostle then suddenly turned the light of the future on to the present. "The end of all things is at hand." The darkness of every day has on it the purple promise of the end. The proper effect of this certainty is then described in its personal and relative aspects. The individual is that they be of "sound mind" and "sober unto prayer." Relatively, love is to be the master motive, and this is to find expression in hospitality and mutual ministration.

The apostle then showed that the fiery trial resulting from loyalty to Christ is inevitable, as partnership in the sufferings of Christ. In such fellowship with His sufferings they are to rejoice, inasmuch as the issue must be that of fellowship in His glory. That result, however, does not follow suffering which is the consequence of sin; if a child of God suffer through wrongdoing, there must be no expectation of

D. Established for Testing in Conflict

glory issuing therefrom. Remembering that the fires through which His children pass are watched by God, Who never allows them to harm His own, let them commit their souls to Him.

Finally the apostle gave instructions as to the orderliness of the Church. The leaders are to care for the flock, not lording it over them, but serving them; not indeed under the authority of the flock, but under that of the Lord and Master, Who is the Chief Shepherd. The younger are to be in subjection. All of them are to gird themselves to service, which is to be characterized by humility, and by freedom from all anxiety.

D. ESTABLISHED FOR TESTING IN CONFLICT

The life of the saint is one of conflict. The apostle named the adversary; he is the devil; he is neither careless nor neutral; his business is the destruction of all good. To those to whom Peter wrote the attitude of the devil was that of a roaring lion. It is not always so. Sometimes his opposition is stealthy and slimy as that of the serpent. At others it is radiant and fascinating as that of an angel. His purpose is always the same, "seeking whom he may devour"; and his method is ever that of *seeking*, watching for the weak moment, the unguarded entrance, the unprepared occasion. The attitude of the Christian toward this foe is to be that of soberness, watchfulness, and actual conflict. An incentive to all this is that we are not alone. Our brethren in the world are all fighting. Our battle is not our own; it is theirs also. They fight for us; and we for them. The strength of conflict is the certainty that the God of all grace will through the process accomplish His purpose.

CONCLUSION

In the last words the apostle indicated the method of the letter, with which we dealt in the introduction; and closed with personal salutations and the benediction of peace.

II PETER—*Christ the Strength of His People*

INTRODUCTION *i. 1-2*	A THE PRINCIPLES OF PRESERVATION *i. 3-21*	B THE PERILS *ii.—iii. 9*	CONCLUSION *iii. 10-18*

I. The Writer and the Readers   **1**
 	
i. Simon Peter
ii. Servant— Apostle
iii. "The like precious faith." (Luke xxii. 32)
	I. The Principles Stated **i. 3-11**
	
	i. Provision. 3-4
	ii. Responsibility. 5-11
	   a. Diligent development. 5-9
	   b. The more diligence. 10-11
		I. Threatening the Power. False Teaching **ii.**
		
		i. The Peril declared. 1-3a
		ii. Judgment announced. 3b-9
		iii. The Peril unmasked. 10-22
			I. The Coming 10-13
			
			II. The Power 14-16

II. His Desire "Knowledge" **2**	**II. The Principles Defended** **i. 12-21**
	
	i. Determination in view of his Exodus. 12-15
	ii. The Vision of the Holy Mount. 16-21
	   a. The Vision. *Power* and *Coming.* 16a
	   b. The Proofs. 16b-21
		II. Threatening the Coming. False living **iii. 1-9**
		
		i. The Peril declared. iii. 1-4
		ii. The Answer. 5-9
			III. Final 17-18

II PETER * * * *

THIS LETTER IS addressed to the same persons as the first. While the purpose of the first was the strengthening of those who were passing through a period of testing from without, this is for their strengthening in view of the dangers threatening them within the Church. The aim of the epistle may be gathered from the concluding exhortation: "Beware," "Grow." It is a solemn warning against the perils that threaten the inner life of the Church, and an exhortation to growth in that "grace and knowledge" in which the perils will be overcome. It may thus be analyzed; Introduction (i. 1, 2); Principles of Preservation (i. 3-21); Perils Threatening (ii.-iii. 9); Conclusion (iii. 10-18).

INTRODUCTION

Through varied experiences the writer had come into possession of the character which the surname "Peter" suggested. As he commenced a letter intended to strengthen his brethren for the testing arising from perils threatening them within the Church, he introduced himself by the names of "Simon Peter," the first of which speaks of his own old life of instability, and the second of the character of stability into which he had been brought. Describing himself as a servant and apostle of Jesus Christ, he addressed his brethren as having a "like precious faith," thus reminding them that the faith which in his case was preserved through the supplication of his Lord, was theirs also. His ultimate desire for them was that they might have knowledge. As the perils against which he was about to warn them resulted from false teaching, so the principle of preservation was that of knowledge.

A. THE PRINCIPLES OF PRESERVATION

In dealing with the principles of preservation, the apostle first stated and then defended them.

The statement of principles consists of a setting forth of the actual facts of the perfect provision, and a declaration of the consequent responsibility of the saints. The provision is described first as to present possession; "all things that pertain unto life and godliness" are granted through the knowledge of Him Who called "by his glory and virtue." This possession is made more sure by the "precious and exceeding great promises." Because of this perfect provision the saints are called to diligence and the development of their resources; and to more diligence, in the light of the things of the eternal Kingdom, wherein all the meaning of participation in the Divine nature will be realized.

Having thus stated the principles of preservation, the apostle defended the truth of his statement. He was conscious of his approaching departure, and expressed his determination to stir them up by putting them in remembrance. There flamed upon him the memory of the Mount of Transfiguration; and the effect which his experiences there had upon him are very evident here. On that mount he had seen the "Power" and "Coming" of the Lord Jesus Christ. These words correspond to the present and future provision with which he had already dealt. On that holy mount moreover he heard the voice of God, and that voice confirmed for

B. *The Perils*

him the prophecies of the past, which were as "a lamp shining in a dark place."

B. THE PERILS

Having thus described the principles of preservation, the apostle now dealt with the perils threatening the Church from within. These are two, the one growing out of the other. The first is that of false teachers, which threatens the power. The second is that of the materialization of mind resulting from their teaching, which threatens the coming.

As in the days of ancient prophecy there were false prophets, so now there will be false teachers; and many will follow, and the way of truth be evil spoken of. The judgment of God against such is sure, and this assertion is defended by the citation of the cases of the casting out of the angels, the destruction of the ancient world, and of the cities of Sodom and Gomorrah. Nevertheless such judgment will be discriminative. "The Lord knoweth how to deliver." The apostle then proceeded to describe more particularly the characteristics of those whom he had in mind. A more scathing description it is not possible to find. The words seem to sting like whips of fire. He described their method. As to themselves, he referred to them as "having eyes full of adultery, and that cannot cease from sin." Their method was that of the enticement of weak souls. With relentless persistence he tore away the attractive outer garments of the false teachers, and revealed the loathsomeness of the self-centered covetousness that lurked behind. This is no dainty handling of false teachers. The terrible manner of it is due to the apostle's consciousness that the effect of false teaching is that of denying the power of Christ, which is the present blessing of the saints. To deny the Lord in any particular is to loosen the bondage of the soul to Him, and to open the door to the incoming of all evil.

False teaching which denies the power of Christ issues in false thinking which questions the coming of Christ. There will be mockers who will walk in lust, and make sport of the great hope of the Church, declaring that things will continue as they have done. To strengthen his readers against the new peril, the apostle reminded them of the prophecies and the commandment of the Lord. The argument that as things have been they remain is contested first by reference to the deluge, and then by the declaration that a fire judgment is reserved for this earth. What appears to be delay is due to the long-suffering of God, with Whom time does not exist.

CONCLUSION

The conclusion consists of a summary of teaching grouped around these two subjects of the coming and the power of the Lord, with a final warning and injunction.

The day of the Lord will come. It will be destructive. The heavens and the elements will be burned up. We may hasten that day by holy living and godliness. It will also be constructive, for there will be "new heavens and a new earth wherein dwelleth righteousness."

The result of this conviction in the experience of the saints should be new appropriation of the power. Personally this means diligence for the creation of the character for which at His coming He will seek. Relatively it means patience during the delay, knowing that it is caused by His long-suffering.

All this leads to the final exhortation, which is twofold.

Conclusion

"Beware"—that marks the attitude of caution. "Grow"—that indicates the necessity for progress. To conclude, there is a brief and comprehensive doxology; glory to the Lord and Saviour, Jesus Christ, "both now," that is, in response to His power, and "for ever," that is, as the result of His coming. Thus the soul is established in Him against all possibilities and perils, both now and for ever.

I JOHN—*Christ and Fellowship with God*

INTRO-DUCTION *1-4*	A FELLOWSHIP WITH GOD. GOD IS LIGHT *i. 5—ii.*	B FELLOWSHIP WITH GOD. GOD IS LOVE *iii.—iv.*	C FELLOWSHIP WITH GOD. GOD IS LIFE *v. 1-12*	CON-CLUSION *v. 13-21*
I. Facts of the Gospel Epitomized 1-2	I. Fellowship with Light i. 5—ii. 11	I. Fellowship with Love iii.	I. Life and Love 1-3	I. "That ye may know" 13-17
II. The Purpose 3-4	II. Perils of Darkness ii. 12-29	II. Perils of Hatred iv.	II. Life and Light 4-12	II. "We know" 18-21

I JOHN * * * *

THIS IS PROBABLY the last apostolic message to the whole Church. If the second and third epistles were written later, they were to individuals. This letter is catholic in the fullest sense of the word, being addressed to no particular church or district, and dealing with the fundamental question of the life which is the true bond of the Church's unity.

A comparison of John xx. 31 and 1 John v. 13 will show the gospel and epistle to be complementary. The gospel was written that men might have life, the epistle that believers might know they had life. In the former we have Divine life as revealed in Christ; in the latter the same life as realized in the Christian. The gospel declares the way of life through the incarnate Son; the epistle unfolds the nature of that life as possessed by the children of God.

The subject of the epistle is that of fellowship with God, into which believers are introduced through their union with Christ. Its divisions mark the subjects dealt with. These subjects overlap in each case. This is the outcome of the fact that they are closely interrelated, the three forming phases of a great whole. They may be indicated thus; Introduction (i. 1-4); Fellowship with God as Light (i. 5-ii.); Fellowship with God as Love (iii.-iv.); Fellowship with God as Life (v. 1-12); Conclusion (v. 13-21).

INTRODUCTION

By way of introduction John affirmed his knowledge, in common with others, of the certainty that eternal life was manifested in the Word. "We have heard . . . we have seen . . . beheld . . . our hands handled." The word "that" refers in each case to a Person. As in the gospel, the "Word" which cannot be touched became flesh which could be touched, so here, "the Word of life," which is a quantity intangible, imponderable, and immeasurable, had yet been touched and handled by men. The purpose of the manifestation was that of bringing men into fellowship with God. This the apostle proceeded to discuss under the three headings of light, love, and life, showing not only the privileges but also the responsibilities of such fellowship.

A. FELLOWSHIP WITH GOD. GOD IS LIGHT

In this division the apostle first dealt with the fellowship of the saints with God in light, and then described the perils of darkness.

The first great message of "the Word of life" to men is that "God is light." This is a truth never to be lost sight of. To forget it is to minimize the meaning of the next declaration that "God is love." The exercise of such fellowship on the part of the believer consists of walking in the light of God. Yet, because of perpetual imperfection even in holy things, there is need of constant cleansing, and this is provided in "the blood of Jesus his Son." Light makes sin known. Sins of the past are forgiven, and the soul is cleansed from unrighteousness. The apostle was careful to state that

-572

he wrote in order that we sin not. He added, however, a gracious declaration concerning the provision of the Advocate Jesus, through Whom sins might be put away. Having stated the nature and conditions of fellowship with God as light, the apostle proceeded to speak of the tests whereby we may know our relation to light, first as to God, and then as to our fellow-men. The test of light is love—love to God exemplified in obedience. The supreme commandment was not new, in that it was the original Divine intention for man. Yet it was new in its new interpretation in Christ, and in the experience of men who in its power love each other.

In approaching the subject of the perils of darkness against which he was about to utter warnings, the apostle, in a beautiful passage, declared the groundwork of his appeal to be the experience of believers in Christ. The perils against which he warned believers were those of materialism, and the false spirit of Antichrist. The description of worldliness is very clear. It consists in "the lust of the flesh," that is, desires which are wholly of the flesh, without the control of the spirit; "the lust of the eyes," that is, desire to see things which minister to the flesh only, evil curiosity to contemplate unholy things; "the vainglory of life," that is, satisfaction and boasting in things which are of the world only, and are passing and perishing. He then described the spirit of Antichrist to be that of denying that Jesus is the Christ, which denial involves also the denial of the Father and the Son. The Church needs to be ever on the watch against such desires or teachings. Her safety consists in the fact that she has the record as received "from the beginning"; and moreover, that she has that anointing of the indwelling Spirit which inter-

prets and explains the things received, so that she has no
need that any one teach her.

B. FELLOWSHIP WITH GOD. GOD IS LOVE

In this division the apostle dealt with the fellowship of
the saints with God in love, and then declared the perils of
hatred.

The love of God is supremely manifest in that we are
called "children of God." All the meaning of this relationship we do not yet know, but this much is certain that eventually we shall be like Him. The present influence of this
hope, born of love, is that he that has it purifies himself. The
apostle proceeded to declare that in Christ there is no need
for any one to sin, and that if a believer do so it must be in
violation of the very life-principle which makes him a child
of God. The test of fellowship with God as love is righteousness of conduct, and love one to another. The result of fellowship with God as love, will be that of hatred toward us on
the part of the world. Yet such hatred is to be answered by
the love of the Christian, such love being the proof of the
presence of the new life. Affirmations of love for the men of
the world, which are not demonstrated by ministry to their
actual needs, are of no value. The apostle then declared the
test by which we may ourselves know that we are of the truth.
The true anxiety of Christian experience is to possess a heart
at rest before God. Doubt or uncertainty in the inward life
is ever productive of harm. The place of peace and power is
that of abiding in Him. To keep His commandments is to
abide in Him, and to abide in Him is to have strength to
keep His commandments. The all-inclusive commandments
are two in number. The first is that we should believe in

B. Fellowship with God. God Is Love

Jesus Christ; and the second is that we should love one another.

Two closely related perils threaten our fellowship with God as love: those of false prophets, and the spirit which actuates them. There is a simple and yet searching test which the children of God are carefully to apply. The testimony of the Spirit of God is to Jesus Christ as having come in flesh. Those who confess not Jesus are those who deny what the Spirit of God affirms concerning Him. All such are of Antichrist. The test of the spirit is the indwelling Spirit. There need be no fear, for the indwelling One is greater than the spirit working in the world; but there must be no carelessness in the matter of testing. The apostle then made an appeal. He used two arguments as he urged the duty of love. First, the nature of God is love, and therefore those begotten of Him should love. The second argument was that of the manifestation of the love of God. He "sent his only begotten Son into the world." That is the last word of love, and upon it the apostle based his appeal. "Beloved, if God so loved us, we ought also to love one another." The argument and appeal now go a step further. The perfect love which has no fear is the true revelation of God. There may be this realization and revelation because "as he is, even so are we in this world." The apostle's consciousness of the glorious perfection of his provision lent strenuousness to his words of application. "If a man say I love God, and hateth his brother, he is a liar." To every person in actual union with God in Christ, love is possible. Moreover, it is not a privilege merely, it is a stern duty. The world waits for the knowledge of God, and can only attain it through His revelation in the love of His children.

C. FELLOWSHIP WITH GOD. GOD IS LIFE

The final subject is that of our fellowship with God in life. This is fundamental, and is here shown to be so. Passing back over the ground traversed, the apostle shows the relation between life and love, and then between life and light.

As to the first, God gives life to the believer. The love of one begotten for the One begetting issues in love for all begotten. In other words, children of the Father love each other. The spring and power of love is life. Fellowship with God in life issues in love.

There is also a close relationship between life and light. Those who are begotten of God overcome the world. Fellowship with the light of God is not possible to those who are alienated from His life. As the fundamental aspect of fellowship with God is fellowship in life, and moreover, as man enters into that life by believing, the apostle now gives the witness upon which faith takes hold. Jesus Christ came by water and blood. He "came by water" in the sense that the baptism in Jordan witnessed to His fellowship with light. He "came by blood" in the sense that the passion baptism witnessed to His fellowship with love. The supreme Witness to this is the Spirit. Thus three bear witness: the Spirit, of life; the water, of light; the blood, of love. These three "agree in one," that is, Jesus. Thus has God borne witness to man. The Son of God possessed, is the life in which men have fellowship with God in light and love.

CONCLUSION

In his concluding words John stated the reason of his writing. His purpose was that of confirmation. The certainty of

Conclusion

life possessed, results in a confidence in God which is calm
and content. That confidence is exercised in intercession,
the limitation of which is clearly marked. The letter closes
with a group of certainties, and an injunction against idols.
The force of the final warning lies in the certainty of the
fellowship of the believer with God in light, and love, and
life.

II. JOHN—*Christ and Fellowship with God*

INTRO-DUCTION *1-4*	A LOVE *5*	B LOVE AND LIGHT *6*	C LIGHT AND LIFE *7-11*	CON-CLUSION *12-13*
I. Addresses and Key Word Truth 1-2 II. Salutation 3 III. The Apostle's Joy 4	The Command-ment	I. Love Defined II. Light Defined	I. A Warning 7 II. Injunction 8 III. A Test 9 IV. A Require-ment 10-11	The Farewell

II JOHN * * * *

THIS SECOND EPISTLE is a concrete application of the principles taught in the first. Its subject is the value of truth in the threefold life of fellowship. Its scheme may be stated thus; Introduction (1-4); Love (5); Love and Light (6); Light and Life (7-9); Conclusion (12, 13).

INTRODUCTION

The repetition of the word "truth" in the address gives the keynote to the letter. The salutation refers to grace, mercy, and peace, which are the effects of truth, the inward sanctifier; and the expression of love, the outward result. This is followed by a declaration of the apostle's joy that the children of the elect lady were found walking in truth.

A. LOVE

The apostle then wrote the central and all-inclusive commandment, and urged her to obey it. It was not a new commandment, but the repetition of that possessed from the beginning.

B. LOVE AND LIGHT

Then followed the statement of supreme importance that love is obedience to light. The commandment heard from the beginning was that of love. Love, therefore, is obedience to the commandment.

C. LIGHT AND LIFE

All already written was preliminary to the warnings which followed, and the necessity for which constituted the real occasion of the letter. Deceivers were gone forth into the world, denying essential truth concerning the Christ. Because love is walking in light, the test of love is light. Any consent to darkness out of a so-called charity is not true love. Loyalty to truth concerning the Person of Christ is the true way of love, and any charity which compromises that is false, and eventually violates love.

The teaching against which the apostle warned the elect lady was progressive teaching. Progress out of first principles is retrogression. The stern requirement of the apostle manifests the sanctified son of thunder, and the determined apostle of love. No hospitality or greeting must be given to those who by false teaching imperil the life, and light, and love, of the believer.

The special teaching of this letter may thus be summarized. Christianity is love. Love is dependent upon the light of truth. To deny the truth is to make love impossible. The continued experience of fellowship is dependent upon the continued fact of fellowship in love and light and life. The continued fact of fellowship is proved by the continued experience of fellowship.

CONCLUSION

The apostle expressed his hope that he might soon see face to face the one to whom he wrote, and sent the salutation of the children of her elect sister.

–580

III JOHN—*Christ and Fellowship with God*

INTRO-DUCTION *1-4*	A GAIUS: LOVE PRACTICED *5-8*	B DIOTREPHES: LOVE VIOLATED *9-10*	C DEMETRIUS: LOVE, LIGHT, LIFE *11-12*	CON-CLUSION *13-14*
I. The Address 1	I. Gaius' Hospitality 5-6a	I. The Reason of Diotrephes' Disobedience 9	I. The Injunction 11a	Anticipation of Meeting
II. The Prayer 2	II. Injunction to continue 6b	II. The Warning 10a	II. Central Statement 11b	A Message of Peace
III. The Apostle's Joy 3-4	III. The Reason 7-8	III. The Expression of Diotrephes' Pride 10b	III. The Example of Demetrius 12	

III JOHN   * * * *

THERE ARE THREE persons previously mentioned in the New Testament bearing the name of Gaius: Gaius of Macedonia (Acts xix. 29), Gaius of Derbe (Acts xx. 4), and Gaius of Corinth (1 Cor. i. 14). The Gaius to whom John wrote may be yet a fourth. It is, however, extremely probable that he was the Gaius of Corinth, for there is similarity between the hospitality which Paul mentioned (Rom. xvi. 23) and that commended by John.

This letter is indeed on the subject of that hospitality as it revealed love, and afforded the apostle an opportunity to utter a warning against schism, which is always due to lack of love. His argument circles around three persons—Gaius, Diotrephes, and Demetrius. It may be divided thus; Introduction (1-4); the Hospitality of Gaius, its Value, Love practised (5-8); the Arrogance of Diotrephes, its Condemnation, Love violated (8-10); the Example of Demetrius, its Cause, Love, Light, Life (11, 12); Conclusion (13, 14).

INTRODUCTION

Very tender and delicate is the introduction. The apostle's recognition of the spiritual health of Gaius when he prayed that his physical prosperity and health might equal it is beautiful. Again the keynote is Truth. As in the letter to the elect lady the apostle had uttered his warnings against a false charity and hospitality, here he commended true love and hospitality. If there is a hospitality impossible to loyalty, to truth, it is equally true there is a kind which such loyalty necessitates and inspires.

A. GAIUS: LOVE PRACTICED

Certain evangelists had been received and entertained by Gaius. For this the apostle commended him, and declared that he would do well to set them forth on their journey, "worthily of God." This is a remarkable phrase, and capable of more than one interpretation. It may mean that Gaius was to see in them the messengers of God, and was to send them forth in a way befitting such sacred calling. It may have reminded Gaius that he was a child of God, and urged him to act accordingly. In all probability it included both these thoughts. The privileges of showing hospitality to the messengers of the Gospel is set forth in the words, "that we may be fellow-workers for the truth."

B. DIOTREPHES: LOVE VIOLATED

In striking contrast to Gaius stands Diotrephes. He had refused to receive some who were recommended to the Church by John, and had gone so far as to cast out of the Church those who did receive them. The whole truth about this man is seen in one of those illuminative sentences in which the character of a man is so often revealed in the Scriptures. "Diotrephes, who loveth to have the pre-eminence." That is the essential violation of love, for "love . . . seeketh not her own." This is an instance of heterodoxy of spirit or temper, rather than of intellect. There is no evidence that this man was teaching false doctrine, but he was not submissive to authority. As is always the case, the unsubmissive one becomes the greatest tyrant, and thus by disobedience he manifests his lack of love. As loyalty to truth is the sphere of love, so also is it the evidence of love. The arrogance of this man shows the governing principle of his life to be selfishness rather than love.

C. DEMETRIUS: LOVE, LIGHT, LIFE

Gaius is urged to imitate good rather than evil, and immediately another change is before us in the introduction of Demetrius. In all likelihood he was the bearer of the letter, and John quoted him in direct contrast to Diotrephes. The central statement of the epistle is found in verse eleven. "He that doeth good is of God; he that doeth evil hath not seen God." The relations of love to life and light are suggested. Doing good is to be interpreted by the subject of the letter, hospitality. Those who act in love thus, do so because they are of God, that is, related to Him in the fellowship of life. Such are Gaius and Demetrius. Those who act in evil by selfishness, do so because they have no fellowship with God in light, not having seen Him.

CONCLUSION

The letter closes with words anticipatory of a meeting, and with a message of peace.

JUDE—*Christ the Perfect and Perfecting Lord*

INTRO-DUCTION *1-3*	A THE DANGER *4-16*	B THE DUTY *17-23*	CON-CLUSION *24-25*
I. The Writer and the Readers **1**	I. Described **4-11** i. Its Nature. **4** ii. Its Peril. **5-7** iii. Its Arrogance. **8-10** iv. Its Doom. **11**	I. Recognition of the Danger **17-19** i. Declared by the Apostles. **17-18** ii. Distinguished by two things. **19**	I. "Him that is able to guard you from stumbling." Continuity
II. Salutation **2**	II. Denounced **12-16** i. Figurative Denunciation. **12-13** ii. Enoch's Prophecy applied to them. **14-15** iii. Final Description. **16**	II. The Personal Duty **20-23** i. Central Clause "Keep yourselves." **21** ii. How this is to be done. **20-21** iii. Duty towards others. **22-23**	II. "To set you before the presence of his glory." Consummation
III. The Writing **3** Change of purpose declared.			III. "To him be glory"

JUDE   * * * *

THE SUBJECT DEALT with in this epistle is that of apostasy—its possibility, peril, and punishment. It solemnly reveals the relation existing between the will of man and the sovereignty of God. Apostasy is shown to be willful return to ungodliness. Two classes are dealt with. Those who "kept not" and are therefore "kept." Those who "keep themselves" and are "kept from stumbling." While man is free to will, he is never freed from the restraining government of God. It is one of the most solemn and searching of the New Testament writings, and cannot be carefully studied without solemn searching of heart. The following analysis may be followed; Introduction (1-3); the Danger described (4-16); the Duty devolving (17-23); Conclusion (24, 25).

INTRODUCTION

Jude introduced himself as brother of James, and servant of Jesus Christ; and his letter was addressed to those who were "called," "beloved," "kept." He wrote in order to urge upon such the necessity for contending earnestly for the faith, and what he meant must be interpreted by all that follows.

A. THE DANGER

The peril threatening those to whom he wrote was created by ungodly men, who, turning grace into an occasion of lasciviousness, denied all authority. The perils of such attitude were illustrated by reference to Israel, angels, and the cities of the plain; all of which were cast out from privilege on account of disobedience. The diversity of these illustrations emphasizes the underlying principle that continuity of privilege is dependent upon continuity of fidelity. The arrogance of the attitude of apostasy is described, and its doom is declared in the pronouncement of woe. Its meaning is revealed as being the way of Cain, which was that of hatred and murder; the error of Balaam, which was that of seduction and lying; and the gainsaying of Korah, which was that of envy and rebellion.

Apostasy is then denounced in a passage full of fiery force. Jude figuratively showed that it means failure to fulfill purpose, and then by quotation of the prophecy of Enoch declared that failure to fulfill purpose must issue in destruction.

The final description of these men reveals their inward fault and motive in two phrases—"walking after lusts," and "for the sake of advantage."

B. THE DUTY

Turning to the subject of the true attitude of believers in the presence of apostasy, he indicated that there must be first a recognition of the danger. It had been foretold by the apostles, and may be known by two distinguishing marks. Men guilty of apostasy are to be known by their influence—"they make separations"; and by their temper—they are "sensual" rather than spiritual.

He then described the sphere and habit of safety, the central charge being, "keep yourselves in the love of God." This is to be done by building on faith, praying in the Spirit, and looking for mercy.

Beyond personal responsibility there is a relative duty. "On some have mercy"—that is, those in doubt; "some save" —that is, such as have been ensnared by the libertines; "on some have mercy with fear"—and here perhaps the reference is to the libertines themselves. This mercy is not to be the condoning of evil, or complicity therewith, but the patient hopefulness that seeks to win all.

CONCLUSION

The apostle closed with a glorious doxology which shows that the writer had no panic in his heart, even though he was profoundly conscious of the surrounding perils. He ascribed to God the Saviour all honor in the immeasurable ages, past and present, for that He is able to accomplish the salvation of His trusting ones in two ways which are all-inclusive; as to continuity, "able to guard you from stumbling"; and as to consummation, "to set you before the presence of his glory."

REVELATION—*The Unveiling of Jesus Christ*

Prologue. i. 1-3.   i. The Book. Its nature, origin, method. 1, 2.
                      ii. The Benediction. 3.
Introduction. i. 4-8.   i. The Mutual Benediction. "To you." "Unto Him." 4-6.
                         ii. Central Truths. 7, 8.

A JESUS CHRIST HIMSELF *i. 9-20*	B JESUS CHRIST AND THE CHURCH *ii., iii.*		C JESUS CHRIST AND THE KINGDOM *iv.—xxii. 5*
I. The Occasion 9-11	**I. Ephesus** Apostolic.	**ii. 1-7**	**I. Millennial Preparation** **iv.—xviii.** i. The Heavenly Order. iv. ii. The Earthly Administration. v. iii. The Procedure. vi.—xviii.

**II. The Vision
12-16**
	II. Smyrna
	
	Persecution.
		ii. 8-11	*a.* Seals. vi.—viii. 5
			   b. Trumpets. viii. 6—ix., xi. 15-19
			     (Parentheses. 1. x.—xi. 14)
			     (2. xii.—xiv.)

III. The Voice 17-18	**III. Pergamum** **ii. 12-17** Patronage.		*c.* Plagues. xv.—xvi. *d.* Fall of Babylon. xvii., xviii.
IV. The Commission 19-20	**IV. Thyatira** **ii. 18-29** Corruption.		**II. The Millennium** **xix.—xx. 8** i. The Inauguration. xix.—xx. 3 ii. The Reign. xx. 4-6
	V. Sardis **iii. 1-6** Reformation.		**III. Millennial Issues** **xx. 7—xxii. 5**
	VI. Philadelphia **iii. 7-13** Evangelization.		i. "After the Thousand Years." xx. 7-10 ii. The Great Assize. xx. 11-15 iii. The Kingdom of the Son. xxi.—xxii. 5
	VII. Laodicea **iii. 14-22** Apostasy.		

Epilogue. xxii. 6-21. i. Final Words of Jesus. 6-19.   ii. Final Words of John. 20-21.

REVELATION * * * *

THE ONLY SATISFACTORY introduction to the book of Revelation is found in the text thereof, which deals with authorship, nature, origin, method, and intention. Its earliest phrase constitutes its title, and indicates its content. It is the "unveiling of Jesus Christ." Our analysis is based upon the supposition that the key to the interpretation of the book is found in the final charge of Jesus to John, "Write therefore the things which thou sawest, and the things which are, and the things which shall come to pass after these."

There is first a Prologue (i. 1-3), followed by an Introduction (i. 4-8). Then follow the three main divisions dealing with the unveiling of Jesus Christ; Jesus Christ Himself (i. 9-20); Jesus Christ and the Church (ii., iii.); Jesus Christ and the Kingdom (iv.-xxii. 5). The book closes with an Epilogue (xxii. 6-21).

PROLOGUE

The foreword constitutes a key to the study of the book as it declares its nature to be that of the unveiling of Jesus Christ; its origin, that God gave the things to His Son to show; and its method, that He signified them by an angel to John. It closes with a blessing pronounced upon those who read, and hear, and keep.

INTRODUCTION

The apostle introduced his writing of the message received with a double benediction; grace and peace to the churches, glory and dominion to Jesus Christ. He then declared that the hidden One is yet to be revealed, and pronounced the Divine name in all its majesty.

A. JESUS CHRIST HIMSELF

The first division of the book deals with what Christ referred to by the phrase "the things which thou sawest." The apostle described the occasion of the coming to him of the unveiling. As to earthly conditions, he was in Patmos in tribulation; as to heavenly condition, he was "in the spirit on the Lord's day." In these circumstances he beheld the vision of the glorious Person of his Lord, as "a son of man," yet infinitely removed from all the sons of men in the splendor of His glory. In the presence of so amazing an unveiling John became "as one dead," and then heard the voice bidding him "fear not," and ultimately commissioning him to write.

B. JESUS CHRIST AND THE CHURCH

There can be no doubt that the seven letters contained in this division were directed to churches actually in existence in the days of John. Nevertheless they reveal a sevenfold condition, lasting through the dispensation of the Church, and almost certainly indicate a process in Church history. That to the church at Ephesus deals with the loss of first love, and had special application to the apostolic period. That to the church at Smyrna deals with the subject of persecution,

C. *Jesus Christ and the Kingdom*

and had special reference to the period from Diocletian (A.D. 303), to that of Constantine (A.D. 313). That to the church at Pergamum deals with the patronage of the world, and had special reference to the period commencing with Constantine, in which the church gained in material splendor. That to the church at Thyatira deals with corruption, and had special reference to the Dark Ages. That to the church at Sardis deals with reformation, and had special reference to the hour of the rebirth of evangelical faith under the reformers. That to the church at Philadelphia deals with the open door for evangelization, and had special reference to the period ushered in by the Puritan movement, which broke into full force in the Evangelical Revival. That to the church at Laodicea deals with apostasy, and describes the final period prior to the advent of the Lord Himself. The careful student of this division will find that its supreme value consists in the unveiling of Jesus Christ in His relation to the Church. His authority, His patience, His judgment, are all set forth, and it is upon these that the mind should principally dwell in the study.

C. JESUS CHRIST AND THE KINGDOM

The final division of the book opens with the phrase, "After these," which is another translation of the same phrase rendered "hereafter" in the commission to John. It indicates that all that is to follow takes place after the conditions described in the previous division, that is, the end of the Church period. In it we see the unveiling of Jesus Christ in the movements which establish the Kingdom in the world. It falls into three sections. The first deals with millennial preparation, and is by far the largest; the second in very brief sentences describes the millennium; while the third has to do with millennial issues.

The subject of millennial preparation is introduced by preliminary pictures of the heavenly order and the earthly administration, and then becomes a symbolic description of the procedure. At the center of everything a Throne is established and occupied. In closest connection therewith are four living ones who in ceaseless worship attest the holiness of the One Who occupies the Throne. Circling around these, four-and-twenty elders declare Him worthy to receive the glory, and the honor, and the power of all created things.

In the hand of the One Who sits upon the Thron᷉ lies the program of events. It is written but sealed, and n᷉ ᷉e can know it. The Lamb by virtue of victory won is able to take the book and unseal it, that the program may be carried out. This fact is heralded by the songs of living ones, of elders, of countless thousands of angels, and of the whole creation of God. Thus, in preparation for a description of the perplexing events which are to follow, it is revealed that holiness is established upon the central Throne, and that it acts though Him Who is the Exponent of the infinite Love.

That part of this section dealing with the procedure of millennial preparation is the most intricate in the whole book. It is a symbolic prophecy of movements occupying seven years, during which evil works itself out to final issues under the government of God. In this there are two great movements, the first dealing with the first three and a half years (vi.-xi.). In this there is an interpolation (x.-xi. 14). The second movement (xii.-xviii.) covers the last three and

C. Jesus Christ and the Kingdom

a half years, and is introduced by an interpolation (xii.-xiv.).

The events immediately following the end of the Church dispensation are symbolically set forth. The first seal is opened, and one representing false authority is seen going "forth conquering and to conquer." The second seal is opened, and carnage and bloodshed follow as the outcome of military despotism. The third seal is opened, and famine follows in the wake of commercial despotism. The fourth seal is opened, and death in its most terrible forms reigns. In the opening of these first four seals the true nature of evil is graphically set forth, as to its strength and weakness. At the opening of the fifth seal the cry of slaughtered saints is heard, and to the martyrs are given the white robes which are the reward of fidelity. The opening of the sixth seal is immediately followed by premonitions of the coming One. The first of four seals revealed the development of lawless government. The fifth gave the cry of the saints, and the answer in heaven. At the opening of the sixth, signs are given of the established order of true government, notwithstanding the apparent victory of the false. Restraining angels are now seen holding in check the hurricanes of Divine judgment, while the sealing of an elect number of the servants of God takes place. From this sealing the seer turns to contemplate a great vision in heaven of a vast multitude lifting the song of salvation. In response to the inquiry of the seer, the angel declares that these have come out of the great tribulation. At last the seventh seal is opened. Heaven is sensible of the stupendous importance of this seal, and its songs are hushed, and prayer is silent for half an hour. Then seven archangels receive trumpets, and prepare themselves to sound.

How long a period elapses between the sounding of the

trumpets we cannot tell. The rapid grouping of the first four would seem to suggest their quick succession. The sounding of the first is followed by a storm and tempest over the earth. The second sounds, and another convulsion, more terrible than the first, follows. The third sounds, and by the touch of a star God changes the character of a third part of the waters of the earth. The fourth angel sounds, and the earth is affected by a display of power among the heavenly bodies. Between the sounding of the fourth and fifth trumpets there is a pause. A flying eagle proclaims a threefold coming woe, and the proclamation is an evidence of the long suffering of God. At the sounding of the fifth trumpet the procedure of judgment takes on a new form. New forces of a spiritual nature produce physical pain and death. The sounding of the sixth trumpet introduces a period in which an army of evil spirits hitherto held in bondage are loosed.

Under the period of the sixth trumpet we have an interlude which chronicles the events preparing the way for the sounding of the seventh and last. A strong angel, full of glorious dignity, gives to the seer a book, and charges him to eat it. Following this, John measures the temple, and two witnesses deliver their testimony for three and a half years. It must be remembered that John is not now describing what he sees, but writing what he is told. The testimony of the witnesses is not a brief one given between the sounding of the sixth and seventh trumpets. Between these soundings he is told that they exercise their ministry during three and a half years. At last the message being so fully delivered that men know it, the witnesses are slain. The seventh angel at length sounds, and the period ushered in includes all the remaining premillennial process.

C. Jesus Christ and the Kingdom

At the sounding of this seventh trumpet John is given a series of visions dealing with the great facts and conditions leading up to the things actually following the sounding of the trumpet. They constitute a restatement of subjects already dealt with in slightly different form. The sign of the woman and the man-child is, as to the woman, that of the external manifestation of loyalty to God, which includes all ages and dispensations; and as to the man-child, that of the coming out of the Church of the First-born at the call of Christ from that which was external only, at the end of the Church period, at the beginning of the seven years. Then follows the war in heaven, and the casting out of Satan half way through the period of tribulation. The scene of conflict is now upon the earth, and Satan is seen against the woman. Still reviewing the processes of the past three and a half years, the seer describes the beasts, and then his attention is turned again to the heavenly order. There we see once more the one hundred and forty-four thousand surrounding the Lamb, while angels in succession set forth the supremacy of God, the fall of Babylon, a warning against the mark of the beast, and the imminence of judgment.

Before commencing the detailed description of the final processes of judgment, John beheld a vision in heaven revealing the prepared order. Standing by a sea of glass, mingled with fire, is a great host of those who have overcome the beast. They are singing the song of Moses and the Lamb. Following this vision of the victorious hosts John beholds the opening Temple in heaven. From thereout come the seven angels having the seven last plagues. The pouring out of these plagues constitutes the final judgments of God upon the earth. The long-continued sin of man has been that of refusal to submit to Divine government, and consequent devotion to the lower side of his nature. Evil has wrought itself out to its most terrible expression, and now judgment proceeds without mercy.

The judgment of Babylon having been announced, there follows an unfolding of its true nature, and a more detailed account of its doom. One of the seven angels calls the seer to behold the judgment of the great harlot. The name upon her forehead commences with the word "MYSTERY." Babylon stands for the whole system of organized godlessness in the history of the human race. From Babel on, this spirit has had definite manifestation in the affairs of men, and has been maintained by material power in some form in every successive age. The angel proceeds to explain to John the meaning of the vision. The beast upon which the woman sits represents the temporal authority which has been the strength of spiritual harlotry. After the angel has thus revealed the history of mystic Babylon under the symbolism of the woman, another angel appears, and with a mighty voice declares the fall of Babylon. Then another voice is heard, this time the voice of God Himself, uttering a call to a remnant, pronouncing an all-inclusive verdict on Babylon, and declaring its sentence of doom. The fall of the city produces entirely opposite effects on earth and in heaven. The whole earth is plunged in mourning; heaven rejoices. A strong angel casts into the sea a millstone, signifying the utter and overwhelming overthrow of Babylon, and the reason thereof is declared.

In the next section we have a brief description of the millennium. This is introduced by an account of heavenly rejoicing. There are three great movements of praise. The

–598

C. Jesus Christ and the Kingdom

first is that of a great multitude in heaven. The second is that of the elders and the living ones. The third is that of a mighty chorus, which John describes by a threefold symbol, as the voice of a great multitude, of many waters, of mighty thunders. Immediately following, the marriage ceremony of the Lamb is described, and Jesus is manifested to the world. It is the coming of the true King into His Kingdom. His name is "The Word of God," that by which He was known when He appeared full of grace and truth. Man in his rebellion is gathered to oppose Him. The battle is immediately joined. There is no indecision, no varying fortunes. It is quick, sharp, decisive, terrible. The King and His armies are supernatural. It is the hour when heaven is touching earth. The spiritualities which men have refused to acknowledge are carrying out a judgment due to blasphemous denial. Victory having thus been obtained over all the manifestation of godlessness on earth, Satan is arrested and imprisoned.

Then follows in brief sentences the only account which this book contains of the actual millennium. It will be a time of perfect earthly government, an absolute monarchy, that of the God-appointed and anointed King.

The final section deals with millennial issues. During the period of perfect government no active rebellion will be possible, but there will still exist an unmanifested capacity for rebellion. At the close of the period Satan will be loosed in order that once again hidden evil may be brought to light for final destruction. Then follows the last apostasy, and fire devours its armies.

John now saw that last assize when the dead, small and great, will be gathered before the Judge. Finally Death and Hades are cast into the lake of fire, and John beholds beyond it the beginning of the great Kingdom of the Son, that glorious reign of the Lamb, in association with His Bride, over an earth and a heaven from which all evil has been finally banished. Toward a city of God, men have looked through long generations, and now at last it comes out of heaven from God. A new order of laughter without tears, of life without death, of singing without mourning, of content without care, of pleasure without pain, will have dawned for the world.

EPILOGUE

The great unveiling is accomplished. What follows is of the nature of ratification and enforcement. The final words of Jesus declare all to be faithful and true, announce His advent, call all trusting souls to Himself, and utter solemn warnings. The final word of John is that of assent and invitation to his Lord, and the benediction pronounced upon all the saints.